The
WRITER'S
ADVISOR

The
WRITER'S
ADVISOR

A Guide to Books and Articles about Writing
Novels, Short Stories, Poetry, Dramatic Scripts,
Screenplays, Magazine Articles, Biographies,
Technical Articles and Books, as Well as a Guide to
Information about Literary Agents, Marketing, and
a Wide Range of Legal and Business Materials of
Interest to Full- and Part-Time Writers

Compiled by Leland G. Alkire, Jr.
Cheryl I. Westerman, *Associate Editor*

GALE RESEARCH COMPANY
BOOK TOWER ● DETROIT, MICHIGAN 48226

Compiled by Leland G. Alkire, Jr.

Cheryl I. Westerman, *Associate Editor*

Gale Research Company Staff

Michaeline R. Nowinski, *Production Editor*
Dennis LaBeau, *Director, Editorial Data Systems*
Miranda C. Herbert, *Supervisor, User Services Department,*
Editorial Data Systems
Elaine Cybulski, *Typist, User Services Department,*
Editorial Data Systems
Barry Trute, *Editorial Data Systems*
Carol Blanchard, *Production Director*
Art Chartow, *Art Director*

Frederick G. Ruffner, *Publisher*
James M. Ethridge, *Executive Vice-President/Editorial*
Dedria Bryfonski, *Editorial Director*

Copyright © 1985 by Leland G. Alkire, Jr.

Library of Congress Cataloging in Publication Data

Main entry under title:

The Writer's advisor.

Includes indexes.
1. Authorship—Bibliography.   I. Alkire, Leland G.
II. Westerman, Cheryl I.
Z5165.W74 1985 [PN145]   016.808′02   84-24715
ISBN 0-8103-2093-2

Printed in the United States of America

FTW

AEF 7696

To Pauline Westerman, 1930-1984,
who was a friend to writers.

"Although sometimes I have felt that I held fire in my hands and spread a page with shining—I have never lost the weight of clumsiness, of ignorance, of aching inability."

—John Steinbeck

Contents

Contents

Contents

Contents

Introduction

Having an idea for a book, a script, or an article is one thing. Knowing what to do with that idea is another matter. This book is designed to meet the unique needs of working writers who are seeking advice and direction. As such, *The Writer's Advisor* will also be of value to technical and creative writing teachers and students, to librarians, and to a variety of other users. It attempts to answer the frequently expressed need for a broad and organized approach to the wealth of advice that exists on the subject of writing both fiction and nonfiction. Even though this book contains thousands of references to such material, it does not pretend to be either comprehensive or exhaustive, nor is it intended as a tool for scholars. *The Writer's Advisor*, thus, is a kind of general purpose key to a manageable treasury of ideas and techniques which may offer each user better control over written language. In that sense, this book represents a kind of referred knowledge about what it is writers do, why they do it, and how others might learn from that collective experience.

The Writer's Advisor is not intended as a collection of magic formulas that will allow "almost anyone" to write with great ability, and there seems little point in debating here the age-old question of whether writing can be taught or not. We know that, given certain minimum levels of talent, one writer can learn from other writers, and, as numerous entries in this book will reveal, many a noteworthy author has served just such an apprenticeship. But we know just as certainly that neither great creativity nor genius can be conferred by such means.

A large number of the articles and books in this work refer to problems of technique. Unlike artful inspiration or creative genius, technique often has more to do with careful planning for effect than it does with the processes of the unconscious. Here, almost anyone can learn something, be it to write a more pithy book review for a local newspaper or a better lead-in for a biographical article, or to create more convincing dialogue in a short story.

In surveying the masses of material that have been printed about the writer's art and craft, one is struck by how little certain noteworthy authors have said about the subject, and how very much certain other equally important authors have left us. Some, such as the poet William Stafford and the short story writer and novelist Joyce Carol Oates, have regularly published such advice and inner reflections. Other writers appear to have been silent on the subject, at least in printed form. If the user questions the poor representation of this or that author, the cause may be due to that author's silence on the subject rather than an oversight by *The Writer's Advisor*. But as stated above, this book makes no attempt to take on the nearly impossible task of listing all that has ever been said on the subject of writing. To have recorded every tract, every fugitive article, and every scholarly study would have defeated the purpose of this book, which is to provide manageable access to widely available materials about writing. Thus, many a worthy critical study and many a competent school exercise book have been excluded. Such decisions have not always been easy, and we are fully aware that someone's favorite book or article may have been overlooked.

What Is Covered?

In general, the materials cited in *The Writer's Advisor* were published between the late 1960s and 1984, but a number of books and articles date from before that time and are included for what should be obvious reasons. At all times we have used as a guide the reasonable needs of the working writer, and, as far as possible, we have included only materials that are widely available through bookstores or libraries.

The decision to provide descriptions of the nearly 800 books listed in *The Writer's Advisor* and merely to record the more than 3,000 magazine articles was prompted by space considerations. The book descriptions vary in length and detail, but whenever a book is seen to be a superior contribution to the literature of authorship, this is clearly indicated.

Of the thirty-four major categories, several address the business aspects of writing. While materials relating to manuscript preparation, marketing, taxation, agents, and the like do not bear directly upon the act of writing, they remain essential elements in the typical writer's day-to-day concerns.

Three Indexes Provided

The author index includes not only the authors of the books and articles contained herein, but also any authors mentioned in the descriptions of such materials. In addition, the numerous interviews appearing in magazine articles have been indexed by interviewee. The resulting system will allow the user to locate references to thoughts about writing by a given author wherever they appear in this work. For increased flexibility, we have also included two additional indexes. One covers book titles; the other is a subject arrangement.

Jorge Luis Borges has said that ". . . a book is not an isolated entity," but that it is ". . . an axis of innumerable relationships." For the many who have asked for organized access to the literature of authorship, here is a beginning. Here, however imperfect, is an "axis of innumerable relationships."

In the recognition that no work such as this can ever be final or complete, we hope to produce frequent revisions of *The Writer's Advisor* in order to record newly published materials and to respond to user suggestions.

Acknowledgments

Among the many individuals at Eastern Washington University who deserve mention for having encouraged or aided in the creation of this book are:

Nancy Aries, former student

Charles Baumann, University Librarian

Sarah Hakim, Reference Assistant

Loren Jorden, Computer Operations Manager

Judith Kaufman, Director, Technical Communications Program

William Kidd, Associate Provost for Faculty Development

Don Lake, Head Reference Librarian

Suzanne Schenk, Interlibrary Loans

Duane Thompson, Vice President and Provost for Academic Affairs

Gratitude must also go to the endlessly resourceful staffs of New York Public Library and the Library of Congress, and to the invaluable assistance of Micki Nowinski and Dedria Bryfonski of Gale Research Company.

Finally, a special word of thanks belongs to Jacques Barzun, Malcolm Cowley, Bill Katz, James McAuley, and Patrick McManus for their early encouragement of the concept that led to this book.

The
WRITER'S
ADVISOR

Novel

"The novel remains still...the most independent, most elastic, most prodigious of literary forms."

—Henry James

Books

1. Allott, Miriam. *Novelists on the Novel.* New York: Columbia, 1959. 336 pp.

   Allott draws on the great English, French, and Russian writers as they expressed themselves about their art in diaries, letters, and notebooks, as well as in passages in their novels. Conveniently divided into major sections such as Characterization, Dialogue, Structural Problems, and Narrative Technique, each of which is introduced by an essay that places the topic in historical perspective.

2. Alter, Robert. *Partial Magic; The Novel as a Self-Conscious Genre.* Berkeley: University of California Press, 1975. 248 pp.

   Examines novels that flaunt artifice through authorial intrusion. Fielding, Sterne, Stendhal, Joyce, and Nabokov receive major attention.

3. Block, Lawrence. *Writing the Novel; From Plot to Print.* Cincinnati: Writer's Digest, 1979. 279 pp.

   In this first-person account of contemporary book-length fiction writing, from category books to serious mainstream novels, Block suggests a kind of market analysis when picking a certain type of novel to write. Advice on plots, notebooks, outlining, drawing on personal experience, rewriting, and advice on "getting published." A lively and informative work by a seasoned veteran.

4. Bocca, Geoffrey. *You Can Write a Novel.* Englewood Cliffs, New Jersey: Prentice-Hall, 1983. 138 pp.

   An author of twenty-six books, including eleven novels, provides candid advice on day-to-day routines, rewriting, plot, dialogue, and style. This work is spiced with examples and advice from other writers.

5. Boulton, Marjorie. *Anatomy of the Novel.* London; Boston: Routledge & Kegan Paul, 1975. 189 pp.

Widely ranging examples (Malamud, James, Woolf, Achebe, Amis, Dickens, Joyce, and Lawrence) are used to chart a course toward verisimilitude in character, scene, plot, and dialogue. Contains an excellent treatment of theme.

6. Braine, John. *Writing a Novel.* New York: Coward, McCann & Geoghegan, 1974. 223 pp.

A narrow "here is how I do it" approach, the most valuable aspect of which is a disciplined and structured system for getting as much down on paper in as short a time as possible. In addition to discussing his own work, he refers to other writers, such as Georges Simenon, who make use of this blitzkrieg method of completing a first draft. Though sometimes pointlessly opinionated, Braine offers professionally reliable advice. He is the author of *Room at the Top.*

7. Buckler, William Earl. *Novels in the Making.* Boston: Houghton Mifflin, 1961. 266 pp.

This collection of prefaces and journal excerpts presents the thinking of seventeen authors, each of whom discuss the problems and perceptions that went into the making of one of his or her novels. From Defoe through Conrad, to Gide and Lawrence, the reader is given not only a sense of the historical development of the novel as a form, but much about the individual efforts involved.

8. Burack, Abraham Saul, editor. *Techniques of Novel Writing.* Boston: Writer, 1973. 305 pp.

Forty different novelists each contribute a short chapter to this anthology and demonstrate a wide variety of approaches. *Techniques of Novel Writing* contains practical advice given by authors who have earned the right to offer it. Joyce Carol Oates, Frank Slaughter, and Norah Lofts are among the contributors.

9. Caserio, Robert L. *Plot, Story, and the Novel.* Princeton, New Jersey: Princeton University Press, 1979. 340 pp.

This is an informed attempt to unravel the narrative versus antinarrative literary positions. Starting with Poe and Dickens, Caserio takes us through the various modern developments that have altered plot and story in the novel. Lawrence, Woolf, Joyce, Conrad, and Nabokov are among the more recent writers discussed in that context.

10. Conrad, Joseph. *Letters from Conrad, 1895-1924.* Edited by Edward Garnett. Indianapolis: Bobbs-Merrill, 1928. 313 pp.

These letters reveal Conrad the writer in his struggles and in his triumphs. One also learns how this subtle and prolific mind was plagued with writer's block!

11. Cowley, Malcolm, and Howard Eppens Hugo. *Lesson of the Masters; An Anthology of the Novel from Cervantes to Hemingway.* New York: Scribner, 1971. 514 pp.

Short excerpts with commentary. Emphasis is on plot and character development.

12. Derrick, Christopher. *The Writing of Novels.* Boston: Writer, 1969. 192 pp.

Derrick cites Faulkner's "Let the writer take up surgery or bricklaying if he is interested in technique," and goes on to advise the reader against theoretical planning and excessive plot considerations. Contains some good advice on manuscript preparation, but generally addresses a wishful audience.

13. Dostoevsky, Fyodor M. *Notebooks for "The Brothers Karamazov."* Chicago: University of Chicago Press, 1971. 279 pp.

14. ———. *Notebooks for "Crime and Punishment."* Chicago: University of Chicago Press, 1967. 246 pp.

15. ———. *Notebooks for "The Idiot."* Chicago: University of Chicago Press, 1967. 254 pp.

16. ———. *Notebooks for "The Possessed."* Chicago: University of Chicago Press, 1968. 431 pp.

17. ———. *Notebooks for "A Raw Youth."* Chicago: University of Chicago Press, 1969. 570 pp.

18. ———. *Unpublished Dostoevsky; Diaries and Notebooks: 1860-1881.* Ann Arbor: Ardis, 1973, 1975, 1976. 3 volumes.

The fragmented record of the author's literary plans, business affairs, intended reading, and comments about the world around him. Not to be confused with the separate and distinct University of Chicago series of notebooks relating to individual novels cited above.

19. Du Maurier, Daphne. *Myself When Young; The Shaping of a Writer.* Garden City, New York: Doubleday, 1977. 204 pp.

This memoir, taken from earlier diaries of the author's formative years, includes the writing apprenticeship that led to her first novel.

20. Forster, Edward Morgan. *Aspects of the Novel.* New York: Harcourt, 1927. 176 pp.

Originally delivered as Clark Lectures at Cambridge, these are the thoughts of a highly regarded novelist on character, plot, pattern, and rhythm in fiction. Drawing on the work of novelists spanning two hundred years, this book is a critical account that bears only peripherally on Forster's own writing. A classic statement on the novel in particular and on fiction in general, it provides a stimulating account of how story and plot differ.

21. Frankau, Pamela. *Pen to Paper; A Novelist's Notebook.* New York: Doubleday, 1962. 237 pp.

    Much more than a handbook on writing, this is an incisive look at the ongoing life of a professional writer.

Fredette, Jean M. *Fiction Writer's Market.* See entry 1109.

22. Gardiner, Harold Charles. *Norms for the Novel.* Garden City, New York: Hanover House, 1960. 166 pp.

    Gardiner, a respected editor and critic, raises basic questions concerning morality in fiction. Graham Greene's *End of the Affair* and *Heart of the Matter* and Betty Smith's *A Tree Grows in Brooklyn* are cited, among other works.

Gardner, John. *The Art of Fiction.* See entry 1113.

23. ———. *On Becoming a Novelist.* New York: Harper & Row, 1983. 150 pp.

    John Gardner, at the time of his recent death, was considered by many to be among the best novelists of his generation. It is no surprise that reviewers have called this work "superbly written" and "eminently useful." In four parts, Gardner discusses the "Writer's Nature," "The Writer's Training and Education," "Publication and Survival," and "Faith."

24. Gibson, Graeme, editor. *Eleven Canadian Novelists.* Toronto: Anansi, 1972. 324 pp.

    These interviews, conducted with Margaret Atwood, Austin Clarke, Matt Cohen, Marian Engel, Timothy Findley, Dave Godfrey, Margaret Laurence, Jack Ludwig, Alice Munro, Mordecai Richter, and Scott Symons, place modern Canadian fiction in perspective.

25. Gide, Andre. *The Counterfeiters, With Journal of "The Counterfeiters."* New York: Alfred A. Knopf, 1955. 432 pp.

    Of principal interest for the light which the Journal sheds on the making of an important novel by a major twentieth-century author.

———. *The Journal of Andre Gide.* See entry 1115.

26. Grabo, Carl Henry. *The Technique of the Novel.* New York: Gordiam Press, 1964. 331 pp.

Designed for the beginning writer, this is a casebook of examples from a variety of novels of recognized merit. Each chapter is concerned with a major technical element, such as plot or point of view. The examples, which are far more useful than Grabo's analysis, are taken from James, Dickens, Zola, Woolf, and the like. Almost no writing has been included for the period since World War II.

27. Halperin, John, editor. *The Theory of the Novel; New Essays.* New York: Oxford, 1974. 396 pp.

Comic forms, aesthetics, narrative, tone, distance, character, illusion, intention, and point of view are investigated by such first-rate critics as Leslie Fiedler and John Halperin.

28. Hicks, Granville, editor. *The Living Novel; A Symposium.* New York: Macmillan, 1957. 230 pp.

Eleven novelists, including Saul Bellow, Ralph Ellison, and Flannery O'Connor, discuss those aspects of modern novel writing that they consider important and sometimes urgent.

29. Hildick, Wallace. *Writing with Care.* New York: David White, 1967. 150 pp.

Discussion, with examples, of the alterations made by Butler to the manuscript for *The Way of All Flesh,* Hardy to the manuscript for *Tess of the D'Urbervilles,* Eliot to the manuscript for *Middlemarch,* and James to the manuscript for *Daisy Miller.* The account of why the changes were made, as well as how they contributed to balance, will give the reader a surer sense of why revision is so important.

30. Humphrey, Robert. *Stream of Consciousness in the Modern Novel.* Berkeley: University of California Press, 1954. 127 pp.

Individual works of James Joyce, Virginia Woolf, Dorothy Richardson, and William Faulkner are examined as being representative of stream of consciousness writing.

31. James, Henry. *The Art of the Novel; Critical Prefaces.* With an introduction by Richard P. Blackmur. New York: Scribners, 1962. 348 pp.

A master renders masterful statements on the specifics of his art.

32. Komroff, Manual. *How to Write a Novel.* New York: Simon and Schuster, 1950. 296 pp.

Called by the *New York Times* a "simple and sound guide," this text for beginners contains carefully selected excerpts from world fiction.

33. Kronenberger, Louis, editor. *Novelists on Novelists; An Anthology.* New York: Doubleday & Company, 1962. 387 pp.

What a notable author of fiction has written about past or contemporary authors has long been considered a clue to the inner workings of his or her own work. In these twenty-eight essays, character sketches, memorials, and reminiscences, one finds assessments by Andre Gide of Fyodor Dostoevsky, E.M. Forster of Marcel Proust, D.H. Lawrence and Graham Greene of Herman Melville, Katherine Anne Porter of Willa Cather, and so on. Kronenberger has made his wise selections on the basis of "...their insight into character, their powers of observation, (and) their creative gifts of memory."

34. Liddell, Robert. *A Treatise on the Novel.* London: J. Cape, 1947. 168 pp.

Filled with careful, scholarly thoughts on fiction, this book is generally regarded as a first-rate work of criticism. Contains an appendix with quotations on writing by noteworthy novelists.

35. Lowry, Malcolm. *Selected Letters.* New York: Lippincott, 1965. 459 pp.

Spanning the years 1928 to 1957, these letters contain numerous literary reflections but are most valuable for the insights one thirty-page letter offers about *Under the Volcano.*

36. Lubbock, Percy. *Craft of Fiction.* New York: Scribners, 1921. 277 pp.

Widely recognized as a classic, this deftly written and cleverly conceived book approaches the traditional novel with lucid concern. It abounds in the details of method used by such giants as Tolstoy, Dostoevsky, Thackeray, and Flaubert. Though it offers no guide to more recent styles of writing, it nevertheless acts as a kind of landmark primer on the heart and substance of the novel.

37. McCormack, Thomas, editor. *Afterwords; Novelists on Their Novels.* New York: Harper & Row, 1969. 231 pp.

Fourteen American and British authors write about one of their works of fiction. Louis Auchincloss comments on the creation of *The Rector of Justin,* Robert Crichton on *The Secret of Santa Vittoria,* John Fowles on *The French Lieutenant's Woman,* Mary Renault on *The King Must Die,* and so on. This volume is full of the kind of shop talk that other writers will find compelling. Also included are Anthony Burgess, Truman Capote, George P. Elliott, William Gass, Mark Harris, Norman Mailer, Ross MacDonald, Wright Morris, and Reynolds Price.

38. McGrady, Mike. *Stranger Than Naked; Or How To Write Dirty Books for Fun and Profit.* New York: Peter H. Wyden, 1970. 213 pp.

An inside look at how twenty-four journalists cooperatively authored the best-selling *Naked Came the Stranger* under the pseudonym Penelope Ashe. In a kind of parody of "how to" books, the author gives a formula for writing sexploitation novels. Humorous, but with a dark side.

39. McHugh, Vincent. *Primer of the Novel.* New York: Farrar-Straus, 1975. 308 pp. (Originally published 1950.)

A treatise having the same high reputation as Lubbock's *Craft of Fiction* and Forster's *Aspects of the Novel,* this work is arranged by such subjects as research, character, dialogue, and aftereffects. Amid a plenitude of technical advice there is an omnipresent sense that each novel is the product of a unique mind and thus cannot be contained by mere formulas. Present also is the suggestion of inner personal reward which may be summed up by a quotation from Henry James, "It may leave him weary and worn; but how, after his fashion, he will have lived!"

40. Mann, Thomas. *The Story of a Novel; The Genesis of Doctor Faustus.* New York: Alfred Knopf, 1961. 242 pp.

Critics have hailed this detailed account of how a great modern novel grew from first idea to completion.

41. Maupassant, Guy de. *The Portable Maupassant.* Edited and with an introduction by Lewis Gallantiere. New York: Viking Press, 1947. 758 pp.

Contains his short but often cited "Essay on the Novel."

42. Mendilow, Adam. *Time and the Novel.* New York: Nevill, 1952. 245 pp.

Of greatest value for its theories on time and the reader, the intrusive author, dialogue, point of view, and psychological duration, this work centers on the time perception of Thomas Wolfe, Franz Kafka, Thomas Mann, Joseph Conrad, James Joyce, Laurence Sterne, Aldous Huxley, and Andre Gide.

43. Meredith, Robert, and John D. Fitzgerald. *Structuring Your Novel; From Basic Idea to Finished Manuscript.* New York: Harper, 1972. 230 pp.

The structure or framework upon which one hangs all the other elements of a novel is discussed with reference to seven key works which range from *Tom Jones* to *The Spy Who Came in from the Cold.*

44. Muir, Edwin. *The Structure of the Novel.* London: Hogarth Press, 1954. 151 pp.

Though Muir's short critical approach to structure has not been so universally recognized as Lubbock's *The Craft of Fiction* or Forster's *Aspects of the Novel,* it remains an important source. It addresses time, space, action, and character from a traditional perspective.

45. Nin, Anais. *The Novel of the Future.* New York: Macmillan, 1968. 214 pp.

In this study of the technique and development of the modern poetic novel, Nin evaluates individual writers whom she sees as having successfully combined poetry and prose. She uses examples from her own work to "analyze and observe the process of creation..." of such literature. In addition, she draws on the work of a sparkling array of modern writers, filmmakers, and other members of the creative community. In her view, the novel of the future will be psychoanalytical and surrealistic.

46. Norris, Frank. *The Responsibilities of the Novelist; and Other Literary Essays.* New York: Haskell House, 1969. 311 pp.

Among these essays by one of the giants of American literature are "The Mechanics of Fiction," "Story-tellers vs. Novelists," and "Fiction Writing as a Business."

47. Perry, Dick. *One Way to Write Your Novel.* Cincinnati: Writer's Digest, 1981. 138 pp.

With a kind of snake-oil rhetoric that will deter some readers, Perry demands two pages per day—no matter what. His zany observations on character, plot, self-editing, and manuscript preparation offer an antidote to novelist's block.

48. Petrakis, Harry Mark. *Reflections; A Writer's Life, A Writer's Work.* Chicago: Lake View Press, 1983. 252 pp.

This impressive and imaginative collection is of interest mainly for its "Journal of a Novel," which discusses the author's difficulties and triumphs while writing the novel *The Year of the Bell.* Just how he overcame the creative and technical obstacles involved will be of direct value to many a practicing novelist.

49. Pritchett, Victor Sawdon. *The Living Novel and Later Appreciations.* New York: Vintage Books, 1964. 467 pp.

A collection of fifty-eight essays on English, European, and American novelistic traditions by a distinguished practitioner.

50. ———. *The Working Novelist.* London: Chatto and Windus, 1965. 203 pp.

This collection of essays gives Pritchett's reflections on other novelists and bears only indirectly on his own work.

51. Robbe-Grillet, Alain. *For a New Novel; Essays on Fiction.* New York: Grove Press, 1966. 175 pp.

Essays on the French *nouveau roman* which Robbe-Grillet says began with Flaubert, Kafka, Proust, Faulkner, and Joyce. This collection was considered a literary event when it originally appeared.

52. Romberg, Bertil. *Studies in the Narrative Technique of the First-Person Novel.* Folcroft, Pennsylvania: Folcroft Library Editions, 1974. 379 pp.

An excellent discussion of the traditional first-person novel with regard to point of view, tenses, and narration. Divides such works into five categories: epic, memoir, diary, epistolary, and mixed.

53. Rubin, Louis D. *The Teller in the Tale.* Seattle: University of Washington Press, 1968. 228 pp.

Taking the position that studies of the novel that leave out the author as teller are likely to miss the point, Rubin comments on Stendhal, Twain, Joyce, James, and several other novelists to show how a sense of reality is furthered by the "authorial personality." Though this book is primarily a work of literary criticism, its significance for practicing novelists goes beyond that of most works of criticism. Though much modern creative writing instruction stresses the elimination of so-called intrusions, the conclusion that may be drawn from Rubin's convincing study is that such eliminations are never entirely successful, nor are they desirable.

54. Sale, Roger, editor. *Discussions of the Novel.* Boston: Heath, 1968. 101 pp.

Reflections on the novel by Nathaniel Hawthorne, Henry James, Ford Madox Ford, Wyndham Lewis, Joseph Conrad, and D.H. Lawrence.

55. Scholes, Robert E. *Approaches to the Novel; Materials for a Poetics.* San Francisco: Chandler, 1966. 314 pp.

This collection of critical essays on the novel draws upon the thinking of Henry James, E.M. Forster, Mark Schorer, Lionel Trilling, and a number of other distinguished authors and critics. Divided into pairs, under categories such as Mimesis, Point of View, Plot, and the Individual and Society, each view is balanced by the thinking of one other writer.

56. Simenon, Georges. *The Novel of Man.* New York: Harcourt, Brace and World, 1964. 59 pp.

A short attempt by a master storyteller at a philosophy of the novel, taking into account both human anxiety and human joy.

57. Steinbeck, John. *Journal of a Novel; The "East of Eden" Letters.* New York: Viking Press, 1969. 182 pp.

As the day-to-day account of the writing of *East of Eden,* this work takes the form of a series of letters sent to Steinbeck's editor Pascal Covici at Viking Press. Its main importance is that it was for Steinbeck "...a kind of arguing ground for the story." Much can also be learned about the author's work habits, down to and including the legendary ritual sharpening of pencils. Above all this is the unfolding of the anguish and joy and loneliness of a major American novelist at work. For anyone who has ever felt his or her writing to be a massive burden, what Steinbeck says toward the end of this work may be meaningful. "Although sometimes I have felt that I held fire in my hands and spread a page with shining—I have never lost the weight of clumsiness, of ignorance, of aching inability."

58. Steinberg, Erwin R. *The Stream of Consciousness Technique in the Modern Novel.* Port Washington, New York: Kennikat Press, 1979. 198 pp.

William James, Sigmund Freud, Henri Bergson, Virginia Woolf, Dorothy Richardson, Marcel Proust, and others define and redefine, inspect and dissect, and generally investigate the major aspects of this technique.

59. Stevick, Philip, editor. *The Theory of the Novel.* New York: The Free Press, 1967. 440 pp.

In fifty-three commentaries, as many distinguished authors and critics express their thoughts about narrative technique, point of view, plot, and six other facets of the novelist's art. Ranging from Miguel de Cervantes and Henry Fielding to Mark Schorer and Phyllis Bentley, this anthology has considerable value for most writers. Extensive bibliography and index.

60. Trenner, Richard, editor. *E.L. Doctorow; Essays and Conversations.* New York: Ontario Review, 1983. 216 pp.

In addition to nine critical essays about Doctorow, this work includes a number of interviews with the author as well as his memorable speech before Congress, "For the Artist's Sake." Included also is Doctorow's essay on literature, "False Documents."

61. Trollope, Anthony. *An Autobiography.* London: Oxford University Press, 1950. 411 pp.

These recollections of a great nineteenth-century British novelist tell of Trollope's early struggles as a writer, his relations with book and magazine publishers, and the secret behind his incredible outpouring of books, as revealed by his work habits.

62. Uzzell, Thomas H. *The Technique of the Novel; A Handbook on the Craft of the Long Narrative.* New York: Citadel Press, 1959. 350 pp.

Taking the position that wisely considered technique offers the novelist a path to lucidity and greater inventive control, Uzzell concentrates on artistic attitudes, characters, viewpoint, and significance in fiction. Over one third of this uncommonly instructive work is given over to the technical analysis of twenty-five outstanding novels.

63. Wallace, Irving. *The Writing of One Novel.* New York: Simon and Schuster, 1968. 250 pp.

Examines the creative processes and sixteen years of labor that went into the writing of Wallace's best seller *The Prize* and represents one of the better statements by a commercial novelist on the burdens of his craft.

64. Wilson, Angus. *Diversity and Depth in Fiction. Selected Writings of Angus Wilson.* New York: Viking, 1984. 303 pp.

The majority of the essays included in this work are critical analyses of the works of other writers. The final portion centers on Wilson's reflections on his own work.

65. Wilson, Colin. *Craft of the Novel.* London: Gollancz, 1975. 256 pp.

In this extended critical essay, Wilson views the historical development of the novel and also expresses his attitudes toward writing and the teaching of writing. He singles out "creative thinking" as a prerequisite to creative writing. Best known for his book *The Outsider,* Wilson is a British novelist and essayist of considerable stature.

66. Wolfe, Thomas. *Story of a Novel.* New York: Scribner's, 1936. 93 pp.

Wolfe's account of how *Look Homeward Angel* came to be written and his confession about the considerable pains of revising and rewriting it. As one critic put it, to read this book is "...almost to be present at an act of creation."

Articles

67. A.B. Guthrie, Jr. (interview). *Publishers Weekly,* vol. 204, October 8, 1973, pp. 58-59.

68. About that novel. Evan Hunter. *Writer,* vol. 91, April 1978, pp. 9-11.

69. Adela Rogers St. John, reliving the good life (interview). *Writer's Digest,* vol. 60, April 1980, pp. 28-32+.

70. Advice to unborn novelists. Pearl S. Buck. *Saturday Review of Literature,* vol. 11, March 2, 1935, pp. 513-514+.

71. All that glitters is not Hollywood, as explained by Joseph Wambaugh. W. Warga. *Writer's Digest,* vol. 63, February 1983, pp. 24-31+.

72. Are there things a novelist shouldn't joke about? (interview). Kurt Vonnegut. *Christian Century,* vol. 93, November 24, 1976, pp. 1048-1050.

73. Battle cries of Leon Uris (interview). *Writer's Digest,* vol. 57, November 1977, pp. 26-27.

74. Best selling novelist tells why she keeps a notebook; excerpt from *Slouching Towards Bethlehem.* Joan Didion. *Writer's Digest,* vol. 51, December 1971, pp. 26-27+.

75. Biographical novel. Irving Stone. *Writer,* vol. 75, January 1962, pp. 9-13.

76. Birth of a saga. R.F. Delderfield. *Writer,* vol. 82, November 1969, pp. 18-21.

77. Born a square; the westerners' dilemma. Wallace Stegner. *Atlantic,* vol. 213, January 1964, pp. 46-50; discussion, vol. 213, March 1964, pp. 40+.

78. C.P. Snow and the realistic novel. E. Miner. *Nation,* vol. 190, June 25, 1960, pp. 554-555.

79. Can the novel still sell? A bookseller's view. Ian Norrie. *Bookseller,* May 15, 1976, pp. 2312-2314.

80. Can the novel still sell? A publisher's view. Phillip Ziegler. *Bookseller,* May 15, 1976, pp. 2314+.

81. Carlos Fuentes (interview). *Kenyon Review,* vol. 5, Fall 1983, pp. 105-118.

82. Category novel. I. Moore. *Writer,* vol. 77, September 1964, pp. 9-13.

83. Character and imagination in the experimental novel. R.S. Ryf. *Modern Fiction Studies,* vol. 20, Autumn 1974, pp. 317-327.

84. Characterization in the romance novel. Laurie McBain. *Writer,* vol. 96, May 1983, pp. 10-12.

85. Characters and personality; the novelist's dilemma. L.S. Roudiez. *French Review,* vol. 35, May 1962, pp. 553-562.

86. Close-up; novelist of suburbia; Mr. Saturday, Mr. Monday, and Mr. Cheever. W. Sheed. *Life,* vol. 66, April 18, 1969, pp. 39-40+.

87. Coincidence in the novel; a necessary technique. W.R. McDonald. *College English,* vol. 29, February 1968, pp. 373-382+.

88. Commanding your material; novel writing. T. Duncan. *Writer,* vol. 79, March 1966, pp. 13-16+.

89. Commitment without empathy; a writer's notes on politics, theatre, and the novel. David Caute. *TriQuarterly,* no. 30, Spring 1974, pp. 51-70.

90. Company; novels of Harold Robbins. *New Yorker,* vol. 45, November 29, 1969, pp. 45-48.

91. Composition and structure of *Tom Sawyer* (Mark Twain). Hamlin L. Hill. *American Literature,* vol. 32, January 1961, pp. 379-392.

92. Confessions of a novelist. *Atlantic Monthly,* vol. 151, April 1933, pp. 385-392.

93. Confessions of the long-distance writer; family sagas. R.F. Delderfield. *Writer,* vol. 84, September 1971, pp. 11-13.

94. Conrad's revisions of *The Secret Agent.* Harold E. Davis. *Modern Language Quarterly,* vol. 19, 1958, pp. 244-254.

95. Conscious craftsman: Ford Madox Ford's manuscript revisions. F. Macshane. *Boston University Studies in English,* vol. 5, 1961, pp. 178-184.

96. Contemporary novel. H.G. Wells. *Fortnightly Review,* vol. 96, November 1911, pp. 860-873; (part of the famous Wells-James dispute).

97. Conversations with James Joyce. Georges Borach. *College English,* vol. 15, March 1954, pp. 325-327.

98. Cosmos of the artist; excerpts from interview. William Faulkner. *Saturday Review,* vol. 45, July 28, 1962, pp. 18-21.

99. Course of composition of *A Connecticut Yankee:* a reinterpretation. (Mark Twain.) Howard G. Baetzhold. *American Literature,* vol. 33, May 1961, pp. 195-214.

100. Day in the life of Joan Didion (interview). John G. Dunne and J. Didion. *Ms.,* vol. 5, February 1977, pp. 65-68+.

101. Dickens at work on *Bleak House:* a critical examination of his memoranda and number plans. H.P. Sucksmith. *Renaissance and Modern Studies,* vol. 9, 1965, pp. 47-85.

102. Dickens at work on the text of *Hard Times.* S. Monod. *Dickensian,* vol. 64, 1968, pp. 86-99.

103. Don't wait to write your novel. E.E. Tigue. *Writer,* vol. 76, September 1963, pp. 25-26.

104. Don't write down to the paperbacks. E. DeRoo. *Writer,* vol. 74, July 1961, pp. 17-19+.

105. Elements of successful novel writing. Frank G. Slaughter. *Writer,* vol. 85, April 1972, pp. 17-19.

106. Elmore Leonard (interview). *Publishers Weekly,* vol. 223, February 25, 1983, p. 32.

107. Empathy follows sympathy. Ed McClanahan. *Writer,* vol. 97, February 1984, pp. 12-13.

108. Every novel is like another planet. H. Lees. *Writer,* vol. 85, October 1972, pp. 12-15.

109. Exclusive interview with Herbert Gold. *Writer's Digest,* vol. 52, September 1972, pp. 29-31+.

110. Finding a plot for your novel. Rick Boyer. *Writer,* vol. 96, July 1983, pp. 14-17.

111. First book. Marsha Parker (interview). *Coda,* vol. 10, June/July 1983, pp. 5-6.

112. First person singular. Donald Hamilton. *Writer,* vol. 97, October 1984, pp. 16-18.

113. First word. M. Millhiser. *Writer,* vol. 95, December 1982, pp. 17-19+.

114. For a new novel. Alain Robbe-Grillet. *Saturday Review,* vol. 49, March 12, 1966, p. 32.

115. Gabriel Garcia Marquez meets Ernest Hemingway. *New York Times Book Review,* vol. 86, July 26, 1981, pp. 1+.

116. Gay Talese (interview). *Writer's Digest,* vol. 53, January 1973, pp. 28-31.

117. Gay Talese (interview continued). *Writer's Digest,* vol. 53, February 1973, pp. 26-31+.

118. George Eliot's notes for *Adam Bede.* Joseph Wiesenfarth. *Nineteenth Century Fiction,* vol. 32, September 1977, pp. 127-165.

119. Giving birth to a novel. Ingrid Rimland. *Writer's Digest,* vol. 59, March 1979, pp. 28-29.

120. Gore Vidal's inner workings (interview). *Writer's Digest,* vol. 55, March 1975, pp. 20-26.

121. Gore Vidal's work habits (interview). *Writer's Digest,* vol. 55, March 1975, pp. 17-19.

122. Graham Greene's second thoughts: the text of *The Heart of the Matter*. D. Higdon. *Studies in Bibliography,* vol. 30, 1977, pp. 249-256.

123. Growing a novel. E. Hyde. *Writer,* vol. 95, August 1982, pp. 16-18+.

124. Guess who writes 70,000 words a week, publishes 24 books a year, and says "Me Tarzan, you Jane" works best in sex scenes (Barbara Cartland). Arturo F. Gonzalez, Jr. *Writer's Digest,* vol. 59, June 1979, pp. 22-24.

125. Harbingers; storytelling in the novel. George P. Elliott. *Writer,* vol. 84, November 1971, pp. 9-10+.

126. Harold Robbins (interview). *New York Times Book Review,* vol. 83, January 29, 1978, p. 36.

127. Heart of Darkness: the manuscript revisions (Joseph Conrad). Jonah Raskin. *Review of English Studies,* New Series, vol. 18, 1967, pp. 30-39.

128. Henry James and the art of revision. I. Traschen. *Philological Quarterly,* vol. 35, 1956, pp. 39-47.

129. How a book grows. F.E. Randall. *Writer,* vol. 85, January 1972, pp. 11-13+.

130. How and why I write the costume novel. F. Yerby. *Harper's Magazine,* vol. 219, October 1959, pp. 145-150.

131. How I write my books. Stanley Ellin, P.D. James, Gregory McDonald, Patricia Highsmith, Len Deighton, Eric Ambler, and Desmond Bagley. *Writer's Digest,* vol. 63, October 1983, pp. 22-29.

132. How to be your own critic. M. Chittenden. *Writer,* vol. 97, February 1984, pp. 14-16.

133. How to get an idea for your novel if you don't already have one. S. Smythe. *Writer's Digest,* vol. 50, March 1970, pp. 20-22.

134. How to write a novel. John Braine. *Writer,* vol. 85, May 1972, pp. 9-10+.

135. How to write a novel. S. Cloete. *Writer,* vol. 77, July 1964, pp. 9-10.

136. How to write a novel. Miguel de Unamuno. *New Review,* August-October 1931, pp. 13-20.

137. How to write a novel. Morris West. *Writer,* vol. 90, May 1977, pp. 9-11.

138. How to write a novel. D. Westheimer. *Writer,* vol. 80, December 1967, pp. 14-15+.

139. How to write a novel synopsis. C. Felice. *Writer,* vol. 94, February 1981, pp. 24-26.

140. How to write a world-famous best-selling novel that will make your name a household word and will make you rich beyond your wildest dreams (satire). E.G. Smith. *Vogue,* vol. 139, March 1, 1962, p. 133; Reply, D. Sayre, vol. 140, September 1, 1962, p. 132.

141. How to write two first novels with your knuckles; G. Jones and editor T. Morrison. D. K. Mano. *Esquire,* vol. 86, December 1976, pp. 62+.

142. Humans are a violent species—we always have been (interview). John Irving. *U.S. News and World Report,* vol. 91, October 26, 1981, pp. 70-71.

143. I live my novel. A. Walden. *Writer,* vol. 84, October 1971, pp. 26-28.

144. I mean, my god, if you can't produce a great American novel for two hundred thou, presold to the flicks, what the hell hope is there for American Literature? S. Brown. *Esquire,* vol. 67, February 1967, pp. 76-77+.

145. Idea to publication; a doctor takes to novel writing. E.M. Goldberg. *Writer,* vol. 86, February 1973, pp. 14-15+.

146. Imperfect ideal of the novel. T. Wright. *Modern Language Review,* vol. 73, January 1978, pp. 1-16.

147. Innocence of Eden—almost; writing the light romance. Linda Jacobs. *Writer,* vol. 87, June 1974, pp. 15-18.

148. Inspiration. Vladimir Nabokov. *Saturday Review of the Arts,* vol. 1, January 1973, pp. 30-32.

149. Interviewing Thomas Berger. *New York Times Book Review,* vol. 85, April 6, 1980, pp. 1+.

150. Introduction for *The Sound and the Fury.* William Faulkner. *Southern Review,* vol. 8, 1972, pp. 705-710.

151. Irving Wallace bends some rules (interview). *Writer,* vol. 78, January 1965, pp. 12-15+.

152. Is Richardson alive? the novel as drama. L. Lerner. *Encounter,* vol. 42, March 1974, pp. 61-64.

153. James Baldwin (interview). *Black Scholar,* vol. 5, December 1973-January 1974, pp. 33-42.

154. James Jones has come home to whistle (interview). *Writer's Digest,* vol. 56, October 1976, pp. 22-26+.

155. James T. Farrell (interview). *Partisan Review,* vol. 50, no. 2, 1983, pp. 266-278.

156. John Hawkes and John Barth talk about fiction. *New York Times Book Review,* vol. 84, April 1, 1979, pp. 7+.

157. John Hawkes (interview). *New Republic,* vol. 181, November 10, 1979, pp. 26-29.

158. Jose Donoso (interview). *Partisan Review,* vol. 49, no. 1, 1982, pp. 23-44.

159. Joseph Heller; some things happen. L. Grobel. *Writer's Digest,* vol. 57, October 1977, pp. 24-25.

160. Journal of a young novelist. Susan Berman. *Writer,* vol. 89, November 1976, pp. 21-22+.

161. Let your novel "come." Janice Elliott. *Writer,* vol. 96, August 1983, pp. 13-14+.

162. Literary horizons; publishing of first novels. Granville Hicks. *Saturday Review,* vol. 52, March 15, 1969, p. 31.

163. Long, long trail; writing a saga. R.F. Delderfield. *Writer,* vol. 84, January 1971, pp. 9-12.

164. Louis L'Amour (interview). *Publishers Weekly,* vol. 204, October 8, 1973, pp. 56-57.

165. Louis L'Amour: writing high in the bestseller saddle. Arturo F. Gonzalez, Jr. *Writer's Digest,* vol. 60, December 1980, pp. 22-29.

166. Lovers, tyrants and other catastrophies (a self-interview by a feminist about women authors of erotica). Francine de Plessiz Gray. *Rolling Stone,* no. 235, March 24, 1977, p. 36+.

167. Ludlum conspiracy; Robert Ludlum. Lawrence Block. *Writer's Digest,* vol. 57, September 1977, pp. 25-26.

168. Lure of the adventure novel. Gordon Gordon. *Writer,* vol. 97, March 1984, pp. 7-9+.

169. Magical world of the novelist. Sidney Sheldon. *Writer,* vol. 93, November 1980, pp. 13-15.

170. Making of a classic; excerpts from interview. Gabriel Garcia Marquez. *Atlas,* vol. 26, July 1950, p. 79.

171. Making of a novel. W.C. Lee. *Writer,* vol. 87, November 1974, pp. 17-19.

172. Man who inspired three novelists. G. Walker. *Cosmopolitan,* vol. 147, August 1959, pp. 42-45.

173. Man who raised the Titanic—and a small fortune (Clive Cussler). Dolores Johnson. *Writer's Digest,* vol. 58, May 1978, pp. 32-33.

174. Marinating of *For Whom the Bell Tolls* (Ernest Hemingway). L. Wagner. *Journal of Modern Literature,* vol. 2, 1977, pp. 533-546.

175. Marquez himself (Gabriel Garcia Marquez). F. MacShane. *New York Times Book Review,* vol. 83, July 16, 1978, pp. 3+.

176. *Master Mariner* and how it grew. Nicholas Monsarrat. *Publishers Weekly,* vol. 215, January 29, 1979, p. 90.

177. Maturing of novel ideas. M. Montgomery. *Writer,* vol. 82, December 1969, pp. 22-24+.

178. Memoirs of a niggling young man; satire. Malcolm Bradbury. *Vogue,* vol. 134, November 1959, pp. 186-188.

179. Metanovel. D.H. Lowenkron. *College English,* vol. 38, December 1976, pp. 343-355.

180. Metaphors for the novel. Philip Stevick. *TriQuarterly,* no. 30, Spring 1974, pp. 127-138.

181. Middle of the book blues. Ten ways to get your novel back on track. Phyllis A. Whitney. *Writer,* vol. 97, July 1984, pp. 9-12.

182. More than plot and character. D. Westheimer. *Writer,* vol. 85, November 1972, pp. 21-23.

183. My first book. Thomas Hinde. *Author,* vol. 91, Winter 1980, pp. 38-39.

184. My first book. Doris Lessing. *Author,* vol. 91, Spring 1980, pp. 11-14.

185. My first novel: good news for unpublished novelists. Candy Schulman. *Writer's Digest,* vol. 63, January 1983, pp. 23-29.

186. My first sale: how I sold my first novel. Alpha Blair. *Writer's Digest,* vol. 62, June 1982, pp. 37-38.

187. Myth of fragility concealing a tough core (interview). Joan Didion. *Saturday Review,* vol. 4, March 5, 1977, p. 24.

188. Name of the game is work; excerpt from *The Writing of One Novel.* Irving Wallace. *Writer,* vol. 81, November 1968, pp. 12-14+.

189. Narrative, time and the open-ended novel. B. Gross. *Criticism,* vol. 8, Fall 1966, pp. 362-376.

190. Nathanael West's revisions of *Miss Lovelyhearts.* C. Daniel. *Studies in Bibliography,* vol. 16, 1963, pp. 232-243.

191. Nicholas Monsarrat's working methods (interview). *Writer's Digest,* vol. 49, August 1969, p. 59.

192. Nine questions to ask yourself before you write your novel. Helene Barnhart. *Writer's Digest,* vol. 63, April 1983, pp. 37-39.

193. No one asked me to write a novel. A. Lurie. *New York Times Book Review,* vol. 87, June 6, 1982, pp. 13+.

194. Notes and comments; excerpts from Nobel Prize address. Aleksandr Solzhenitzyn. *New Yorker,* vol. 48, September 9, 1972, p. 29.

195. Notes of a novelist. J. Berry. *Nation,* vol. 189, November 14, 1959, pp. 351-354.

196. Notes on a second novel. F. Salas. *Writer,* vol. 84, February 1971, pp. 12-15.

197. Notes on writing a novel. John Hawkes. *TriQuarterly,* vol. 30, Spring 1974, pp. 109-126.

198. Notes on writing a novel; excerpt from *Afterwords: Novelists on Their Novels.* J. Fowles. *Harper's,* vol. 237, July 1968, pp. 88-90+.

199. Novel and the market. Surveys of fiction. David Lodge. *Encounter,* vol. 47, September 1976, pp. 69-76.

200. Novel approach. M. Mather. *Writer,* vol. 81, March 1968, pp. 12-14+.

201. Novel art. David Paul. *Twentieth Century,* vol. 153, June 1953, pp. 436-442.

202. Novel art: II. David Paul. *Twentieth Century,* vol. 153, October 1953, pp. 294-301.

203. Novel as an expression of the writer's vision of the world. S. Eile. *New Literary History,* vol. 9, Autumn 1977, pp. 115-128.

204. Novel bites man. Dan Wakefield. *Atlantic,* vol. 226, August 1970, pp. 72-78; same, *Writer,* vol. 83, November 1970, pp. 11-13+; reply with rejoinder. Philip Roth. *Atlantic,* vol. 226, October 1970, p. 28.

205. Novelist and his theme. T.C. Turner. *Writer,* vol. 76, December 1963, pp. 12-14+.

206. Novelist and his trade. John Moore. *Writer,* vol. 80, October 1967, pp. 13-16.

207. Novelist as village idiot. U. Zilinsky. *Writer,* vol. 83, December 1970, pp. 24-26.

208. Novelist's dilemma. R.G. Kelly. *Writer,* vol. 76, March 1963, pp. 7-9+.

209. Novelist's identity crisis. H. Van Slyke. *Writer,* vol. 90, November 1977, pp. 11-14.

210. Novelists responsibility. L.P. Hartley. *English,* vol. 13, Summer 1961, pp. 172-177.

211. Novel view of the novel (satire). Jesse Hill Ford. *Americas,* vol. 12, August 1960, pp. 38-39.

212. On the first-person novel. M. Glowinski. *New Literary History,* vol. 9, Autumn 1977, pp. 103-114.

213. Ordinary thoughts on the writing of a novel. J. Guest. *Writer,* vol. 90, January 1977, pp. 11-14+.

214. Oysters and a novelist's art. J. Wain. *New Republic,* vol. 151, August 8, 1964, pp. 23-24.

215. Phenomenology and the form of the novel; toward an expanded critical method. D.W. Townsend, Jr. *Philosophy and Phenomenological Research,* vol. 34, March 1974, pp.331-338.

216. Philip Roth (interview). *Mademoiselle,* vol. 53, August 1961, pp. 254-255.

217. Picture your fiction. After everyday sights have made a movie in your mind, you are ready to start writing your novel. Jerry McGuire. *Writer's Digest,* vol. 58, January 1978, pp. 32-33.

218. Plotting the children's novel. Joan Aiken. *Writer,* vol. 95, April 1982, pp. 14-17; May 1982, pp. 15-17.

219. Plot-tone conflict; a new key to the novel. R. Stanton. *College English,* vol. 29, May 1968, pp. 602-607.

220. Prince of the paperback literati. Tom Robbins. *New York Times Magazine,* February 12, 1978, pp. 16-17.

221. Problem with a poetics of the novel. W.L. Reed. *Novel,* vol. 9, Winter 1976, pp. 101-113.

222. Problems and accomplishments in the editing of the novel. G.T. Tanselle. *Studies in the Novel,* vol. 7, Fall 1975, pp. 323-360.

223. Process of writing a novel; excerpts from address, March 1970. James Dickey. *Writer,* vol. 83, June 1970, pp. 12-13.

224. PW interviews: John Fowles. *Publishers Weekly,* vol. 206, November 25, 1974, pp. 6-7.

225. PW interviews: Peter Benchley. *Publishers Weekly,* vol. 205, February 11, 1974, pp. 8-9.

226. PW interviews: Walker Percy. *Publishers Weekly,* vol. 211, March 21, 1977, pp. 6-7.

227. Questions they never asked me. Walker Percy. *Esquire,* vol. 88, December 1977, pp. 170-172+.

228. Real secret of Santa Vittoria. Robert Crichton. *Writer,* vol. 82, July 1969, pp. 13-14+.

229. Realism in the novel. D. Goldknopf. *Yale Review,* vol. 60, October 1970, pp. 69-84.

230. Recipe for a novel. J.M. McClary. *Writer,* vol. 85, August 1972, pp. 9-12+.

231. Research is a snap (use of photos to aid description in novel). Jacqueline Briskin. *Writer's Digest,* vol. 59, February 1979, pp. 26-28.

232. Richard Condon; bestsellers are his business. Arturo F. Gonzalez, Jr. *Writer's Digest,* vol. 56, November 1976, pp. 22-25.

233. Rise of the housewife novelist. R. Wetzsteon. *Saturday Review,* vol. 7, November 1980, pp. 49-52.

234. Risks and rewards in writing the saga novel. S. Howatch. *Writer,* vol. 90, June 1977, pp. 11-13+.

235. Roots of a novel. Jane Gilmore Rushing. *Writer,* vol. 88, July 1975, pp. 9-11+.

236. Roots of Alex Haley's writing career. Jeffrey Elliot. *Writer's Digest,* vol. 60, August 1980, pp. 20-27+.

237. Rx for novelists. H. Van Slyke. *Writer,* vol. 87, July 1974, pp. 11-14.

238. Self-begetting novel. S.G. Kellman. *Western Humanities Review,* vol. 30, Spring 1976, pp. 119-128.

239. Self-control techniques of famous novelists (with introduction and discussion by J.J. Pear). Irving Wallace. *Journal of Applied Behavior Analysis,* vol. 10, Fall 1977, pp. 515-525.

240. Setting and a sense of world in the novel. A. Gelley. *Yale Review,* vol. 62, December 1972, pp. 186-201.

241. Setting and background in the novel. Mary Stewart. *Writer,* vol. 77, December 1964, pp. 7-9.

242. Silence of the novel. John Preston. *Modern Language Review,* vol. 74, April 1979, pp. 257-267.

243. Sinclair Lewis and rules. Adelyne Berg. *Writer,* vol. 74, August 1961, pp. 12-13+.

244. Some modest proposals on the novel. Gerald Green. *Writer,* vol. 82, June 1969, pp. 19-23.

245. Some reflections of a popular novelist. J.B. Priestley. *Essays and Studies,* vol. 18, 1932, pp. 149-159.

246. Space of the novel. E. Marcotte. *Partisan Review,* vol. 41, no. 2, 1974, pp. 263-272.

247. Steel writer: Stirling Silliphant (interview). *Writer's Digest,* vol. 64, March 1984, pp. 39-42.

248. Stephen Crane's revision of *Maggie: A Girl of the Street.* R.W. Stallman. *American Literature,* vol. 26, January 1955, pp. 528-536.

249. Story behind a record-breaking sale; writing *The French Passion.* D. DuPont. *Writer,* vol. 90, November 1977, pp. 15-17.

250. Such good writing; an interview with Lois Gould. Jane Bakerman. *Writer's Digest,* vol. 60, September 1980, pp. 24-28.

251. Talking with John Irving (interview). *Redbook,* vol. 158, November 1981, pp. 12+.

252. Technique of counterpoint. M. Roston. *Studies in the Novel,* vol. 9, Winter 1977, pp. 378-388.

253. Technique of the novel. F. Marcus. *English Journal,* vol. 51, October-December 1962, pp. 449-458, pp. 527-535, pp. 609-616; vol. 52, January 1963, pp. 1-8.

254. Television techniques for novel writing. T. Willis. *Writer,* vol. 91, June 1978, pp. 14-17+.

255. Temporal form in the novel. J. Miel. *MLN,* vol. 84, December 1969, pp. 916-930.

256. Tense and novel. R. Pascal. *Modern Language Review,* vol. 57, January 1962, pp. 1-11.

257. That first novel and after. V.G. Myer. *Times Educational Supplement,* vol. 2889, October 2, 1970, pp. 21-22.

258. That lively corpse; the novel. Richard Powell. *Writer,* vol. 78, October 1965, pp. 12-14+.

259. Thomas Gifford; the bestsell factor. S.L. Muellner. *Writer's Digest,* vol. 57, July 1977, pp. 50-51.

260. Thorned words of Colleen McCullough. Kay Cassill. *Writer's Digest,* vol. 60, March 1980, pp. 32-36.

261. Time and the novelist. David Paul. *Partisan Review,* vol. 21, November/December 1954, pp. 636-649.

262. Time and transition in the novel. Margaret Culkin Banning. *Writer,* vol. 87, October 1974, pp. 11-13+.

263. Timely and timeless young adult novel. Laurie Glieco. *Writer,* vol. 97, March 1984, pp. 22-23.

264. To get in a famous last word, better find a good first one; opening lines from famous novels. M. Olmert. *Smithsonian,* vol. 9, November 1978, p. 212.

265. To make a short story long. Orson S. Card. *Writer's Digest,* vol. 60, September 1980, pp. 20-23.

266. Total revolution in the novel. Richard Gilman. *Horizon,* vol. 4, January 1962, pp. 96-101.

267. Toward a definition of the novella. J. Gibaldi. Studies in Short Fiction, vol. 12, Spring 1975, pp. 91-97.

268. Truth and Nat Turner; an exchange. William Styron. *Nation,* vol. 206, April 22, 1968, pp. 544-547.

269. Versions of *Brave New World* (Aldous Huxley). R. Wilson. *Library Chronicle of the University of Texas,* vol. 8, Spring 1968, pp. 28-41.

270. Viewpoint in the novel. W. Graham. *Writer's Digest,* vol. 52, October 1972, pp. 25-26+.

271. What makes a good novel? R.P. Ashley. *English Journal,* vol. 60, May 1971, pp. 596-598+.

272. What plot means in the novel. D. Goldknopf. *Antioch Review,* vol. 29, Winter 1969-1970, pp. 483-496.

273. What should a novel be? adaptation of address, 1970. Al Dewlen. *Writer,* vol. 84, July 1971, pp. 16-17.

274. What to do till the novel comes. S. Jameson. *Writer,* vol. 84, April 1971, pp. 14-15.

275. Where does a novel begin? S. Grafton. *Writer,* vol. 83, February 1970, pp. 17-19.

276. Where writers dare not fear to tread (physical research for novels). *Writer's Digest,* vol. 59, September 1979, pp. 20-25.

277. Who reads the literary novel? Peter H. Mann. *Bookseller,* November 24, 1979, pp. 2356-2357.

278. Who wrote Thomas Wolfe's last novels? (allegedly written by editor E. Aswell). J. Halberstadt. *New York Review of Books,* vol. 28, March 19, 1981, pp. 51-52.

279. Why John Irving is so popular. J. Epstein. *Commentary,* vol. 73, June 1982, pp. 59-63.

280. Why novelists go wrong. J.W. Krutch. *Theatre Arts,* vol. 43, June 1959, pp. 12-14.

281. Why they aren't writing the great American novel anymore; comparison of 19th century novels with 20th century journalism; with appendices. Tom Wolfe. *Esquire,* vol. 78, December 1972, pp. 152-159+.

282. Writer as moralist. Saul Bellow. *Atlantic,* vol. 211, March 1963, pp. 58-62.

283. Writer's Digest interview; Lawrence Durrell. *Writer's Digest,* vol. 55, November 1975, pp. 18-20.

284. Writing a first novel. Erica Jong. *Twentieth Century Literature,* vol. 20, October 1974, pp. 262-269.

285. Writing a first novel. Part I. *Writer,* vol. 97, October 1984, pp. 26-30.

286. Writing a first novel. Part II. *Writer,* vol. 97, November 1984, pp. 21-24.

287. Writing a first novel; comments by newly published novelists. *Writer,* vol. 88, March 1975, pp. 24-29; April 1975, pp. 22-25; May 1975, pp. 22-25; June 1975, pp. 23-27.

288. Writing a first novel; symposium. *Writer,* vol. 80, January 1967, pp. 16-18; vol. 81, January 1968, pp. 20-26; February 1968, pp. 18-22; March 1968, pp. 20-30; April 1968, pp. 25-33; May 1968, pp. 20-27; June 1968, pp. 27-37; vol. 84, October 1971, pp. 20-23; November 1971, pp. 19-25.

289. Writing an adventure novel. H. Innes. *Writer,* vol. 88, February 1975, pp. 17-18.

290. Writing a novel. E. Hardwick. *New York Review of Books,* vol. 20, October 18, 1973, pp. 33+.

291. Writing and selling your first novel. Kelly Cherry. *Writer,* vol. 96, April 1983, pp. 18-21.

292. Writing novels for children. C. Aaron. *Writer,* vol. 86, July 1973, pp. 21-22+.

293. Writing paperback originals. M. Williams. *Writer,* vol. 82, April 1969, pp. 24-26.

294. Writing the documentary novel. B. Deal. *Writer,* vol. 81, September 1968, pp. 11-13+.

295. Writing the episodic novel. R. White. *Writer,* vol. 77, May 1964, pp. 9-12.

296. Writing the first-second-third-fourth novel. G.S. Wright, Jr. *Writer,* vol. 89, April 1976, pp. 23-24+.

297. Writing the historical romance. Robyn Carr. *Writer's Digest,* vol. 63, July 1983, pp. 38-40.

298. Writing the roman a clef. John Leggett. *Writer,* vol. 93, February 1980, pp. 15-17.

Drama and Musical Theatre

"A drama must be shaped so as to have a spire of meaning."
—John Galsworthy

Books

299. Anderson, Maxwell. *Off Broadway; Essays About the Theatre.* New York: William Sloane Associates, 1947. 91 pp.

Ten essays on playmaking by a master of that art. Filled with faith in the power of the theatre, but mainly concerned with Anderson's "on Broadway" efforts, rather than his works of a non-commercial or experimental nature.

300. Archer, William. *Play-Making, A Manual of Craftsmanship.* With a new introduction by John Gessner. New York: Dover, 1960. 277 pp.

Considered by many observers to be the finest statement on the subject. First published in 1912, it retains a wealth of specific suggestions on theme, climax, anticlimax, probability, obligatory scenes, foreshadowing, interest, and the psychology of character.

301. Baker, George P. *Dramatic Technique.* New York: DeCapo, 1976. 532 pp.

Contains numerous technical insights, some of which may not be found elsewhere.

302. Bentley, Eric R. *The Playwright as Thinker; A Study of Drama in Modern Times.* New York: Harcourt, Brace & World, 1946. 382 pp.

Expresses Bentley's conviction that the theater should be a moral and aesthetic force as opposed to Broadway and Hollywood shallowness. Using as examples a number of outstanding nineteenth- and twentieth-century dramatists, he relates them to their times, cultures, and dramatic traditions. There is little in this book that will tell the reader how to write a play, but much about the question of seriousness and quality in playwriting.

303. Boulton, Marjorie. *The Anatomy of Drama.* London: Routledge and Kegan Paul, 1960. 212 pp.

Intending her book to be a "...contribution to literary criticism," Boulton nevertheless gives us many practical insights about setting, character, and plot in drama. Her analysis of dialogue is particularly noteworthy.

304. Brecht, Bertolt. *Brecht on Theatre; The Development of an Aesthetic.* New York: Hill and Wang, 1964. 294 pp.

Arranged in chronological order, these notes and theoretical writings give the reader a sense of how Brecht's ideas evolved. "A Short Organum for the Theatre," Brecht's most complete statement of his revolutionary philosophy of the theatre, is also included.

305. Brustein, Robert. *The Theatre of Revolt; An Approach to Modern Drama.* Boston: Little, Brown, 1964. 435 pp.

Eight playwrights (Ibsen, Strindberg, Chekhov, Shaw, Brecht, Pirandello, O'Neill, and Genet) are examined with regard to dramatic rebellion, methods, and influences. One of the "...decisive books on modern theatre."

306. Chekhov, Anton. *Letters.* New York: Harper, 1973. 494 pp.

From early student days to his position as master of fiction and drama, Chekhov reveals the literary concerns of a lifetime, including the preoccupations that accompanied *The Seagull, Three Sisters,* and *The Cherry Orchard.*

307. ———. *Letters on the Short Story, the Drama, and Other Literary Topics.* New York: Minton, Balch and Co., 1924. 358 pp.

Among these letters are a number that bear upon Chekov's dramatic art.

308. Chekhov, Michael. *To the Director and Playwright.* Compiled by Charles Leonard. New York: Harper & Row, 1963. 329 pp.

A highly respected director's reflections on the how and why of twentieth-century directing and playwriting and its genesis in the techniques of the great Russian playwrights and directors.

309. Clark, Barrett H. *European Theories of Drama.* New York: Crown, 1947. 576 pp.

Considered fundamental by many observers, this work moves from Aristotle to the mid-twentieth century. Of great value is the diary for O'Neill's *Mourning Becomes Electra.*

310. Cole, Toby, editor. *Playwrights on Playwriting; The Meaning and Making of Modern Drama From Ibsen to Ionesco.* Introduction by John Gassner. New York: Hill and Wang, 1960. 299 pp.

An anthology of prefaces, public statements, and introductions by Bertolt Brecht, William Archer, Thornton

Wilder, Emile Zola, J.M. Synge, August Strindberg, T.S. Eliot, Henrik Ibsen, Eugene O'Neill, Sean O'Casey, and Eugene Ionesco, among others. Organized in two sections, "Credos and Concepts" and "Creations," the first explores critical and technical concepts, while the second records the thinking of fifteen playwrights about their own works.

311. Egri, Lajos. *The Art of Dramatic Writing; Its Basis in the Creative Interpretation of Human Motives.* Introduction by Gilbert Miller. New York: Simon & Schuster, 1946. 294 pp.

A classic work which remains in print.

312. Engle, Lehman. *The Making of a Musical.* New York: Macmillan, 1977. 157 pp.

Provides numerous examples to support the theories presented, including techniques of "book" writing for the musical in its many forms.

313. Esslin, Martin. *The Theatre of the Absurd.* New York: Anchor, 1961. 364 pp.

One of the best introductory texts on the subject.

314. Frankel, Aaron. *Writing the Broadway Musical.* New York: Drama Book Specialists, 1977. 182 pp.

More specialized than Engle (above), this somewhat "starstruck" approach not only addresses scriptwriting, music, and stage direction, but also provides a useful survey of the professional responsibilities of the many categories of individuals, on stage and behind the scenes, who bring a musical to life. Examples are mainly from *My Fair Lady* and *Company.*

315. Fugard, Athol. *Notebooks 1960-1977.* New York: Knopf, 1984. 237 pp.

An internationally-acclaimed South African playwright reveals how he transformed people and events into art.

316. Funke, Lewis. *Playwrights Talk about Writing; Twelve Interviews.* Chicago: Dramatic, 1975. 307 pp.

Includes interviews of Neil Simon, Howard Sackler, Lillian Hellman, Edward Albee, Arthur Miller, John Osborne, Tom Stoppard, William Gibson, and Jean Kerr.

317. Gallaway, Marian. *Constructing a Play.* With a forward by Tennessee Williams. Englewood Cliffs, New Jersey: Prentice-Hall, 1950. 380 pp.

Gallaway's text is obligatory reading for the apprentice playwright. It is perceptive of and sensitive to the wide variety of forms that good playscripts can take. The main emphasis is on scenario building, with considerable attention to action, complications, and other aspects of plot. Dialogue and characterization, by intent, receive less attention. This book will not make one a playwright, but according to Tennessee Williams, "What Marian Gallaway is offering is not a way to shortcut your own natural growth, but ways to avoid unnatural growth."

318. Gibson, William. *Two for the Seesaw and Seesaw Log.* New York: Bantam, 1962. 199 pp.

A detailed account of the path leading to the production of a Broadway play as seen by the playwright. This has been called by Peter Kline, "One of the best studies of the professional playwright's life ever written."

319. Granville-Barker, Harley. *On Dramatic Method.* New York: Hill and Wang, 1956. 191 pp.

An accomplished director offers essays on the theatre, many of which bear on the art of writing plays. Based on the distinguished lectures given by Granville-Barker at Trinity College, Cambridge, *On Dramatic Method* sets forth various laws of the theatre as seen in the works of playwrights from Aeschylus to Ibsen.

320. Grebanier, Bernard D.N. *Playwriting; How to Write for the Theater.* New York: Barnes and Noble, 1979. 386 pp.

Called eminent and practical by reviewers, this lucid study, which offers frequent examples, tells how to select a theme, form a plot, create characters, and develop dialogue. Some attention is given to television writing.

321. Greenwood, Ormerod. *The Playwright; A Study of Form, Method, and Tradition in the Theatre.* London: Pitman, 1950. 214 pp.

A highly recommended historical survey of playwriting which covers Greek, Elizabethan, Restoration, and modern playwrights.

322. Hart, Moss. *Act One.* New York: Random House, 1959. 444 pp.

The autobiography of an important playwright and director which, in addition to entertaining us with lively anecdotes, tells much about the "dolors and doldrums" of playwriting. Like *Two for the Seesaw and Seesaw Log* (see entry 318), *Act One* follows a play from inception to production.

323. Hoare, John Edward. *The Psychology of Playwriting; Audience, Writer, Play.* New York: Dramatists Play Service, 1949. 211 pp.

The illusion created by playwright and actors is seen as a delicate fabric which can be torn aside at any moment. How the illusion is maintained, how themes and symbols are used, and how characters are created are the subjects of this book, which uses examples from Ibsen, Hellman, Wilder, and Wilde.

324. Hogarth, Basil. *How to Write Plays.* London: Pitman, 1933. 158 pp.

Though long out of print, this work retains the same high value as the previously mentioned classic by Archer.

325. Hull, Raymond. *Profitable Playwriting.* New York: Funk and Wagnalls, 1969. 257 pp.

A Canadian playwright gives instructions for conceiving plots, developing characters, and sustaining action. The examples he uses from his own writing are none too convincing, but his discussions of technique, marketing, and character development in both playwriting and television writing will properly inform the beginner on the essentials. Considerable attention is given to dialogue and tension.

326. Ionesco, Eugene. *Notes and Counter Notes; Writings on the Theatre.* New York: Grove Press, 1964. 271 pp.

Letters, critical statements, and interviews make up the bulk of this collection of writings by a major twentieth-century dramatist of the absurd. The section called "testimony" includes essays such as "How I write."

327. Izakowitz, David. *Dramatists Sourcebook 1982-83.* New York: Theatre Communications Group, 1982, (annual). 192 pp.

From the publisher: "...opportunities for playwrights, translators, composers, lyricists, and librettists. Includes theatre submission guidelines, grants, contests, and much more."

328. Kerr, Walter. *How Not to Write a Play.* New York: Simon & Schuster, 1955. 245 pp.

A distinguished drama critic views playwriting in America, shows the traditions, both here and abroad, that have influenced it, and then goes on to illustrate how playwrights are still writing in imitation of Chekhov and Ibsen. Though hardly a text on writing plays, this work of popular criticism offers many suggestions about what makes for quality scripts. Some of Kerr's remarks about contemporary theatre have become dated, but this remains an indispensable work.

329. Kline, Peter. *The Theatre Student; Playwriting.* New York: Richards Rosen Press, 1970. 186 pp.

Intended mainly for public school use, this introductory text treats the critical and technical aspects of playwriting. It tells how to create dialogue, plot, and characters, and how to revise. An appendix contains scenes from student written plays.

330. Langner, Lawrence. *The Play's the Thing*. New York: Putnam, 1960. 258 pp.

Based on information and experience from the Theatre Guild, this guide to writing commercial drama continues to provide insight and practical advice. The chapters on lyrical productions and rewriting are particularly valuable. Langner was a distinguished producer and also co-authored a Broadway hit.

331. Lawson, John Howard. *Theory and Technique of Playwriting*. With a new introduction. New York: Hill and Wang, 1960. 313 pp.

An uneven but basically sound text which leans toward the philosophical at the expense of the practical.

332. Leach, Robert. *How to Make a Documentary Play; A Handbook for Drama Teachers and Youth Leaders*. Glasgow, Scotland: Blackie & Son, 1975. 115 pp.

Leach attempts to show the essentials of recreating "...factual material in a theatrical idiom." From the choice of subject to the actual performance of the play, Leach offers step-by-step guidance.

333. Mabley, Edward Howe. *Dramatic Construction; An Outline of Basic Principles. Followed by Technical Analyses of Significant Plays by Sophocles and Others*. Philadelphia: Chitton, 1972. 430 pp.

Detailed analysis of twenty-four plays with regard to plot, conflict exposition, development, dialogue, and other considerations of concern to playwrights.

334. MacGowan, Kenneth. *Primer of Playwriting*. New York: Random House, 1951. 210 pp.

Taking the position that a great amount of nonsense has been written about playwriting, this respected guide stresses plot, character, and emotional unity. Exposition, relation of early material to later scenes, the conflict of wills, complication, and suspense are also given emphasis. MacGowan produced plays for Eugene O'Neill and films for a number of major studios. Filled with common sense and uncommon advice.

335. Matthews, Brander, editor. *Papers on Playmaking*. With a preface by Henry W. Wells. Freeport, Long Island, New York: Books for Libraries, 1970. 312 pp.

Contains essays and letters on writing plays by Lope de Vega, Alexandre Dumas, Wolfgang Goethe, Carlo Goldoni, and Victorien Sardou.

336. Miller, J. William. *Modern Playwrights at Work.* New York: Samuel French, 1968. 576 pp.

The methods, work habits, and influences of eight playwrights are related to specific plays. Those covered are Henrik Ibsen, August Strindberg, Anton Chekhov, George Bernard Shaw, John Galsworthy, Luigi Pirandello, Eugene O'Neill, and Tennessee Williams.

337. Niggli, Josefina. *New Pointers on Playwriting.* Boston: Writer, 1967. 166 pp.

Techniques such as suspense, dialogue, characterization, and conflict are successfully demonstrated in this introduction to play and script writing. Examples range from Sophocles and Shakespeare to Arthur Miller and Edward Albee.

338. Polti, Georges. *The Thirty-Six Dramatic Situations.* Boston: Writer, 1977, 181 pp.

Polti draws on classics of literature to categorize situations into classes and subclasses. He has attached an extensive index to the plays, novels, and authors cited in this unique resource.

339. Priestley, John Boynton. *The Art of the Dramatist; A Lecture Together with Appendix and Discursive Notes.* London: Heinemann, 1973. 91 pp.

As theorist and practitioner, Priestley provides what has been called a valuable addition to the "... list of good books on the technique of writing plays."

340. Raphaelson, Samson. *The Human Nature of Playwriting.* New York: Macmillan, 1949. 267 pp.

Cited by *Library Journal* as "...one of the best books on playwriting...." Seen by Arthur Miller as a work that will offer aid to the "...talented but foundering..." writer. Not a text nor a set of rules, but a stimulus to the creative process.

341. Shaw, George Bernard. *Plays and Players; Essays on the Theatre.* New York: Oxford University Press, 1952. 350 pp.

These critical essays and reviews range from Shakespeare to Ibsen and reveal the fierce loyalty that Shaw brought to the dramatic form.

342. ———. *Shaw on Theatre.* Edited by E.J. West. New York: Hill and Wang, 1958. 320 pp.

Further essays by Shaw, which appeared in a wide range of magazines and newspapers, will have general appeal, but are most valuable for the approaches they take to individual theatrical practices.

343. Smiley, Sam. *Playwriting; The Structure of Action.* Englewood Cliffs, New Jersey: Prentice-Hall, 1971. 315 pp.

This comprehensive text is addressed to "...all playwrights—beginners, interns, and professionals." It is a tightly organized, information-packed account which deals not only with writing plays, but also with the role of the playwright in the production of the play. Additional material appears on aesthetic theory, audiences, and script marketing. An impressive amount of analysis and background reading obviously went into its making.

344. Stanislavski, Konstantin S. *Building a Character.* New York: Theatre Arts Books, 1962. 292 pp.

Widely accepted advice to actors and directors which will have value for writers, particularly in those chapters dealing with character building, speech tempo, and accentuation.

345. ———. *Creating a Role.* New York: Theatre Arts, 1961. 271 pp.

Like the above work, these classic statements on roles, inner tone, and external circumstances should be considered required reading for scriptwriters and playwrights.

346. Van Druten, John. *Playwright at Work.* New York: Harper, 1952. 210 pp.

The author of *I Am a Camera* provides heartening counsel about both method and instinct in writing plays. Less "how to" in approach than "how I do," this book, in addition, is simply good reading.

347. Wager, Walter. *The Playwrights Speak.* New York: Delacorte, 1958. 290 pp.

These interviews, conducted by the former editor of *Playbill* and *Show,* include eleven dramatists. They are Arthur Miller, Edward Albee, Friedrich Duerrenmatt, John Osborne, William Inge, Eugene Ionesco, Harold Pinter, Peter Weiss, Tennessee Williams, John Arden, and Arnold Wesker.

348. Williams, Tennessee. *Cat on a Hot Tin Roof.* New York: New Directions, 1955. 173 pp.

Includes revisions of the third act with comments by Williams.

Articles

349. Adapting to success: writing the adaptation. Tim Kelly (playwright). *Writer's Digest,* vol. 63, March 1983, pp. 33-37.

350. After commitment (interview). Arthur Miller. *Theatre Journal,* vol. 32, May 1980, pp. 196-204.

351. Album of a play doctor. Stanley Kauffman. *American Scholar,* vol. 47, Winter 1977-78, pp. 87-94.

352. All comes clear at last, but the readiness is all. T.B. Stroup. *Comparative Drama,* vol. 10, Spring 1976, pp. 61-77.

353. Ambushes for the audience towards a high comedy of ideas (interview). Tom Stoppard. *Theatre Quarterly,* vol. 4, May 1974, pp. 3-17.

354. American writer: the American theatre. Arthur Miller. *Michigan Quarterly Review,* vol. 21, Winter 1982, pp. 4-20.

355. Art in microcosm: the manuscript stages of Beckett's *Come And Go.* Breon Mitchell. *Modern Drama,* vol. 19, September 1976, pp. 245-254.

356. Art of the theater: Arthur Miller (interview). *Paris Review,* no. 38, Summer 1966, pp. 61-98.

357. Art of the theater: Edward Albee (interview). *Paris Review,* no. 39, 1966, pp. 92-121.

358. Art of the theatre: Harold Pinter (interview). *Paris Review,* no. 39, Fall 1966, pp. 12-37.

359. Art of the theatre; Lillian Hellman (interview). *Paris Review,* no. 33, Winter 1965, pp. 64-95.

360. Arthur Miller on plays and playwriting (interview). *Modern Drama,* vol. 19, December 1976, pp. 375-384.

361. Audience as jury. D.A. Borchardt. *Players Magazine,* vol. 50, Fall-Winter 1975, pp. 10-15.

362. Barker's bite (interview). H. Barker. *Plays and Players,* vol. 23, December 1975, pp. 36-39.

363. Before you write your play. An eight point, step-by-step outline. Lavonne Mueller. *Writer,* vol. 97, February 1984, pp. 17-20.

364. Better a bad night in Bootle (interview). J. McGrath. *Theatre Quarterly,* vol. 5, September 1975, pp. 39-54.

365. Between absurdity and the playwright. William Oliver. *Educational Theatre Journal,* vol. 15, October 1963, pp. 224-235.

366. Beverly Cross (interview). *Plays and Players,* vol. 26, June 1979, p. 10.

367. Business of dealing with the business. Dennis McIntyre. *Michigan Quarterly Review*, vol. 21, Winter 1982, pp. 48-56.

368. Case for plot in modern drama. B.O. States. *Hudson Review*, vol. 20, Spring 1967, pp. 49-61.

369. Changing Cannan (interview). D. Cannan. *Plays and Players*, vol. 24, October 1976, pp. 37+.

370. Character and theatre: psychoanalytic notes on modern realism. D.M. Kaplan. *Tulane Drama Review*, vol. 10, Summer 1966, pp. 93-108; Reply, M. Kirby, vol. 11, Winter 1966, pp. 207-208.

371. Cognitive complexity and theatrical information processing: audience responses to plays and characters. W. Gourd. *Communication Monographs*, vol. 44, June 1977, pp. 136-151.

372. Commitment without empathy; a writer's notes on politics, theatre, and the novel. David Caute. *Triquarterly*, no. 30, Spring 1974, pp. 51-70.

373. Confessions of a playwright. William Saroyan. *World Review*, April 1949, pp. 9-13; May 1949, 33-35.

374. Creating what is normal; Edward Bond (interview). *Plays and Players*, vol. 23, December 1975, pp. 9-13.

375. Diary of a playwriting bursary. Bill Martin. *Theatre Quarterly*, vol. 10, Summer 1980, pp. 17-25.

376. Discovering the theatre. Eugene Ionesco. *Tulane Drama Review*, vol. 4, September 1959, pp. 3-18.

377. Documentary drama from the revue to the tribunal. G. Mason. *Modern Drama*, vol. 20, September 1977, pp. 263-277.

378. Dumb waiter: undermining the tacit dimension. A.E. Quigley. *Modern Drama*, vol. 21, March 1978, pp. 1-11.

379. Education of a playwright. Ronald E. Mitchell. *Players Magazine*, May 1941, pp. 8, 36.

380. End of playwriting. T. Dorst. *Antioch Review*, vol. 31, Summer 1971, pp. 255-265.

381. Energy: and the small discovery of dignity (interview). M. Hay and S. Trussler. *Theatre Quarterly*, vol. 10, Autumn/Winter 1981, pp. 3-14.

382. Equal first. J. Byrne. *Plays and Players*, vol. 26, April 1979, pp. 15-16.

383. Eugene Ionesco opens fire. *World Theatre*, vol. 3, no. 3, Autumn 1959, pp. 171-202.

384. Family in modern drama. Arthur Miller. *Atlantic*, vol. 197, April 1956, pp. 35-41.

385. Famous playwright's first awful flop; excerpt from *Act One.* Moss Hart. *Life,* vol. 47, August 24, 1959, pp. 82-86+.

386. Fish in the sea: playwright's note. J. McGrath. *Plays and Players,* vol. 22, April 1975, pp. 8-10.

387. Five ways to sell your play. Sam Smiley. *Writer's Digest,* vol. 51, December 1971, pp. 22-25.

388. Flight into lunacy. M. Valency. *Theatre Arts,* vol. 44, August 1960, pp. 8-11+.

389. Form and the dramatic text. J.A. Withey. *Educational Theatre Journal,* vol. 12, October 1960, pp. 205-211.

390. Gorky on playwriting. M. Gorky. *Yale Theatre,* vol. 7, Winter 1976, pp. 25-32.

391. Grammar for being elsewhere. H.P. Abbott. *Journal of Modern Literature,* vol. 6, February 1971, pp. 39-46.

392. Growth of images. Adrienne Kennedy. *Drama Review,* vol. 21, December 1977, pp. 43-48.

393. Guidelines for the beginning playwright. Louis E. Catron. *Writer,* vol. 94, November 1981, pp. 22-25.

394. Hey, stupid, where's the glass? experiences of propman author of *Agatha Sue, I Love You* (interview). A. Einhorn. *New Yorker,* vol. 42, November 12, 1966, pp. 54-55.

395. *Highest Tree* and how it grew. D. Schary. *Theatre Arts,* vol. 43, November 1959, pp. 10-13.

396. Hotel Universe: playwriting and the San Francisco mime troup. W. Kelb. *Theatre,* vol. 9, Spring 1978, pp. 15-20.

397. How I write my self-plays. R. Foreman. *Drama Review,* vol. 21, December 1977, pp. 5-24.

398. How to be your own best critic. T. Noice. *Writer's Digest,* vol. 55, September 1975, p. 18.

399. How to break into the theatre. M. Stehlik. *Writer's Digest,* vol. 55, September 1975, pp. 14-15.

400. How to write a play. Edward Albee. *USA Today,* vol. 107, April 1979, pp. 11-12.

401. How to write a play. M. Monigle. *Writer's Digest,* vol. 50, January 1970, p. 40.

402. How to write and sell that play. Tim Kelly. *Writer's Digest,* vol. 57, May 1977, pp. 19-23.

403. I thought I was hallucinating. Robert Wilson. *Drama Review,* vol. 21, December 1977, pp. 75-78.

404. I write these messages that come. M.I. Fornes. *Drama Review,* vol. 21, December 1977, pp. 25-40.

405. Inarticulations—the failure of American tragedy. R. Hayman. *Drama,* no. 707, Winter 1972, pp. 45-51.

406. Interview with Jerry Mayer. *Theatre,* vol. 9, Summer 1978, pp. 93-94.

407. Interview with Timothy Findley. *Canadian Literature,* no. 91, Winter 1981, pp. 49-55.

408. Interviews with Edward Bond, Arnold Wesker, and K.H. Stoll. *Twentieth Century Literature,* vol. 22, December 1976, pp. 411-432.

409. Jack Gelber talks about surviving in the theater (interview). *Theatre,* vol. 9, Spring 1978, pp. 46-58.

410. Joan Holden and the San Francisco mime troupe. R. Cohn. *Drama Review,* vol. 24, June 1980, pp. 41-50.

411. Language and action in the drama. A.S. Cooke. *College English,* vol. 28, October 1966, pp. 15-25.

412. Language of the theatre. E.L. Doctorow. *Nation,* vol. 228, June 2, 1979, pp. 637-638.

413. Languages of drama. R. Rosenburg. *Educational Theatre Journal,* vol. 15, March 1963, pp. 1-16.

414. Lines worth speaking. *Drama,* no. 80, Spring 1966, p. 15.

415. *Long Day's Journey Into Night:* from early notes to finished play (Eugene O'Neill). J.E. Barlow. *Modern Drama,* vol. 22, March 1979, pp. 19-28.

416. Make 'em laugh (interview). Neil Simon. *Plays and Players,* vol. 24, September 1977, pp. 12-15.

417. Making up the well-made plays for today. M. Leigh and M. Bradwell. *Plays and Players,* vol. 23, October 1975, pp. 12-16.

418. Man of the theatre; writing *Monkey Mountain* (interview). D. Walcott. *New Yorker,* vol. 47, June 26, 1971, pp. 30-31.

419. Metaphors, mad dogs, and old-time cowboys (interview). S. Shepard. *Theatre Quarterly,* vol. 4, August 1974, pp. 3-16.

420. Model for epic theatre. Bertolt Brecht. *Sewanee Review,* July-September 1949, pp. 425-436.

421. Murder games (interview). A. Shaffer. *Plays and Players,* vol. 27, October 1979, pp. 10-13.

422. Myths of present-day playwriting. H.M. Teichmann. *Writer,* vol. 75, April 1962, pp. 36-38.

423. New force on the theatrical horizon; dramaturge. D.B. Wilmeth. *USA Today,* vol. 107, March 1979, p. 66.

424. Notes on *The Best Man.* G. Vidal. *Theatre Arts,* vol. 44, July 1960, pp. 8-9.

425. Observations on the theatre. Maxim Gorky. *English Review,* April 1924, pp. 494-498.

426. Odets at center stage (interview). *Theatre Arts,* vol. 47, May 1963, pp. 16-19+; June 1963, pp. 28-30+.

427. On Kleist (interview). Eric R. Bentley. *Theatre,* vol. 11, Summer 1980, pp. 102-103.

428. On literary theatre (dramatic illusion). M. Kirby. *Drama Review,* vol. 18, June 1974, pp. 103-113.

429. On the nature of theatre; excerpts from *The Diary of Max Frisch. Tulane Drama Review,* vol. 6, no. 4, Spring 1962, pp. 3-11.

430. On the playwright's condition. *Theatre Crafts,* vol. 1, November/ December 1967, pp. 30-37.

431. Opportunities for playwrights (markets, contests, awards, and prizes). *Writer,* vol. 96, September 1983, pp. 25-30.

432. *Our Town*—from stage to screen; a correspondence between Thornton Wilder and Sol Lesser. *Theatre Arts,* vol. 24, November 1940, pp. 815-824.

433. Play construction; excerpts from *The Play's the Thing.* Lawrence Langner. *Writer,* vol. 76, February 1963, pp. 17-24.

434. Playmaker; or, The dramatic side of life. R. Sposet and T. Asad. *English Journal,* vol. 63, March 1974, pp. 80-81.

435. Plays that never get written. A. Pryce-Jones. *Theatre Arts,* vol. 47, October 1963, pp. 18-19.

436. Playwright and the contemporary world. J. Glassner. *Theatre Arts,* vol. 48, January 1964, pp. 22-23+.

437. Playwright and the rhythm of the seasons (interview). C. Fry. *Theatre Quarterly,* vol. 9, Autumn 1979, pp. 69-74.

438. Playwright as puppet. D. Rush. *Writer's Digest,* vol. 54, April 1974, pp. 18-21.

439. Playwrights and the stationary carrot. C. Farrington. *Theatre Arts,* vol. 46, February 1962, pp. 21-23.

440. Playwright's problem. Discussion between John Boynton Priestley and L.A.G. Strong. *Listener,* vol. 25, 1941, pp. 445-446.

441. Playwriting, a unique discipline. Jeffrey Sweet. *Writer,* vol. 85, April 1972, pp. 31-33.

442. Playwriting—getting started. Jeffrey Sweet. *Writer,* vol. 96, September 1983, pp. 22-24+.

443. Playwriting: hints from a first reader; with list of theaters. J. Calender. *Writer,* vol. 91, January 1978, pp. 16-20.

444. Playwriting without intermission; with a list of play publishers. J. McDonough. *Writer's Digest,* vol. 55, September 1975, pp. 16-17.

445. Poetry in playwriting. E.M. Browne. *Drama,* no. 83, Winter 1966, pp. 31-34.

446. Practice of playwriting. M.C. Chase. *Writer,* vol. 76, June 1963, pp. 17-19.

447. Probing Pinter's play; *The Homecoming;* with interview with Harold Pinter. H. Hewes. *Saturday Review,* vol. 50, April 8, 1967, pp. 56+.

448. Problem of realism in modern drama. J. Hristic. *New Literary History,* vol. 8, Winter 1977, pp. 311-318.

449. Realism in the American theatre. Mary McCarthy. *Harper's Magazine,* vol. 223, July 1961, pp. 45-52.

450. Reinvention of form. Jean-Claude van Itallie. *Drama Review,* vol. 21, December 1977, pp. 65-74.

451. Retrospective technique and its implications for tragedy. C.A. Hallett. *Comparative Drama,* vol. 12, Spring 1978, pp. 3-21.

452. Rhythmic language in the theatre. L.W. Cor. *Modern Language Quarterly,* vol. 22, September 1961, pp. 302-306.

453. Rx for stuck playwrights. Louis E. Catron. *Writer,* vol. 97, September 1984, pp. 20-23+.

454. Scavengers and scalpels on Broadway. Louis Kronenberger. *Theatre Arts,* vol. 46, February 1962, pp. 16-17+.

455. Scenario: talk with Robert Wilson (interview). *Dance Scope,* vol. 10, Fall 1975, pp. 11-21.

456. Sense of what should follow (interview). Arnold Wesker. *Theatre Quarterly,* vol. 7, Winter 1977-78, pp. 5-24.

457. Setting off down the golden pathway. J. Harding. *Plays and Players,* vol. 21, August 1974, pp. 27-29.

458. Snoo Wilson: enfant terrible of the English stage (interview). *Modern Drama,* vol. 24, December 1981, pp. 424-435.

459. Some uses of the "frame" in playwriting. Barnard Hewitt. *Quarterly Journal of Speech,* vol. 32, no. 4, 1946, pp. 480-484.

460. Staging of a play: notebooks and letters behind Elia Kazan's staging of *J. B.* Archibald McLeish. *Esquire,* vol. 50, May 1959, pp. 144-158.

461. Survival notes; a journal. Tennessee Williams. *Esquire,* vol. 78, September 1972, pp. 130-134+.

462. Theater of commitment; excerpt from address. Eric R. Bentley. *Commentary,* vol. 42, December 1966, pp. 63-72.

463. Theatre: an interview. Jean Paul Sartre. *Evergreen Review,* vol. 4, no. 11, 1960, pp. 143-152.

464. Theatre and the coming revolution (interview). A. Baraka. *Theatre Quarterly,* vol. 8, Autumn 1978, pp. 29-35.

465. Theatre of form and anti-form. Walter Kerr. *Horizon,* vol. 3, March 1961, pp. 42-47.

466. Theatre of light, space, and time (interview). Snoo Wilson. *Theatre Quarterly,* vol. 10, Spring 1980, pp. 3-18.

467. Thoughts on playwriting. R. Anderson. *Writer,* vol. 83, September 1970, pp. 12-14+.

468. Tom Stoppard. B.K. Snader. *Writer's Digest,* vol. 61, February 1981, pp. 18-19.

469. Toward a poetic of modern realistic tragedy. Alfred Schwarz. *Modern Drama,* vol. 9, September 1966, pp. 136-146.

470. Toward a theory of dramatic literature for a technological age. J. Fuegi. *Educational Theatre Journal,* vol. 26, December 1974, pp. 433-440.

471. Twenty-five years hard: a playwright's personal retrospective. A. Plater. *Theatre Quarterly,* vol. 7, Spring 1977, pp. 34-42.

472. Two pages a day. M. Terry. *Drama Review,* vol. 21, December 1977, pp. 59-64.

473. Two people in a room; playwriting (interview). Harold Pinter. *New Yorker,* vol. 43, February 25, 1967, pp. 34-36.

474. Uses of incongruity. W. Gray. *Educational Theatre Journal,* vol. 15, December 1963, pp. 343-347.

475. Verse drama. J. Garlington. *Texas Quarterly,* vol. 18, Summer 1975, pp. 119-121.

476. Verse in the theatre: the language of tragedy. M. Halpern. *Massachusetts Review,* vol. 8, Winter 1967, pp. 137-148.

477. Vision shared. Carson McCullers. *Theatre Arts,* April 1950, pp. 28-30.

478. Visualization, language, and the inner library. Sam Shepard. *Drama Review,* vol. 21, December 1977, pp. 49-58.

479. What you should know about staging your play. Carolyn Lane. *Writer,* vol. 96, May 1983, pp. 13-14.

480. Where to get new plays produced. *Writer,* vol. 93, August 1980, pp. 23-28.

481. Wickedest man in the world (interview). Snoo Wilson. *Plays and Players,* vol. 22, December 1974, pp. 36-38.

482. Working inside the system: a playwright's opinion. R. Bolt. *World Theatre,* vol. 13, Summer 1964, pp. 37-40.

483. Writing a stage play. J. Neipris. *Writer,* vol. 91, November 1978, pp. 17-19+.

484. Writing children's theatre is no child's play. William Brohuagh and Dennis Chaptman. *Writer's Digest,* vol. 59, August 1979, pp. 29-32.

485. Writing for values. William Oliver. *Educational Theatre Journal,* vol. 12, no. 3, October 1960, pp. 191-199.

486. Writing life; Edward Albee. Bob Woggon. *Writer's Digest,* vol. 60, October 1980, pp. 18+.

487. Writing plays for amateurs. J. Henderson. *Writer,* vol. 74, February 1961, pp. 15-19.

Television, Radio, and Film

"Television is now so desperately hungry for material that they're scraping the top of the barrel."

—Gore Vidal

Books

488. Baddeley, W. Hugh. *Technique of Documentary Film Production.* New York: Hastings House, 1975. 283 pp.

A full treatment of the documentary film which covers research, terminology, and dealing with the unpredictable.

489. Bayer, William S. *Breaking Through, Selling Out, Dropping Dead.* New York: Macmillan, 1971. 227 pp.

Flip in tone and shallow in content, this work may appeal to beginners in the cinematic arts, but it will be no substitute for the better texts in the field.

490. Bliss, Edward, and John M. Patterson. *Writing News for Broadcast.* 2nd revised edition. New York: Columbia University Press, 1978. 220 pp.

Maintaining its status as the standard resource in the field, the second edition explains technical terms while offering broader perspectives on the craft. Actual scripts are used to illustrate conventional and innovative forms.

491. Bluem, A. William. *Documentary in American Television.* New York: Hastings House, 1965. 311 pp.

Considered by many as having the same definitive status as Rotha's *Documentary Film.*

492. Blum, Richard. *Television Writing; From Concept to Contract.* New York: Hastings House, 1980. 184 pp.

A pleasant beginner's text which offers, among other things, advice on how not to write scripts. The section on public television writing is welcome and infrequently found in works of this type.

493. Brady, Ben. *Keys to Writing for Television and Film.* 3rd edition. Dubuque, Iowa: Kendall/Hunt, 1978. 281 pp.

Brady shares his twenty-five years of experience as a producer, director, broadcast executive, and writer to give us expert views on story, realism, conflict, theme, action, character development, dialogue, and plot. In addition, he provides a chapter on camera language, a glossary of terms, and a number of illustrative scripts. Brady produced such series as *Perry Mason, Have Gun Will Travel,* and *Rawhide.*

Brenner, Alfred. *The T.V. Scriptwriter's Handbook.* See entry 4248.

494. British Broadcasting Corporation. *Writing for the BBC; A Guide for Professional and Part-time Freelance Writers on Possible Markets for Their Work Within the British Broadcasting Corporation.* London: British Broadcasting Corporation, 1977. 75 pp.

495. Bronfeld, Stewart. *Writing for Film and Television.* Englewood Cliffs, New Jersey: Prentice-Hall, 1981. 144 pp.

This middling introductory text places heavy emphasis on the use of camera, dialogue, and other technical aspects. It says less about the use of imagination and is remarkably deficient in concrete examples. Reviewers have suggested that it is overly optimistic about the marketing of manuscripts.

496. Burr, Keith. *The Screenwriter's Guide; The Handbook for Film and Television Sales with the Names and Addresses of Over 2100 Producers and Agents Worldwide.* New York: New York Zoetrope, 1982. 159 pp.

This directory claims to be the most complete resource of its kind. Entries frequently include telephone numbers as well as addresses. Introductory matter includes advice on script length, format, style, and legal protection.

497. Coe, Michelle E. *How to Write for Television; A Primer for the Creative Writer Covering Commercials, Interviews, Narratives, Newscasts, Serials, Musicals, and Institutional Promotions.* New York: Crown, 1980. 149 pp.

Though sketchy at times, the information in this work is an accurate account by an experienced professional television writer.

498. Conrad, Jon J. *The TV Commercial; How It Is Made.* New York: Van Nostrand Reinhold, 1983. 160 pp.

This comprehensive work covers most aspects of production and technology associated with commercials. Examples by and personal recollections of the author abound.

499. Cousin, Michelle. *Writing a Television Play.* Boston: Writer, 1975. 202 pp.

Cousin, a successful television writer, tells briefly about dramatic construction, exposition, theme, plot, character, dialogue and markets. Nearly half of her book is given over to sample scripts which convert theory into craft.

500. Edmonds, Robert. *Scriptwriting for the Audio-Visual Marketplace.* New York: Teachers College Press, 1978. 185 pp.

Sample materials and advice about writing for television, radio, films, filmstrips, and other nonprint media in an instructional context.

501. Eisenstein, Sergei. *Film Form and Film Sense.* 2 vols. Cleveland: World, 1963.

Memorable reflections by a great pioneer filmmaker on the film as word and image and on the synchronization of the senses.

502. Evans, Elwyn. *Radio; A Guide to Broadcasting Techniques.* London: Barrie & Jenkins, 1977. 175 pp.

An overview of the subject which provides worthwhile information on scripting, plays, and interviews. Evans was in charge of the BBC radio training section.

503. Field, Stanley. *Professional Broadcast Writer's Handbook.* Blue Ridge Summit, Pennsylvania: TAB Books, 1974. 396 pp.

Making use of a wide variety of scripts and styles, Field offers analyses and examples of commercials, dramas, documentaries, religious and children's programs, and instructional formats. Along with Edgar Willis's *Writing Scripts for Television, Radio, and Film* (see entry 545) and Robert L. Hilliard's *Writing for Television and Radio* (see entry 512), this work is a basic text of high reputation.

504. ———. *Television and Radio Writing.* Boston: Houghton Mifflin, 1958. 544 pp.

Filled with sample scripts and analyses that address the basics of dramas, series, educational programs, children's programs, news, talk shows, and the like from broadcasting of another era.

505. Field, Syd. *Screenplay; The Foundations of Screenwriting.* New expanded edition. New York: Delacorte, 1982. 246 pp.

Contains valuable practical advice which will appeal to both amateurs and professionals. Treats structuring of the story, restraint in camera directions, and a wide variety of purely mechanical writing tips. Character, scene, and collaboration are also covered in detail by this highly regarded short text. Excerpts from the scripts for *Chinatown* and *Silver Streak* are included.

506. Froug, William. *The Screenwriter Looks at the Screenwriter.* New York: Macmillan, 1972. 352 pp.

Twelve screenwriters review their careers and discuss their relationships with directors and other writers. More is revealed about the difficult environment of the screenwriter than about the craft, but this highly rated book remains essential reading. Interviewees are Lewis John Carlino, William Bowers, Walter Brown Newman, Jonathan Axlerod, Ring Lardner, Jr., I.A.L. Diamond, Buck Henry, David Giler, Nunnally Johnson, Edward Anhalt, Stirling Silliphant, and Fay Konin.

507. Giustini, Rolando. *The Filmscript; A Writer's Guide.* Englewood Cliffs, New Jersey: Prentice-Hall, 1980. 243 pp.

Takes the reader from original idea through screenplay and storyboard by using one of Giustini's own scripts. Considered by reviewers to be a good introduction to the subject.

508. Goldman, William. *Adventures in the Screen Trade; A Personal View of Hollywood and Screenwriting.* New York: Warner Books, 1983. 418 pp.

There are so many valuable aspects to this book that no short description can do it justice. Goldman, with almost twenty years of screenwriting experiences that include *Marathon Man, All the President's Men,* and *The Great Santini,* provides both amusing and appalling personal anecdotes which bear on the internal workings of filmmaking and film writing. The final portion of this work is devoted to a series of practical examples of the assertions he has made up to that point. In doing so, he converts one of his own stories into a screenplay and then allows a designer, a cinematographer, an editor, a composer, and a director to tell how they might respond to the script if it were filmed. In the process, the restrictions and limitations set by other people upon the screenwriter are made very clear. Goldman, one of our most highly paid screenwriters, has given us a lively look behind the scenes.

509. Goodman, Evelyn. *Writing Television and Motion Picture Scripts That Sell.* Chicago: Contemporary Books, 1982. 219 pp.

This tightly knit work includes step-by-step instructions on such essentials as script formats and selecting an agent. But its greatest value lies in an approach to dramatic structure that relies upon interactive diagrams as well as upon examples from noteworthy films and television productions. However, those seeking guidance about convincing dialogue will have to look elsewhere.

510. Greene, Robert S. *Television Writing; Theory and Technique.* Revised edition. Foreword by Robert Montgomery. New York: Harper, 1956. 274 pp.

Covers script format and analysis, visual writing structure, and adaptations mainly for television dramas.

511. Hall, Mark W. *Broadcast Journalism; An Introduction to News Writing.* New York: Hastings House, 1978. 156 pp.

An accepted "nuts and bolts" text, according to *Journalism Quarterly.*

512. Hilliard, Robert L. *Writing for Television and Radio.* 3rd edition. New York: Hastings House, 1981. 461 pp.

This edition maintains the work's previous position as one of the best books available on the subject. With an abundance of sample scripts to support the theories presented, the chapters range from the basic elements of production, through music and variety programs and plays, to women's and ethnic programs. The bibliographies at the end of each chapter refer to many related publications in the communication field. Accompanied by a comprehensive index, this book is an exhaustive and trustworthy introductory text.

513. Hulke, Malcolm. *Writing for Television in the 70s.* London: Adam and Charles Black, 1974. 263 pp.

Taking the position that television writing is, more than most forms, a craft to be learned, this British view of the subject treats technical "tricks," fiction techniques of dialogue and characterization, script mechanics, marketing, censorship, and libel. Script excerpts from a number of television series are included.

Kauffman, Stanley. *Albums of Early Life.* See entry 4254.

514. Lee, Robert, and Robert Misiorowski. *Script Models.* New York: Hastings House, 1978. 96 pp.

This short reference work, which assumes a prior understanding of basic principles, provides sample scripts for a wide variety of formats. The section called "writers' aids" provides data on agents and manuscript preparation, lists media forms and abbreviations, and offers a valuable set of suggested additional readings.

515. Luhr, William, and Peter Lehman. *Authorship and Narrative in the Cinema.* New York: Putnam, 1977. 320 pp.

A study of how directors transform scripts. Called by the critics "sensible" and "seminal," and viewed as one of the most important works on film criticism in recent years.

516. McCavitt, William E. *Radio and Television; A Selected, Annotated Bibliography.* Metuchen, New Jersey: Scarecrow Press, 1978. 241 pp.

Over fifty years of broadcast literature are covered, including a wide range of authorship materials.

517. McGuire, Jerry. *How to Write, Direct, and Produce Effective Business Films and Documentaries.* Blue Ridge Summit, Pennsylvania: TAB Books, 1978. 292 pp.

This is a valuable introduction to 16mm film production which draws on the author's wide experiences as a writer and director of business films.

518. Maddux, Rachel, Stirling Silliphant, and Neil D. Isaacs. *Fiction into Film; A Walk in the Spring Rain.* New York: Dell, 1969. 239 pp.

This valuable source begins with the full text of Rachel Maddux's story and then gives the full text of Silliphant's screenplay adaptation, after which Isaacs provides an extended commentary on the transformations involved, up to and including filming and editing. In the process, the reader is thoroughly immersed in production terms and technical details. The text is complemented by an ample selection of photographs of the film crew, actors, and sets. The combined result is an enlightening view of how a simple story was brought to life by a wide variety of talented people, among whom were Ingrid Bergman and Anthony Quinn.

519. Maloney, Martin, and Paul Max Rubenstein. *Writing for the Media.* Englewood Cliffs, New Jersey: Prentice-Hall, 1980. 293 pp.

A better-than-average text which advises apprenticeship, research, and hard work. The major emphasis is on dramatic scripts, but some attention is also given to nonfiction forms, such as news, advertising, and documentaries. Covers creative thinking, script formats, and marketing.

520. Miller, William. *Screenwriting for Narrative Film and Television.* New York: Hastings House, 1980. 256 pp.

Along with Syd Field's *Screenplay,* this is one of several recent first-rate texts on the subject. By means of theory and extensive example, issues such as creativity, character, invention, suspense, comedy, and documentary techniques are competently dealt with.

521. Munro, Kate. *Writing Radio and Television Scripts.* New York: McGraw-Hill, 1966. 160 pp.

Uses examples from Canadian radio and television to focus on drama in broadcasting.

522. Nash, Constance, and Virginia Oakey. *Screen-Writer's Handbook.* New York: Harper & Row, 1978. 149 pp.

How-to and how-not-to. Includes interviews with Ernst Lehman, Gene Wilder, Robert Evans, and Delbert Mann.

523. ———. *Television Writer's Handbook.* New York: Harper & Row, 1978. 186 pp.

Interviews with television writers, agents, and producers are included, in addition to a broad discussion of the basics.

524. Nicol, Eric Patrick. *One Man's Media, and How to Write for Them.* Toronto: Holt, Rinehart and Winston of Canada, 1973. 135 pp.

Written from a Canadian perspective, this short conversational work discusses writing for magazines, newspapers, radio, and television in ways that will more likely amuse and divert than instruct.

525. Orlik, Peter B. *Broadcast Copywriting.* Boston: Allyn and Bacon, 1978. 439 pp.

This well illustrated text covers both radio and television advertising and promotion and includes production terminology. Appendices contain radio and television codes, consumer survey guidelines, and network standards. "It's about time that someone put together a well conceived text-book dealing with broadcast copywriting," said *Journalism Quarterly.*

526. Parker, Norton S. *Audiovisual Script Writing.* New Brunswick, New Jersey: Rutgers University Press, 1968. 330 pp.

Called "solid," "practical," and "indispensable" by reviewers, this book covers the training film, the documentary, the filmed report, the film story, and the persuasion film, as well as the basic theory behind visual media.

527. Peck, William. *Anatomy of Local Radio-TV Copy.* Blue Ridge Summit, Pennsylvania: TAB Books, 1976. 95 pp.

This short but informative approach to writing commercial advertising copy discusses usage, cliches, motivation, sales, and production techniques.

528. Ravage, John W. *Television; The Director's Viewpoint.* Boulder, Colorado: Westview Press, 1978. 184 pp.

These interviews offer insight about the interactions between directors and their producers, actors, and others, including writers.

529. Reiss, David. *MASH; The Exclusive Story of TV's Most Popular Show.* New York: Bobbs-Merrill, 1980. 160 pp.

Amid biographical data, awards, and fan mail, there are plot summaries and other indications of how scripts were transformed into a winning series.

530. Rilla, Wolf. *The Writer and the Screen; Writing for Film and Television.* New York: Morrow, 1974. 191 pp.

A veteran film and television writer and producer discusses language, characters, dialogue, and plot, and illustrates these with filmscript segments. Finally, Rilla deftly transforms a story into screenplay and television scripts.

531. Roberts, Edward B. *Television Writing and Selling.* Boston: Writer, 1967. 504 pp.

Dealing mainly with television playwriting, to the exclusion of nonfiction studio forms, this effort makes ample use of excerpted scripts to discuss setting, special effects, camera directions, time transitions, and adaptions of existing literary works. The author has served as script editor for the original Armstrong Theatre, faculty member of the Yale School of Drama, and story editor for the CBS Television Network.

532. Root, Wells. *Writing the Script; A Practical Guide for Films and Television.* New York: Holt, Rinehart and Winston, 1980. 252 pp.

Elements of dramatic story lines, realities of the marketplace, and sound advice about each industry make up this practical survey.

533. Rotha, Paul, Sinclair Road, and Richard Griffith. *Documentary Film; The Use of the Film Medium to Interpret Creatively and in Social Terms the Life of the People as It Exists in Reality.* New York: Hastings House, 1964. 412 pp.

Recognized as "the classic treatise" on the subject, this definitive work covers naturalist, realist, news, and propaganda traditions in the documentary film.

534. Rouverol, Jean. *Writing for the Soaps.* Cincinatti: Writer's Digest, 1984. 252 pp.

Contains anecdote and practical advice about scriptwriting for the soap operas.

535. Serling, Rod. *Patterns; Four Television Plays with the Author's Personal Commentaries.* New York: Simon and Schuster, 1957. 246 pp.

Includes two of his Emmy winning scripts, *Patterns* and *Requiem For a Heavyweight* and may be considered required reading for all prospective television dramatists.

536. Settel, Irving. *How to Write Television Comedy.* Boston: Writer, 1958. 228 pp.

Chapters on writing jokes, making people laugh, stunt writing, and situation comedy by Settel, Leonard Hole, Sidney Reznick, Bob Howard, Art Henley, and other professionals from the period.

537. Stemple, Tom. *Screenwriter; The Life and Times of Nunnally Johnson.* San Diego: Barnes, 1980. 269 pp.

This biocritical analysis of a man who was acknowledged as one of Hollywood's top script craftsmen contains priceless information about apprenticeship and matured professionalism.

538. ———. *Screenwriting.* New York: A.S. Barnes, 1982. 192 pp.

Liberal quotations from screenwriters on work habits, block, marketing research, and mistakes to be avoided make up this unpedantic survey.

539. Straczynski, J. Michael. *The Complete Book of Scriptwriting.* Cincinnati: Writer's Digest, 1982. 288 pp.

Covers television, radio, films, and theatre, and makes ample use of actual scripts to illustrate specific problems and points. A glossary of terms and an inventory of movie and television producers complete this valuable work.

540. Taylor, Cecil P. *Making a Television Play; A Complete Guide from Conception to BBC Production. Based on the Making of the Play, "Charles and Cromwell," for BBC Thirty Minute Theatre.* London: Oriel Press, 1970. 88 pp.

According to Taylor, "In this book, I am throwing open my workshop to writers and others interested in the craft and giving them an opportunity of working with me through one particular job—the development and writing of a thirty minute television play."

541. Terrell, Niel. *The Power Technique of Radio-TV Copywriting.* Blue Ridge Summit, Pennsylvania: TAB Books, 1971. 222 pp.

The hard sell, the soft sell, and the intermediate sell are all examined and illustrated in this advertising copy handbook. Audience motivation, writing mechanics, and client relationships are but a few of the topics covered.

542. Trapnell, Coles. *Teleplay; An Introduction to Television Writing.* Revised edition. New York: Hawthorne, 1974. 245 pp.

This introductory text surveys camera terminology, script mechanics, writing for actors, outlining, and a wide variety of other topics related to television drama, including characterization, dialogue, comedy, and marketing. Nearly eighty pages are devoted to the complete teleplay script for James Moser's *What Is the Truth?* A short history of the Writers Guild of America is also included.

543. Vale, Eugene. *Technique of Screen and Television Writing.* Englewood Cliffs, New Jersey: Prentice-Hall, 1982. 302 pp.

Unfortunately for the reader, there is very little in this otherwise worthwhile effort that has to do with television writing. For those seeking information about scriptwriting in general and filmscripts in particular, this work contains wise counsel and instructive examples.

544. Wertheim, Arthur Frank. *Radio Comedy.* New York: Oxford University Press, 1979. 439 pp.

Script excerpts from the golden age of radio comedy and analysis of the techniques of the great radio comics.

545. Willis, Edgar E., and Camille D'Arienzo. *Writing Scripts for Television, Radio, and Film.* New York: Holt, Rinehart and Winston, 1981. 322 pp.

In one of the better guides to writing for popular media, Willis and D'Arienzo have brought together a current, useful, and well-organized book. The discussions of scripts, including those for *Norma Rae* and episodes of *Lou Grant,* are particularly relevant, as are the examples of both bad and good writing. This lively work covers such diverse topics as news, interviewing, daytime drama, the documentary, and the docudrama.

546. Wylie, Max. *Radio and Television Writing.* New York: Rinehart, 1952. 635 pp.

With the current renewed interest in radio drama, this book remains a valuable source, but those segments dealing with television must be read in conjuction with more recent books on television writing. Includes much of the material that appeared in Wylie's *Radio Writing,* published in 1939.

547. ———. *Writing for Television.* New York: Cowles, 1970. 456 pp.

Part lament over television's creative decline, part wise advice on how to write for television, and part analysis of sample scripts, this is a first-rate effort by a veteran of radio and television writing and production.

Articles

548. And now a few words on writing for radio. Bob Jacobs. *Writer's Digest,* vol. 57, April 1977, pp. 15-19.

549. And now a word from the copywriter (radio). Patricia Fox. *Writer's Digest,* vol. 58, September 1978, pp. 21-23.

550. BBC Radio fees: getting a better deal. Ian Rowland-Hill. *Author,* vol. 89, Autumn 1978, pp. 107+.

551. Bill Kerby (interview). *Film Comment,* vol. 16, January/February 1980, pp. 51-53.

552. Buck Henry in the twentieth century (film scriptwriter). Jim Fragale. *Writer's Digest,* vol. 59, August 1979, pp. 22-24.

553. Business of dealing with the business (film and TV). D. McIntyre. *Michigan Quarterly Review,* vol. 21, Winter 1982, pp. 48-56.

554. Cheever on writing for TV (interview). *Horizon,* vol. 24, December 1981, pp. 56-57.

555. Closer and closer to real (interview). M. Ross and B. West. *Writer's Digest,* vol. 53, August 1973, pp. 16-26.

556. Cloudland remembered. S.J. Perelman. *Film Comment,* vol. 14, March 1978, p. 25.

557. Comedy writers. G. Ace. *Saturday Review,* vol. 48, January 23, 1965, p. 10.

558. Considering *All Things Considered* (public radio). *Writer's Digest,* vol. 56, July 1976, pp. 42-43.

559. Creating television stories and characters. Stewart Bronfeld. *Writer,* vol. 94, October 1981, pp. 15-17+.

560. Day in the Life: Cyra McFadden (television author). *Esquire,* vol. 91, February 13, 1979, pp. 85-86.

561. Dialing for radio dollars. Ted Schwarz. *Writer's Digest,* vol. 58, September 1978, pp. 18-21.

562. Don't look now, we're being followed (chase scenes in scripts). Alan A. Armer. *Writer's Digest,* vol. 59, April 1979, pp. 36-39.

563. Elmore Leonard: screenwriter (interview). *Publishers Weekly,* vol. 223, February 25, 1983, p. 32.

564. Elusive, John Collier (screenwriter): Tom Milne and John Collier. *Sight and Sound,* vol. 45, Spring 1976, pp. 104-108.

565. Eureka (interview). T. Milne (screenwriter). *Sight and Sound,* vol. 51, Autumn 1982, pp. 280-285.

566. Fantasy and culture on television. B. Stein. *Society,* vol. 16, March 1979, pp. 89-94.

567. Fiction and film: a search for new sources. Stephen Koch. *Saturday Review,* vol. 52, December 27, 1969, pp. 12-14+.

568. Filmwriting; excerpt from *Breaking Through, Selling Out, Dropping Dead.* William S. Bayer. *Writer's Digest,* vol. 54, February 1974, pp. 44-45.

569. Four-letter screen writer; slap shot writer, N. Dowd. J. Maslin. *Newsweek,* vol. 89, March 7, 1977, pp. 68-69.

570. Freelancing TV editorials. Cookie McGee. *Writer's Digest,* vol. 59, October 1979, pp. 28-29.

571. French Uncles (motion pictures). A. Insdorf. *Film Comment,* vol. 16, September/October 1980, pp. 19+.

572. From computer screen to silver screen: word processing software for scriptwriters. Barbara Elman. *Writer's Digest,* vol. 63, October 1983, pp. 35-38.

573. Funnier, Billy, funnier (reminiscences of writer of "special" material—musical arrangements for TV shows). Billy Barnes. *TV Guide,* vol. 24, August 28, 1976, pp. 28+.

574. George Toliver on one-liners (television). G. Toliver. *Writer's Digest,* vol. 54, February 1974, pp. 10-11.

575. Getting a foothold in television. E.L. Musto. *Writer,* vol. 89, March 1976, pp. 21-23.

576. Gloria Katz—Willard Huyck (interview). *Film Comment,* vol. 11, March 1975, pp. 47-53.

577. Graham Greene: on the screen (interview). *Catholic World,* vol. 209, August 1969, pp. 218-221.

578. Goodbye to Mr. Stark (motion pictures). R. Lardner, Jr. *Nation,* vol. 232, February 7, 1981, pp. 149-152.

579. Great scriptwriter race. (How George Toliver writes TV scripts). G. Toliver. *TV Guide,* vol. 22, August 17, 1974, pp. 31+.

580. Hanging out; works of S. Stern (motion pictures). R.A. Aurthur. *Esquire,* vol. 83, February 1975, pp. 10+.

581. Hollywood phrasebook. Frederic Raphael. *Listener,* vol. 97, June 23, 1977, pp. 815-816.

582. Hollywood screenwriter: take 2 (interview). R. Gordon. *Film Comment,* vol. 14, July 1978, pp. 33-47.

583. Hollywood; writers and directors as authors of films. P. Bogdanovich. *Esquire,* vol. 79, March 1973, pp. 55-56+.

584. How a high school class in Utah sold a TV script. N. Vogel. *Writer's Digest,* vol. 53, February 1973, pp. 21-23+.

585. How Patricia Resnick came to write the script of "9 to 5." E. Attias and Mimi White. *Ms.,* vol. 9, January 1981, pp. 44-46+.

586. How Peggy Elliott broke down barriers and broke into TV writing. Sherall Scharlach. *Writer's Digest,* vol. 59, November 1979, pp. 26-27+.

587. How to sell your television script. Richard Blum. *Writer,* vol. 94, February 1981, pp. 19-23.

588. How to write and sell for TV. *Writer,* vol. 97, July 1984, pp. 13-16.

589. How to write the film documentary. B. Hampe. *Writer's Digest,* vol. 55, September 1975, pp. 19-21.

590. How to write the teleplay outline; excerpt from *An Introduction to Television Writing.* Coles Trapnell. *Writer's Digest,* vol. 55, September 1975, pp. 9-10.

591. Illustrated man (interview). Ray Bradbury. *Sight and Sound,* vol. 43, Spring 1974, pp. 96-100.

592. In the American grain: an interview with Robert Getchell (screenwriter). *Sight and Sound,* vol. 45, Summer 1976, pp. 140-144.

593. It's here! Hollywood's ninth era! L.M.K. Carson. *Esquire,* vol. 83, February 1975, pp. 65-75.

594. ITV scriptwriter's checklist. B. Frye. *Training and Development Journal,* vol. 32, March 1978, pp. 14-19.

595. John Milius is not as bad as his movies (interview). *Writer's Digest,* vol. 55, September 1975, p. 22.

596. *Kane Mutiny;* interview with O. Welles. P. Bogdanovich. *Esquire,* vol. 78, October 1972, pp. 999-1005.

597. Lost art of writing for television. Vance Bourjaily. *Harper's Magazine,* vol. 219, October 1959, pp. 151-157.

598. Mamet in Hollywood (writing the screenplay for *The Postman Always Rings Twice).* D. Mamet. *Horizon,* vol. 24, February 1981, pp. 54-55.

599. Memoirs of a sitcom writer. Barry Meadow. *Writer's Digest,* vol. 59, May 1979, pp. 28-30+.

600. Method to the madness; writing for situation comedies. J.C. Cavella. *Writer's Digest,* vol. 55, April 1975, pp. 12-13.

601. *My dinner With Andre.* W. Shawn. *Sight and Sound,* vol. 51, Spring 1982, pp. 118-120.

602. My first sale: How I started at the top and worked my way down (television). Bonnie Souleles. *Writer's Digest,* vol. 64, November 1984, p. 35.

603. My word is his bond: a view from the back room: writing and producing *Thunderball.* R. Maibaum. *Esquire,* vol. 63, June 1965, pp. 73+.

604. Norman Lear: *Playboy* interview. *Playboy,* vol. 23, March 1976, pp. 53+.

605. Perelman in Cloudsville. Mel Calman and S.J. Perelman. *Sight and Sound,* vol. 47, Autumn 1978, pp. 248-249.

606. Pinter in no man's land: the Proust screenplay. D. Davidson. *Contemporary Literature,* vol. 34, Spring 1982, pp. 157-170.

607. Playwright in films. R. Bolt. *Saturday Review,* vol. 45, December 29, 1963, pp. 15-16.

608. Postman's words (interview). D. Mamet (screenwriter). *Film Comment,* vol. 17, March/April 1981, pp. 21-24.

609. Producer's assistant always rings once; writing scripts for movies different from writing books. J. Greenfield. *New West,* vol. 2, October 10, 1977, p. 74.

610. Sample page of TV script. *Writer's Digest,* vol. 48, December 1968, p. 65.

611. Sample TV script. *Writer's Digest,* vol. 53, August 1973, p. 43.

612. Screenwriting techniques from a Hollywood insider. R.N. Flint Dille. *Writer's Digest,* vol. 63, July 1983, pp. 34-37.

613. Scribes of Hollywood. Clancy Sigal. *Listener,* vol. 98, October 20, 1977, pp. 497-498.

614. Scriptwriter and director: interview with Walter Hill. *Movie,* vol. 26, Winter 1978/1979, pp. 29-42.

615. Secret mind; excerpt from Afterword to *Anthem Sprinters and Other Antics.* Ray Bradbury. *Writer,* vol. 78, November 1965, pp. 13-16.

616. Selling the comedy bit. G.Q. Lewis. *Writer's Digest,* vol. 51, September 1971, p. 31.

617. Selling TV spot news and features. Dave Derkacy. *Writer's Digest,* vol. 59, January 1979, pp. 32-35.

618. Should the new TV writer go to Hollywood? H. Meinert and D. Marsh. *Writer's Digest,* vol. 51, June 1971, pp. 32-35+.

619. Six weeks, four drafts, and half a nervous breakdown later; agonies of writer of series "Jigsaw John." Al Martinez. *TV Guide,* vol. 24, March 27, 1976, pp. 24+.

620. So you want to write a movie.... J.G. Dunne. *Atlantic,* vol. 234, July 1974, pp. 38-46.

621. Steadiest market for films; writing for educational or industrial films. N. Vogel. *Writer's Digest,* vol. 52, April 1972, pp. 26-27+.

622. Steel writer: Stirling Silliphant (interview). *Writer's Digest,* vol. 64, March 1984, pp. 39-42.

623. Storyboarding: visual scripting for better movies. M. Kruse-Smith. *Petersen's Photographic Magazine,* vol. 7, April 1979, pp. 76-78+.

624. Subconsciousness raising, scriptwriter C. Schnee. R. Scheib. *Film Comment,* vol. 17, January/February 1981, pp. 24-32.

625. Super (market) scriptwriter (interview). J. Bateman. *Writer's Digest,* vol. 57, April 1977, pp. 38-39.

626. Sylvester Stallone's rocky road to *Rocky* (interview). *Writer's Digest,* vol. 57, July 1977, pp. 29-30.

627. Talking about *The Shining* with Diane Johnson (interview). *Chicago Review,* vol. 33, Summer 1981, pp. 75-79.

628. Television and film writing. N. Vogel. October 1969, pp. 22+; December 1969, pp. 18-20+; vol. 50, February 1970, pp. 44-46; April 1970, pp. 42+.

629. This Oscar (sob) really belongs to all those whom... L. Conger. *Writer,* vol. 80, August 1967, pp. 9-10.

630. TV copywriter. Kirk Polking. *Writer's Digest,* vol. 48, June 1968, 56-62+.

631. Twelve steps to TV scripts that sell. Joseph Hanania. *Writer's Digest,* vol. 60, April 1980, pp. 36-39.

632. Two ways to write a script. C. Willeford. *Writer's Digest,* vol. 55, September 1975, p. 20.

633. Visualizing and writing video programs. S. Floyd. *Training and Development Journal,* vol. 33, December 1979, pp. 24-28.

634. Wall of glass; some notes on the writer in television. Robert Furnival. *Encore, the Voice of Vital Theatre,* vol. 5, no. 4, Nov.-Dec. 1958, pp. 29-34.

635. Where could I meet other screenwriters? (interview). R.P. Jhabvala. *Sight and Sound,* vol. 48, Winter 1978-79, pp. 15-18.

636. Who knows what opportunities lurk in the heart of radiodrama? J. Michael Straczynski. *Writer's Digest,* vol. 61, May 1981, pp. 34-39.

637. William Goldman (interview). *Publishers Weekly,* vol. 223, March 18, 1983, pp. 26-27.

638. With the eyes of a demon: writing for television today. H. Ellison. *Writer's Digest,* vol. 56, July 1976, pp. 15-21.

639. Woman behind *Nashville* (interview). J. Tewkesbury. *Ms.,* vol. 4, July 1975, pp. 22+.

640. Writer and Hollywood. B. Schulberg. *Harper's Magazine,* vol. 219, October 1959, pp. 132-137.

641. Writer in American films; with interviews. S. Farber. *Film Quarterly,* vol. 21, Summer 1968, pp. 2-13.

642. Writer (interview). A. Jacobs. *Film Quarterly,* vol. 22, Winter 1968, pp. 2-14.

643. Writers' dilemma; Writers Guild of America conference discusses the question of writer control. A. Knight. *Saturday Review,* vol. 52, April 26, 1969, p. 51.

644. *Writing a Television Play:* excerpt. Michelle Cousin. *Writer,* vol. 88, November 1975, p. 20-23.

645. Writing and selling the TV documentary. Joseph Hanania. *Writer's Digest,* vol. 59, October 1979, pp. 25-30.

646. Writing for films. M. Bragg. *Times Literary Supplement,* vol. 3474, September 26, 1968, pp. 1076-1077.

647. Writing for motion pictures. J. Wald. *Writer,* vol. 74, February 1961, pp. 5-6+.

648. Writing for Saturday morning television. Ted Pedersen and Martha Humphreys. *Writer's Digest,* vol. 60, February 1980, pp. 26-31.

649. Writing for television. B. Schultz. *Writer,* vol. 80, May 1967, pp. 17-18+.

650. Writing for television. Robert Wales. *Author,* vol. 89, Winter 1978, pp. 182-185.

651. Writing for television: two novelists' problem. Robert Henniques. *BBC Quarterly,* vol. 7, no. 2, Summer 1952, pp. 89-93.

652. Writing life: Karen Hall (television scriptwriter). *Writer's Digest,* vol. 63, June 1983, pp. 18-19.

653. Writing on the screen. M.S. Dworkin. *Educational Forum,* vol. 40, March 1976, pp. 289-296.

654. Writing radio commercials. David Campiti. *Writer's Digest,* vol. 63, November 1983, pp. 30-33.

655. Writing the business film. Jerry McGuire. *Writer's Digest,* vol. 60, September 1980, pp. 29-32.

656. Writing the teleplay. F. Gruber. *Writer,* vol. 72, June 1959, pp. 16-17+.

657. You ought to be in pictures. E.S. Stevens. *Writer's Digest,* vol. 57, October 1977, pp. 43-45.

658. You some kind of ecology freak? Problem of writing a TV script on location. George Toliver. *TV Guide,* vol. 23, January 4, 1975, pp. 11+.

Poetry

"Like a piece of ice on a hot stove the poem must ride on its own melting."

—Robert Frost

Books

659. Aiken, Conrad. *Ushant; An Essay.* New York: Oxford, 1971. 365 pp.

This journey into the mind of a major American poet has been hailed by Malcolm Cowley and Mark Schorer as one of the most significant of American literary autobiographies.

660. Bly, Robert. *Talking All Morning.* (Poets on Poetry Series.) Ann Arbor: University of Michigan Press, 1980. 308 pp.

This book, from the consistently high quality Poets on Poetry Series, discusses how poets grow, poets and politics, translation, and isolation. Bly received the National Book Award in 1968.

Borges, Jorge Luis. *Borges on Writing.* See entry 1073.

661. Brooks, Cleanth, and Robert Penn Warren. *Understanding Poetry.* 4th edition. New York: Holt, Rinehart and Winston, 1976. 602 pp.

One of the most widely respected and extensive anthology-criticisms available. Essential reading for the beginning poet.

662. Cahn, Sammy. *The Songwriter's Rhyming Dictionary.* New York: New American Library, 1984. 159 pp.

Contains some 50,000 entries which are organized by vowel sound and number of syllables. This well-conceived work by a noted songwriting professional has received excellent reviews.

663. Davie, Donald. *Trying to Explain.* (Poets on Poetry Series.) Ann Arbor: University of Michigan Press, 1979. 213 pp.

"Meant for serious readers who are trying to make sense of the 20th-century poetic landscape."

Davis, Sheila. *The Craft of Lyric Writing.* See entry 4250.

664. Deutsch, Babette. *Poetry Handbook; A Dictionary of Terms.* New York: Harper & Row, 1982. 224 pp.

Compiled without illusions about "how complex the stuff of poetry is," Deutsch's book has become a standard reference source.

665. Dickey, James. *Self-Interviews.* Recorded and edited by Barbara Reiss and James Reiss. Garden City, New York: Doubleday, 1970. 190 pp.

Personal reflections on the poet's life and creative wellsprings, as well as analysis of specific poems such as "Buckdancer's Choice" and "The Friend."

666. Eliot, T.S. *On Poetry and Poets.* New York: Octagon Books, 1975. 308 pp.

Sixteen enduring essays and addresses,including "The social function of poetry," "The music of poetry," and "The three voices of poetry."

667. ———. *The Waste Land; A Facsimile and Transcript of the Original Draft, Including the Annotations of Ezra Pound.* New York: Harcourt, Brace, Jovanovich, 1971. 149 pp.

668. Engle, Paul, and Joseph Langland. *Poet's Choice.* New York: Dial Press, 1962. 303 pp.

The comments of 100 poets, each on one of his or her own poems, with regard to revision, sources, and purpose.

669. Francis, Robert. *Pot Shots at Poetry.* (Poets on Poetry Series.) Ann Arbor: University of Michigan Press, 1980. 220 pp.

Covers adjectives in poetry, what poets get away with, and the basis of a good poetry reading.

670. Frost, Robert. *Interviews with Robert Frost.* New York: Holt, Rinehart and Winston, 1966. 295 pp.

This collection begins in 1915 and ends in 1962.

671. ———. *Robert Frost on Writing.* Edited by Elaine Barry. New Brunswick, New Jersey: Rutgers University Press, 1973. 188 pp.

These letters, prefaces, reviews, and interviews set forth Frost's critical theories and practical impressions of other writers' works and at the same time reveal his attitudes toward his own literary efforts.

672. Gibbons, Reginald, editor. *The Poet's Work; Twenty-Nine Masters of Twentieth Century Poetry on the Origins and Practice of Their Art.* Boston: Houghton Mifflin, 1979. 305 pp.

A broad range of modernist poets discuss their own works in this wise and sophisticated anthology. Part one deals with poetic motivation, while part two addresses the more technical aspects of poetic creation. Among those included are Paul Valery, Frederico Garcia Lorca, Boris Pasternak, Fernando Pessca, Eugenio Montale, Wallace Stevens, Seamus Heaney, Denise Levertov, Wendell Berry, Hart Crane, Delmore Schwartz, W.H. Auden, Karl Shapiro, Gary Snyder, George Seferis, and Rene Char.

673. Graves, Robert. *On Poetry; Collected Talks and Essays.* New York: Doubleday, 1969. 597 pp.

Called outrageous and cranky by the critics, this highly personal set of reflections makes war on a variety of poets of established reputation. Its greatest value lies in its defense of Graves's own methods. To quote Graves, "Verse is a craft, poetry a way of life."

674. Haines, John. *Living Off the Country; Essays on Poetry and Place.* (Poets on Poetry Series.) Ann Arbor: University of Michigan Press, 1981. 188 pp.

A recipient of a Guggenheim and an Amy Lowell scholarship, Haines was also Poet Laureate of Alaska for four years. He discusses, among other topics, form, line and color, the burdens of a literary education, and making a poem significant.

675. Hall, Donald. *Goatfoot Milktongue Twinbird; Interviews, Essays, and Notes on Poetry 1970-76.* (Poets on Poetry Series.) Ann Arbor: University of Michigan Press, 1978. 224 pp.

Being a poet today, the creative process, free verse, work routines, and failure are all addressed.

Harding, Rosamond Evelyn Mary. *An Anatomy of Inspiration.* With an appendix on *The Birth of a Poem* by Robert B.M. Nichols. See entry 3953.

676. Hartmann, Sadakichi. *Conversations with Walt Whitman.* New York: E.P. Coby, 1895. 51 pp.

The product of a series of meetings the author had with Whitman, this slim volume gives only a little information about Whitman's views of his own writing.

677. Hochman, Sandra. *Streams; Life-Secrets for Writing Poems and Songs.* Englewood Cliffs, New Jersey: Prentice-Hall, 1978. 188 pp.

The gem-like reminiscences and advice of an acclaimed poet and novelist about the nature of experience, uses of the past, and the means of deriving inspiration from other writers.

678. Hughes, Ted. *Poetry Is.* New York: Doubleday, 1970. 101 pp.

Based on the author's BBC children's programs, this slim book shows by explanation and example how Roethke,

Eliot, Plath, and Dickinson handle a variety of simple subjects such as animals, wind and weather, people, and landscapes. This is a simple, truthful book which is addressed to anyone wanting to learn about poetry and its creation. The author is an award-winning poet and the husband of the late Sylvia Plath.

Hugo, Richard. *The Triggering Town: Lectures and Essays on Poetry and Writing.* See entry 4253.

679. Ignatow, David. *Notebooks.* Chicago: Swallow Press, 1974. 375 pp.

This "irregular autobiography of the poet" covers the years 1940 through 1971 and contains countless writer's reflections such as, "By keeping the door open to my room I am saying that writing is not outside my life. I am not interested in simply exploring myself. I keep the door open to get the sounds of the world also."

680. ———. *Open Between Us.* (Poets on Poetry Series.) Ann Arbor: University of Michigan Press, 1980. 296 pp.

Discusses "...what poets are doing—and why."

681. Jerome, Judson. *Poet and the Poem.* Cincinnati: Writer's Digest, 1979. 399 pp.

This serviceable "how to" and "where to" approach to content in poetry had its origins in a monthly column for the *Writer's Digest.* Taking the position that any book about the writing of poetry must also be a book about the reading of poetry, Jerome covers meter, line units, diction, imagery, symbolism, and the like. He counsels hard work, risk, and the nurturing of vision.

682. ———. *Poet's Handbook.* Cincinnati: Writer's Digest, 1980. 224 pp.

Jerome calls this work a "companion volume" to the *Poet and The Poem* (see entry 681) in which the emphasis is on technique rather than content. This popular introduction to the subject defines terms and illustrates techniques in a way that should appeal to beginners.

683. Kennedy, X.J. *Introduction to Poetry.* 5th edition. Boston: Little, Brown, 1982. 484 pp.

A sensitive and widely accepted approach to classical forms such as meter, rhyme, stanza, and line configuration. A respected basic text that leans toward poetry of long-standing reputation.

684. Kinnell, Galway. *Walking Down the Stairs; Selections From Interviews.* (Poets on Poetry Series.) Ann Arbor: University of Michigan Press, 1978. 128 pp.

Discusses self-expression, translation, reading of poetry,
and being an American poet today.

685. Kostelanetz, Richard. *Old Poetries and the New.* (Poets on Poetry
Series.) Ann Arbor: University of Michigan Press, 1981. 316 pp.

Kostelanetz, a Guggenheim fellow and Pulitzer-Prize
winner, addresses rules in poetry, text-sound, intermedia,
and the concept of the polyartist.

686. Kumin, Maxine. *To Make a Prairie; Essays on Poets, Poetry, and
Country Living.* (Poets on Poetry Series.) Ann Arbor: University of
Michigan Press, 1979. 161 pp.

A Pulitzer-Prize winner discusses form, revision, and risk.

687. Kunitz, Stanley. *A Kind of Order, A Kind of Folly; Essays and
Conversations.* New York: Little, 1975. 320 pp.

A distinguished poet examines his and other poets' creative
resources, establishes a philosophy of poetry, and concludes
with a provocative series of aphorisms on the spirit and
essences of poetry.

688. Levine, Philip. *Don't Ask.* (Poets on Poetry Series.) Ann Arbor:
University of Michigan Press, 1981. 174 pp.

Eight interviews covering such diverse topics as can real be
romantic and what are the advantages of being discovered
late? Levine has been poet-in- residence at several
universities and has twice received the National Book
Critics Circle Award.

689. Lowes, John L. *The Road to Xanadu.* New York: Random, 1978. 614
pp.

Memorable study of the creativity and labor that went into
the making of Samuel Taylor Coleridge's "Rime of the
Ancient Mariner" and "Kubla Khan."

690. Neruda, Pablo. *Memoirs.* New York: Farrar Straus, 1977. 370 pp.

These recollections of a Nobel laureat contain gem-like
assessments of the poet's craft such as the chapter "Poetry
is an occupation."

691. Perrine, Laurence. *Sound and Sense; An Introduction to Poetry.* 5th
edition. New York: Harcourt, Brace, Jovanovich, 1982. 377 pp.

Intended for those who wish to undertake the serious study
of poetry, this work has long enjoyed a warm critical
reception. It concentrates on why poets use certain
elements and the value of these to both poet and reader.
The work includes a large number of illustrative poems as
well as a working glossary.

692. Rilke, Rainer Maria. *Letters to a Young Poet*. New York: W.W. Norton, 1934. 128 pp.

This is the wise, kind, and utterly unique voice of a master poet speaking to those who would follow, as well as to a single correspondent. The letters urge development of individual style, mastery of language, and purity of emotion. For example: "If your daily life seems poor, do not blame it; blame yourself, tell yourself that you are not poet enough to call forth its riches; for to the creator there is no poverty and no poor indifferent place."

693. Roethke, Theodore. *On the Poet and His Craft; Selected Prose*. Seattle: University of Washington Press, 1965. 154 pp.

Sometimes comic and satiric and sometimes deadly serious, these are the working thoughts of a brilliant poet. They include, among other fine essays, "Some remarks on rhythm," "How to write like somebody else," "Open letter," and "On identity." To quote Philip Booth in *The Christian Science Monitor,* "Wherever there is a library, and somewhere in it a lost young poet fumbling in the stacks in need of self-courage, this book must be."

694. ———. *Straw for the Fire; From the Notebooks of Theodore Roethke, 1943-1963*. Edited by David Wagoner. Garden City, New York: Doubleday, 1972. 262 pp.

These poems, reflections, illustrations, and manuscript excerpts reveal Roethke in rare and raw creative form.

695. Sarton, May. *At Seventy. A Journal*. New York: Norton, 1984. 344 pp.

These wide-ranging reflections bear on the work of other writers and on Sarton's own continuing efforts as a poet.

696. Scott, A.F. *Poet's Craft; A Course in the Appreciation of Poetry Based on the Study of Holograph Manuscripts, Earlier and Later Versions of Printed Poems, Transpositions of Prose into Verse, and Contrasted Translations*. Cambridge: Cambridge University Press, 1957. 219 pp.

These poems by Milton, Blake, Wordsworth, Byron, Shelley, Keats, Tennyson, Browning, Hopkins, and Coleridge appear with their authors' revisions. In them one can sense the sweat of creation.

697. Shapiro, Karl Jay. *Essay on Rime*. New York: Random, 1945. 72 pp.

A clever combination of essay and poetry which reviews the subject and critically charts its future.

698. ———. *Primer for Poets: Three Essays; What the Poet Knows, the True Artificer, and the Career of the Poet*. Lincoln: University of Nebraska Press, 1953. 73 pp.

A notable poet and critic addresses the "tangled shapes of modern poetry."

699. Shapiro, Karl Jay, and Robert Beum. *A Prosody Handbook.* New York: Harper, 1965. 214 pp.

According to the authors, prosody refers to "...tempo and sound, pause and flow, line and stanza, rhyme and rhymelessness," and is vital to any analysis of poetry. This admirable work covers all of these and includes an extended glossary.

700. Simpson, Louis. *Company of Poets.* (Poets on Poetry Series.) Ann Arbor: University of Michigan Press, 1981. 358 pp.

A Pulitzer-Prize-winning poet addresses the shape of American poetry today, the question of popularity, and his expectations for the next generation of poets.

701. Sitwell, Edith. *A Poet's Notebook.* Westport, Connecticut: Greenwood, 1950. 276 pp.

The personality and poetic preferences of a great lady and a great poet are revealed in this graceful "common place book" of quotations and notes.

702. Skelton, Robin. *Practice of Poetry.* New York: Barnes and Noble, 1972. 184 pp.

Combines an analysis of the work of modern poets with a treatment of the techniques of diction, verse, rhythm, and stanza forms. Less convincing are the efforts to teach inspiration and imagination.

703. Smith, Barbara Hernstein. *Poetic Closure; A Study of How Poems End.* Chicago: University of Chicago Press, 1968. 289 pp.

In this lucid, coherent, and original work, poetic structure, integrity, dynamic effect, and completeness are examined for clues to finality of expression in William Shakespeare, T.S. Eliot, Robert Graves, Ben Jonson, John Keats, John Milton, Walt Whitman, and William Butler Yeats.

704. Stafford, William. *Writing "The Australian Crawl"; Views on the Writer's Vocation.* (Poets on Poetry Series.) Ann Arbor: University of Michigan Press, 1979. 161 pp.

Drawing on materials originally generated for articles, interviews, and conferences, Stafford reveals his sources of inspiration, work methods, and opinions on writing. Seeing poetry as "truth that has learned jujitsu," Stafford stresses privacy and receptivity as prime requisites for his kind of creation. Such issues as revision of poems, social issues in poetry, and the influence of other poets on his work emerge in ways that cannot fail to move the reader and influence his or her own writing. Graceful reflections by a major American poet.

705. Stevens, Wallace. *Letters of Wallace Stevens.* New York: Knopf, 1966. 890 pp.

Contains over 800 letters, as well as excerpts from his journals. To quote from the *New York Times,* "Few poets in their letters have talked so freely about their art and their intentions...." And to quote Stanley Kunitz, "Students of Stevens will rejoice at the number of letters in which he patiently elucidates the most difficult of his poems, line by line and image by image—the most extensive commentary that any major poet has ever provided on his own work."

706. Tate, Allen. *The Language of Poetry.* New York: Russell & Russell, 1960. 125 pp.

Essays read at Princeton University by a distinguished critic and poet.

707. Trefethen, Florence. *Writing a Poem.* Boston: Writer, 1975. 224 pp.

With an emphasis on control, discipline, depth, and quality, Trefethen draws upon the examples set by Robert Graves, Wallace Stevens, Robert Frost, Maxine Kumin, Sylvia Plath, A.E. Housman, and others to provide definitions of terms and explanations of technique. This is a commendable introductory text, which covers verse forms, imagery, figurative language, revision, getting rid of rhetoric, and avoiding excessive sentimentality.

708. Untermeyer, Louis. *Pursuit of Poetry; A Guide to Its Understanding and Appreciation with an Explanation of Its Forms and a Dictionary of Poetic Terms.* New York: Simon & Schuster, 1969. 318 pp.

Of its two principal parts, the first broadly examines the relationship of the unconscious to the conscious mind, inspiration, sound in words, and other theoretical elements. Part two contains the dictionary of terms as well as a discussion of technique.

709. Wakoski, Diane. *Toward a New Poetry.* (Poets on Poetry Series.) Ann Arbor: University of Michigan Press, 1979. 335 pp.

The pioneer poet, mythology in poetry, the music of poetry, and image and digression are all discussed in the context of "good" poetry.

710. Wood, Clement. *Poets' and Songwriters' Guide; The Complete Book of Scansion for Writers of Poetry, Verse, Song Lyrics, and Prose.* New York: Valiant House, 1948. 240 pp.

Scansion, we are reminded, "...is the division of verse or prose into its rhythmical units, called feet." Wood gives attention to prose and prose verse, free verse, accent verse, meter and metric verse, gracenote verse, and various other types of verse, such as durational and syllable count. Though long out of print, this book remains a reasoned analysis and competent history of the subject. It is of strikingly immediate value to poets.

711. ———. *Poets' Handbook.* Cleveland: World, 1946. 466 pp.

Called "an omnibus of verse technique" by its author, this standard source ranges from dramatic poetry to light and occasional verse. Rhythm and accent are dealt with in depth, as are rhyme and stanza patterns.

712. ———. *Unabridged Rhyming Dictionary.* New York: World, 1971. 1040 pp.

Intended for poets, versifiers, songwriters, advertising writers, and students of poetics, this monumental work contains not only an extensive dictionary arranged by rhyme forms but also general chapters that provide advice on allusions, cliches, kinds of poetry, stanza forms, fixed forms, the mechanics of rhyme, self-taught versification, and the use of musical and singable words.

713. Yeats, William Butler. *Essays and Introductions.* New York: Macmillan, 1961. 530 pp.

Contains, among other writings, "What is popular poetry," "The symbolism of poetry," and "A general introduction to my work."

714. ———. *Memoirs.* New York: Macmillan, 1972. 318 pp.

Combines Yeats's *Journal,* which was begun in 1908, and the first draft of his autobiography.

Articles

715. A.R. Ammons (interview). *Contemporary Literature,* vol. 21, Spring 1980, pp. 173-190.

716. Andrei Voznesensky and Allen Ginsberg: a conversation. *Paris Review,* no. 78, 1980, pp. 149-177.

717. Art of language. John Ciardi. *Saturday Evening Post,* vol. 232, March 19, 1960, pp. 22-23+.

718. Art of poetry (interview).

Conrad Aiken. *Paris Review,* no. 42, 1968, pp. 97-124.
W.H. Auden. *Paris Review,* no. 57, 1973-74, pp. 32-69.
John Berryman. *Paris Review,* no. 53, 1972, pp. 177-207.
Joseph Brodsky. *Paris Review,* no. 83, 1982, pp. 82-126.
Robert Creeley. *Paris Review,* no. 44, 1968, pp. 155-187.

James Dickey. *Paris Review,* no. 65, 1976, pp. 52-88.

T.S. Eliot. *Paris Review,* no. 21, 1959, pp. 46-70.

Robert Frost. *Paris Review,* no. 24, 1960, pp. 88-120.

Allen Ginsberg. *Paris Review,* no. 37, 1966, pp. 13-55.

Robert Graves. *Paris Review,* no. 47, 1969, pp. 119-145.

David Ignatow. *Paris Review,* no. 76, 1979, pp. 54-99.

Stanley Kunitz. *Paris Review,* no. 83, 1982, pp. 205-246.

Philip Larkin. *Paris Review,* no. 84, 1982, pp. 42-72.

Peter Levi. *Paris Review,* no. 76, 1979, pp. 120-154.

Robert Lowell. *Paris Review,* no. 25, 1961, pp. 56-95.

Archibald MacLeish. *Paris Review,* no. 58, 1973-74, pp. 52-81.

James Merrill. *Paris Review,* no. 84, 1982, pp. 185-219.

Marianne Moore. *Paris Review,* no. 26, 1961, pp. 56-66.

Pablo Neruda. *Paris Review,* no. 51, 1971, pp. 149-175.

Charles Olson. *Paris Review,* no. 49, 1970, pp. 177-204.

Ezra Pound. *Paris Review,* no. 28, 1962, pp. 22-51.

May Sarton. *Paris Review,* no. 89, 1983, pp. 80-110.

George Seferis. *Paris Review,* no. 50, 1970, pp. 56-9.

Anne Sexton. *Paris Review,* no. 52, 1971, pp. 158-191.

Stephen Spender. *Paris Review,* no. 77, 1980, pp. 118-154; discussion, Spring 1981, pp. 280-307.

Andrei Voznesensky. *Paris Review,* no. 78, 1980, pp. 94-109.

John Hall Wheelock. *Paris Review,* no. 67, 1976, pp. 156-172.

Richard Wilbur. *Paris Review,* no. 72, 1977, pp. 69-105.

William Carlos Williams. *Paris Review,* no. 32, 1964, pp. 111-151.

James Wright. *Paris Review,* no. 62, 1975, pp. 34-61.

Yevgeny Yevtushenko. *Paris Review,* no. 34, 1965, pp. 97-115.

719. Auden on poetry; a conversation with Stanley Kunitz. *Atlantic,* vol. 218, August 1966, pp. 94-102.

720. Audre Lorde (interview). *American Poetry Review,* vol. 9, March/April 1980, pp. 18-21.

721. Between suicide and revolution: the poet as role-player. E. Lucie-Smith. *Saturday Review,* vol. 2, April 19, 1975, pp. 14-18.

722. Charles Wright (interview). *Partisan Review,* vol. 50, no. 4, 1983, pp. 566-575.

723. Choir from the soul: a conversation with Anne Sexton. *Massachusetts Review,* vol. 19, Spring 1978, pp. 69-88.

724. Confessions of an American poet. Louis Simpson. *New York Times Magazine,* May 2, 1965, pp. 30-31+.

725. Decade of my poetry. J. Carrera Andrade. *Americas,* vol. 22, July 1970, pp. 9-13.

726. Definition implied. H. Behn. *Horn Book,* vol. 43, October 1967, pp. 561-564.

727. Dialogue with Robert Penn Warren on *Brother to Dragons* (interview). *Southern Review,* vol. 16, Winter 1980, pp. 1-17.

728. Did I mean that? John Ciardi. *Saturday Review,* vol. 48, January 16, 1965, p. 19.

729. Discovery of a voice. T. Paulin. *Times Literary Supplement,* vol. 4006, January 4, 1980, pp. 3-4.

730. Echoing Howl (advice from Allen Ginsberg). Michael Schumacher. *Writer's Digest,* vol. 64, May 1984, pp. 32-36.

731. Education of a poet: a conversation between Mark Strand and Nolan Miller (interview). *Antioch Review,* vol. 39, Winter 1981, pp. 106-118; Spring 1981, pp. 181-192.

732. Emily Dickinson: poetry and punctuation. E.P. Stamm. *Saturday Review,* vol. 46, March 30, 1963, pp. 26-27+; reply, T. Ward, April 27, 1963, p. 25; rejoinder, May 25, 1963, p. 23.

733. Environment of poetry. John Ciardi. *Saturday Review,* vol. 42, September 19, 1959, pp. 13-15+.

734. Everyone wants to be published, but.... J. Ciardi. *Writer,* vol. 89, August 1976, pp. 20-22.

735. Excerpts from *Write Me Another Verse.* D. McCord. *Horn Book,* vol. 46, August 1970, pp. 364-369.

736. Experience of the poem. A. Stanford. *Writer,* vol. 80, December 1967, pp. 20-23.

737. Ferlinghetti improvises. Lawrence Ferlinghetti. *Cimmaron Review,* vol. 16, 1971, pp. 27-34.

738. Finding what the world is trying to be: a conversation with William Stafford. *American Poetry Review,* vol. 4, July/August 1975, pp. 28-30.

739. Form and pressure in poetry. Stephen Spender. *Times Literary Supplement,* vol. 69, October 23, 1970, pp. 1226-1228.

740. Freelancing with poetry. Peter Porter. *Author,* vol. 88, Spring 1977, pp. 16-19.

741. From open house to the greenhouse: Theodore Roethke's poetic breakthrough. D. Bogen. *ELH,* vol. 47, Summer 1980, pp. 399-418.

742. From poetic thinking to concrete interpretation. D. Halliburton. *Papers on Language & Literature,* vol. 17, Winter 1981, pp. 71-79.

743. Function of stanzaic form. Milton A. Kaplan. *English Journal,* vol. 60, January 1971, pp. 47-53.

744. Gay sunshine (interview). Allen Ginsberg. *College English,* vol. 36, 1974, pp. 392-400.

745. Gerard Manley Hopkins on the origin of language. Michael Sprinker. *Journal of the History of Ideas.* vol. 41, January/March 1980, pp. 113-128.

746. Getting organized: poet's information sources. Judson Jerome. *Writer's Digest,* vol. 55, February 1975, pp. 36-38.

747. Grammar and meaning in poetry. S.B. Greenfield. *PMLA,* vol. 82, October 1967, pp. 377-387.

748. Handwritings on the wall; use of graffiti. S. Spann. *English Journal,* vol. 62, November 1973, pp. 1163-1165.

749. Haphazard poetry collecting. Richard Eberhart. *Chicago Review,* vol. 24, Spring 1973, pp. 57-70.

750. Having become a writer: some reflections. William Stafford. *Northwest Review,* vol. 13, 1973, pp. 90-92.

751. How poets make a living, if any. Kenneth Rexroth. *Harper's Magazine,* vol. 234, February 1967, pp.90-92+.

752. How poets use imagery to stimulate the reader's sense of sight, sound, taste, smell, and touch. Florence Trefethen. *Writer,* vol. 97, September 1984, pp. 24-26.

753. How to market your poetry. *Writer,* vol. 86, March 1973, pp. 27-31.

754. How to write good poetry and get it published. L.E. Sissman. *Writer,* vol. 83, October 1970, pp. 18-21.

755. How to write like somebody else. Theodore Roethke. *Yale Review,* vol. 48, March 1959, pp. 336-343.

756. Howard Nemerov (interview). *Massachusetts Review,* vol. 22, Spring 1981, pp. 43-57.

757. Inspiration and experience. W.K. Seymour. *Contemporary Review,* vol. 204, October 1963, pp. 185-188.

758. Inspiration and work: how poetry gets to be written (with a reply by M. Anania). K. Koch. *Comparative Literary Studies,* vol. 17, June, part 2, 1980, pp. 206-223.

759. Inspiration, insight, and the creative process in poetry. A. Rothenberg. *College English,* vol. 32, November 1970, pp. 172-176+.

760. Interval in a Northwest writer's life, 1950-1973. William Stafford. *Northwest Review,* vol. 13, 1973, pp. 6-9.

761. Irish genius. W. Allen. *New Republic,* vol. 172, February 1975, pp. 14-16.

762. Ishmael Reed (interview). *American Poetry Review,* vol. 7, January/ February 1978, pp. 32-36.

763. James Laughlin (interview). *American Poetry Review,* vol. 10, November/December 1981, pp. 19-32.

764. James Wright: the pure clear word (interview). *American Poetry Review,* vol. 9, May/June 1980, pp. 19-30.

765. Karla Hammond (interview). *American Poetry Review,* vol. 10, September/October 1981, pp. 15-18.

766. Kathleen Spivack (interview). *Massachusetts Review,* vol. 21, Fall 1980, pp. 540-547.

767. Leslie Ullman (interview). *American Poetry Review,* vol. 10, January/ February 1981, pp. 8-12.

768. Letter to a foreign friend. George Seferis. *Poetry,* vol. 105, October 1964, pp. 50-59.

769. Letter to Ezra Pound. T.S. Eliot. *Nine,* vol. 1, Summer 1950, pp. 178-179.

770. Life of the modern poet. John Berryman. *Times Literary Supplement,* vol. 3703, February 23, 1973, pp. 193-195.

771. Lyrics, heroic and otherwise. R.D. Spector. *Saturday Review,* vol. 52, March 15, 1969, pp. 33-35.

772. Making of "Mother Rosarine." Maxine Kumin. *Writer,* vol. 83, April 1970, pp. 19-21.

773. Market for poetry: the poets' view, the publishers' view. *Writer,* vol. 95, December 1982, pp. 23-27.

774. Max Jacob on poetry. J.M. Schneider. *Modern Language Review,* vol. 69, April 1974, pp. 290-296.

775. Memo from a poetry editor. E. Bartlett. *Writer's Digest,* vol. 55, December 1975, p. 20.

776. My wonderful lousy poem. B. Schulberg. *Reader's Digest,* vol. 89, August 1966, pp. 67-69.

777. Norman Dubie (interview). *American Poetry Review,* vol. 7, July/ August 1978, pp. 7-11.

778. On having a poem; adaptation of address. B.F. Skinner. *Saturday Review,* vol. 55, July 15, 1972, pp. 32-35.

779. On poetry. Robert Graves. *Virginia Quarterly Review,* vol. 43, Spring 1967, pp. 196-219.

780. On the methods and ambitions of poetry. A. Hecht. *Hudson Review,* vol. 18, Winter 1965-66, pp. 481-505.

781. On the poet, James Wright. P. Serchuk. *Modern Poetry Studies,* vol. 10, no. 2/3, pp. 85-90.

782. Origins of a poem. Denise Levertov. *Michigan Quarterly Review,* vol. 7, Autumn 1968, pp. 233-238.

783. Pablo Neruda; from *Memoirs. American Poetry Review,* vol. 5, September/October 1976, pp. 21-28.

784. Poem takes shape. J. Wheatcroft. *Journal of Creative Behavior,* vol. 4, Spring 1970, pp. 103-112.

785. Poet in his poems; address, October 17, 1968. H. Rajo. *Poetry,* vol. 113, March 1969, pp. 413-420.

786. Poet in the world. Denise Levertov. *American Poetry Review,* vol. 1, 1972, pp. 16-18.

787. Poet remembers his life. Vicente Aleixandre. *Nation,* vol. 226, March 4, 1978, p. 248.

788. Poet speaks for the records (business files). Marzi Kaplan. *Writer's Digest,* vol. 59, July 1979, pp. 32-33+.

789. Poetry and family: an interview with Karl Shapiro. *Prairie Schooner,* vol. 55, Fall 1981, pp. 3-31.

790. Poetry and folklore: some points of affinity. S.J. Sackett. *Journal of American Folklore,* vol. 77, April 1964, pp. 143-153.

791. Poetry and happiness. Richard Wilbur. *Shenandoah,* vol. 20, Summer 1969, pp. 3-23.

792. Poetry as discovery. A. Stanford. *Writer,* vol. 92, August 1979, pp. 20-22.

793. Poetry in a time of crack-up. Robert Penn Warren. *New York Review of Books,* vol. 15, January 7, 1971, pp. 32-33.

794. Poetry market is a poetry market is a poetry market. *Writer's Digest,* vol. 55, December 1975, pp. 22-23.

795. Poetry readings; why go to them, why give them? Mark Nepo. *Coda,* vol. 11, November/December 1983, pp. 1+.

796. Poetry without rhyme—or even thees and thous; using Japanese forms. J.C. Soule. *Writer's Digest,* vol. 57, January 1977, p. 29.

797. Poet's letter to a beginner. May Sarton. *Writer,* vol. 75, April 1962, pp. 19-21+.

798. Poets on poetry. *Writer,* vol. 82, March 1969, p. 30.

799. Poet's workshop. Florence Trefethen. *Writer,* vol. 96, January 1983, pp. 22-25.

800. Pointers for poets. D.D. Guyer. *Writer,* vol. 77, December 1964, pp. 27+.

801. Pound's battle with time. V. Miller. *Yale Review,* vol. 66, December 1976, pp. 193-208.

802. Principle of apprenticeship: Donald Justice's poetry. T. Swiss. *Modern Poetry Studies,* vol. 1, 1980, pp. 44-58.

803. Principle of composition. K. Burke. *Poetry,* vol. 99, October 1961, pp. 46-53.

804. Problems and delights of revision. May Sarton. *Writer,* vol. 79, December 1966, pp. 20-22.

805. Rhetorical structure in contemporary Afro-American poetry. R. T. Sheffery. *CLA Journal,* vol. 24, September 1980, pp. 97-107.

806. Rhyme does pay. Selma Glasser. *Writer,* vol. 87, December 1974, pp. 25-27+.

807. Rhymes with reasons (includes poetry markets). Agnes W. Thomas. *Writer's Digest,* vol. 59, January 1979, pp. 26-31.

808. Richard Hugo (interview). *Contemporary Literature,* vol. 22, Spring 1981, pp. 139-152.

809. Robert Duncan (interview). *Contemporary Literature,* vol. 21, Autumn 1980, pp. 513-548.

810. Robert Frost: on the dialects of poetry. S.N. Liebman. *American Literature,* vol. 52, May 1980, pp. 265-278.

811. Robert Frost on vocal imagination, the merger of form and content. Eric W. Carlson. *American Literature,* vol. 33, January 1962, pp. 519-522.

812. Robert Lowell's apprenticeship and early poems. J.B. Rollins. *American Literature,* vol. 52, March 1980, pp. 67-83.

813. Robert Penn Warren: a conversation on poetry. *South Atlantic Quarterly,* vol. 80, Summer 1981, pp. 272-280.

814. Sandra McPherson (interview). *American Poetry Review,* vol. 10, September/October 1981, pp. 15-20.

815. Silkin's stand. Jon Silkin. *Writer's Digest,* vol. 64, October 1984, pp. 6-7.

816. Some notes on organic form. Denise Levertov. *Poetry,* vol. 106, September 1965, pp. 420-425.

817. Some recollections of the Poetry Club at the University of Chicago. George Campbell. *Poetry,* vol. 107, November 1965, pp. 110-117.

818. Staying carefully ignorant. William Stafford. *Writer,* vol. 95, February 1982, pp. 16-17.

819. Stephen Spender: a conversation with Robert Dana. *American Poetry Review,* vol. 6, November/December 1977, pp. 14-19.

820. Stevens on the genesis of a poem. F. Doggett. *Contemporary Literature*, vol. 16, Autumn 1975, pp. 463-477.

821. Stray thoughts on Roethke and teaching. Richard Hugo. *American Poetry Review*, vol. 3, January/February 1974, pp. 50-53.

822. Surviving as a poet. Peter Redgrove. *Author*, vol. 90, Spring 1979, pp. 23+.

823. T.S. Eliot talks about his poetry. *Columbia University Forum*, vol. 2, Fall 1958, pp. 1-14.

824. Ten rules for poets. E.P. LaSelle. *Writer*, vol. 74, June 1961, pp. 18-20.

825. Third dimension of poetic expression; or, Language and harmony. D. Gostuski. *Musical Quarterly*, vol. 55, July 1969, pp. 372-383.

826. Three revolutions of modern poetry. S. Burnshaw. *Sewanee Review*, vol. 70, Summer 1962, pp. 418-450.

827. Time and the poet. P. Davison. *Writer*, vol. 80, August 1967, pp. 20-21.

828. Time and the poetic imagination. E. Staiger. *Times Literary Supplement*, vol. 3213, September 27, 1963, pp. 747-748.

829. Time is a waiting woman: new poetic icons. R. Gustafson. *Midwest Quarterly*, vol. 16, April 1975, pp. 318-327.

830. Toward a rhetoric of spatial form: some implications of Frank's theory. L.D. MacNeil. *Comparative Literature Studies*, vol. 17, December 1980, pp. 355-367.

831. Tropes and blocks. John Bayley. *Modern Language Review*, vol. 73, October 1978, pp. 748-754.

832. Vision and revision. D. Holmes. *Writer*, vol. 80, April 1967, pp. 39-42.

833. Visit with Eberhart. *New York Times Book Review*, vol. 83, January 1, 1978, pp. 10+.

834. What are pomes? H. Petroski. *Journal of Modern Literature*, vol. 3, April 1974, pp. 1021-1026.

835. What the poetry editor of *Esquire* is like: interview with James Dickey. *Writer's Digest*, vol. 54, October 1974, pp. 16-20.

836. What the poetry judge was looking for; excerpt from *The Poet and the Poem*. Judson Jerome. *Writer's Digest*, vol. 54, October 1974, pp. 13-15.

837. William Blake's revision of *The Tyger*. Martin Nurmi. *PMLA*, vol. 71, September 1956, pp. 669-685.

838. William Carlos Williams (interview). *Massachusetts Review,* vol. 14, Winter 1973, pp. 130-148.

839. William Stafford (interview). *American Poetry Review,* vol. 10, November/December 1981, pp. 8-11.

840. Words for young writers, from *The Notes of Theodore Roethke;* compiled by David Wagoner. Theodore Roethke. *Saturday Review,* vol. 51, June 29, 1968, pp. 14-15+.

841. Writer's Digest poetry fifty (markets). Thomas Clark. *Writer's Digest,* vol. 64, September 1984, pp. 20-29.

842. Writing children's verse. A. Fisher. *Writer,* vol. 76, April 1963, pp. 21-24.

843. Writing poems. Donald Hall. *Writer,* vol. 84, February 1971, pp. 19-21.

844. Writing poems to sell. D.D. Guyer. *Writer's Digest,* vol. 57, September 1977, pp. 52-53.

845. Writing *The Australian Crawl.* William Stafford. *College Composition and Communication,* vol. 15, February 1964, pp. 12-15.

846. Zen in the heartland: an interview with Lucien Stryk. *Modern Poetry Studies,* vol. 1, 1980, pp. 22-37.

847. Zen poetry: a conversation with Lucien Stryk. *American Poetry Review,* vol. 6, July/August 1977, pp. 33-36.

Story, Short and Otherwise

"That's another story."

—Laurence Sterne

Books

848. Bates, Herbert Frost. *The Modern Short Story; A Critical Survey.* Boston: Writer, 1972. 231 pp.

Intended as guidance for apprentice short story writers, this work "... sets out to be a study of certain established writers from Poe and Gogol to the present-day who have practiced the short story as a craft separate from the novel." Contains assertions on the writer's art by Leo Tolstoy, H.G. Wells, Rudyard Kipling, Katherine Mansfield, A.E. Coppard, and Ernest Hemingway.

849. Bentley, Phyllis E. *Some Observations on the Art of Narrative.* Folcroft, Pennsylvania: Folcroft, 1973. 50 pp.

This brief critical introduction stresses the various forms of narrative and the use of summary and is regarded by many as a small classic because of its wise use of examples and its convincing style.

850. Berdan, J. *Fourteen Stories From One Plot. Based on "Mr. Fothergill's Plot."* New York: Oxford, 1932. 287 pp.

G.K. Chesterton, Frank Swinnerton, A.E. Coppard, Rebecca West, and others, each present a short story based on the same plot. This collection is unique in what it sets out to do, which is to show us how different authors handle a common idea. Each story is accompanied by a short commentary by the editor.

851. Boggess, Louise. *How to Write Short Stories That Sell.* Cincinnati: Writer's Digest, 1980. 212 pp.

This work will appeal mainly to those interested in formula short fiction.

852. Boynton, Robert W., and Maynard Mack, editors. *Introduction to the Short Story.* Rochelle Park, New Jersey: Hayden, 1972. 286 pp.

Stories by James Thurber, Frank O'Connor, Ray Bradbury, and others are included in this anthology and are accompanied by their authors' comments on form and theme.

853. Burnett, Hallie. *On Writing the Short Story.* New York: Harper, 1983. 192 pp.

An author and seasoned editor of *Story* magazine discusses plot, style, characterization, work habits, and marketing in ways that assume prior knowledge on the part of the reader. Also included are comments from a variety of other established short story writers as well as an admirable group of sample stories.

854. Burnett, Whit, editor. *The Modern Short Story in the Making.* New York: Hawthorne Books, 1964. 405 pp.

Includes exemplary short stories with comments by the author of each.

Chekhov, Anton. *Letters on the Short Story, the Drama, and Other Literary Topics.* See entry 307.

855. Dickson, Frank A., and Sandra Smythe. *Handbook of Short Story Writing.* Cincinnati: Writer's Digest, 1981. 238 pp.

An anthology of articles that originally appeared in *Writer's Digest* and that covers conflict, dialogue, characterization, plot, and marketing.

856. Elwood, Maren. *Write the Short Short.* Boston: Writer, 1959. 348 pp.

Uses 175 short shorts to discuss specific aspects of this form.

857. Fox, Edward S. *How to Write Stories that Sell.* Boston: Writer, 1969. 132 pp.

Concentrates on specific story problems in a mass market perspective.

Fredette, Jean M. *Fiction Writer's Market.* See entry 1109.

858. Gavin, Marian. *Writing Short Stories for Pleasure and Profit.* Boston: Writer, 1973. 129 pp.

This introductory overview addresses personal experience and personal emotion stories, basic story patterns, do's and don'ts of story writing, and step-by-step diagnosis of ailing stories. The chapter that contains "one hundred and two self starters" has the potential for unblocking beginning writers.

859. Gilkes, Lillian, and Warren Bower, editors. *Short Story Craft; An Introduction to Short Story Writing.* New York: Macmillan, 1949. 501 pp.

This collection of stories ranges widely from Thomas Wolfe and Dorothy Parker to Erskine Caldwell and Walter Van

Tilberg Clark. The first ninety-seven pages record the thinking of the editors on technical theory and marketing of short stories.

860. Hardy, Barbara Nathan. *Tellers and Listeners; The Narrative Imagination.* London: Althone Press, 1975. 279 pp.

From traditional folktales to stream of consciousness novels, the storyteller's art is examined and illustrated for technique, form, success, and failure.

861. Hildick, Wallace. *Thirteen Types of Narrative.* New York: Clarkson N. Potter, 1970. 136 pp.

A discussion of the strengths and weaknesses of a variety of narrative forms, this compelling study relies on established literary figures for instruction and example. Multiple voices, epistology, diary, and stream of consciousness are but a few of the techniques included.

862. Hills, Rust. *Writing in General and the Short Story in Particular; An Informal Textbook.* Boston: Houghton Mifflin, 1977. 159 pp.

Taking a cynical view of the majority of how-to-write books, as well as of most college and university writing courses, Hills offers his own book, not as a new approach, but merely as an account of the basic techniques generally employed in writing quality fiction. It is filled with witty, aphoristic advice and germane (if sparse) examples, and it conveys to the reader some sense of the real demands of the contemporary quality short story market. However, the glibness of language, which is initially so appealing, is not accompanied by the critical depth we might have expected from one who was the fiction editor for *Esquire* during the 1960s. In sum, *Writing in General* is a good once-over-lightly introduction which should be supplemented by other reading.

863. Kempton, Kenneth Payson. *Short Stories for Study.* Chosen and appraised by Kenneth Payson Kempton. Cambridge: Harvard University Press, 1953. 351 pp.

This collection, with commentary, is intended to help writers discover solutions to their own writing problems. Each story is used as an example of a principle or technique. The commentary suggests how successful, in each case, the story is in reaching the theoretical objective and is quick to indicate when and where the story falls short. The stories have been taken from such sources as *The New Yorker, Yale Review,* and *Commentary.* Kempton's analyses of these stories, as well as his spirited asides, are both artful and sound.

864. Knight, Damon. *Creating Short Fiction; A Practical Approach to Unlock the Magic of Writing Within You.* Cincinnati: Writer's Digest, 1981. 215 pp.

A veteran short fiction writer, editor, and teacher draws on the experiences of over thirty years to provide an inspirational system and a working method.

865. Meredith, Robert, and John Fitzgerald. *The Professional Story Writer and His Art.* New York: Thomas Y. Crowell, 1963. 467 pp.

A serviceable text that addresses itself to both "literary quality" stories and commercial fiction. Strong emphasis on technique and craftsmanship, characterization, avoidance of cliches and stereotypes, and use of exaggerated complications in plot. Over a third of the book is devoted to sample stories, and these are accompanied by criticisms and corrections in each case.

866. O'Connor, Frank. *The Lonely Voice; A Study of the Short Story.* Cleveland: World Publishing, 1963. 220 pp.

A distinguished introductory text on the subject by an uncommonly able short story writer of solid reputation. Uses examples from Turgenev, Chekhov, Maupassant, Mansfield, Lawrence, and Coppard and concentrates on the concept of the "submerged population group" in characterization and plot.

867. O'Faolain, Sean. *The Short Story.* New York: Devin-Adair, 1951. 370 pp.

A forthright discussion and defense of craftsmanship and superior technique in the short story which relies on eight masterful stories by such writers as Henry James, Ernest Hemingway, and Frank O'Connor.

868. Peeples, Edwin Augustus. *A Professional Storywriter's Handbook.* Garden City, New York: Doubleday, 1960. 282 pp.

As an organized handbook, this book fails almost any reasonable definition of that term. However, it does provide a means of getting its readers to think about what makes for controlled and competently written fiction.

869. St. John, Adela Rogers. *How to Write a Story and Sell It.* Port Washington, New York: Kennikat Press, 1969. 217 pp.

A successful mass market story writer offers hints and provides examples for improving technique.

870. Sansom, William. *The Birth of a Story.* Toronto: Irwin Clarke (Chatto), 1972. 121 pp.

Sansom, an accomplished short story writer, shows how one of his published stories came to be written. Using pages reproduced from the original manuscripts, he takes us from

handwritten draft through revised, typed draft, at each
stage and line-by-line showing how the germ of an idea
evolved into a finished story. An initial chapter giving
Sansom's general thoughts on short story writing as well as
his methods and work habits is followed by the analysis
and the manuscripts for "No Smoking on the Apron." To
use the author's own words: "this book is not about quality,
but about how, personally, one author goes about things. A
kind of peep-show, in case of interest." While the story
used as an example is not outstanding, the methods
employed to explain its creation are.

871. Toliver, Harold Earl. *Animate Illusions; Explorations of Narrative Structure.* Lincoln: University of Nebraska Press, 1974. 412 pp.

A critically perceptive survey of narrative forms in
literature. Novels, epics, and parables are examined for the
effects that narrative has on the material they deal with.

Welty, Eudora. *The Eye of the Story; Selected Essays and Reviews.* See entry 1183.

Articles

872. Algebraic semantics for narrative. E. Kahn. *Linguistics,* no. 141, December 1, 1974, pp. 27-33.

873. All's well that ends well (story endings). James McKimmey. *Writer's Digest,* vol. 62, June 1983, pp. 33-36.

874. Anatomy of a story. D. Whitcomb. *Writer,* vol. 81, July 1968, pp. 12-14+.

875. Anatomy of a true adventure story. H.D. Steward. *Writer,* vol. 79, May 1966, pp. 13-17.

876. Angling for that short story sale. M.F. Shyer. *Writer,* vol. 89, July 1976, pp. 9-11.

877. Art of storytelling. D. Athas. *South Atlantic Quarterly,* vol. 73, Spring 1974, pp. 256-260.

878. Art of storytelling. H. Innes. *Writer,* vol. 72, March 1959, pp. 8-9+.

879. Art of the short story. E. Hemingway. *Paris Review,* no. 79, Spring 1981, pp. 85-102.

880. Beginning and the middle of your story. F.A. Rockwell. *Writer,* vol. 76, October 1963, pp. 13-16+.

881. Beginnings. E.S. Connell, Jr. *Writer,* vol. 83, September 1970, pp. 9-11.

882. Betting on a grand thing (short stories in periodicals). J. Neugeboren. *Nation,* vol. 231, December 13, 1980, pp. 645-648.

883. Big secret. R. McInerny. *Writer,* vol. 84, February 1971, pp. 9-11.

884. Birth of a story. Lajos Egri. *Writer,* vol. 78, June 1965, pp. 20-22.

885. Black and bright humor; comic vision in the modern short story. C.T. Whaley. *Southwest Review,* vol. 61, Autumn 1976, pp. 370-383.

886. Brevity takes time. M. Costigan. *Writer,* vol. 95, October 1982, pp. 9-11+.

887. Building a story around a single character. David Walton. *Writer,* vol. 96, October 1983, pp. 21-23+.

888. Building tension in the short story. Joyce Carol Oates. *Writer,* vol. 79, June 1966, pp. 11-12+.

889. Butter the size of a walnut; recipe for a story. I. Foster. *Writer,* vol. 79, December 1966, pp. 23-25.

890. Can you state your story in a sentence? J.D. Lucey. *Writer's Digest,* vol. 50, December 1970, pp. 27+.

891. Categories of literary narrative. T. Todorov. *Papers on Language and Literature,* vol. 16, Winter 1980, pp. 3-36.

892. Cheap repository tracts and the short story. S. Pickering. *Studies in Short Fiction,* vol. 12, Winter 1975, pp. 15-21.

893. Checkpoints for your short story. M. Chittenden. *Writer,* vol. 94, August 1981, pp. 15-18.

894. Confessions of a storyteller; address, July 1965. Frank G. Slaughter. *ALA Bulletin,* vol. 59, December 1965, pp. 1003-1005.

895. Counter trend; fiction in *Redbook.* P. Nathan. *Publishers Weekly,* vol. 207, June 2, 1975, p. 36.

896. Credo of a storyteller; excerpt from *Points of View.* William Somerset Maugham. *Saturday Evening Post,* vol. 231, March 21, 1959, pp. 38-39+.

897. Descriptive detail in your story. Jinger Hoop Griswold. *Writer,* vol. 97, July 1984, pp. 17-19+.

898. Detail makes the difference; heightening story impact. Peggy Simson Curry. *Writer,* vol. 84, November 1971, pp. 13-15+.

899. Developing story ideas. E. Jensen. *Writer,* vol. 81, February 1968, pp. 9-11+.

900. Discoveries by hindsight. A. Heinemann. *Writer,* vol. 82, October 1969, pp. 20-21+.

901. Eighteen checkpoints for your story. J.Z. Owen. *Writer,* vol. 77, April 1964, pp. 11-15.

902. Empathy and the short story. M. Wallace. *Writer,* vol. 81, August 1968, pp. 11-13.

903. Everybody change places! M.J. Amft. *Writer,* vol. 82, December 1969, pp. 12-13.

904. Everything can be too much. E. Allen. *Writer,* vol. 88, June 1975, pp. 18-19+.

905. Eye of the story. Eudora Welty. *Yale Review,* vol. 55, December 1965, pp. 265-274.

906. Fall dead without mentioning it. L.G. Erdman. *Writer,* vol. 72, April 1959, pp. 9-11.

907. Feel of a story. C.R. Bittle. *Writer,* vol. 75, June 1962, pp. 15-16.

908. Fiction fifty (top short story markets). *Writer's Digest,* vol. 63, August 1983, pp. 22-31; (see also entry 976).

909. Fiction from fact. V.M. Gillette. *Writer,* vol. 84, April 1971, pp. 11-13.

910. Fiction in the literary magazines; letters from editors. *Writer,* vol. 85, October 1972, pp. 25-27.

911. Fiction markets; alive and kicking! P. Sandhage. *Writer's Digest,* vol. 56, August 1976, pp. 38-45.

912. Fifty self-starters for fiction writers; excerpts from *Writing Short Stories for Pleasure and Profit.* Marian Gavin. *Writer,* vol. 77, February 1964, pp. 11-13+.

913. Filing cabinet. F.E. Randall. *Writer,* vol. 79, February 1966, pp. 11-13.

914. Finding the right shape for your story. Gail Godwin. *Writer,* vol. 88, September 1975, pp. 9-11.

915. First aid for story-sag. J.Z. Owen. *Writer,* vol. 83, October 1970, pp. 14-17.

916. First hundred words are the hardest. M. Constiner. *Writer,* vol. 75, November 1962, pp. 24-26.

917. Five writing problems in the short story. Jean Chimsky. *Writer's Digest,* vol. 51, May 1971, pp. 24-27+.

918. Four principles of story writing. E. Malpass. *Writer,* vol. 81, September 1968, pp. 14-16.

919. Four rules for the short story. S.W. Taylor. *Writer,* vol. 76, February 1963, pp. 7-9.

920. Four story forms: drama, film, comic strip, narrative. G.H. Thompson. *College English,* vol. 37, November 1975, pp. 265-280.

921. Furnishing the rooms. K. Reed. *Writer*, vol. 77, March 1964, pp. 20-21+.

922. Genesis of a story. Peggy Simson Curry. *Writer*, vol. 75, December 1962, pp. 7-10.

923. Genius and the craftsman. K. Hurlbut. *Writer*, vol. 88, October 1975, pp. 15-17+.

924. Give your fiction the movie treatment. Maia Wojciechowska. *Writer*, vol. 88, September 1975, pp. 18-19.

925. Giveaway. B. Ledecky. *Writer*, vol. 88, June 1975, pp. 11-12.

926. Good fiction, plain and fancy; fiction in *Redbook* and in little magazines. G. Lyons. *Nation*, vol. 225, October 22, 1977, pp. 405-406.

927. Hello! I love you! tantalizing leads to stories. A. Wohl. *Writer's Digest*, vol. 53, September 1973, pp. 22-23.

928. How different readers perceive magazine stories and characters. R.A. LeBouef and M. Matre. *Journalism Quarterly*, vol. 54, Spring 1977, pp. 50-57.

929. How not to write a short story; excerpts from *Prize Stories from Seventeen*. B. Rosmond. *Writer*, vol. 82, August 1969, pp. 22-24+.

930. How to find your real story. S.L. Stebel. *Writer*, vol. 90, March 1977, pp. 22-23.

931. How to get to page one. J. Savage. *Writer*, vol. 81, January 1968, pp. 9-11+.

932. How to give your story a face lift. H. Schellenberg. *Writer's Digest*, vol. 56, August 1976, pp. 58-59.

933. How to plot your story. Edward S. Fox. *Writer*, vol. 76, December 1963, pp. 21-24+.

934. How to turn fact into fiction; newspapers as story sources. G. Antonich. *Writer's Digest*, vol. 51, April 1971, pp. 37-39+.

935. In the beginning...; how to catch and hold your reader. Lee Smith. *Writer*, vol. 96, December 1983, pp. 9-11+.

936. International symposium of the short story: part one. Christina Stead and others. *Kenyon Review*, vol. 30, 1968, pp. 443-477.

937. International symposium of the short story: part two, United States. William Saroyan and others. *Kenyon Review*, vol. 31, 1969, pp. 58-62.

938. Is slant a dirty word? C. Turner. *Writer's Digest*, vol. 48, July 1968, pp. 53-54+.

939. Is your story different enough? D.J. Marlowe. *Writer,* vol. 79, December 1966, pp. 17-19.

940. Isaac Babel talks about writing; excerpts from *Years of Hope.* K.G. Paustovskii. *Nation,* vol. 208, March 31, 1969, pp. 406-407.

941. Joyous encounter. G.H. Freitag. *Writer,* vol. 81, August 1968, pp. 19-20.

942. Kiss, a gun, a tear, a smile. J. McKimmey. *Writer,* vol. 83, September 1970, pp. 15-17.

943. Let nothing your readers dismay; writing a Christmas story. L. Conger. *Writer,* vol. 84, December 1971, pp. 7-8.

944. Let's build a story. Edward S. Fox. *Writer,* vol. 77, June 1964, pp. 17-20+.

945. Look, you're standing on a story. Margaret Hill. *Writer's Digest,* vol. 56, July 1976, pp. 28-29.

946. Love stories that solve problems. H.L. Coffer. *Writer,* vol. 89, April 1976, pp. 14-16+.

947. Magazine short story. M. Constiner. *Writer,* vol. 73, June 1960, pp. 12-13+.

948. Making of a short story. J. Cowley. *Writer,* vol. 93, September 1980, pp. 13-15+.

949. Method-acting the first-person story. S. Hearon. *Writer,* vol. 87, August 1974, pp. 11-13.

950. Mood of your story. M.J. Waldo. *Writer,* vol. 78, April 1965, pp. 12-13+.

951. Multiply by two. D. Betts. *Writer,* vol. 85, September 1972, pp. 11-12+.

952. Mutato nomine (story titles). L. M. Harris. *Writer,* vol. 76, January 1963, pp. 16-18+.

953. My reluctant magician. Richard Powell. *Writer,* vol. 83, February 1970, pp. 11-14+.

954. Myths and realities about short story writing. Catherine Brady. *Writer,* vol. 96, July 1983, pp, 11-13.

955. New traditions, old innovations; writing a Christmas story. L. Conger. *Writer,* vol. 90, December 1977, pp. 9-10.

956. Nine rules for cutting a story. D. Booth. *Writer's Digest,* vol. 48, August 1968, pp. 25-27.

957. Notes for a young writer; excerpt from *Come Along With Me.* S. Jackson. *Writer,* vol. 94, January 1981, pp. 18-21+.

958. Of necessity, major events, and boxcars. E. Hannibal. *Writer,* vol. 91, June 1978, pp. 22-24.

959. On sale: a technique for breaking into the short story market. Hal Blythe and Charlie Sweet. *Writer's Digest,* vol. 62, December 1982, pp. 40-43.

960. People at work; fiction bonus. Peggy Simson Curry. *Writer,* vol. 88, December 1975, pp. 13-15+.

961. Pictures as inspiration for creativity. R. Osterweis. *English Journal,* vol. 57, January 1968, pp. 93-95.

962. Plotting short stories. Dan Marlowe. *Writer,* vol. 97, August 1984, pp. 9-11+.

963. Poe's extension of his theory of the tale. H.E. Smith. *Modern Philology,* vol. 16, 1918, pp. 195-203.

964. Point of the story; excerpt from *The Eye of the Story.* Eudora Welty. *New York Times Book Review,* vol. 83, March 5, 1978, pp. 3+.

965. Point of view in the short story. T. Springstubb. *Writer,* vol. 94, February 1981, pp. 15-18.

966. Plotting the short story. H. Whittington. *Writer's Digest,* vol. 52, November 1972, pp. 25-26+.

967. Price of a story. G. Sire. *Writer,* vol. 75, September 1962, pp. 12-14.

968. Proverbs and originality in modern short fiction. F.A. DeCaro. *Western Folklore,* vol. 37, January 1978, pp. 30-38.

969. Put your reader on the scene. E. Hyde. *Writer,* vol. 91, November 1978, pp. 15-16+.

970. Put your story on stage. N.B. Owen. *Writer,* vol. 73, June 1960, pp. 7-9.

971. Reading and writing of short stories. Eudora Welty. *Atlantic Monthly,* vol. 183, February 1949, pp. 54-58; March 1949, pp. 46-49.

972. Recipe for a short story. Sister Christine. *Writer,* vol. 82, December 1969, pp. 17-21.

973. *Redbook* fiction, from the inside. J. Johnson. *Writer,* vol. 90, November 1977, pp. 18-21.

974. Rhythm of a story. M.A. Rodgers. *Writer,* vol. 80, November 1967, pp. 19-21.

975. Rules; and when to break them. E. Hyde. *Writer,* vol. 89, August 1976, pp. 11-14.

976. Second fifty; fifty more great markets for fiction. *Writer's Digest,* vol. 63, August 1983, pp. 22-31; (see also entry 908).

977. Second fifty. Fifty more great markets for short fiction. *Writer's Digest,* vol. 64, August 1984, p. 24.

978. Selling touch. C. Boyd. *Writer,* vol. 81, January 1968, pp. 16-17+.

979. Short fiction in the market place. F.J. Soman. *Writer,* vol. 85, December 1972, pp. 17-20+.

980. Short history of a short-story writer. I. Gold. *Commonweal,* vol. 84, May 13, 1966, pp. 223-224.

981. Short scripts and the short story. E.W. Nold. *English Journal,* vol. 61, March 1972, pp. 377-380.

982. Short-short. V. Henry. *Writer's Digest,* vol. 50, February 1970, pp. 24-26.

983. Short-short and the gimmick. T. Burnam. *Writer,* vol. 79, June 1966, pp. 16-17.

984. Short-short story. R.W. Alexander. *Writer,* vol. 80, August 1967, pp. 17-18.

985. Short stories: bridges to vision. P.D. Boles. *Writer,* vol. 84, March 1971, pp. 9-11.

986. Short stories: how to begin and how to end. D. Bates. *Writer,* vol. 79, January 1966, pp. 19-20+.

987. Short stories: preface to an episode in life. B. Plagemann. *Writer,* vol. 78, June 1965, pp. 14-15+.

988. Short stories: their past, present, and future. *Publishers Weekly,* vol. 198, December 1970, pp. 12-15.

989. Short story checklist. H. Joseph Chadwick. *Writer's Digest,* vol. 51, November 1971, p. 33; vol. 52, January 1972, p. 27.

990. Short story heroine. M.F. Shyer. *Writer,* vol. 95, November 1982, pp. 12-13+.

991. Short story not made easy. S. Litsey. *Writer,* vol. 73, January 1960, pp. 12-14+.

992. Short-story workshop. J. Strong. *English Journal,* vol. 59, September 1970, pp. 811-814+.

993. Short story writing tips. Louise Boggess. *Writer's Digest,* vol. 54, August 1974, pp. 12-14.

994. Silent snow, secret snow: the short story as poem. B. Graham. *English Journal,* vol. 57, May 1968, pp. 693-695.

995. Sorry, your story's too pat. L. Ryker. *Writer's Digest,* vol. 49, June 1969, pp. 45-47.

996. Sound of the story. J. Buechler. *Writer,* vol. 80, June 1967, pp. 19-21.

997. Speaking about short stories. Joyce Carol Oates: Interview. *Studies in Short Fiction,* vol. 18, Summer 1981, pp. 239-243.

998. Stories complete on two pages. T. Aguallo. *Writer,* vol. 91, September 1978, pp. 18-20.

999. Stories I guess I won't write. Herbert Gold. *Atlantic,* vol. 224, August 1969, pp. 39-42.

1000. Stories without plot. M. Granbeck. *Writer's Digest,* vol. 50, January 1970, pp. 45-46.

1001. Story behind a story; excerpt from *Further Confessions of a Story Writer.* Paul Gallico. *Writer,* vol. 74, November 1961, pp. 7-9.

1002. Story box. D. Whitcomb. *Writer,* vol. 83, September 1970, p. 27.

1003. Story is a love affair. N.B. Owen. *Writer,* vol. 75, October 1962, pp. 22-23.

1004. Story value. J. Bentham. *Writer,* vol. 72, August 1959, pp. 16-17.

1005. Story's trigger. W.E. Henning. *Writer,* vol. 73, March 1960, pp. 19-20.

1006. Storyteller and his audience. O. Ruhen. *Writer,* vol. 73, October 1960, pp. 7-9+.

1007. Storyteller's creed. Frank G. Slaughter. *Writer,* vol. 75, November 1962, pp. 13-15.

1008. Storyteller's shoptalk. Raymond Carver. *New York Times Book Review,* vol. 86, February 15, 1981, pp. 9+.

1009. Storytellers' street. S. Babb. *Writer,* vol. 74, October 1961, pp. 5-7+.

1010. Storytelling old and new. E. Spencer. *Writer,* vol. 85, January 1972, pp. 9-10+.

1011. Storytelling's tarnished image. Malcolm Cowley. *Saturday Review,* vol. 54, September 25, 1971, pp. 25-27+.

1012. Substance of fiction; excerpts from *The Story: A Critical Anthology.* Mark Schorer. *Writer,* vol. 80, June 1967, pp. 14-18+.

1013. Surprised by tears. L. Conger. *Writer,* vol. 89, January 1976, pp. 7-8.

1014. Take a sentimental journey (emotion and action). Mary E. Nutt. *Writer,* vol. 96, September 1983, pp. 13-15.

1015. Tell them a story. J. McKimmey. *Writer,* vol. 75, August 1962, pp. 7-9.

1016. Telling stories. Dennis Potter. *New Society,* May 15, 1975, pp. 419-420.

1017. Ten guideposts to a salable story. H. Shiek. *Writer,* vol. 73, March 1960, pp. 15-16.

1018. Testing short story technique. L. Paul. *Writer,* vol. 75, March 1962, pp. 10-11+.

1019. Theory of the silver bullet. L.S. Bernstein. *Writer,* vol. 90, August 1977, pp. 28-29.

1020. Three key questions; writing a believable story. John Ball. *Writer,* vol. 86, December 1973, pp. 11-13+.

1021. Through the maze to the story. M.J. Gerber. *Writer,* vol. 88, April 1975, pp. 9-11+.

1022. Till (violent) death do us part. George P. Elliott. *Writer,* vol. 82, October 1969, pp. 15-16.

1023. To writers of magazine fiction; symposium. *Writer,* vol. 75, December 1962, pp. 22-27.

1024. Top nonpaying markets; thirty top fiction markets where payment is measured in terms other than dollar signs. *Writer's Digest,* vol. 63, August 1983, p. 83.

1025. Towards a theory of narrative. S. Chatman. *New Literary History,* vol. 6, Winter 1975, pp. 295-318.

1026. Trade secrets. Diane Lefer. *Writer,* vol. 96, December 1983, pp. 12-15.

1027. Trade winds. Herbert R. Mayes. *Saturday Review,* vol. 51, January 27, 1968, pp. 12-13.

1028. Turning experience into fiction. S. Coffman. *Writer,* vol. 93, December 1980, pp. 20-22.

1029. Turning novel cuts into short stories. R.E. Hayes. *Writer's Digest,* vol. 51, July 1971, pp. 28-29+.

1030. Twelve rules for story dissection. Howard E. Hill. *Writer's Digest,* vol. 50, February 1970, p. 26.

1031. Two-level story. V. Sneider. *Writer,* vol. 84, June 1971, pp. 21-22.

1032. Unique effect of the short story: a reconsideration and an example. C.E. May. *Studies in Short Fiction,* vol. 13, Summer 1976, pp. 289-297.

1033. Unmatched pearls: advice on magazine fiction writing. M. Campbell. *Writer,* vol. 87, August 1974, pp. 17-19+.

1034. Use threefold magic; build suspense into your story. J.Z. Owen. *Writer,* vol. 77, October 1964, pp. 18-20+.

1035. Using an original formula. Lois Duncan. *Writer,* vol. 84, November 1971, pp. 11-12+.

1036. Using the what-if technique. L.S. Cardozo. *Writer,* vol. 72, November 1959, pp. 14-15+.

1037. Video short story. S. Moro, and D. Fleming. *English Journal,* vol. 65, March 1976, pp. 60-63.

1038. View from the upstairs porch. S.F. Ciulla. *Writer,* vol. 76, November 1963, pp. 9-11.

1039. Watch out for this writing trap. R. Zacks. *Writer,* vol. 73, April 1960, pp. 15-16.

1040. Wayward reader. C. Fadiman. *Holiday,* vol. 36, November 1964, pp. 26+.

1041. Well-tempered story. T. Solotaroff. *Nation,* vol. 226, June 3, 1978, pp. 669-670+; June 10, 1978, pp. 701-702+.

1042. What a short-short is. Marjorie Lee. *Writer,* vol. 81, June 1968, pp. 16-18+.

1043. What happens? what if? what then? B. Robinson. *Writer,* vol. 79, September 1966, pp. 9-11+.

1044. What I learned from four top fiction editors. M. Joerden. *Writer's Digest,* vol. 50, September 1970, pp. 24-25.

1045. What is a story? A. Vivante. *Writer,* vol. 92, January 1979, pp. 16-18.

1046. What makes a good story? Norah Lofts. *Writer,* vol. 87, March 1974, pp. 11-12+.

1047. What makes us write? excerpts from *Introduction to Selected Stories.* Nadine Gordimer. *Writer,* vol. 89, October 1976, pp. 23-24.

1048. What's wrong with your story? Joseph Hansen. *Writer,* vol. 89, October 1976, pp. 16-19.

1049. Where does a story begin? Lajos Egri. *Writer,* vol. 77, November 1964, p. 15.

1050. Where it comes from. M. Taube. *Writer,* vol. 81, June 1968, pp. 25-26.

1051. Why did my story get rejected? M.Z. Bradley. *Writer,* vol. 96, February 1983, pp. 15-16.

1052. Why I write short stories. J. Cheever. *Newsweek,* vol. 92, October 1978, pp. 24-25.

1053. Why Lori can't sell—and Janet can. M.C. Shecktor. *Writer's Digest,* vol. 56, November 1976, p. 29.

1054. Women can sell to men's magazines. M. Raphael. *Writer,* vol. 86, May 1973, p. 27.

1055. Women's fiction today; it's a fast track: writing for periodicals. E. Jensen. *Writer's Digest,* vol. 56, August 1976, pp. 22-23.

1056. Wonderful idea for a story. C.R. Bittle. *Writer,* vol. 74, July 1961, pp. 15-16.

1057. *Writer's Digest* fiction fifty. Top short story markets. *Writer's Digest,* vol. 64, August 1984, pp. 16-25.

1058. Writing action scenes. R.S. Aldrich. *Writer,* vol. 94, February 1981, pp. 27-28+.

1059. Writing for the *Kenyon Review.* George Lanning. *Writer,* vol. 80, October 1967, pp. 31-32.

1060. Writing from the dark side. The horror short story. Steve Rasnic Tem. *Writer,* vol. 97, May 1984, pp. 16-19+.

1061. Writing romantic short stories. R. Pilcher. *Writer,* vol. 93, November 1980, pp. 16-17+.

1062. Writing short stories; excerpts from *Mystery and Manners.* Flannery O'Connor. *Writer,* vol. 83, January 1970, pp. 17-19+.

1063. Writing the short-short. M.J. Waldo. *Writer,* vol. 73, September 1960, pp. 8-10.

1064. Writing your first story. E.R. Hutchison. *Writer,* vol. 74, February 1961, pp. 10-11+.

1065. Yes, Virginia, there still are formula stories. R.L. Sargent. *Writer's Digest,* vol. 48, February 1968, pp. 44-47+.

1066. You need someone to love. M.J. Amft. *Writer,* vol. 88, March 1975, pp. 17-19.

1067. Your story's climax. J.C. Clark. *Writer,* vol. 72, December 1959, pp. 13-15.

1068. Your story's too episodic. S. Smythe. *Writer's Digest,* vol. 51, March 1971, pp. 36-37+.

1069. Your technique is showing. M. Wilson. *Writer,* vol. 80, January 1967, pp. 19-21.

Fiction Technique, Including General Creative Forms

"They say it is good, but it is just at this point that the real work begins."

—Tolstoy

Books

1070. Bement, Douglas. *The Fabric of Fiction.* New York: Harcourt, Brace and Company, 1948. 644 pp.

Retaining its reputation as one of the best of the post World War II works on fiction writing, this combination of theory and anthology blends the two in a way that sheds considerable light on the processes of dialogue, theme, setting, and thought in relation to characterization. An appendix provides selections by authors on their techniques and methods. Included are Eric Knight, Amy Lowell, Edna Ferber, Joel Chandler Harris, and William McFee.

1071. Benet, Steven Vincent. *Steven Vincent Benet on Writing; A Great Writer's Letters of Advice to a Young Beginner.* Edited and with comment by George Abbe. Brattleboro, Vermont: Greene Press, 1974. 111 pp.

The first section of this book is an attempt by George Abbe to categorize the advice he received from Benet into a working system. We are given advice on how to choose a theme, how to avoid cliches, and so on. The second half of the book consists of the letters, sent by Benet to Abbe between 1935 and 1943, which allowed Abbe to write the first half of the book. How much of the first half is Abbe's thinking and how much is Benet's is sometimes hard to determine. The book nonetheless abounds with wise suggestions.

1072. Block, Lawrence. *Telling Lies for Fun and Profit; A Manual for Fiction Writers.* New York: Arbor House, 1981. 240 pp.

Based on articles written for *Writer's Digest,* this work is a useful blend of theory and practice.

1073. Borges, Jorge Luis. *Borges on Writing.* New York: Dutton, 1973. 173 pp.

The product of three separate discussions held at Columbia University in 1971, this work gives Borges's views of his story, "The End of the Novel," as well as analyses of a number of his poems.

1074. Bowen, Elizabeth. *Seven Winters; Memories of a Dublin Childhood;* and *Afterthoughts; Pieces of Writing.* New York: Alfred Knopf, 1962. 272 pp.

Along with her deeply perceptive recollections of childhood are a series of "afterthoughts" that present Bowen's beliefs about writing fiction. The latter have been variously praised as "essential" reading and "indispensable documents" on the writer's craft.

1075. Bowen, Elizabeth, and others. *Why Do I Write? An Exchange of Views between Elizabeth Bowen, Graham Greene, and V.S. Pritchett.* With a preface by V.S. Pritchett. New York: Haskell House, 1975. 58 pp.

These letters address the fiction writer in a society as both citizen and reformer in ways that will help every imaginative author define his or her purpose.

1076. Brace, Gerald Warner. *The Stuff of Fiction.* New York: Norton, 1969. 156 pp.

Style, dialogue, setting, point of view, characters, theme, and plot are discussed in reference to how Poe, Hawthorne, Joyce, Conrad, and other authors actually handled such considerations. In fact, it is this continual citing of work habits and methods that gives the book its principal value. Brace, in addition, presents his concepts and evidence with wit and dexterity. Contains an appendix listing novels and authors the author considers essential reading for any writer.

1077. Brashers, Howard Charles. *Creative Writing; Fiction, Drama, Poetry, and Essay.* Cincinnati: American Book Company, 1968. 476 pp.

Brashers makes use of numerous examples from mainstream literature for purposes of analysis. The usual programmed approaches to technique are found here.

1078. Breit, Harvey. *The Writer Observed.* Cleveland, Ohio: World Publishing Company, 1976. 287 pp.

Brief character sketches of, and short interviews with, sixty notable authors, including T.S. Eliot, Aldous Huxley, Robert Penn Warren, Joyce Cary, Jean Stafford, and William Faulkner.

1079. Brooks, Cleanth. *The Scope of Fiction.* New York: Appleton-Century-Crofts, 1960. 336 pp.

A shorter version of *Understanding Fiction* (see entry 1080).

1080. Brooks, Cleanth, and Robert Penn Warren. *Understanding Fiction.* 2nd edition. New York: Appleton-Century-Crofts, 1959. 688 pp.

One of the most valuable sources on the subject, this anthology-text employs stories as diverse as those by Rudyard Kipling and Flannery O'Connor to uncover action, characterization, and meaning in the short story. Each story is followed by an "interpretation" and several discursive questions. The comparison of one story with others is an important part of the analysis.

1081. Brown, Francis, editor. *Opinions and Perspectives from the "New York Times Book Review."* Boston: Houghton Mifflin, 1964. 441 pp.

In this collection of critical and literary essays taken from a ten-year span of *The New York Times Book Review,* sixty-two writers and critics discuss their own and others' literary efforts. The names of the contributors will be recognized by anyone familiar with American letters. Robert Penn Warren discusses "How a Story Was Born and How, Bit by Bit, It Grew;" Wallace Stegner tells of writing in "The American Vein;" V.S. Pritchett tells us that "In Writing, Nothing Fails Like Success;" and so on. A triumph of lively commentary and a treasury of clear-sighted counsel.

1082. Burnett, Hallie, and Whit Burnett. *Fiction Writer's Handbook.* Preface by Norman Mailer. New York: Harper, 1975. 200 pp.

Whit and Hallie Burnett were for many years the guiding force behind the magazine *Story.* Their *Handbook* ranges from style and narrative development to editing. It also sheds light on the beginning careers of many notable writers and is an optimistic collection of imparted wisdom by two dedicated and influential teachers and editors.

1083. Burns, Alan, and Charles Sugnet, editors. *Imagination on Trial; British and American Writers Discuss Their Working Methods.* London: Allison and Busby, 1982. 170 pp.

Interviews with twelve British and American writers on the subjects of inspiration, work habits, and the subtleties of imagination. Included are J.G. Ballard, Eva Figes, John Gardner, Wilson Harris, John Hawkes, B.S. Johnson, Tom Mallin, Michael Moorcock, Grace Paley, Ishmael Reed, Allan Sillitoe, and one of the editors, Alan Burns.

1084. Butler, Samuel. *The Notebooks of Samuel Butler.* Selections arranged and edited by Henry Festing Jones; with an introduction by Francis Hackett. New York: Dutton, 1907. 437 pp.

Random observations about the human condition and the arts, including writing. Said F. Scott Fitzgerald in a letter to Max Perkins, "Every young author ought to read Samuel Butler's Notebooks."

1085. Caldwell, Erskine. *Writing in America.* New York: Phaedra, 1968. 133 pp.

Caldwell takes the position that writing is a perilous business and a hard one to learn. He rejects the concept of the natural-born novelist as quickly as he does the idea that art and profit do not mix. Amid much advice, he still finds time to address what he calls the "...fire in the heart and fever in the mind" which is the essence of the creative spirit. *Writing in America* is short, filled with opinion, and mainly of interest to Caldwell fans.

1086. Cary, Joyce. *Art and Reality; Ways of the Creative Process.* New York: Harper, 1958. 175 pp.

The intuitions that lead the writer through character, description, plot, and ultimately to meaning and truth are explored with reference to Hardy, Lawrence, Zola, Tolstoy, and others. The basic understandings that are reflected in Cary's memorable novels are explicitly revealed in this simple but rewarding essay on writing in particular and the arts in general.

1087. Cassill, Ronald Verlin. *Writing Fiction.* 2nd edition. Englewood Cliffs, New Jersey: Prentice-Hall, 1975. 174 pp.

According to numerous observers, this is one of the better short texts dealing with the writing of fiction. It relies on six short stories as points of departure for lively (if brief) discussions of unity, plot, tone, character, scene, dialogue, and the like. Making no claim that readers of his book will become professional writers, Cassill promises only that those who work at their writing with some sense of responsibility will "...overcome narrowness and fear by giving order, measure, and significance to the flux of experience constantly dinning into our lives." Cassill is a widely published author of novels, short stories, and articles. He has been a teacher of writing at Columbia, Harvard, Brown, and the University of Iowa.

1088. Cather, Willa. *Willa Cather on Writing; Critical Studies on Writing as an Art.* New York: Alfred A. Knopf, 1949. 126 pp.

Short reflections on her own and others' fiction, including a letter to *Commonweal* describing the forging of *Death Comes for the Archbishop.*

1089. Conrad, Joseph. *Conrad's Prefaces to His Works.* Freeport, New York: Books for Libraries, 1971. 218 pp.

The genesis of Conrad's tales and novels is revealed by their maker in these brief admissions of technique and inspiration.

1090. ———. *Joseph Conrad on Fiction.* Edited by Walter F. Wright. Lincoln, Nebraska: University of Nebraska Press, 1964. 236 pp.

Contains letters and literary reflections, as well as notes and prefaces, that shed light on the author's individual works.

1091. Cowley, Malcolm. *The Literary Situation.* New York: Viking Press, 1958. 259 pp.

To quote Cowley: "Here, I am trying to discuss whole categories of books... My new book deals with mid-century Americans as professional writers and unprofessional readers." He presents, in a series of essays, his views on war novels, "new" fiction, and naturalism. His extended comments on the natural history of the American writer tell of the day-to-day aspects of being a writer and the forces that impel people to write in the first place. This is a bright and entertaining view of American letters.

1092. Dembo, L.S., and Cyrena N. Pondrom. *The Contemporary Writer; Interviews with Sixteen Novelists and Poets.* Madison: University of Wisconsin Press, 1972. 296 pp.

Fiction section includes John Hawkes, John Barth, Saul Bellow, Vladimir Nabokov, I.B. Singer, Jorge Luis Borges, Sara Lidman, Per Sundman, and James Merrill. Poetry section includes Kenneth Rexroth, George Oppen, Carl Rakosi, Charles Reznikoff, Louis Zukofsky, Gwendolyn Brooks, and George Baker.

1093. DeVoto, Bernard Augustine. *The World of Fiction.* Boston: Writer, 1956. 299 pp.

DeVoto, a novelist and Pulitzer-Prize-winning historian, presents his views on the relationship between the person who writes a novel and the person who reads it. He addresses the questions of why people read fiction and what techniques and skills are required for the writing of it. This is neither a handbook for writers nor a critical treatise, but it can be used by writers, critics, and general readers to good advantage. It received laudatory reviews in the *New Republic, New Yorker,* and *New York Times Book Review,* and it remains a thoughtful and stimulating study.

1094. Dos Passos, John. *The Fourteenth Chronicle; Letters and Diaries of John Dos Passos.* Ipswich, Massachusetts: Gambit, 1973. 662 pp.

This collection spans the years from 1910 to 1970 and contains more than a little insight about the making of the author's major works.

1095. Dreiser, Theodore. *Notes on Life.* University, Alabama: University of Alabama Press, 1974. 346 pp.

Dreiser addresses emotion, creative energy, and a host of other topics in these explosive and sometimes disturbing musings.

1096. Edel, Leon. *The Prefaces of Henry James.* Folcroft, Pennsylvania: Folcroft Press, 1970. 136 pp.

This is an extended essay on the theories and methods of fiction as expressed by James in the prefaces he wrote for the definitive edition of his novels and tales. Less concerned with standard literary criticism than with an exposition of what motivated James, both Edel and James shed much light on the creative process.

1097. Eliot, George. *A Writer's Notebook, 1854-1879 and Uncollected Writings.* Edited by Joseph Wiesenfarth. Charlottesville: University of Virginia Press, 1981. 301 pp.

Contains notes on the readings Eliot did for such classics as *The Mill on the Floss* and *Adam Bede.*

1098. Ellison, Ralph. *Shadow and Act.* New York: Random, 1964. 317 pp.

Twenty years of essays by a principled writer who comments at length on the Black experience in general and on writing as a Black in particular.

1099. Engle, Paul, editor. *On Creative Writing.* New York: Dutton, 1964. 244 pp.

Under each of the headings, Short Story, Article, Poetry, Novelist, and Play, there appears a summary essay which is followed by illustrative excerpts from Anton Chekhov, James Baldwin, Edgar Allan Poe, Richard Wilbur, William Carlos Williams, Wallace Stevens, Leo Tolstoy, Stephen Crane, George Eliot, Samuel Beckett, and George Bernard Shaw. Engle has been a poet, fiction writer, editor of several O'Henry Prize anthologies, and teacher at the Iowa Writer's Workshop.

1100. Faulkner, William. *Faulkner in the University; Class Conferences at the University of Virginia, 1957-1958.* Edited by Frederick L. Gwynn and Joseph L. Blother. New York: Random House, 1965. 294 pp.

Dialogues that demonstrate "...the working of the writer's mind and the qualities of his character." Contains a wealth of information about individual works of fiction as seen by the man who wrote them.

1101. ———. *Lion in the Gate; Interviews with William Faulkner, 1926-1962.* New York: Random House, 1968. 298 pp.

1102. Fisher, Vardis. *God or Caesar? The Writing of Fiction for Beginners.* Caldwell, Idaho: Caxton Printers, 1953. 271 pp.

The late Vardis Fisher was an able and prolific novelist who fell short of greatness. His cogent reflections and advice on writing present his philosophy of the subject. His remarks on language, style, and scene flow with ease and conviction, and one comes away with the sense that Fisher genuinely wished to communicate with other writers about the things he held most dear.

1103. Fitzgerald, F. Scott. *Correspondence.* Edited by Matthew J. Bruccoli and others. New York: Random House, 1980. 640 pp.

Moving communications to his wife, daughter, Max Perkins, Ernest Hemingway, Edmund Wilson, and others. Along with the burdens and loneliness, we share his thoughts on the writer's art.

1104. ———. *The Crackup.* Edited by Edmund Wilson. New York: New Directions, 1956. 347 pp.

Amid the obsessions with personal adjustment, or the lack thereof, a sustained thread of the author's technical concerns shows through.

1105. ———. *Notebooks of F. Scott Fitzgerald.* New York: Harcourt Brace Jovanovich, 1980. 357 pp.

Though many of these random observations made by Fitzgerald between 1932 and 1940 are commonplace, the remainder provide an audience with creative vision.

1106. Flaubert, Gustave. *The Selected Letters of Gustave Flaubert.* Translated and edited with an introduction by Francis Steegmuller. New York: Vintage Books, 1957. 310 pp.

The author of *Madame Bovary* reveals his artistic concerns to a number of other great authors, including Emile Zola and George Sand.

1107. Ford, Ford Madox. *Critical Writings.* Edited by Frank MacShane. Lincoln: University of Nebraska Press, 1964. 167 pp.

These essays express Ford's conviction that the function of fiction was to give an objective account of the actual world. Included are letters to other writers and the introduction to Hemingway's *A Farewell to Arms.* The essay "Techniques" is of particular interest to the fiction writer.

1108. Foster-Harris, William. *The Basic Formulas of Fiction.* Norman, Oklahoma: University of Oklahoma Press, 1967. 146 pp.

Starting from the premise that works of modern fiction are solutions in "...moral arithmetic," Foster-Harris literally uses arithmetic equations to show how to develop plot and conflict. He uses a similarly prescriptive approach for viewpoint and character. His analysis is not entirely convincing, but it may help some beginning writers to organize their thoughts.

1109. Fredette, Jean M. *Fiction Writer's Market, 1983-84; How to Get Your Short Stories and Novels Published.* Cincinnati: Writer's Digest, 1983. 672 pp.

Lists over 1,200 magazine and book publishers who regularly publish fiction and includes editors' names, addresses, rates of pay, and other valuable data. Also included are a series of short essays on fiction technique and fiction publishing, as well as lists of awards and contests, writers' organizations, agents, and a glossary of fiction terms.

1110. Frenkel, James. *Make More Money Writing Fiction Than You Would Without This Book!* New York: Arco, 1983. 224 pp.

With an emphasis on genre fiction, this work covers author-publisher relations, career management, and other essentials for surviving in the fiction market.

1111. Fuchs, Esther. *Encounters with Israeli Authors.* Marblehead, Maine: Micah, 1983. 92 pp.

Interviews with nine outstanding authors, including Amalia Kahana Carmon (often called the Jewish Virginia Woolf), S. Yizhar, Itamar Yaoz-Kest, A.B. Yehoshua, and Aharon Appelfeld.

1112. Gado, Frank. *First Person; Conversations on Writers and Writing.* Schenectady, New York: Syracuse University Press, 1973. 159 pp.

These extended interviews were conducted with Glenway Wescott, John Dos Passos, Robert Penn Warren, John Updike, John Barth, and Robert Coover.

1113. Gardner, John. *The Art of Fiction; Notes on Craft for Young Writers.* New York: Knopf, 1984. 187 pp.

The late and widely admired John Gardner starts with his definition of fiction as a "vivid and continuous dream" that must be transferred to the mind of the reader. He then discusses and illustrates the basic elements of fiction in a way that will benefit almost any new writer.

1114. ———. *On Moral Fiction.* New York: Basic Books, 1978. 214 pp.

Addresses the failure of morality in recent fiction and its replacement with literature that is nihilistic and absurdist. Moral fiction, in the author's view, should test values in an effort to determine a path to human fulfillment.

1115. Gide, Andre. *The Journal of Andre Gide: 1889-1949.* 4 vols. New York: Knopf, 1947-1951.

Comments and criticism on other writers, on work habits and periods of block, and on books read are combined with the reflections of a long literary life in this monumental memoir.

1116. Goodman, Theodore. *The Techniques of Fiction; An Analysis of Creative Writing.* New York: Crowell, Collier, 1961. 288 pp.

A critical discussion of the mechanics of fiction as exemplified by the works of traditional writers. Goodman treats conflict, image, pattern, character, emotion, fictional ideas, and style in ways that establish firm theories, but leaves specific applications to his readers.

1117. Gorky, Maxim. *The Autobiography of Maxim Gorky.* Introduction by Abraham Armolinsky. New York: Collier Books, 1962. 639 pp.

Brings together all three previously published autobiographies of Gorky: *My Childhood, In the World,* and *My Universities.*

1118. Graham, John. *Craft So Hard to Learn; Conversations with Poets and Novelists about the Teaching of Writing.* Edited by George Garrett. Caldwell, New Jersey: William Morrow, 1972. 93 pp.

This slim volume reflects the attitudes of the authors and poets interviewed by Graham, such as Richard Wilbur, James Dickey, and William Harrison. Along the way, a few insights emerge about teaching students to write with polished technique, but the interviews are far too short to give any depth to these ideas.

1119. ———. *The Writer's Voice; Conversations with Contemporary Writers.* Conducted by John Graham; edited by George Garrett. New York: Morrow, 1973. 294 pp.

Interviews with nineteen poets and fiction writers who attended the 1970 Hollins College Conference in Creative Writing and Cinema in which opinions on writing and the creative process are expressed by the well known and not so well known. The reader will find memorable comments by Richard Wilbur, James Dickey, and Ralph Ellison, among others. Given the limitations of the interview technique, this is a better than average collection. George Garrett, author of *Death of the Fox,* has written a short biography of each writer as well as what he calls a "snapshot" (brief description of the person) for each.

1120. Greene, Graham. *A Sort of Life.* New York: Simon and Schuster, 1971. 220 pp.

Of most immediate value to writers for the light it sheds on the beginnings of Greene's career as an author.

1121. Hale, Nancy. *The Realities of Fiction; A Book about Writing.* Boston: Little, Brown, 1962. 247 pp.

Stressing mental attitudes that allow for maximum freedom of action in one's writing, Nancy Hale at the same time calls for disciplined imagination as a prerequisite for writing fiction. Those looking for a tightly organized "here's how" approach may be disappointed, but Hale soars and swoops and ascends on "thermals" of the spirit which are largely ignored by run-of-the-mill books about fiction writing. She assumes that the reader is capable both of nuance and of complex perception.

1122. Hardy, Thomas. *The Collected Letters.* 2 vols. Oxford: Oxford University Press, 1978; 1980.

In the first two volumes of a projected seven-volume set, these letters reveal Hardy's literary efforts as they unfolded.

1123. Hawthorne, Nathaniel. *Journals.* (various editions)

Broad evidence for the value of keeping a detailed journal. Creative insights abound in these random thoughts and regular musings.

1124. Heckelmann, Charles N. *Writing Fiction for Profit.* New York: Coward-McCann, 1968. 256 pp.

Speaking from experience as the author of more than twenty published novels (Westerns) and hundreds of short stories and articles, Heckelmann discusses the usual technical aspects of writing fiction, such as dialogue and characterization. Drawing on his experience as a book and magazine editor, he also treats the business end of writing. Though he gives able advice on manuscript submission and on what happens "behind the scenes" in the editor's office, his comments on marketing have become somewhat dated due to the changes in the book and magazine publishing world over the past decade and a half.

Hemingway, Ernest. *Ernest Hemingway on Writing.* See entry 3955.

1125. Hemingway, Ernest. *Selected Letters, 1917-1961.* Edited by Carlos Baker. New York: Scribner's, 1981. 948 pp.

Glimpses of the many Ernest Hemingways, from youth to old age, with continual references to his craft.

1126. Hubert, Karen M. *Teaching and Writing Popular Fiction; Horror, Adventure, Mystery, and Romance in the American Classroom.* New York: Teachers & Writers Collaborative, 1976. 235 pp.

Part writing advice, part teaching advice, and part anthology, this work defies easy description. It will, however, inspire and instruct those wishing to write or teach the writing of category fiction.

1127. Hunt, Percival. *The Gift of the Unicorn; Essays on Writing.* Pittburgh: University of Pittsburgh Press, 1965. 120 pp.

Neither critical nor technical in approach, these short inspirational essays are full of apt quotations and sound opinions on writing, past and present.

1128. James, Henry. *The Art of Fiction, and Other Essays.* Introduction by Morris Roberts. New York: Charles Scribner's Sons, 1948. 240 pp.

These eleven essays present James's theories of fiction.

1129. ———. *The Notebooks of Henry James.* Edited by F.O. Mathiessen and Kenneth B. Murdock. Oxford: Oxford University Press, 1948. 425 pp.

An illuminating record of the writer's creative life over a span of thirty years. Comparable to Dostoevsky's *Notebooks,* Flaubert's *Letters,* and Hawthorne's *Journals.*

1130. ———. *Theory of Fiction.* Edited with an introduction by James E. Miller, Jr. Lincoln: University of Nebraska Press, 1972. 366 pp.

Excerpts from James's writings about his craft. Arranged by broad headings such as "the writer and his imagination," "characters," "point of view," and "meaning and theme," this book provides insights not possible to attain by simply reading James at random.

1131. Kafka, Franz. *Letters to Felice.* New York: Schocken Books, 1973. 620 pp.

Amid the soul-bearing to Felice we find Kafka sending manuscripts and forming himself as a writer.

1132. Kennedy, X.J. *Introduction to Fiction.* 2nd edition. Boston: Little, Brown, 1979. 421 pp.

Like the author's *Introduction to Poetry* (see entry 683), a standard and widely accepted text on the subject.

1133. Knott, William C. *The Craft of Fiction.* Revised edition. Reston, Virginia: Reston Publishing Co., 1977. 191 pp.

Beginning with a section on the financial risks implicit in a shrinking fiction market, Knott goes on to define fiction and to discuss technical elements such as dialogue and point of view. Comments on marketing techniques and the writer's life round out this text for beginners. Written on the same basic plan as Knott's *The Craft of Non-Fiction* (see entry 2836).

1134. Koontz, Dean R. *Writing Popular Fiction.* Cincinnati: Writer's Digest, 1981. 309 pp.

Koontz divides modern fiction into "mainstream and category." "Category," which is the subject of this book, includes mystery, suspense, gothic romance, western, science fiction-fantasy, and erotica. Koontz discusses general elements common to all and then devotes a chapter to each. Generally, this book provides a knowledgeable analysis, backed by apt examples, though some readers will balk at his generalizations and others will find the treatment of each category far too short. At the very least, this book offers definitions and guidelines for writing a variety of modern popular forms, including Harold Robbins-style *roman a clef* novels.

1135. Kuehl, John. *Write and Rewrite; A Study of the Creative Process.* New York: Meredith Press, 1967. 308 pp.

By placing first-draft efforts of distinguished authors alongside the finished product, Kuehl has provided a unique and much needed approach to understanding the process. Kuehl contacted each author included in the anthology and asked for first draft materials of their published works. Thus, the reader is afforded a view of how such contemporary writers as Philip Roth, Eudora Welty, Robert Penn Warren, William Styron, and John Hawkes revise their initial efforts. At times the reader has the illusion of peering over the author's shoulder as needless authorial intrusions are crossed out and as clumsy dialogue is set right. Each selection is chosen to illustrate a problem as seen by its own author. Kuehl and the writers who so generously allowed a peek beneath the curtain of creativity deserve our gratitude.

1136. Liddell, Robert. *Some Principles of Fiction.* Bloomington: Indiana University Press, 1954. 162 pp.

This highly regarded work takes up where its predecessor volume, *A Treatise on the Novel* (see entry 34), left off. Questions such as the relationship of quality and content and the nature of good prose are discussed, as well as a variety of technical problems such as summary and scene.

1137. London, Jack. *No Mentor but Myself; A Collection of Articles, Essays, Reviews, and Letters on Writing and Writers.* Edited by Dale L. Walker; foreword by Howard Lachtman. Port Washington, New York: Kennikat Press, 1979. 197 pp.

Reveals the concerns of a major American writer for his craft and the generous impulse to share this concern with young writers. As should be expected, the commentary is pithy and direct.

Lubbock, Percy. *Craft of Fiction.* See entry 36.

1138. Macauley, Robie, and George Lanning. *Technique in Fiction.* New York: Harper & Row, 1964. 227 pp.

The authors are convinced that the best way to learn technique is to hear about it from great writers. In that sense, this is not a how-to-do-it book but rather a how-it-was-done book. From story origin to final meaning, the concepts are always presented in the context of what Conrad or Lawrence or Gogol or a host of other writers wrote or thought about their writing. This is a balanced and useful study of technique in traditional fiction, but obviously less so for the study of technique in more recent and innovative forms.

1139. McGraw, Eloise Jarvis. *Techniques of Fiction Writing.* Boston: Writer, 1959. 209 pp.

Competent advice about pace, rhythm, suspense, realistic description, and other devices for holding reader attention. McGraw views plot and character as inseparable elements and provides recipes for creating and combining both. One wonders why this book is no longer in print, since it does such an above-average job of explaining dialogue and style, as well as the aforementioned topics.

1140. Mansfield, Katherine. *Journal of Katherine Mansfield.* New York: Knopf, 1927. 255 pp.

The impressions of a mind only sometimes at peace with itself but always sensitive and very alone.

1141. ———. *The Scrapbook of Katherine Mansfield.* New York: Knopf, 1940. 280 pp.

Fragments that reveal the joys and burdens of being both female and an accomplished writer.

1142. Mathieu, Aron M. *The Creative Writer.* Cincinnati: Writer's Digest, 1961. 528 pp.

Contains, among others, excerpts from William Saroyan, Erskine Caldwell, and Ken Purdy on writing.

1143. Maugham, William Somerset. *The Summing Up.* New York: Doubleday, 1938. 310 pp.

"Matured conclusions" about the trials and errors of the author's profession.

1144. ———. *A Writer's Notebook.* Freeport, Long Island, New York: Greenwood Press, 1970. 367 pp.

Maugham has condensed fifteen of his notebooks, the first of which dates from 1892, into this volume. His intention in publishing it is to reveal "...the technique of literary production and...the process of creation." An interesting volume of aphorisms and reflections which only occasionally bear upon the subject of writing as a sustained and complex effort.

1145. Miller, Henry. *Henry Miller on Writing.* Selected by Thomas H. Moore from the published and unpublished works of Henry Miller. New York: New Directions, 1964. 216 pp.

Miller discusses the early influence of art and other writers on his work, as well as his efforts to perfect his style. "The Author at Work" shows, in part, how Henry Miller went about writing his books. Miller's writing "commandments" are also listed, in addition to his daily work schedules. To quote from his editors, "Some of the most rewarding pages in Henry Miller's book concern his self-education as a writer. He tells, as few great writers ever have, how he set his goals, how he discovered the excitement of using words, how the books he read influenced him, and how he learned to draw on his own experiences."

1146. Miller, James E., Jr. *F. Scott Fitzgerald; His Art and His Technique.* New York: New York University Press, 1964. 173 pp.

An exacting evaluation of the technical growth of Fitzgerald which charts the influences of Mencken, Conrad, James, and H.G. Wells.

1147. Minot, Stephen. *Three Genres; The Writing of Fiction, Poetry, and Drama.* Englewood Cliffs, New Jersey: Prentice-Hall, 1981. 326 pp.

Minot examines each of three art forms with regard to the creative processes involved. Intended neither as a "how to" approach nor as a path to commercial success, this readable survey stresses dynamics and self-criticism, while providing a few excellent examples from the works of established writers. *Three Genres* can be recommended for its thoughtful definitions alone. The abundance of additional material makes it a valuable one-of-a-kind contribution to the literature. Completed by an excellent glossary-index.

1148. Morgan, Louise. *Writers at Work.* London: Chatto and Windus, 1931. 71 pp.

Eight articles on William Butler Yeats, Richard Aldington, Sinclair Lewis, Sylvia Townsend Warner, Edgar Wallace, Wyndham Lewis, Somerset Maugham and A.E. Coppard.

1149. Morris, Wright. *About Fiction; Reverent Reflections on the Nature of Fiction with Irreverent Observations on Writers, Readers, and Other Abuses.* New York: Harper & Row, 1975. 182 pp.

Morris, the author of many novels, terms this book "propaganda in the interests of good fiction."

1150. Nabokov, Vladimir. *Speak Memory.* New York: Putnam, 1966. 316 pp.

An outstanding autobiography containing frequent references to his fiction in the form of lucid self-criticism.

1151. Newquist, Roy. *Counterpoint.* Foreword by Mark Van Doren. New York: Simon & Schuster, 1967. 653 pp.

Interviews with sixty-three authors, columnists, and publishers. The subjects of these interviews provide many informative asides about writing and publishing. The authors interviewed reveal how certain of their books began and were completed. Technical hints on rewriting, inspiration, and plain hard work are variously dealt with. Unfortunately, such comments are randomly placed, and the book lacks an index. Newquist's book is, thus, more likely to provide relaxed discovery by the fireside than it is to act as a ready-reference source. Some of the writers interviewed are Louis Auchincloss, Erskine Caldwell, Truman Capote, Bruce Catton, Jessica Mitford, C.P. Snow, Helen MacInnes, and Peter DeVries.

1152. O'Connor, Flannery. *The Habit of Being.* Letters edited and with an introduction by Sally Fitzgerald. New York: Farrar, 1979. 617 pp.

In a series of transcendent letters to fellow authors such as Robert Lowell and John Hawkes, a gifted artist reveals her writing methods and addresses the relationship between sin and fate in human experience.

1153. ———. *Mystery and Manners; Occasional Prose.* Selected and edited by Sally Fitzgerald and Robert Fitzgerald. New York: Farrar, Straus, and Giroux, 1969. 237 pp.

Articles and essays on short story and novel writing with regard to religion, the South, and O'Connor's own accomplishments as a writer.

1154. O'Connor, William V. *Forms of Modern Fiction; Essays Collected in Honor of Joseph Warren Beach.* Minneapolis: University of Minnesota Press, 1948. 305 pp.

Ideas on technique from Mark Schorer, Allen Tate, and others who know.

1155. O'Hara, John. *"An Artist Is His Own Fault"; John O'Hara on Writers and Writing.* Introduced by Matthew J. Bruccoli. Carbondale: Southern Illinois University Press, 1977. 226 pp.

A fine collection of the late John O'Hara's interviews, lectures, speeches, reviews, and essays. Recognized by critics for his "ear for speech" and his "eye for detail," he employed what he called "pre-paper discipline," which involved great care and planning prior to the writing act. Thoughts on dialogue, detail, characterization, fiction writing as social history, and psychological truth by a novelist and short story writer whose readers have numbered in the millions.

1156. Owen, Jean Z. *Professional Fiction Writing; A Practical Guide to Modern Techniques.* Boston: Writer, 1974. 133 pp.

A short text for beginning fiction writers which covers the expected basics of theme, plot, dialogue, and character as well as a number of related topics. The quotations and examples are apt, and Owen's advice is generally sound, as far as it goes. Addresses both quality fiction and commercial stories, but her emphasis is on the latter.

1157. Peck, Robert N. *Secrets of Successful Fiction.* Cincinnati: Writer's Digest, 1980. 119 pp.

In twenty-two short chapters, Peck attempts to introduce writers of all ages to the essentials of the craft. In a number of cases the "secrets" remain undisclosed.

1158. Porter, Katherine Anne. *The Days Before.* New York: Harcourt, Brace, 1952. 273 pp.

These critical essays and book prefaces span a period of thirty years, and while the majority bear on the writing of other authors, much can be inferred about Porter's own techniques.

1159. Prestwood, Edward. *The Creative Writer's Phrase-Finder.* Palm Springs, California: ETC Publications, 1984. 364 pp.

Contains over 9,000 short phrases organized under such headings as people, nature, behavior, time, and actions. Under people we find "nature had cheated her," "heart of flint," "blind prey to impulses," and "an expert flatterer." The assumption is that even the best of writers sometimes bog down.

1160. Rehder, Jessie. *The Young Writer At Work.* New York: The Odyssey Press, 1962. 274 pp.

Jessie Rehder judiciously selects passages from the works of major fiction writers in order to illustrate how to create effective plots, develop and breathe life into characters, and reveal theme. In most cases, the author who wrote the selection is quoted again with regard to his or her attitudes toward the subject matter or fictional technique involved. Rehder introduces the short chapters thus formed and concludes each with suggested exercises. The result is a superior fiction writing text which is concerned with artistic rather than purely commercial ends.

1161. Reid, Mildred. *Writers: Why Stop Now?* Contoocook, New Hampshire: Burkhaven, 1962. 224 pp.

Based on articles that have appeared in a variety of periodicals, Reid's book is mainly on fiction techniques such as conflict, characterization, pace, endings, flashback, and viewpoint.

1162. Reynolds, Paul Revere. *The Writing and Selling of Fiction.* New York: Doubleday, 1965. 175 pp.

Drawing on a lifetime of experience as a literary agent, Reynolds discusses the basics of fiction writing, aspects of the publishing industry, and the launching of a first novel. May be compared with Meredith's *Writing to Sell* (see entry 3725).

1163. Richter, David H. *Fable's End; Completeness and Closure in Rhetorical Fiction.* Chicago: University of Chicago Press, 1974. 214 pp.

Richter defines rhetorical fiction as being based less on plot than on themes, attitudes, and doctrines. In this context he discusses the works of writers as recent as Pynchon, Golding, Bellow, and Heller. This is a valuable resource for anyone wishing to write or even understand the modern open-form novel.

1164. Roberts, Kenneth. *I Wanted to Write.* New York: Doubleday, 1949. 471 pp.

The autobiography of a novelist and popular magazine writer who gained critical and financial success. Recollections of the difficulties and rewards of a writing career, as well as the day-to-day struggles.

1165. Roberts, Thomas John. *When Is Something Fiction?* Carbondale, Illinois: Southern Illinois University Press, 1972. 144 pp.

Intention, value, and genre are examined in this critical essay which incidentally bears on technique and craft.

1166. Rockwell, F.A. *Modern Fiction Techniques.* 2nd revised edition. Boston: Writer, 1969. 292 pp.

Standard techniques for writing novels and short stories are competently described and illustrated.

1167. Rodman, Selden. *Tongues of Fallen Angels.* New York: New Directions, 1974. 271 pp.

Conversations with Jorge Luis Borges, Robert Frost, Ernest Hemingway, Pablo Neruda, Stanely Kunitz, Gabriel Garcia Marquez, Octavio Paz, Norman Mailer, Allen Ginsberg, Vinicus de Moraes, Joao Cabral de Melo Neto, and Derek Wolcott. Most valuable for its views of the Latin American writers of genius.

1168. Roth, Philip. *Reading Myself and Others.* New York: Farrar, Straus, and Giroux, 1975. 269 pp.

Essays on his own and others' art which explore the nature of literature and Jewish writing.

1169. Russell, John. *Style in Modern British Fiction.* Baltimore: Johns Hopkins, 1978. 196 pp.

James Joyce's *Dubliners,* D.H. Lawrence's *The Lost Girl* and *Kangaroo,* E.M. Forster's *Howard's End* and *A Passage to India,* Wyndham Lewis's *Tar* and *Self Condemned,* and Henry Green's *Back and Concluding* are examined minutely for cadence, suffix use, forms of negation, and other matters of style.

1170. Schorer, Mark. *The World We Imagine; Selected Essays.* New York: Farrar, Straus, and Giroux, 1968. 402 pp.

Technique considered by a master critic.

1171. Sloane, William. *The Craft of Writing.* Edited by Julia Sloane. New York: Norton, 1979. 123 pp.

Called "perceptive" and "practical" by reviewers, these notes on fiction from Sloane's Bread Loaf Writers' Conference lectures cover narration, scene, character, and dialogue.

1172. Smith, Bertha W., and Virginia C. Lincoln, editors. *Writing Art; Authorship as Experienced and Expressed by the Great Writers.* Boston and New York: Houghton Mifflin, 1931. 277 pp.

The editors draw upon diaries, letters, journals, and other sources to give us quotations on the subject of writing from Emily Dickinson, O. Henry, Samuel Coleridge, Alexandre Dumas, Dante, Fyodor Dostoevsky, and Leo Tolstoy, to mention only a few. The quotations may serve to inspire rather than to give detailed instructions, and frequently the reader may inquire as to why some of the selections were included at all.

1173. Somerlott, Robert. *The Writing of Modern Fiction.* Boston: Writer, 1972. 147 pp.

Somerlott sees his book as a problem-solving device for serious writers. He begins by dismissing the casual dreamer who would like to write but does not put ink or type to paper. He also indicates, early on, his suspicions of any how-to book on writing that promises "never-fail systems." His book is about writing fiction in all its forms, not just the art novel or the literary short story. It tells how to develop one's powers of observation and how to bend reality to the needs of plot and story line. Perhaps the strongest elements of this book are the chapters on character and voice or point of view. Somerlott advises, unlike John Braine, that the short outline is better for the first draft. Somerlott is a seasoned novelist and short story writer, having published with *Atlantic, Harpers,* and many other national magazines.

1174. Steinbeck, John. *A Life in Letters.* Edited by Elaine Steinbeck and Robert Wallsten. New York: Viking Press, 1975. 848 pp.

No other major fiction writer's letters reveal more of the preoccupations and outright anguish that are the serious novelist's lot. For example: "Nine tenths of a writer's life do not admit of any companion nor friend nor associate. And until one makes peace with loneliness and accepts it as a part of the profession, as celibacy is a part of priesthood, until then there are times of dreadful dread. I am just as terrified of my next book as I was of my first."

1175. Stevenson, Robert Louis. *Learning to Write; Suggestions and Counsel from Robert Louis Stevenson.* Edited by J.W. Rogers, Jr. New York: C. Scribner's Sons, 1920. 225 pp.

Contains the famous article on self-taught writing from *A College Magazine,* in addition to thoughts on realism, story, and style.

1176. Surmelian, Leon Z. *The Techniques of Fiction Writing; Measure and Madness.* Introduction by Mark Schorer. New York: Doubleday, 1968. 255 pp.

A lucid guide to plot, character, and scene that instructs through examples from Woolf, Joyce, Tolstoy, Flaubert, Christopher Isherwood, and William Saroyan, to name a few. As the *New York Times Book Review* said of this remarkably balanced effort, "...no one since E.M. Forster or Percy Lubbock has brought so much faith and good will...to the task of examining and evaluating the elusive workings of fiction."

1177. Sutherland, James. *Fiction and the Fiction Industry.* London: Athlone Press, 1978. 231 pp.

A study of the present state of fiction book publishing in Britain, along with predictions for the future which take into account immediate weaknesses and the potential for a healthy transformation.

1178. Swain, Dwight V. *Techniques of the Selling Writer.* Norman: University of Oklahoma Press, 1974. 330 pp. (First edition published in 1965 as *Tricks and Techniques of the Selling Writer.*)

This book is intended to help the would-be fiction writer to become a "commercially-oriented professional." It stresses hard work and sustained enthusiasm as prerequisites. It is filled with do's and don'ts, some of which are valid and a few of which are questionable. At times, the reader wishes for fewer opinions and more examples, but Swain's book remains a perceptive account of fiction technique, in which the uses of tension, reader interest, story movement, and planning are explored in ways not common to other books on writing.

1179. Turner, Katherine C. *Writing; The Shapes of Experience.* Boulder, Colorado: Pruett, 1967. 186 pp.

Turner addresses an audience of beginners in this skillfully constructed text. She begins with the premise that effective reading leads to good creative writing. She then goes on to show how personal experience adds individual and indelible uniqueness. Her chapters on dialogue, point of view, and story detail are valuable reading for writers of any level. Her abundant examples are first-rate, as is her book as a whole.

1180. Twain, Mark. *Mark Twain's Notebooks and Journals.* 3 vols. Berkeley: University of California Press, 1975-1980.

1181. Watkins, Floyd C., and Carl F. Knight, editors. *Writer to Writer; Readings on the Craft of Writing.* Boston: Houghton Mifflin, 1966. 243 pp.

This anthology draws on the thoughts of William Saroyan, John Ciardi, William Faulkner, John Steinbeck, Ernest Hemingway, and many others on topics related to writing. Most of the selections are short and to the point.

1182. Waugh, Evelyn. *The Letters of Evelyn Waugh.* Edited by Mark Amory. New Haven: Ticknor and Fields, 1980. 664 pp.

These 840 acerbic and sometimes brilliant letters repeatedly demonstrate the link between Waugh's artistic expression and his Catholicism.

1183. Welty, Eudora. *The Eye of the Story; Selected Essays and Reviews.* New York: Random, 1977. 355 pp.

Called "delightful" and a "treasure" by critics, this shrewd set of reflections contains Welty's well known "Place in Fiction" and "Looking at Short Stories."

1184. West, Ray Benedict. *The Art of Writing Fiction.* New York: Thomas Y. Crowell, 1968. 304 pp.

Part short story anthology, part practical advice about both short story and novel writing, and part critical commentary. Each story has been chosen to illustrate a particular aspect of technique, such as action, character, setting or theme, and each story is followed by West's commentary. Addressed to the beginning writer, this work uses the stories of established authors. West is an accomplished short story writer in his own right.

1185. Wharton, Edith N. *The Writing of Fiction.* New York: Octagon Books, 1967. 178 pp.

Originally published in 1924, Wharton's book begins by addressing the stream of consciousness writing of the time, with reminders that even the greatest writers of the past

"...have made use of the stammering and murmurings of the half-conscious mind." There, however, she parts company, preferring form and structure. Under the chapter headings "Telling a short story," "Constructing a novel," and "Character and situation," Wharton goes on to explain her critical and artistic views through reference to Tolstoy, Proust, and other traditional authors. She tells little about her own day-to-day writing methods and techniques.

1186. Whitney, Phyllis A. *Guide to Fiction Writing.* Boston: Writer, 1982. 133 pp.

With an emphasis on romantic novels, Whitney discusses story line, character development, and emotional content, as well as work routines and keeping a notebook. The anecdotes from the life of this best-selling fiction writer will please most readers.

1187. Wolfe, Thomas. *The Notebooks of Thomas Wolfe.* 2 vols. Chapel Hill: University of North Carolina Press, 1970.

These grandiloquent, inventive, and chaotic thoughts, drafts of letters, and outlines of fictional works in progress span the years from 1926 to 1938.

1188. ———. *Thomas Wolfe's Purdue Speech; "Writing and Living."* Edited from the dictated and revised typescript, with an introduction and notes by William Braswell and Leslie A. Field. West Lafayette, Indiana: Purdue University Studies, 1964. 133 pp.

Wolfe used only a portion of this typescript when he addressed the students and faculty of Purdue in 1938. Written three years after *The Story of a Novel* (see entry 66), this is in many ways an extension and further development of the ideas expressed in that book.

———. *The Story of a Novel.* See entry 66.

1189. Woolf, Virginia. *Common Reader; First Series.* New York: Harcourt, Brace, 1953. 246 pp.

Described by Stewart Sherman as being "about writing for writers," these essays range from Chaucer to the "hypothetical young novelist whose book will be reviewed in tomorrow's newspaper." Addressing the so-called "common reader" as opposed to the critic and scholar, this collection of twenty essays sets forth Woolf's positions with regard to literature and its creation.

1190. ———. *A Writer's Diary; Being Extracts from the Diary of Virginia Woolf.* Edited by Leonard Woolf. New York: Harcourt, Brace, 1954. 356 pp.

For extended treatment, see the more recently published complete diaries of Woolf.

Articles

1191. Action! Action! Action (tips for writing action sequences). Dean R. Koontz. *Writer's Digest,* vol. 61, August 1981, pp. 36-39.

1192. Advice can be dangerous. W. Brown. *Writer,* vol. 78, January 1965, pp. 19-21.

1193. Aim for the heart. P. Gallico. *Writer,* vol. 80, September 1967, pp. 11-12+.

1194. Alien subject. A. Myrer. *Writer,* vol. 81, November 1968, pp. 9-11+.

1195. Angle of vision. Rosellen Brown. *Writer,* vol. 90, September 1977, pp. 15-18+.

1196. Anthony Burgess (interview). *Modern Fiction Studies,* vol. 27, Autumn 1981, pp. 429-452.

1197. Approach to authorship. W. Penfield. *Writer,* vol. 74, March 1961, pp. 5-9+.

1198. Are you dreaming on paper? E.K. Woolvin. *Writer,* vol. 73, April 1960, pp. 12-14.

1199. Art of faction. Norah Lofts. *Writer,* vol. 94, August 1981, pp. 10-11+.

1200. Art of fiction (interview).

> Nelson Algren. *Paris Review,* no. 11, 1955, pp. 36-58.
> Kingsley Amis. *Paris Review,* no. 64, 1975, pp. 39-72.
> James Baldwin. *Paris Review,* no. 91, Spring 1984, pp. 48-82.
> Donald Barthelme. *Paris Review,* vol. 23, Summer 1981, pp. 181-210.
> Saul Bellow. *Paris Review,* no. 36, 1966, pp. 49-73.
> Heinrich Boll. *Paris Review,* no. 87, 1983, pp. 66-87.
> Jorge Luis Borges. *Paris Review,* no. 40, 1967, pp. 116-164.
> Anthony Burgess. *Paris Review,* no. 56, 1973-74, pp. 119-163.
> William Burroughs. *Paris Review,* no. 35, 1965, pp. 13-49.
> James M. Cain. *Paris Review,* no. 73, 1978, pp. 117-138.
> Erskine Caldwell. *Paris Review,* no. 86, Winter 1982, pp. 126-157.
> Truman Capote. *Paris Review,* no. 16, 1957, pp. 34-51.
> Raymond Carver. *Paris Review,* no. 89, 1983, pp. 192-234.
> Louis-Ferdinand Celine. *Paris Review,* no. 31, 1964, pp. 138-146.
> Blaise Cendrars. *Paris Review,* no. 37, 1966, pp. 105-

132.

John Cheever. *Paris Review,* no. 67, 1976, pp. 39-66.
Jean Cocteau. *Paris Review,* no. 32, 1964, pp. 12-37.
Simone de Beauvoir. *Paris Review,* no. 34, 1965, pp. 23-40.
Joan Didion. *Paris Review,* no. 74, 1978, pp. 142-163.
Isak Dinesen. *Paris Review,* no. 14, 1956, pp. 43-59.
J.P. Donleavy. *Paris Review,* no. 63, 1975, pp. 122-166.
John Dos Passos. *Paris Review,* no. 46, 1969, pp. 147-172.
Margaret Drabble. *Paris Review,* no. 74, 1978, pp. 40-65.
Lawrence Durrell. *Paris Review,* no. 22, 1960, pp. 32-61.
Ilya Ehrenburg. *Paris Review,* no. 26, 1961, pp. 99-117.
Stanley Elkin. *Paris Review,* no. 66, 1976, pp. 54-86.
Ralph Ellison. *Paris Review,* no. 8, 1955, pp. 54-71.
William Faulkner. *Paris Review,* no. 12, 1956, pp. 28-52.
John Gardner. *Paris Review,* no. 75, 1979, pp. 36-74.
William Gass. *Paris Review,* no. 70, 1977, pp. 61-94.
Nadine Gordimer. *Paris Review,* no. 88, 1983, pp. 82-127.
William Goyen. *Paris Review,* no. 68, 1976, pp. 58-100.
Joseph Heller. *Paris Review,* no. 60, 1973-74, pp. 126-147.
Ernest Hemingway. *Paris Review,* no. 18, 1958, pp. 60-89.
Aldous Huxley. *Paris Review,* no. 23, 1960, pp. 57-80.
Guillermo Cabrera Infante. *Paris Review,* no. 87, 1983, pp. 154-195.
Christopher Isherwood. *Paris Review,* no. 57, 1973-74, pp. 138-182.
James Jones. *Paris Review,* no. 20, 1959, pp. 34-55.
Jack Kerouac. *Paris Review,* no. 43, 1968, pp. 61-105.
Jerzy Kosinski. *Paris Review,* no. 54, 1972, pp. 183-207.
Mary McCarthy. *Paris Review,* no. 27, 1962, pp. 58-94.
Norman Mailer. *Paris Review,* no. 31, 1964, pp. 28-58.
Bernard Malamud. *Paris Review,* no. 61, 1975, pp. 40-64.
Henry Miller. *Paris Review,* no. 28, 1962, pp. 129-159.
Vladimir Nabokov. *Paris Review,* no. 41, 1967, pp. 92-111.
Joyce Carol Oates. *Paris Review,* no. 74, 1977, pp. 198-226.
Frank O'Connor. *Paris Review,* no. 17, 1957, pp. 42-64.
Dorothy Parker. *Paris Review,* no. 13, 1956, pp. 72-87.
Boris Pasternak. *Paris Review,* no. 24, 1960, pp. 42-69.
Katherine Anne Porter. *Paris Review,* no. 29, 1963, pp. 87-114.

Anthony Powell. *Paris Review,* no. 73, 1978, pp. 45-79.
Jean Rhys. *Paris Review,* no. 76, 1979, pp. 218-237.
Francoise Sagan. *Paris Review,* no. 14, 1956, pp. 82-89.
Irwin Shaw. *Paris Review,* no. 75, 1979, pp. 248-262.
Georges Simenon. *Paris Review,* no. 9, 1955, pp. 70-90.
Isaac Bashevis Singer. *Paris Review,* no. 44, 1968, pp.
   53-73.
John Steinbeck. *Paris Review,* no. 48, 1969, pp. 161-188.
John Steinbeck (continued). *Paris Review,* no. 63, 1975,
   pp. 180-194.
James Thurber. *Paris Review,* no. 10, 1955, pp. 34-49.
P.L. Travers. *Paris Review,* no. 86, Winter 1982, pp.
   210-224.
John Updike. *Paris Review,* no. 45, 1968, pp. 84-117.
Gore Vidal. *Paris Review,* no. 59, 1973-74, pp. 130-165.
Kurt Vonnegut. *Paris Review,* no. 69, 1977, pp. 56-103.
Robert Penn Warren. *Paris Review,* no. 16, 1957, pp.
   112-140.
Evelyn Waugh. *Paris Review,* no. 30, 1963, pp. 73-85.
Eudora Welty. *Paris Review,* no. 55, 1972, pp. 72-97.
Jessamyn West. *Paris Review,* no. 71, 1977, pp. 141-159.
Rebecca West. *Paris Review,* vol. 23, Spring 1981, pp.
   117-164.
Angus Wilson. *Paris Review,* no. 17, 1957, pp. 88-105.
P.G. Wodehouse. *Paris Review,* no. 64, 1975, pp. 149-
   171.
Marguerite Young. *Paris Review,* no. 71, 1977, pp. 59-
   75.

1201. Art of writing fiction. F. Martinez-Bonati. *New Literary History,* vol.
   11, Spring 1980, pp. 425-434.

1202. Artist in the labyrinth; design or dasein? R. Macksey. *Modern
   Language Notes,* vol. 77, May 1962, pp. 239-256.

1203. Attention, please! E. Corbett. *Writer,* vol. 75, March 1962, pp. 15-17.

1204. Audience of one. J.L. Toohey. *Writer,* vol. 75, October 1962, p. 30.

1205. Author as fiction. W. Sheed. *Commonweal,* vol. 78, September 6,
   1963, pp. 535-536.

1206. Back to beginnings. P.M. Daltry. *Writer,* vol. 78, July 1965, pp. 14-
   15.

1207. Being a writer. Sherwood Anderson. *20th Century Literature,* vol.
   23, February 1977, pp. 1-16.

1208. Bernard Malamud on writing fiction (interview). *Writer's Digest,* vol.
   52, July 1972, pp. 22-23.

1209. Beyond the obvious. A.S. Turnbull. *Writer,* vol. 90, September 1977,
   pp. 23-24.

1210. Blueprint for Negro literature. Richard Wright. *Amistad,* vol. 2, 1971, pp. 3-20.

1211. Borges on Borges (interview). *American Scholar,* vol. 38, Summer 1969, pp. 452-458.

1212. Bringing it all back home. S. O'Connell. *Atlantic,* vol. 225, January 1970, pp. 92-95.

1213. Bringing it back; writer's nostalgia. E. Savage. *Writer,* vol. 87, December 1974, pp. 15-16.

1214. But where do you get your ideas? M.F. Shyer. *Writer,* vol. 83, May 1970, pp. 19-20.

1215. Choosing details that count. E. Taylor. *Writer,* vol. 83, January 1970, pp. 15-16+.

1216. Commitment and action. E. Hannibal. *Writer,* vol. 83, December 1970, pp. 11-14.

1217. Confessions of a rookie fiction writer. D. Downing. *Writer,* vol. 95, September 1982, pp. 15-17.

1218. Contrast. B. Roer. *Writer,* vol. 77, June 1964, pp. 23-24.

1219. Conversation on The Blood Oranges. John Hawkes and Robert E. Scholes. *Novel,* vol. 5, Spring 1972, pp. 197-207.

1220. Conversation with Isaac Bashevis Singer (interview). *Chicago Review,* vol. 31, Spring 1980, pp. 53-60.

1221. Conversation with John Gardner (interview). *Atlantic,* vol. 239, May 1977, pp. 43-47.

1222. Conversation with Richard Stern (interview). *Chicago Review,* vol. 31, Winter 1980, pp. 98-108.

1223. Conversations with yourself; the interior monologue. D. Sanderson. *Writer's Digest,* vol. 53, September 1973, pp. 24-26.

1224. Craft as mirror. M. Jones. *Sewanee Review,* vol. 82, Winter 1974, pp. 179-189.

1225. Craft of Fiction in Far Tortuga; Peter Matthiessen (interview). *Paris Review,* no. 60, 1973-74, pp. 79-82.

1226. Creating mood in fiction. P.D. Boles. *Writer,* vol. 73, August 1960, pp. 5-7+.

1227. Creative energy and fiction writing. R. McKenna. *Writer,* vol. 76, June 1963, pp. 7-9+.

1228. Credo for fiction writers. P. Combs. *Writer,* vol. 73, September 1960, pp. 5-7+.

1229. Cure for halfwayitis. E.J. McGraw. *Writer,* vol. 83, August 1970, pp. 18-20+.

1230. Dear young writer. E.R. Mirrielees. *Writer,* vol. 75, August 1962, pp. 16-17.

1231. Decoding the secrets to selling popular fiction. Roy Sorrels and Megan Daniel. *Writer's Digest,* vol. 61, April 1981, pp. 31-34.

1232. Delta factor. Walker Percy. *Southern Review,* vol. 11, January 1975, pp. 29-64.

1233. Details! Details! S. Eclov. *Writer,* vol. 84, January 1971, pp. 19-21.

1234. Discipline and anger. D. Shetzline. *Writer,* vol. 83, June 1970, pp. 9-11+.

1235. Discovering the form for your fiction. G. Godwin. *Writer,* vol. 89, December 1976, pp. 11-14.

1236. Disguised fiction. Joyce Carol Oates. *PMLA,* vol. 89, 1974, pp. 580-581.

1237. Do-it-yourself fiction writing. J. Hinchman. *Writer,* vol. 85, March 1972, pp. 19-21.

1238. Does genius have a gender? Janet Burroway and C. Ozick. *Ms.,* vol. 6, December 1977, pp. 56-57+.

1239. Dog engulfed by sand; abstraction and irony. Malcolm Bradbury. *Encounter,* vol. 51, November 1978, pp. 51+.

1240. Don't blame the editors. Sloan Wilson. *Writer,* vol. 95, July 1982, pp. 12-13+.

1241. Don't clean the refrigerator. G.L. Tassone. *Writer,* vol. 80, October 1967, pp. 29-30.

1242. Don't let your mother look over your shoulder. Nancy Thayer. *Writer,* vol. 97, June 1984, pp. 10-12+.

1243. Don't lick the stamp yet. B. Robinson. *Writer,* vol. 76, September 1963, pp. 11-13+.

1244. Don't start with too much. K. Kay. *Writer,* vol. 76, April 1963, pp. 10-13.

1245. Dramatic conflict-fiction. John Foster West. *Writer,* vol. 85, June 1972, pp. 19-21.

1246. Duet of Cheevers (interview). *Newsweek,* vol. 89, March 14, 1977, pp. 68-70+.

1247. Eccentric like a Fox (William Price Fox) (interview). *Writer's Digest,* vol. 57, February 1977, p. 41.

1248. Element of you. A. Cavanaugh. *Writer,* vol. 80, August 1967, pp. 22-23.

1249. Elements of fiction. S.L. Rubinstein. *Writer,* vol. 82, January 1969, pp. 21-24.

1250. Eleven check points for writers. Mildred Gordon and Gordon Gordon. *Writer,* vol. 75, January 1962, pp. 14-17.

1251. Elizabeth Bowen talks about writing. *Mademoiselle,* vol. 51, July 1960, pp. 89+.

1252. Embracing the world; Donald Bartheleme (interview). *Southwest Review,* vol. 67, Spring 1982, pp. 121-137.

1253. Empathy unlimited. E. Pearson. *Writer,* vol. 76, February 1963, pp. 25-26.

1254. Erica Jong (interview). *Writer's Digest,* vol. 61, June 1981, pp. 20-25.

1255. Erskine Caldwell (interview). *Georgia Review,* vol. 36, Spring 1982, pp. 83-101.

1256. Eudora Welty (interview). *Senior Scholastic,* vol. 89, December 9, 1966, supp. 18.

1257. Events, happenings, credibility, fictions. Richard G. Stern. *Yale Review,* vol. 57, June 1968, pp. 577-585.

1258. Exclusive interview with Morris West. *Writer's Digest,* vol. 51, February 1971, pp. 30-33+.

1259. Exclusive re-visit with Evan Hunter. *Writer's Digest,* vol. 51, April 1971, pp. 24-26.

1260. Exercise in emotion. Omer Henry. *Writer's Digest,* vol. 56, April 1976, p. 42.

1261. Expand or contract? E. Lee. *Writer,* vol. 76, December 1963, pp. 18-20+.

1262. Experience and fiction; excerpts from *Come Along With Me.* S. Jackson. *Writer,* vol. 82, January 1969, pp. 9-14+.

1263. Experiment in collaboration. L. Bergson and R. McMahon. *Writer,* vol. 81, October 1968, pp. 14-16+.

1264. Experimenting with perspective. B. Rohde. *Writer,* vol. 91, January 1978, pp. 9-12+.

1265. Exploration in writing. Gordon Gordon and Mildred Gordon. *Writer,* vol. 82, November 1969, pp. 9-12.

1266. Explore your own world. Sloan Wilson. *Writer,* vol. 91, July 1978, pp. 9-12+.

1267. F. Scott Fitzgerald (interview). *Saturday Review,* vol. 43, November 5, 1960, pp. 26+.

1268. Fact into fiction. F.A. Rockwell. *Writer,* vol. 96, June 1983, pp. 19-21+.

1269. Facts about co-writing fiction. Laurie Lawlor. *Writer's Digest,* vol. 60, July 1980, p. 24.

1270. Facts about fiction; Irving Wallace (interview). *Writer,* vol. 96, February 1983, pp. 7-11+.

1271. Facts of fiction. M. Dickens. *Writer,* vol. 81, June 1968, pp. 21-24.

1272. Fall dead without mentioning it. L.G. Erdman. *Writer,* vol. 72, April 1959, pp. 9-11.

1273. Fall of the house of fiction. Gore Vidal. *Times Literary Supplement,* February 20, 1976, pp. 182-183.

1274. Feel of writing; excerpt from *Realities of Fiction.* Nancy Hale. *Saturday Review,* vol. 45, September 8, 1962, pp. 16-18.

1275. Fiction and the suspension of disbelief. Eva Schaper. *British Journal of Aesthetics,* vol. 18, Winter 1978, pp. 31-44.

1276. Fiction is a battleground. M. Franco. *Writer's Digest,* vol. 53, March 1973, pp. 25-26+.

1277. Fiction of self-begetting. S.G. Kellman. *MLN,* vol. 91, December 1976, pp. 1243-1256.

1278. Fiction strategy; excerpts from *Tricks and Techniques of the Selling Writer.* Dwight V. Swain. *Writer,* vol. 79, November 1966, pp. 15-19.

1279. Fiction technique and style: some comparisons. David Madden. *Writer's Digest,* vol. 51, August 1971, pp. 24-26+.

1280. Fiction vs. incident. Judson Jerome. *Writer's Digest,* vol. 55, July 1975, pp. 46-48.

1281. Fiction writing: conceptions and misconceptions; Page Stegner (interview). *Writer,* vol. 86, August 1973, pp. 14-17.

1282. Fiction's all-seeing I. Robert Somerlott. *Writer,* vol. 82, February 1969, pp. 11-15.

1283. Finding the straw for the bricks. Norah Lofts. *Writer,* vol. 75, July 1962, pp. 17-19.

1284. First day's interview, Norman Mailer. *Paris Review,* vol. 7, Summer-Fall 1961, pp. 140-153.

1285. Five pluses for fiction; judging what you write. G. Owen. *Writer,* vol. 87, January 1974, pp. 16-17.

1286. Five w's and how! L. Floren. *Writer's Digest,* vol. 57, July 1977, pp. 39-40+.

1287. *Floating Opera and Second Skin.* John Hawkes. *Mosaic,* vol. 8, 1974, pp. 17-28.

1288. For writing out loud! L. Conger. *Writer,* vol. 79, August 1966, pp. 7-8.

1289. Form in fiction. A. Vivante. *Writer,* vol. 89, June 1976, pp. 19-21.

1290. Fortunate failures. S.K. Boyd. *Writer,* vol. 79, August 1966, pp. 13-15+.

1291. Found paradise (satire). G. Keillor. *New Yorker,* vol. 47, September 18, 1971, pp. 32-33.

1292. Four tests for a paragraph. J. Ball. *Writer,* vol. 90, January 1977, pp. 15-16+.

1293. Fresh fresh fresh eye. M. Williams. *Writer,* vol. 76, August 1963, pp. 13-14+.

1294. From facts to fiction; physician turned writer; reprint. Walker Percy. *Writer,* vol. 80, October 1967, pp. 27-28+.

1295. From unseen author to unseen reader. F. Brookhouser. *Writer,* vol. 74, June 1961, pp. 5-8.

1296. Gail Godwin (interview). *Writer,* vol. 96, October 1983, pp. 15-17.

1297. Games writers play. J. Porter. *Writer,* vol. 84, December 1971, pp. 9-10+.

1298. Gathering facts for fiction. S. Hearon. *Writer,* vol. 91, February 1978, pp. 15-16+.

1299. Getting caught in the middle. H. Schellenberg. *Writer's Digest,* vol. 57, January 1977, pp. 24-25.

1300. Getting sharp focus in your fiction. E. Lindemann. *Writer's Digest,* vol. 48, December 1968, pp. 45-47+.

1301. God in a box and how to avoid him; planning the end. A. Coppel. *Writer,* vol. 87, December 1974, pp. 20-21.

1302. God out of the machinery. R. Maloney. *Atlantic,* vol. 226, October 1970, pp. 144-145.

1303. Gold mine of experience. C. Brink. *Writer,* vol. 90, August 1977, pp. 11-14.

1304. Good writing is rewriting. E.J. McGraw. *Writer,* vol. 75, May 1962, pp. 8-11+.

1305. Great man syndrome; Saul Bellow and me. S. Dworkin. *Ms.,* vol. 5, March 1977, pp. 72-73.

1306. Greek myths in pop fiction; Jason and Medea's love story. D. Goleman. *Psychology Today,* vol. 9, April 1976, pp. 84+.

1307. Guns of Avallone; M.A. Avallone, Jr. (interview). *Writer's Digest,* vol. 56, October 1976, pp. 38-39.

1308. Happy ending. M.J. Rolfs. *Writer,* vol. 85, August 1972, pp. 13-14.

1309. Hello, young writers. M.D. Lane. *Writer,* vol. 73, May 1960, pp. 12-14+.

1310. Hortense Calisher (interview) (reprint). *Writer's Digest,* vol. 49, March 1969, pp. 58-60+.

1311. How I go about it. P.H. Bonner. *Writer,* vol. 75, October 1962, pp. 9-12.

1312. How I write. Eudora Welty. *Virginia Quarterly Review,* vol. 31, Spring 1955, pp. 240-251.

1313. How to be a writer. Sloan Wilson. *Writer,* vol. 75, April 1962, pp. 13-16.

1314. How to be an expert on anything. Frank G. Slaughter. *Writer,* vol. 90, July 1977, pp. 11-13.

1315. How to choose a thought. G.H. Freitag. *Writer,* vol. 74, January 1961, pp. 18-19+.

1316. How to get to the core of salable fiction ideas. Bill Pippin. *Writer's Digest,* vol. 62, September 1983, pp. 26-29.

1317. How to make an idea work. Al Dewlen. *Writer,* vol. 76, August 1963, pp. 18-19.

1318. How to put emotion into your story. E.S. Fox. *Writer,* vol. 76, January 1963, pp. 12-15+.

1319. Hush! Beth is dying! E. Ibbotson. *Writer,* vol. 87, February 1974, pp. 11-14.

1320. I always begin on page one. A. Iverson. *Writer,* vol. 74, November 1961, pp. 11-13.

1321. I remember Androcles. E. Jensen. *Writer,* vol. 77, April 1964, pp. 7-10.

1322. Idea hits you. E.J. McGraw. *Writer,* vol. 72, December 1959, pp. 19-22+.

1323. Impending event. V. Sneider. *Writer,* vol. 81, April 1968, pp. 16-18.

1324. Importance of being sincere. F. Baldwin. *Writer,* vol. 75, April 1962, pp. 31-32+.

1325. Importance of irrelevancies. C. Bartholomew. *Writer,* vol. 74, February 1961, pp. 7-9+.

1326. In and out of universal city; reflections on the new journalism and the old fiction. B. DeMott. *Antioch Review,* vol. 29, Spring 1969, pp. 15-24.

1327. In the beginning... E. Ibbotson. *Writer,* vol. 84, August 1971, pp. 9-12.

1328. Interior world: an interview with Eudora Welty. *Southern Review,* vol. 7, October 1972, pp. 711-735.

1329. Intuitive fiction writer. Janice Elliott. *Writer,* vol. 85, October 1972, pp. 9-11.

1330. Involvement; action and reaction. O. Ruhen. *Writer,* vol. 84, February 1971, pp. 16-18.

1331. It just ain't natural; plausibility. W.C. Lee. *Writer,* vol. 87, April 1974, pp. 19-21.

1332. John Gardner (interview). *English Studies,* vol. 62, December 1981, pp. 509-524.

1333. John Irving (interview). *Contemporary Review,* vol. 23, Winter 1982, pp. 1-18.

1334. John Jakes has a fever, a writing fever (interview). *Writer's Digest,* vol. 57, January 1977, pp. 22-23.

1335. Keep it brief and blend it in. D. James. *Writer's Digest,* vol. 49, July 1969, pp. 50-52+.

1336. Keep the reader where the action is. William C. Knott. *Writer's Digest,* vol. 56, June 1976, pp. 24-25.

1337. Know-how and experience. Phyllis A. Whitney. *Writer,* vol. 74, November 1961, pp. 24+.

1338. Language of fiction. Robert E. Scholes. *Wisconsin Studies in Contemporary Literature,* vol. 8, Autumn 1967, pp. 574-577.

1339. Leading with your write; how to add punch to fiction leads. Dorothy Francis. *Writer's Digest,* vol. 61, January 1981, pp. 46-47.

1340. Leap to imagination. J. Weston. *Writer,* vol. 83, August 1970, pp. 12-14.

1341. Learn all about it and throw it away. Anthony Burgess. *New Society,* December 20/27, 1979, supplement ii-iv.

1342. Leaving the reader satisfied. Phyllis A. Whitney. *Writer,* vol. 90, April 1977, pp. 13-16+.

1343. Let's hear it for sex and violence; too much or too little? Lawrence Block. *Writer's Digest,* vol. 63, November 1983, pp. 24-29.

1344. Letter to a fiction writer. B.J. Chute. *Writer,* vol. 80, October 1967, pp. 9-12.

1345. Letter to a still unknown author; entertainment in political thrillers. M. Avallone. *Writer,* vol. 82, February 1969, pp. 21-22+.

1346. Life with father. William Burroughs. *Esquire,* vol. 76, September 1971, pp. 113-115+.

1347. Literary life anything but romantic; excerpts from address. Wallace Stegner. *Intellect,* vol. 106, September 1977, p. 107.

1348. Literature of exhaustion. John Barth. *Atlantic,* vol. 220, August 1967, pp. 29-34.

1349. Lovely way through life. John Updike. *Southwest Review,* vol. 66, Autumn 1981, pp. 341-350.

1350. Lure of I, the tyranny of he. R.F. Delderfield. *Writer,* vol. 85, July 1972, pp. 11-12+.

1351. Magnificent trifles. Robert Somerlott. *Writer,* vol. 79, October 1966, pp. 16-19.

1352. Make a list. M. Deasy. *Writer,* vol. 85, February 1972, pp. 16-17+.

1353. Make it happen. R. Gatenby. *Writer,* vol. 84, August 1971, pp. 17-19+.

1354. Making of a fiction writer. Bernard Malamud. *Writer,* vol. 97, January 1984, pp. 9-11.

1355. Mapping out successful fiction. Roy Sorrels and Megan Daniel. *Writer's Digest,* vol. 61, December 1981, pp. 32-34+.

1356. Mary Stolz (interview). *English Journal,* vol. 64, October 1975, pp. 84-86.

1357. Mastering fictionese (adherence to truth rather than facts, faces, or personalities). Gerald Petievich. *Writer,* vol. 97, August 1984, pp. 12-14.

1358. Meanwhile back at the ranch... R. Gatenby. *Writer,* vol. 91, December 1978, pp. 9-12+.

1359. Metaphors and confusions. D.M. Monaghan. *Canadian Literature,* no. 67, Winter 1976, pp. 64-73.

1360. More fiction writing tips; A. Burgess (interview). *Writer's Digest,* vol. 55, August 1975, p. 13.

1361. Mr. M. interviews himself. Norman Mailer. *New York Times Book Review* Section, September 17, 1967, pp. 6-7, 40.

1362. Nature and aim of fiction; excerpt from *Mystery and Manners.* Flannery O'Connor. *Writer,* vol. 82, October 1969, pp. 11-14+.

1363. Neural neighborhoods and other concrete abstracts. J. McElroy. *TriQuarterly,* no. 34, Fall 1975, pp. 201-217.

1364. Never insult a Yiddish typewriter, and other gentle wisdom from Isaac Bashevis Singer. Helen Benedict. *Writer's Digest,* vol. 60, May 1980, pp. 36-38.

1365. Never lead with a dead dog. Nancy McCarthy. *Writer's Digest,* vol. 63, December 1983, pp. 30-32.

1366. New big one (satire). R. Lipez. *Atlantic,* vol. 241, January 1978, pp. 88-89.

1367. New heaven and earth. Joyce Carol Oates. *Saturday Review*, vol. 55, November 1972, pp. 51-54.

1368. Not all our words are sacred. M. Franco. *Writer*, vol. 91, May 1978, pp. 11-14.

1369. Not what-if but how-he. J. Christopher. *Writer*, vol. 81, November 1968, pp. 15-17+.

1370. Notes on the internal life. N. Clad. *Writer*, vol. 75, June 1962, pp. 17-18+.

1371. Notes on writing. Carson McCullers. *Writer*, vol. 85, March 1972, pp. 17-18.

1372. Now I sit me down; pleasing the editor. W. Chamberlain. *Writer*, vol. 79, February 1966, pp. 22-24.

1373. Old-fashioned and up-to-the-minute. H. Van Slyke. *Writer*, vol. 88, November 1975, pp. 14-16.

1374. Old writers never die—they just scrawl away. Frank G. Slaughter. *Writer*, vol. 93, February 1980, pp. 9-10.

1375. On feminism and creation. Anais Nin. *Michigan Quarterly Review*, vol. 13, 1974, pp. 4-13.

1376. On words. R. Godden. *Writer*, vol. 75, September 1962, pp. 17-19.

1377. On words, singleness of mind, and the genius loci. M. Benary-Isbert. *Horn Book*, vol. 40, April 1964, pp. 202-209.

1378. On writing. Vardis Fisher. *South Dakota Review*, vol. 11, August 1973, pp. 106-107.

1379. One pin and a fish hook. M.S. Foster. *Writer*, vol. 79, April 1966, pp. 9-12+.

1380. One, two, three... L. Conger. *Writer*, vol. 80, October 1967, pp. 7-8.

1381. One way through the woods. Richard Martin Stern. *Writer*, vol. 90, February 1977, pp. 11-13.

1382. Ones that got away. A.E. Jones. *Writer*, vol. 78, May 1965, pp. 17-18+.

1383. Only way to fly. C. Bartholomew. *Writer*, vol. 83, April 1970, pp. 15-18.

1384. Opening sentence. J.Z. Owen. *Writer*, vol. 86, October 1973, pp. 20-22+.

1385. Opinion; notes on writing. Katherine Anne Porter. *Mademoiselle*, vol. 69, October 1969, pp. 14+.

1386. Opportunity is like a train. Phyllis A. Whitney. *Writer*, vol. 87, November 1974, pp. 11-13+.

1387. Particular bent. D. Gilman. *Writer,* vol. 85, July 1972, pp. 9-10.

1388. Philip Roth, writing and the powers that be (interview). *American Poetry Review,* vol. 3, July/August 1974, pp. 18-20.

1389. Plan ahead. A. Heinemann. *Writer,* vol. 78, December 1965, pp. 14-16.

1390. Porter on prose. Katherine Anne Porter and Margarette Hosback. *Writer's Digest,* vol. 57, November 1977, p. 6.

1391. Possession of Doraine Moore (satire). *Writer's Digest,* vol. 53, September 1973, pp. 28-31.

1392. Psychology; towards a science of fiction. R.L. Gregory. *New Society,* May 23, 1974, pp. 439-441.

1393. Put it in the deep-freeze. Mildred Gordon and Gordon Gordon. *Writer,* vol. 89, April 1976, pp. 9-13.

1394. PW interviews: Jane Flaum Singer. *Publishers Weekly,* vol. 225, June 15, 1984, pp. 84-85.

1395. PW interviews: Joyce Carol Oates. *Publishers Weekly,* vol. 213, June 26, 1978, pp. 12-13.

1396. PW interviews: Paul Theroux. *Publishers Weekly,* vol. 210, July 26, 1976, pp. 10-11.

1397. Quality and opinion. S. Epstein. *Writer,* vol. 76, July 1963, pp. 7-9+.

1398. Questions they never asked me. Walker Percy. *Esquire,* vol. 88, December 1977, pp. 170-172+.

1399. Random thoughts on fiction writing. Norah Lofts. *Writer,* vol. 89, July 1976, pp. 12-14.

1400. Readers are collaborators. M. Williams. *Writer,* vol. 74, August 1961, pp. 5-6+.

1401. Reading myself. Philip Roth. *Partisan Review,* vol. 40, no. 393, pp. 404-417.

1402. Realm of emotion. P.S. Curry. *Writer,* vol. 79, February 1966, pp. 14-18+.

1403. Realistic goals for fiction writers. M. Bonham. *Writer,* vol. 86, November 1973, pp. 16-18.

1404. Recent trends in writing and publishing; excerpts from address. J. Cheever. *Intellect,* vol. 105, July 1976, pp. 11-12.

1405. Relevance without meaning. Robert Penn Warren. *Intercollegiate Review,* vol. 7, 1971, pp. 149-152.

1406. Reminiscences; a conversation with Robert Penn Warren (interview). *Southern Review,* vol. 16, October 1980, pp. 782-798.

1407. Reporting fiction. M.R. Myers. *Writer,* vol. 91, October 1978, pp. 11-13.

1408. Richard Hughes (interview). *New Yorker,* vol. 45, June 28, 1969, pp. 30-31.

1409. Rules of the game. M.A. Rodgers. *Writer,* vol. 78, September 1965, pp. 11-14+.

1410. Rules to write by. D. Gaines. *Writer,* vol. 80, January 1967, pp. 14-15.

1411. Satisfying element. Phyllis A. Whitney. *Writer,* vol. 78, February 1965, pp. 11-14+.

1412. Second thoughts about fiction. A.B. Holland. *Writer's Digest,* vol. 49, May 1969, p. 20.

1413. Second time around. Mildred Gordon and Gordon Gordon. *Writer,* vol. 91, April 1978, pp. 12-15.

1414. Secret mind; excerpt from afterword to *Anthem Sprinters and Other Antics.* R. Bradbury. *Writer,* vol. 78, November 1965, pp. 13-16.

1415. Section of an interview between Norman Mailer and David Young. *Notre Dame Review,* vol. 1, 1974, pp. 5-9.

1416. Self-awarenesss and beyond. J. Bayley. *Times Literary Supplement,* vol. 72, July 27, 1973, pp. 853-854.

1417. Sense of audience. H. Alpert. *Writer,* vol. 73, December 1960, pp. 10-11+.

1418. Sense of balance. R.A. Knowlton. *Writer,* vol. 80, April 1967, pp. 17-19+.

1419. Shape of fiction; notes towards a possible classification of narrative discourses. E. Donato. *MLN,* vol. 86, December 1971, pp. 807-822.

1420. Shaping of a writer. J. McKimmey. *Writer,* vol. 73, December 1960, pp. 5-9.

1421. Shaw as influence, Laughton as teacher. Ray Bradbury. *Shaw Review,* vol. 16, 1973, pp. 98-99.

1422. Sheer fiction; mind and the fabulist's mirage. P. West. *New Literary History,* vol. 7, Spring 1976, pp. 549-561.

1423. Short story or novel? J. Rikhoff. *Writer,* vol. 79, October 1966, pp. 11-15.

1424. Signs of the times. T.W. Molyneux. *American Scholar,* vol. 42, Autumn 1973, pp. 663-670.

1425. Silk purses for sale. L. Conger. *Writer,* vol. 74, June 1961, pp. 9-11.

1426. Slick pattern. M.F. Shyer. *Writer,* vol. 78, August 1965, pp. 12-14.

1427. Some deadly sins. Mildred Gordon and Gordon Gordon. *Writer,* vol. 85, May 1972, pp. 11-13.

1428. Some fiction terms. A. McIlnay. *Writer's Digest,* vol. 52, June 1972, pp. 31-32+.

1429. Some questions and answers. Saul Bellow. *Ontario Review,* vol. 3, 1975, pp. 51-60.

1430. Some tricks of the trade. J. Van de Wetering. *Writer,* vol. 91, December 1978, pp. 23-24+.

1431. Sources and processes in the writing of fiction. Warrene Piper. *American Journal of Psychology,* vol. 43, 1931, pp. 188-201.

1432. Southern imagination: an interview with Eudora Welty and Walker Percy. William F. Buckley, Jr. *Mississippi Quarterly,* Fall 1973, pp. 493-576.

1433. Springboard to fiction. Phyllis A. Whitney. *Writer,* vol. 89, October 1976, pp 11-15.

1434. Starting out in Chicago. S. Bellow. *American Scholar,* vol. 44, Winter 1974, pp. 71-77.

1435. Stop, look, and listen! L.T. Henderson. *Writer,* vol. 73, May 1960, pp. 5-7.

1436. Stream of conscience as a form of fiction. A. Friedman. *Hudson Review,* vol. 17, Winter 1964-65, pp. 537-546.

1437. S-t-r-e-t-c-h what you know. Elizabeth Davis. *Writer,* vol. 85, January 1972, pp. 16-17+.

1438. Structuralism; its implications for the performance of prose fiction. M.F. Hopkins. *Communication Monographs,* vol. 44, June 1977, pp. 93-105.

1439. Structures of fiction. Frank Kermode. *MLN,* vol. 84, December 1969, pp. 891-915.

1440. Struggling against the plaid; an interview with Eudora Welty. *Southwest Review,* vol. 66, Summer 1981, pp. 255-266.

1441. Style and the fiction writer. M. Wallace. *Writer,* vol. 89, February 1976, pp. 18-21+.

1442. Suspense in fiction. E. Ogilvie. *Writer,* vol. 83, January 1970, pp. 11-14.

1443. Swann's way (interview). L. Swann. *Writer's Digest,* vol. 56, October 1976, pp. 39-40.

1444. Taking notes for fiction. M. Edwards. *Writer,* vol. 88, October 1975, pp. 21-22+.

1445. Taking self-inventory. L.D. Peabody. *Writer,* vol. 78, August 1965, pp. 26-28.

1446. Teaching and study of writing. Eudora Welty. *Western Review,* vol. 14, Spring 1950, pp. 167-168.

1447. Technique of fiction. Allen Tate. *Sewanee Review,* vol. 52, 1944, pp. 210-225.

1448. Ten commandments for the beginning writer. B.S. Levin. *Writer,* vol. 83, June 1970, p. 13.

1449. Ten tips for writers. M. Shulman. *Writer,* vol. 74, August 1961, pp. 10-11.

1450. Ten tips for writing success. H.R. Smith. *Writer,* vol. 74, December 1961, pp. 14-15+.

1451. That certain feeling. G. Taber. *Writer,* vol. 77, February 1964, pp. 14-16.

1452. That certain smile. L. Conger. *Writer,* vol. 74, December 1961, pp. 5-8.

1453. That vital first page. V.H. Findlow. *Writer,* vol. 72, March 1959, pp. 12-14.

1454. Theatrical opener. T.J. McCauley. *Writer,* vol. 80, February 1967, pp. 26-28.

1455. There must be more to love than death (interview). Kurt Vonnegut. *Nation,* vol. 231, August 2-9, 1980, pp. 128-132.

1456. Thinking man's waste land; excerpts from address. Saul Bellow. *Saturday Review,* vol. 48, April 3, 1965, p. 20.

1457. Thoughts on writing. James A. Michener. *Writer,* vol. 75, May 1962, pp. 12-13+.

1458. Three hints for successful revision. J.H. Ford. *Writer,* vol. 73, September 1960, pp. 11-12.

1459. Throw your heart over. Norah Lofts. *Writer,* vol. 78, December 1965, pp. 11-13+.

1460. Tickets a writer needs. S. Stevens. *Writer,* vol. 81, December 1968, pp. 27-29+.

1461. Time to live, a time to write. S. Wilkinson. *Writer,* vol. 81, July 1968, pp. 9-11+.

1462. Tips for busy beginners. Tom McCormick. *Writer,* vol. 78, February 1965, pp. 29-31.

1463. To a young Southern writer. Jesse Hill Ford. *Southern Review,* vol. 4, Spring 1968, pp. 291-298.

1464. Touching the heart of your reader. C. Cookson. *Writer,* vol. 87, December 1974, pp. 11-14.

1465. Touchstone in writing fiction. S. Epstein. *Writer,* vol. 77, October 1964, pp. 9-11+.

1466. Treasure hunt of research. A. Seton. *Writer,* vol. 75, April 1962, pp. 33-35.

1467. Tricks of the fiction writing trade. R. McInerny. *Writer,* vol. 86, October 1973, pp. 11-13.

1468. Trouble with trouble. R.A. Knowlton. *Writer,* vol. 76, June 1963, pp. 15-16+.

1469. Trust the back of your mind. M.R. Gardner. *Writer,* vol. 74, April 1961, pp. 14-15+.

1470. Turning unhappiness into money; the fiction market revisited. David Lodge. *Encounter,* vol. 51, July 1978, pp. 63-69.

1471. Two contemporary views on fiction; Iris Murdoch and Muriel Spark. Patricia Stubbs. *English,* vol. 23, Autumn 1974, pp. 102-110.

1472. Two-for-one beginning. E. Jensen. *Writer,* vol. 73, October 1960, pp. 11-13+.

1473. Two writers talk it over. James Jones and William Styron. *Esquire,* vol. 60, July 1963, pp. 57-59.

1474. Unconscious literary use of traditional material. G.F. Dalton. *Folklore,* vol. 85, Winter 1974, pp. 268-275.

1475. Unique/universal in fiction. Joyce Carol Oates. *Writer,* vol. 86, January 1973, pp. 9-12.

1476. Using the force. Phyllis A. Whitney. *Writer,* vol. 92, January 1979, pp. 11-15.

1477. Versatility. W.F. Nolan. *Writer,* vol. 81, March 1968, pp. 9-11+.

1478. Visualizing fiction on paper. D. Uhnak. *Writer,* vol. 87, June 1974, pp. 9-11+.

1479. Watch out for this writing trap. R. Zacks. *Writer,* vol. 73, April 1960, pp. 15-16.

1480. Welcome to the fiction marketplace. Richard Curtis (literary agent). *Writer's Digest,* vol. 63, March 1983, pp. 22-26.

1481. What I learned from four top fiction editors. M. Joerden. *Writer's Digest,* vol. 50, September 1970, pp. 24-25.

1482. What is stream of consciousness technique. *PMLA,* vol. 65, 1950, pp. 337-345.

1483. What makes a fiction writer? B.J. Chute. *Writer,* vol. 90, October 1977, pp. 9-11.

1484. What you do know can hurt you. J. McKimmey. *Writer*, vol. 90, June 1977, pp. 18-20.

1485. What you know. H. Wolitzer. *Writer*, vol. 91, March 1978, pp. 11-14.

1486. What's in it for me? Isaac Bashevis Singer. *Harper's Magazine*, vol. 231, October 1965, pp. 172-173.

1487. When scalpel sharpens pen; reprint. Frank G. Slaughter. *Writer*, vol. 81, July 1968, pp. 15-18.

1488. When the writer comes of age. B.J. Chute. *Writer*, vol. 76, May 1963, pp. 10-14.

1489. Where do you start? C. Edwards. *Writer*, vol. 77, December 1964, pp. 20-22+.

1490. Who can afford to write for money? D. Hamilton. *Writer*, vol. 81, June 1968, pp. 19-20+.

1491. Why fiction? A.B. Glasscock. *Writer*, vol. 89, March 1976, pp. 11-14.

1492. Why is your writing so violent? Joyce Carol Oates. *New York Times Book Review*, vol. 86, March 29, 1981, pp. 15+.

1493. Why look, here comes one now. S. Koperwas. *Writer's Digest*, vol. 55, August 1975, pp. 11-12.

1494. With eyes wide open. E. Caldwell. *Writer*, vol. 74, September 1961, pp. 5-7.

1495. With the help of my reader. J.L. Latham. *Writer*, vol. 75, December 1962, pp. 19-20+.

1496. Words into fiction. *Southern Review*, vol. 1 (new series), July 1965, pp. 543-553.

1497. Workshop trio. P.D. Boles. *Writer*, vol. 90, May 1977, pp. 15-17.

1498. World too much with us. Saul Bellow. *Critical Inquiry*, vol. 2, 1975, pp. 1-9.

1499. Write what you feel. S.L. Stebel. *Writer*, vol. 83, March 1970, pp. 26-27.

1500. Write what you want to read. Elizabeth Forsythe Hailey. *Writer*, vol. 96, March 1983, pp. 9-11+.

1501. Writer and the concept of adulthood. Wallace Stegner. *Daedalus*, vol. 105, Fall 1976, pp. 39-48.

1502. Writer as conjurer. L. Wibberley. *Writer*, vol. 75, February 1962, pp. 5-7+.

1503. Writer at work. John Boynton Priestley. *New Statesman*, vol. 71, April 1, 1966, p. 461.

1504. Writer has to care. E.E. Gordon. *Writer,* vol. 73, February 1960, pp. 16-17+.

1505. Writers at Work; fact into fiction. Paul Ferris. *Author,* vol. 85, Summer 1974, pp. 75-77.

1506. Writer's audience is always a fiction. W.J. Ong. *PMLA,* vol. 90, January 1975, pp. 9-21.

1507. Writer's craft. Andre Maurois. *Saturday Review,* vol. 43, November 19, 1960, pp. 19-22+.

1508. Writers in glass houses. D. Betts. *Writer,* vol. 88, February 1975, pp. 9-11.

1509. Writer's real world. S. Stevens. *Writer,* vol. 84, July 1971, pp. 11-12+.

1510. Writer's sermon. S. Jameson. *Writer,* vol. 75, October 1962, pp. 13-15.

1511. Writing about the west. William Eastlake. *South Dakota Review,* vol. 11, Autumn 1973, pp. 87-88.

1512. Writing fiction today. D. Shannon. *Writer,* vol. 83, October 1970, pp. 11-13.

1513. Writing genre fiction for a living: bodice rippers and WWII adventures. *Coda,* vol. 9, September/October 1981, pp. 1+.

1514. Writing in depth. E. Bachmann. *Writer,* vol. 81, October 1968, pp. 26-28.

1515. Writing techniques and freedom. M. Shedd. *Writer,* vol. 81, May 1968, pp. 13-15+.

1516. Yet another interview with B. Bonnet; fiction as nonfiction. *Nation,* vol. 202, February 14, 1966, pp. 193-194.

1517. Your first resource; yourself. Winifred Madison. *Writer,* vol. 89, December 1976, pp. 23-26.

1518. Your life in action. C.L. Evans. *Writer,* vol. 90, February 1977, pp. 21-22+.

1519. Your secret writing weapons. P. Gunn. *Writer,* vol. 85, December 1972, pp. 26-27.

Characterization, Voice, and Viewpoint

"Characters in decay is the theme of the great bulk of superior fiction."

—H.L. Mencken

Books

1520. Elwood, Maren. *Characters Make Your Story.* Boston: Writer, 1973. 303 pp.

In this comprehensive approach to the subject, Elwood discusses the interaction of characters, individual motives and emotions, plot and character, visual techniques, the portrayal of thoughts in a character, and the fostering of characterization skills by observing real life conversations and interactions. Elwood also covers specialized techniques for short stories, broadcast scripts, stage drama, and screenplays. To quote Elwood, who has been a successful agent and writing teacher, "Literary talent cannot be taught. But the mechanics of expression (without which talent will never be realized) unquestionably can."

1521. Fugate, Francis L. *Viewpoint; Key to Fiction Writing.* Boston: Writer, 1968. 184 pp.

This competent, in-depth analysis of a technique that is integral to both formula and serious fiction also relates viewpoint to characterization, dialogue, time, and background. Each type of viewpoint, from first person to omniscient, is examined in detail to show advantages, disadvantages, and over-all effect. Fugate is an experienced freelance fiction writer and writing teacher.

1522. Walcutt, Charles Child. *Man's Changing Mask; Modes and Methods of Characterization in Fiction.* Minneapolis: University of Minnesota Press, 1966. 368 pp.

Walcutt investigates characterization as a function of action and intellect. In doing so he explores a broad range of characters, from Hamlet to Herzog, and succeeds in showing how character is formulated, revealed, and developed, while at the same time maintaining a readable, if not compelling, style. *Man's Changing Mask* is one of the most comprehensive and systematic studies of characterization available. Though the reader may disagree

131

with the assessment of individual writers, it is balanced, informed and perceptive.

1523. Wallace, Irving. *The Fabulous Originals; Lives of Extraordinary People Who Inspired Memorable Characters in Fiction.* New York: Knopf, 1956. 317 pp.

The character Sherlock Holmes was inspired by his real life prototype, Dr. Joseph Bell. Deacon William Brodie served as the model for both Dr. Jeckyll and Mr. Hyde. These and eighteen other examples show us how the lives of actual persons have been transformed by well-known authors into memorable characters in fiction. Part biography, part literary detection, Wallace's investigations provide the fiction writer with a number of engrossing insights into the process of character creation.

See also the chapters on Fiction Technique (page 91), Novel (page 1), Story, Short and Otherwise (page 75), and Drama (page 25) for book annotations containing numerous references to the use of characterization.

Articles

1524. Ancestry of your characters. S. Hearon. *Writer,* vol. 89, February 1976, pp. 11-13.

1525. Ashtrays in a vacuum. L. Conger. *Writer,* vol. 76, May 1963, pp. 15-17.

1526. Astro-logical way to create fictional characters. Patti Heffernan. *Writer's Digest,* vol. 61, October 1981, p. 39.

1527. Author's voice in story. E.A. Parker. *Elementary English,* vol. 47, April 1970, pp. 483-485.

1528. Balancing plot and character. E. Cadell. *Writer,* vol. 75, February 1962, pp. 17-18+.

1529. Beginning with character. S.D. Siegel. *College Composition and Communication,* vol. 25, May 1974, pp. 200-203.

1530. Building a story around a single character. David Walton. *Writer,* vol. 96, October 1983, pp. 21-23+.

1531. Building characters from the ground up. G. Owen. *Writer,* vol. 90, January 1977, pp. 17-19.

1532. Building reader identification. A. Coppel. *Writer,* vol. 85, June 1972, pp. 9-11.

1533. Caring. Margery F. Brown. *Writer,* vol. 88, August 1975, pp. 15-16.

1534. Case of slander. J. Greenberg. *Writer,* vol. 88, November 1975, pp. 11-13+.

1535. Case of the wooden Indian. V.K. Smiley. *Writer,* vol. 73, October 1960, pp. 18-19.

1536. Castings. Lawrence Block. *Writer's Digest,* vol. 57, October 1977, pp. 10+.

1537. Character and consciousness. John Bayley. *New Literary History,* vol. 5, Winter 1974, pp. 225-235.

1538. Character, closure, and impressionist fiction. N. Armstrong. *Criticism,* vol. 19, Fall 1977, pp. 317-337.

1539. Character of character. H. Cixous. *New Literary History,* vol. 5, Winter 1974, pp. 383-402.

1540. Characterization. P. Ernst. *Writer,* vol. 75, September 1962, pp. 14-16.

1541. Characterization. William Harrison. *Writer,* vol. 83, June 1970, pp. 21-23+.

1542. Characterization. A. Vivante. *Writer,* vol. 88, February 1975, pp. 12-13.

1543. Characterization and moral judgements. J.T. Laney. *Journal of Religion,* vol. 55, October 1975, pp. 405-414.

1544. Characterization in fiction. C.E. Eisinger. *Wisconsin Studies in Contemporary Literature,* vol. 8, Summer 1967, pp. 463-467.

1545. Characterization in the romance novel. Laurie McBain. *Writer,* vol. 96, May 1983, pp. 10-12.

1546. Characterization; love it or leave it. J. Mekeel. *Media & Methods,* vol. 6, April 1970, p. 60.

1547. Characterization—the long and the short of it. D.J. Marlowe and A.F. Nussbaum. *Writer,* vol. 86, April 1973, pp. 15-16+.

1548. Characters in fiction. Mary McCarthy. *Partisan Review,* vol. 28, March/April 1961, pp. 171-191.

1549. Characters in wanderland. M. Dutton. *Writer,* vol. 83, October 1970, pp. 22-24.

1550. Children are people. N.L. Babson. *Writer,* vol. 74, June 1961, pp. 16-17.

1551. Coming to terms with a character. A. Chamberlain. *Writer,* vol. 84, August 1971, pp. 25-26+.

1552. Conceiving of character. R. Beach. *Journal of Reading,* vol. 17, April 1974, pp. 546-551.

1553. Control of character. R. Savage. *Writer,* vol. 76, August 1963, pp. 7-9.

1554. Craftsmanship and character. P.D. Boles. *Writer,* vol. 87, November 1974, pp. 14-16.

1555. Creating the "outcast" character. Evelyn Mayerson. *Writer,* vol. 94, May 1981, pp. 10-13+.

1556. Crux of plot: moment of decision. F.A. Rockwell. *Writer,* vol. 74, April 1961, pp. 5-7+.

1557. Developing an original person. R.K. Carlson. *Elementary English,* vol. 41, March 1978, pp. 268-278+.

1558. Discovering persons in fiction. D.H. Otto. *Education,* vol. 82, November 1961, pp. 166-168.

1559. Don't forget the people; three dimensional characters. P.C. Smith. *Writer,* vol. 87, August 1974, pp. 23-24+.

1560. Dynamic duos. R.M. Adams. *Sewanee Review,* vol. 86, Fall 1978, pp. 527-538.

1561. Elusive secret; creating memorable characters. H.D. Jordan. *Writer,* vol. 80, December 1967, pp. 24-26.

1562. Everybody change places. M.J. Amft. *Writer,* vol. 82, December 1969, pp. 12-13.

1563. Eye-witness narrator. V. Case. *Writer,* vol. 72, July 1959, pp. 8-9.

1564. Fathers and sons in American fiction. E. Rovit. *Yale Review,* vol. 53, December 1963, pp. 248-257.

1565. Fiction versus reality. Richard Stern. *Writer,* vol. 73, June 1960, pp. 10-11.

1566. Fiction writer and human behavior. J.C. Clark. *Writer,* vol. 74, November 1961, pp. 14-15+.

1567. Find out where they hurt, and why. D. McCleary. *Writer,* vol. 75, November 1962, pp. 27-28+.

1568. First person singular. Donald Hamilton. *Writer,* vol. 97, October 1984, pp. 16-18.

1569. Getting it together. H. Crews. *Writer,* vol. 84, June 1971, pp. 9-11.

1570. Getting to know them. Norah Lofts. *Writer,* vol. 83, November 1970, pp. 9-10+.

1571. Getting to know your characters. V. Henry. *Writer,* vol. 77, August 1964, pp. 23-25.

1572. Give your characters free rein. G. Roark. *Writer,* vol. 83, July 1970, pp. 13-15.

1573. Giveaway. B. Ledecky. *Writer,* vol. 88, June 1975, pp. 11-12.

1574. Glad you dropped in. E. Jensen. *Writer,* vol. 87, April 1974, pp. 13-15.

1575. Goals. F.A. Rockwell. *Writer,* vol. 77, September 1964, pp. 19-21.

1576. Grain in the silo. E.K. Woolvin. *Writer,* vol. 76, November 1963, pp. 20-21+.

1577. Hand is quicker than the I; first person viewpoint. W. Shore. *Writer,* vol. 79, April 1966, pp. 17-19.

1578. Help your characters be themselves. Phyllis A. Whitney. *Writer,* vol. 94, March 1981, pp. 7-10+.

1579. How different readers perceive magazine stories and characters. R.A. LeBouef and M. Matre. *Journalism Quarterly,* vol. 54, Spring 1977, pp. 50-57.

1580. How important is conflict? Edward S. Fox. *Writer,* vol. 73, November 1960, pp. 11-14.

1581. How people sound. Marjorie Lee. *Writer,* vol. 82, September 1969, pp. 13-15+.

1582. How to bring your characters to life. F.A. Rockwell. *Writer,* vol. 81, August 1968, pp. 21-24+.

1583. How to build your characters. Marjorie Lee. *Writer,* vol. 86, August 1973, pp. 20-22+.

1584. How to characterize. Edward S. Fox. *Writer,* vol. 74, April 1961, pp. 13-15+.

1585. How to live with a hero. John D. MacDonald. *Writer,* vol. 77, September 1964, pp. 14-16+.

1586. How to put emotion into your story. Edward S. Fox. *Writer,* vol. 76, January 1963, pp. 12-15+.

1587. Humane comedy. S.S. Kenny. *Modern Philology,* vol. 75, August 1977, pp. 29-43.

1588. Identity problem. A. Broyard. *New York Times Book Review,* vol. 86, March 15, 1981, p. 39.

1589. I loved the way you described Aunt Mary... E. Hawes. *Writer,* vol. 82, March 1969, pp. 15-16+.

1590. Importance of being sincere. Faith Baldwin. *Writer,* vol. 75, April 1962, pp. 31-32+.

1591. In search of a character. Graham Greene. *Harper's Magazine,* vol. 224, January 1962, pp. 66-74.

1592. Incongruity: character vs. setting. Frances L. Shine. *Writer,* vol. 87, June 1974, pp. 22-24.

1593. Inside Uriah Heep. Nina Bawden. *Writer,* vol. 82, May 1969, pp. 9-11.

1594. It's all in your point of view. E.J. McGraw. *Writer,* vol. 74, January 1961, pp. 11-15.

1595. Journey; destination unknown. F.E. Randall. *Writer,* vol. 81, March 1968, pp. 15-17.

1596. Just a bunch of words: how to develop believable characters. Colleen Reece. *Writer's Digest,* vol. 61, November 1981, pp. 28-31.

1597. Keep moving forward. D.C. DeJong. *Writer,* vol. 76, June 1963, pp. 20-21.

1598. Learn to write in scenes. William Barrett. *Writer,* vol. 75, August 1962, pp. 13-16.

1599. Life and depth of story characters. A. Glimm. *Writer,* vol. 88, August 1975, pp. 9-11+.

1600. Likes attract: how to create likeable characters in your fiction. J.Z. Owen. *Writer's Digest,* vol. 57, June 1977, pp. 31-32+.

1601. Living other lives. Caroline Leavitt. *Writer,* vol. 96, March 1983, pp. 12-14.

1602. Long, long trail. R.F. Delderfield. *Writer,* vol. 84, January 1971, pp. 9-12.

1603. Make 'em laugh, make 'em cry. W. Chamberlain. *Writer,* vol. 73, July 1960, pp. 16-17.

1604. Make your characters live. Curtis Casewit. *Writer,* vol. 74, July 1961, pp. 13-15.

1605. Making your characters live and move. D. Betts. *Writer,* vol. 89, January 1976, pp. 9-13.

1606. Mannequins, or characters? J.Z. Owen. *Writer,* vol. 84, September 1971, pp. 17-19.

1607. Method-acting the first-person story. S. Hearon. *Writer,* vol. 87, August 1974, pp. 11-13.

1608. Mind's construction: characters at cross purposes. W. Witte. *Modern Language Review,* vol. 58, July 1963, pp. 326-334.

1609. More notes on characters' thoughts. J. Haugland. *Writer's Digest,* vol. 48, July 1968, p. 55.

1610. More than plot and character. D. Westheimer. *Writer,* vol. 85, November 1972, pp. 21-23.

1611. Motivate your characters. Jean L. Backus. *Writer,* vol. 97, September 1984, pp. 16-19.

1612. New lit; giving fictitious names to people who may be recognizable. G. Ace. *Saturday Review,* vol. 50, March 18, 1967, p. 5.

1613. No mirrors, please! D. Gardiner. *Writer,* vol. 77, January 1964, pp. 16-19.

1614. Old comedy and character: some comments. R.G. Ussher. *Greece & Rome,* vol. 24, April 1977, pp. 71-19.

1615. Participant past imperfect. A.B. Malec. *Writer,* vol. 82, August 1969, pp. 19-21.

1616. People and characters. B.H. Deal. *Writer,* vol. 84, April 1971, pp. 16-18.

1617. People, not plot. J. Rikhoff. *Writer,* vol. 90, March 1977, pp. 15-18.

1618. People on your pages. Peggy Simson Curry. *Writer,* vol. 86, March 1973, pp. 16-18+.

1619. People we write about. N.L. Babson. *Writer,* vol. 72, December 1959, pp. 8-10.

1620. Person and plot. S. Epstein. *Writer,* vol. 79, May 1966, pp. 9-12.

1621. Point of no return. Shelly Lowenkopf. *Writer,* vol. 96, August 1983, pp. 20-22+.

1622. Point of view: experiment in living. M. Franco. *Writer,* vol. 86, September 1973, pp. 11-14.

1623. Practice of writing. H.D. Jordan. *Writer,* vol. 75, November 1962, pp. 22-23.

1624. Putting your characters in their place. P.R. Zerger. *Writer,* vol. 89, June 1976, pp. 13-15.

1625. Reading this all the way through will build your character; excerpts from *The Craft of Fiction.* William C. Knott. *Writer's Digest,* vol. 53, July 1973, pp. 15-17.

1626. Real and made-up people. Kingsley Amis. *Times Literary Supplement,* vol. 72, July 27, 1973, pp. 847-848.

1627. Simple line of belief. G.H. Freitag. *Writer's Digest,* vol. 48, July 1968, pp. 65-67.

1628. Slake's limbo: in which a book switches authors. F. Holman. *Horn Book,* vol. 52, October 1976, pp. 479-485.

1629. Stop that stereotype! R. Chamberlin. *Writer,* vol. 76, November 1963, pp. 26-27.

1630. Stories are about people. L. Wibberley. *Writer,* vol. 78, August 1965, pp. 9-11+.

1631. Style, allusion, and the manipulation of viewpoint. David Hurry. *Critical Quarterly,* vol. 23, Summer 1981, pp. 61-71.

1632. Tagging your characters. Janice Young Brooks. *Writer's Digest,* vol. 58, March 1978, pp. 34-35.

1633. Thematic unity and the homogenization of character. R. Levin. *Modern Language Quarterly,* vol. 33, March 1972, pp. 23-29.

1634. Theory and model for the structural analysis of fiction. F. Ferrara. *New Literary History,* vol. 5, Winter 1974, pp. 245-268.

1635. There, but for the grace of God; reader-identification problem. L. Conger. *Writer,* vol. 87, July 1974, pp. 7-9.

1636. This time with feeling. J. Hinchman. *Writer,* vol. 87, July 1974, pp. 18-20.

1637. Those magic one-liners. E. Jensen. *Writer,* vol. 78, January 1965, pp. 9-11.

1638. Till (violent) death do us part. George P. Elliott. *Writer,* vol. 82, October 1969, pp. 15-16.

1639. To meet and to know. Thomas Williams. *Writer,* vol. 89, September 1976, pp. 17-18+.

1640. Trouble with trouble. R.A. Knowlton. *Writer,* vol. 76, June 1963, pp. 15-16+.

1641. Twenty questions to ask a character. Winifred Madison. *Writer,* vol. 96, November 1983, pp. 15-17+.

1642. Universe of ready made characters: zodiac signs of literary characters. W.J. Watkins. *Writer's Digest,* vol. 49, August 1969, pp. 38-39.

1643. Use your senses to improve characterization. B. Deane. *Writer,* vol. 89, August 1976, pp. 26-27.

1644. Verbs and people. F. Rickett. *Writer,* vol. 80, January 1967, pp. 11-13.

1645. Viewpoint. Anthony Burgess. *Times Literary Supplement,* vol. 71, June 16, 1972, p. 686.

1646. Viewpoint. J. Willett. *Times Literary Supplement,* vol. 72, November 2, 1973, p. 1342.

1647. Viewpoint: a persuasive light; excerpt from *Creating Fiction From Experience.* Peggy Simson Curry. *Writer,* vol. 84, March 1971, pp. 17-18+.

1648. Voice: study in characterization. G. Taylor. *English Journal,* vol. 57, October 1968, pp. 992-994.

1649. Weaving the web of story: archetype and image as the bearers of the tale. M. Lasser. *Children's Literature in Education,* vol. 10, Spring 1979, pp. 4-10.

1650. Whatever happened to Peggy? E. Allen. *Writer,* vol. 78, June 1965, pp. 11-13.

1651. Where do characters come from? C. Edwards *Writer,* vol. 77, March 1964, pp. 10-12+.

1652. Where the action is. E. Jensen. *Writer,* vol. 85, February 1972, pp. 11-13+.

1653. Which viewpoint? Edward S. Fox. *Writer,* vol. 75, June 1962, pp. 19-21+.

1654. Who am I? V. Athanas. *Writer,* vol. 73, August 1960, pp. 18-19.

1655. Writing about my neighbors. E. Seifert. *Writer,* vol. 74, October 1961, pp. 12-14.

1656. You can change puppets to people. H. Hinckley. *Writer,* vol. 78, May 1965, pp. 12-16.

1657. You need someone to love. M.J. Amft. *Writer,* vol. 88, March 1975, pp. 17-19.

1658. Your characters need backbone. M. Nord. *Writer's Digest,* vol. 56, June 1976 pp. 48-49.

Dialogue

"We had been talking as old friends should talk, about nothing, about everything."

—Lillian Hellman

See the chapters on Fiction Technique (page 91), Novel (page 1), Story, Short and Otherwise (page 75), and Drama (page 25) for book annotations containing numerous references to the use of dialogue.

Articles

1659. Dialogue. P. Duganne. *Writer,* vol. 76, April 1963, pp. 19-20.

1660. Dialogue can save your story. H.L. Coffer. *Writer,* vol. 87, October 1974, pp. 14-16+.

1661. "Dialogue," said the writer, "is a fantastic tool for enriching and enlivening your fiction." Robyn Carr. *Writer's Digest,* vol. 64, February 1984, pp. 35-37.

1662. Dialogue that is music. R.O. Bristow. *Writer,* vol. 86, November 1973, pp. 21-22+.

1663. Dialogue that speaks volumes. M.F. Shyer. *Writer,* vol. 87, March 1974, pp. 13-14+.

1664. Dialogue with distinction. Peggy Simson Curry. *Writer,* vol. 77, July 1964, pp. 11-13+.

1665. Diction in Warren's *All the King's Men.* R. Glenn Martin. *English Journal,* vol. 58, November 1969, pp. 1169-1174.

1666. Don't tell it, say it. E. Jensen. *Writer,* vol. 76, February 1963, pp. 14-16.

1667. Fine art of eavesdropping. Gordon Gordon and Mildred Gordon. *Writer,* vol. 80, September 1967, pp. 16-17+.

1668. Five ways to strengthen fiction with dialogue. Loren D. Estleman. *Writer's Digest,* vol. 63, March 1983, pp. 27-28.

1669. From movies to talkies; dialogue in fiction. M. Edwards. *Writer,* vol. 89, November 1976, pp. 11-14.

1670. He said she said. Lawrence Block. *Writer's Digest,* vol. 57, February 1977, pp. 13+.

1671. How people sound. Marjorie Lee. *Writer,* vol. 82, September 1969, pp. 13-15+.

1672. How to use dialogue. Edward S. Fox. *Writer,* vol. 74, November 1961, pp. 16-18+.

1673. How you talk! E.J. McGraw. *Writer,* vol. 73, June 1960, pp. 18-22+.

1674. Humane comedy. S.S. Kenny. *Modern Philology,* vol. 75, August 1977, pp. 29-43.

1675. Letting your characters have their say. Jeffrey Sweet. *Writer,* vol. 88, January 1975, pp. 15-17.

1676. Monologue on dialogue. Harvey Jacobs. *Writer,* vol. 88, July 1975, pp. 12-14.

1677. Secrets of dynamic dialogue. Alan A. Armer. *Writer's Digest,* vol. 60, November 1980, pp. 20-24.

1678. Simon retorts... exclaims... states... Simon says. Colleen Reece. *Writer's Digest,* vol. 64, January 1984, pp. 27+.

1679. Six functions of dialogue in fiction. Charles N. Heckelmann. *Writer's Digest,* vol. 51, June 1971, pp. 24-27.

1680. Sound of the story. J. Buechler. *Writer,* vol. 80, June 1967, pp. 19-21.

1681. Sounds of fiction. M. Franco. *Writer,* vol. 84, October 1971, pp. 11-13.

1682. Uses and abuses of dialogue. Bill Pronzini. *Writer,* vol. 84, May 1971, pp. 12-14+.

1683. Using dialogue in the outdoor article. T. Wendelburg. *Writer,* vol. 84, January 1971, pp. 27-29.

1684. Writing dialogue. K. Reed. *Writer,* vol. 79, August 1966, pp. 16-17.

1685. Writing dialogue. N.B. Gerson. *Writer,* vol. 83, August 1970, pp. 15-17.

Plot and Theme

"There is nothing better fitted to delight the reader than change of circumstances and varieties of fortune."
—Cicero

Books

1686. Dipple, Elizabeth. *Plot.* London: Methuen, 1970. 73 pp.

An extended essay on the elements of plot and how the concept of plot has evolved in modern criticism.

1687. Phillips, Henry Albert. *The Universal Plot Catalog; An Examination of the Elements of Plot Material and Construction, Combined with a Complete Index and a Progressive Category in Which the Source, Life and End of All Dramatic Conflict and Plot Matter Are Classified, Making the Work a Practical Treatise.* Norwood, Pennsylvania: Norwood Editions, 1976. 162 pp.

Phillips is to plot ideas what Roget is to synonyms. Taking the position that universal themes make for the most effective story lines, he goes on to distinguish between plot fragments and matured plots. He then presents his plot catalog, an elaborate arrangement of abstract concepts, emotions, and personal attributes which are intended to stimulate plot ideas. Mainly of historical interest.

1688. Rabkin, Eric S. *Narrative Suspense; "When Slim Turned Sideways...."* Ann Arbor: University of Michigan Press, 1973. 192 pp.

Rabkin has closely read many well-known works of literature in order to discover the mechanics behind books and plays that rivet our attention from the first page or scene. This theoretical description of suspense goes beyond mere plot and into thematic development, character development and style. Rabkin arrives at the conclusion that some kind of suspense is fundamental to all great works of literature and applies this assertion to a variety of genres.

1689. Reid, Mildred. *Writers; Let's Plot!* Contoocook, New Hampshire: Burkhaven Press, 1958. 136 pp.

Reid explores methods and techniques of plot construction in short stories, detective fiction, westerns, romantic fiction, and other forms. In doing so she discusses reverse order, chronological plotting, and plots inspired by names, titles, themes, and locale.

1690. Rockwell, F.A. *How to Write Plots That Sell.* Foreword by Ray Bradbury. Chicago: H. Regnery, 1975. 279 pp.

Ever read a newspaper story or hear an anecdote that would make a good plot for a novel, story, or script? Rockwell explains how and where to look for plots. He categorizes plot and possible sources and then deals with each division under chapter headings such as "Quotations," "Plotting from the Classics," "Bible Stories," and "Plotting from Values." In the final part of the book, Rockwell offers advice on fully developing the plot idea. Throughout the book he presents examples from a variety of literary styles and genres to support his theories.

1691. Young, James N. *101 Plots Used and Abused.* Boston: Writer, 1946. 53 pp.

Young gives brief outlines of much-used plots which he suggests can be reclothed by clever writers.

See also the chapters on Fiction Technique (page 91), Story, Short and Otherwise, (page 75), and Drama (page 25) for book annotations containing numerous references to the use of plot.

Articles

1692. Action, action description, and narrative. T.A. Van Dijk. *New Literary History,* vol. 6, Winter 1975, pp. 273-294.

1693. Alien subject. A. Myrer. *Writer,* vol. 81, November 1968, pp. 9-11+.

1694. Ashtrays in a vacuum. L. Conger. *Writer,* vol. 76, May 1963, pp. 15-17.

1695. Back to beginnings; reprint. P.M. Daltry. *Writer,* vol. 78, July 1965, pp. 14-15.

1696. Balancing plot and character. E. Cadell. *Writer,* vol. 75, February 1962, pp. 17-18+.

1697. Brainstorming by yourself; plot cards. D. Whitcomb. *Writer's Digest,* vol. 49, February 1969, pp. 54-58.

1698. Conflict and how to build it. Dwight V. Swain. *Writer,* vol. 78, December 1965, pp. 22-26; vol. 79, January 1966, pp. 21-28+.

1699. Day the real Queen Mary nearly turned over at sea; idea for the *Poseidon Adventure.* P. Gallico. *Saturday Evening Post,* vol. 244, Fall 1972, pp. 69+.

1700. Dynamics of form. V.R. Lowe. *Writer,* vol. 77, March 1964, pp. 16-19+.

1701. Elusive plot. D. Eden. *Writer,* vol. 85, December 1972, pp. 9-10+.

1702. Every writer needs a turquoise horse. L. Baker. *Writer,* vol. 90, June 1977, pp. 14-17.

1703. Excitement for sale. Mildred Gordon and Gordon Gordon. *Writer,* vol. 86, November 1973, pp. 13-15.

1704. Finding a theme. Gordon Gordon. *Critical Quarterly,* vol. 22, Spring 1980, pp. 5-11.

1705. First things second. Lawrence Block. *Writer's Digest,* vol. 57, August 1977, pp. 10+.

1706. Goals. F.A. Rockwell. *Writer,* vol. 77, September 1964, pp. 19-21.

1707. How much of a story is real? Mary Stolz. *Writer,* vol. 80, March 1967, pp. 9-10+.

1708. How to devise an ingenious plot. R. Gatenby. *Writer,* vol. 88, October 1975, pp. 11-14.

1709. How to turn an incident into a plot. K. Corey. *Writer's Digest,* vol. 52, September 1972, pp. 32-33+.

1710. I remember Androcles. E. Jensen. *Writer,* vol. 77, April 1964, pp. 7-10.

1711. Importance and unimportance of plot; excerpt from *Writing in General and the Short Story in Particular.* Rust Hills. *Writer,* vol. 91, October 1978, pp. 14-17.

1712. Letting the well fill; ideas for stories. M.J. Gerber. *Writer,* vol. 86, March 1973, pp. 14-15.

1713. Meanwhile, back at the plot... W. Walden. *Saturday Review,* vol. 48, January 2, 1965, pp. 19-20.

1714. Modes of fiction: a plot morphology. E.A Tilley. *College English,* vol. 39, February 1976, pp. 692-706.

1715. My literary deep-freeze. B. Gilman. *Writer,* vol. 72, July 1959, pp. 16-17+.

1716. New themes, old techniques. M.E. Nutt. *Writer,* vol. 87, June 1974, pp. 12-14.

1717. Norms of the plot. Norman Friedman. *Journal of General Education,* vol. 8, 1955, pp. 241-253.

1718. On plot in modern fiction: Hardy, James, and Conrad. Walter O'Grady. *Modern Fiction Studies,* vol. 9, 1965, pp. 107-115.

1719. Person and plot. S. Epstein. *Writer,* vol. 79, May 1966, pp. 9-12.

1720. Plausibility. V. Thiessen. *Writer,* vol. 76, October 1963, pp. 21-23+.

1721. Plot. A. Vivante. *Writer,* vol. 90, April 1977, pp. 29-32.

1722. Plot, a pattern created by people. Peggy Simson Curry. *Writer,* vol. 78, February 1965, pp. 20-26+.

1723. Plot blueprints. F.A. Rockwell. *Writer,* vol. 77, May 1964, pp. 16-21.

1724. Plot for your reader. L. Fisher. *Writer,* vol. 74, June 1961, pp. 12-14.

1725. Plot is an invention. W.H. Upson. *Writer,* vol. 75, April 1962, pp. 28-30+.

1726. Plot isn't a dirty word. Z. Popkin. *Writer,* vol. 82, July 1969, pp. 11-12.

1727. Plot—motivation—plot. Michael A. Banks. *Writer's Digest,* vol. 63, June 1983, pp. 35-37.

1728. Plot patterns and frame of mind. Edwin Augustus Peeples. *Writer,* vol. 72, December 1959, pp. 5-7+.

1729. Plot, plot, who's got a plot? Robert Fish. *Writer,* vol. 82, April 1969, pp. 22-23+.

1730. Plot to sell. H. Montgomery. *Writer's Digest,* vol. 48, March 1968, pp. 48-51+.

1731. Plots and people. Hillary Waugh. *Writer,* vol. 82, December 1969, pp. 9-11+.

1732. Plots and plans. P. Ketchum. *Writer,* vol. 78, June 1965, pp. 23-25.

1733. Plots brew in Kansas; L.V. Roper. B. Townsend. *Writer's Digest,* vol. 57, March 1977, pp. 30-31.

1734. Plotting can be play. Allen Saunders. *Writer's Digest,* vol. 63, March 1983, p. 32.

1735. Plotting short stories. Dan Marlowe. *Writer,* vol. 97, August 1984, pp. 9-11+.

1736. Plotting without pain. E.J. McGraw. *Writer,* vol. 72, June 1959, pp. 5-11.

1737. Plottings. Max Byrd. *Writer,* vol. 96, November 1983, pp. 9-11+.

1738. Problematic of ending in narrative. J.H. Miller. *Nineteenth Century Fiction,* vol. 33, June 1978, pp. 3-7.

1739. Rhetorics of the plot. R. Christ. *World Literature Today,* vol. 52, Winter 1978, pp. 38-44.

1740. Second thoughts about sources. A.B. Holland. *Writer's Digest,* vol. 48, May 1968, p. 13.

1741. Sense of a beginning. G. Watson. *Sewanee Review,* vol. 86, Fall 1978, pp. 539-548.

1742. Sensing endings. Frank Kermode. *Nineteenth Century Fiction,* vol. 33, June 1978, pp. 144-158.

1743. Slick pattern. M.F. Shyer. *Writer,* vol. 78, August 1965, pp. 12-14.

1744. Snowflakes and people. L. Conger. *Writer,* vol. 88, December 1975, pp. 7-8.

1745. Story, yes! Outline, no! M.F. Shyer. *Writer,* vol. 85, April 1972, pp. 20-21.

1746. Stuff of a plot. M.F. Shyer. *Writer,* vol. 80, May 1967, pp. 15-16.

1747. Substance of fiction; excerpts from *The Story: A Critical Anthology.* Mark Schorer. *Writer,* vol. 80, June 1967, pp. 14-18+.

1748. Tell them a story. J. McKimmey. *Writer,* vol. 75, August 1962, pp. 7-9.

1749. Theme and variations. D.K. Findlay. *Writer,* vol. 75, February 1962, pp. 10-11+.

1750. Theme in fiction. Gerald Warner Brace. *Massachusetts Review,* vol. 11, Winter 1970, pp. 180-185.

1751. There's gold in the fine print, personals columns as basis for stories. L.F. Reed. *Writer's Digest,* vol. 49, February 1969, pp. 51-53.

1752. This time with feeling. J. Hinchman. *Writer,* vol. 87, July 1974, pp. 18-20.

1753. Thoughts on plots. Joan Aiken. *Writer,* vol. 81, May 1968, pp. 9-12+.

1754. Tiger by the tail. V.N. McCall. *Writer,* vol. 81, October 1968, pp. 17-19.

1755. Towards a theory of narrative. S. Chatman. *New Literary History,* vol. 6, Winter 1975, pp. 295-318.

1756. Tricking the reader for fun and profit. D. Whitcomb. *Writer's Digest,* vol. 48, November 1968, pp. 44-47+.

1757. Twists, angles, and gimmicks. M. Corson. *Writer,* vol. 76, May 1963, pp. 18-20+.

1758. What is a plot? K. Egan. *New Literary History,* vol. 9, Spring 1978, pp. 455-473.

1759. Where do plots start? H. Hinckley. *Writer,* vol. 80, February 1967, pp. 19-20+.

1760. Where the action is. E. Jensen. *Writer's Digest,* vol. 57, September 1977, pp. 27-28.

1761. You can't use coincidence, unless... F.A. Rockwell. *Writer's Digest,* vol. 48, October 1968, pp. 48-52+.

1762. Your plot is contrived. C. Armstrong. *Writer,* vol. 80, October 1967, pp. 17-19.

Setting: Time and Place, Including Flashback

"Some places speak distinctly."
—Robert Louis Stevenson

Books

1763. Lutwack, Leonard. *The Role of Place in Literature.* Syracuse, New York: Syracuse University Press, 1984. 274 pp.

A scholarly investigation of the relationship between place and metaphor, mainly in British and American fiction.

Mendilow, Adam. *Time and the Novel.* See entry 42.

1764. Welty, Eudora. *Place in Fiction.* New York: House of Books, 1957. 31 pp.

In this abridgement of lectures prepared for the Conference on American Studies in Cambridge, England, Welty stresses the importance of detail, "both mundane and poetic," in giving a sense of place and therefore making a work of fiction credible.

See also the chapters on Fiction Technique (page 91), Novel (page 1), Story, Short and Otherwise (page 75), and Drama (page 25) for book annotations containing numerous references to the use of setting.

Articles

1765. Aesthetics of time in narrative fiction. J.H. Maclay. *The Speech Teacher,* vol. 18, September 1969, pp. 194-196.

1766. Background and foreground in fiction. J.C. Oates. *Writer,* vol. 80, August 1967, pp. 11-13.

1767. Background as plus-value. G. Armoury. *Writer,* vol. 76, September 1963, pp. 19-20+.

1768. Background; the most important character. E. Ogilvie. *Writer,* vol. 79, July 1966, pp. 11-14.

1769. Background vs. setting. D.J. Marlowe. *Writer,* vol. 76, February 1963, pp. 12-13+.

1770. Crossing the river of time. M.J. Waldo. *Writer,* vol. 76, April 1963, pp. 7-9.

1771. Description: how much is enough. Rex Burns. *Writer,* vol. 97, March 1984, pp. 13-15.

1772. Dream device in fiction. Francis L. Shine. *Writer,* vol. 93, February 1980, pp. 22-24.

1773. Faraway places. F. Crane. *Writer,* vol. 73, July 1960, pp. 13-15.

1774. Flashback. G. Swarthout. *Writer,* vol. 75, July 1962, pp. 15-16+.

1775. Flashback alternative. John Ball. *Writer,* vol. 94, August 1981, pp. 12-14.

1776. Flashback, the flavor of experience. Peggy Simson Curry. *Writer,* vol. 73, August 1960, pp. 11-13.

1777. Flashbacks and flashforwards. E. Mirabelli, Jr. *Writer,* vol. 83, December 1970, pp. 15-17+.

1778. Flashbacks, transitions, and time (excerpt from *Guide to Fiction Writing).* Phyllis A. Whitney. *Writer,* vol. 95, May 1982, pp. 7-11.

1779. How to make a scene. B. Townsend. *Writer's Digest,* vol. 56, December 1976, pp. 22-23.

1780. In our time: the interchapters as structural guides to a psychological pattern. D.J. Leigh. *Studies in Short Fiction,* vol. 12, Winter 1975, pp. 1-8.

1781. In search of a story: the setting as source. K. Paterson. *Writer,* vol. 91, April 1978, pp. 16-19.

1782. Incongruity, character vs. setting. Francis L. Shine. *Writer,* vol. 87, June 1974, pp. 22-24.

1783. Learn to write in scenes. William Barrett. *Writer,* vol. 75, August 1962, pp. 13-16.

1784. Make your background come alive; excerpt from *Techniques of Fiction Writing.* E.J. McGraw. *Writer,* vol. 74, October 1961, pp. 17-20+.

1785. Making a scene. M. Franco. *Writer,* vol. 95, June 1982, pp. 15-17+.

1786. Map is not a journey. Phyllis A. Whitney. *Writer,* vol. 78, November 1965, pp. 7-12.

1787. Other times, other places. A. Heinemann. *Writer,* vol. 86, July 1973, pp. 14-15+.

1788. Passing the time. J.A. Hodge. *Writer,* vol. 89, March 1976, pp. 18-20+.

1789. Past recaptured. J.M. Kertzer. *Canadian Literature,* no. 65, Summer 1975, pp. 74-85.

1790. Place in Fiction. E. Welty. *South Atlantic Quarterly,* vol. 76, Autumn 1977, pp. 438-453.

1791. Place setting. A. Cavanaugh. *Writer,* vol. 84, January 1971, pp. 16-18+.

1792. Present tense in *Jane Eyre.* Edgar F. Shannon. *Nineteenth Century Fiction,* vol. 10, no. 2, September 1955, pp. 141-145.

1793. Presenting the past. A. Vivante. *Writer,* vol. 84, May 1971, pp. 9-11.

1794. Scene in fiction. F. Bennett. *Writer,* vol. 75, November 1962, pp. 19-21.

1795. Setting a scene. E. Taylor. *Writer,* vol. 78, July 1965, pp. 9-11.

1796. Setting for suspense; the where of your story. J. Lutz. *Writer,* vol. 87, July 1974, pp. 21-23.

1797. Setting in the historical novel. Jane Gilmore Rushing. *Writer,* vol. 97, September 1984, pp. 13-15.

1798. Some notes on time in fiction. Eudora Welty. *Mississippi Quarterly,* vol. 26, Fall 1973, pp. 483-492.

1799. Ticket to Timbuktu; writing about unfamiliar places. Norah Lofts. *Writer,* vol. 80, June 1967, pp. 11-13.

1800. Time and sensibility. D. Daiches. *Modern Language Quarterly,* vol. 25, December 1964, pp. 486-492.

1801. Time and the writer. F.E. Randall. *Writer,* vol. 86, December 1973, pp. 14-16+.

1802. Time and transition. Peggy Simson Curry. *Writer,* vol. 79, September 1966, pp. 18-20+.

1803. Time was, a long time coming. John Foster West. *Writer,* vol. 78, August 1965, pp. 15-18.

1804. Transition tricks; taking your reader from here to there. F.A. Rockwell. *Writer,* vol. 74, December 1961, pp. 11-13+.

1805. Transitions; behind the scenes magic. E.J. McGraw. *Writer,* vol. 81, October 1968, pp. 22-25+.

1806. Uses of the past in fiction writing. B.H. Deal. *Writer,* vol. 75, June 1962, pp. 7-9.

1807. Western regional writers and the uses of place. F. Erisman. *Journal of the West,* vol. 19, January 1980, pp. 36-44.

1808. Westerns: fiction's last frontier. Loren D. Estleman. *Writer,* vol. 94, July 1981, pp. 19-21.

1809. What about flashbacks? Edward S. Fox. *Writer,* vol. 77, November 1964, pp. 16-18.

1810. What is a scene? Edward S. Fox. *Writer,* vol. 78, October 1965, pp. 17-20.

1811. What you should know about using the flash-back in fiction. M. Prieto. *Writer's Digest,* vol. 49, May 1969, pp. 44-47.

1812. When scenery becomes character. A. Chamberlain. *Writer,* vol. 95, August 1982, pp. 12-15+.

1813. Where it happens; backgrounds for fiction. Phyllis A. Whitney. *Writer,* vol. 85, January 1972, pp. 14-15+.

1814. Writing action scenes. R.S. Aldrich. *Writer,* vol. 94, February 1981, pp. 27-28+.

1815. Writing from background. M.P. Strachan. *Writer,* vol. 81, April 1968, pp. 34-35.

1816. You-are-thereness in fiction. J. Williams. *Writer,* vol. 80, April 1967, pp. 20-21+.

1817. You can get there from here; good transitions. E. Jensen. *Writer,* vol. 86, June 1973, pp. 9-11+.

Realism

"The stupendous fact that we stand in the midst of reality will always be something far more wonderful than anything we do."

—Henry Miller

Books

1818. Curry, Peggy Simson. *Creating Fiction from Experience.* Boston: Writer, 1975. 148 pp.

The meaningful fictional expression of ideas and emotions that are rooted in experience is the end goal of this short work which contains some useful suggestions on observation and characterization.

See also the chapters on Fiction Technique (page 91), Novel (page 1), Story, Short and Otherwise (page 75), and Drama (page 25) for book annotations containing numerous references to the use of realism.

Articles

1819. Absorbing reality into fiction. Margaret Culkin Banning. *Writer,* vol. 90, October 1977, pp. 12-14+.

1820. Against realism: some thoughts on fiction, story, and reality. Q.G. Kraft. *College English,* vol. 31, January 1970, pp. 344-354.

1821. Challenge of linguistic realism; dilemmas in drama and literature. M. Pei. *Saturday Review,* vol. 49, April 23, 1966, pp. 27-28+.

1822. Creating the illusion of reality. Hal Charles. *Writer,* vol. 97, April 1984, pp. 15-17.

1823. Details: the source of power. S.L. Rubenstein. *Writer,* vol. 96, May 1983, pp. 15-16+.

1824. Down to the quick: the use of daily reality in writing fiction. J. Langton. *Horn Book,* vol. 49, February 1973, pp. 24-30.

1825. Fact in fiction. Mary McCarthy. *Partisan Review,* vol. 27, Summer 1960, pp. 438-458.

1826. Fact in fiction. N.B. Gerson. *Writer,* vol. 91, July 1978, pp. 16-18.

1827. Flirting with guilt and tyranny. E. Larson. *Harper's,* vol. 225, December 1977, pp. 95-98+; Reply, G. Lyons, *Nation,* vol. 226, January 7, 1978, pp. 24-27.

1828. From realism to reality. Alain Robbe-Grillet. *Evergreen Review,* vol. 10, 1966, pp. 50-53, 83.

1829. Gathering facts for fiction. S. Hearon. *Writer,* vol. 90, February 1978, pp. 15-16+.

1830. Heroics of realism. G. Hartman. *Yale Review,* vol. 53, October 1963, pp. 26-35.

1831. Is the problem of literary realism a pseudo-problem? M. Peckham. *Critique,* vol. 12, 1970, pp. 95-112.

1832. Library closes at nine; importance of research and personal observation. J. Gores. *Writer,* vol. 83, July 1970, pp. 16-19.

1833. Literary realism redefined. J.W. Loofbourow. *Thought,* vol. 45, Autumn 1970, pp. 433-443.

1834. Literature and social change. L. Lerner. *Journal of European Studies,* vol. 7, December 1977, pp. 231-252.

1835. London letter. Anthony Burgess. *American Scholar,* vol. 37, Spring 1968, pp. 312-315.

1836. Notes on the rhetoric of anti-realist fiction. A.J. Guerard. *TriQuarterly,* no. 30, Spring 1974, pp. 3-50.

1837. Old drama and the new: the emerging poetic of modern realism. Alfred Schwarz. *Symposium,* vol. 20, Winter 1966, pp. 343-366.

1838. Realism as a practical and cosmic joke. A. Welsh. *Novel,* vol. 9, Fall 1975, pp. 23-39.

1839. Realism with a difference. G.J. Becker. *Modern Language Quarterly,* vol. 26, December 1965, pp. 606-610.

1840. Reality in fiction: no laughing matter. G. Kums. *English Studies,* vol. 53, December 1972, pp. 523-531.

1841. Realms of reality. Mark Taylor. *Claremont Reading Conference Yearbook,* vol. 30, 1966, pp. 67-77.

1842. Right way to write about what you know (verisimilitude). Hal Blythe and Charlie Sweet. *Writer's Digest,* vol. 64, April 1984, pp. 25-27.

1843. Style and sacrament in modernist writing. H.N. Schneidau. *Georgia Review,* vol. 31, Summer 1977, pp. 427-452.

1844. Truth in fiction. M.P. Betts. *Writer,* vol. 74, September 1961, pp. 20+.

1845. Truth is no excuse. G. Dessart. *Writer,* vol. 85, July 1972, pp. 22-23.

1846. Way it is. B.J. Chute. *Writer,* vol. 86, June 1973, pp. 12-13.

1847. Writers, speak now! Excerpt from *Creating Fiction From Experience.* Peggy Simson Curry. *Writer,* vol. 77, February 1964, pp. 7-10.

Writing for Children and Young People

"It is one of my rules in life not to believe a man who may happen to tell me that he has no interest in children."
— Charles Dickens

Books

1848. Aiken, Joan. *The Way to Write for Children.* New York: St. Martin's, 1983. 93 pp.

Aiken, an award-winning author of juvenile and mystery books, discounts the notion of writing for children as a simple art and approaches its complexity through discussions of picture books, teen novels, fantasy, humor, historical novels, and several other forms. No recent book on the subject has been more widely praised for its high standards and wise approach to taboo subjects.

1849. Blishen, Edward, editor. *The Thorny Paradise; Writers on Writing for Children.* Harmondsworth, Middlesex: Kestral Books, 1975. 176 pp.

The preoccupations, working methods, and pleasures of writing children's literature are examined by a distinguished group of authors, including Richard Adams, Joan Aiken, Nina Bawden, Helen Cresswell, Penelope Farmer, Nicholas Fisk, Jane Gardam, Leon Garfield, John Gordon, Russell Hoban, C. Walter Hodges, Mollie Hunter, Ursula LeGuin, Philippa Pearce, K.M. Peyton, Ian Serraillier, Catherine Storr, Rosemary Sutcliff, John Rowe Townsend, Geoffrey Trease, Jill Paton Walsh, and Barbara Willard.

1850. Colby, Jean. *Writing, Illustrating and Editing Children's Books.* New York: Hastings House, 1967. 318 pp.

A valuable chapter on "how not to write" specifies writing excesses and lapses that give editors mal de manuscript. Though sometimes plodding and preachy, this book offers an insider's perspectives and gives a detailed analysis of age groups and the limits publishers set for books in each group. Several chapters are devoted to illustration, typography, and book design. However, readers should be aware that some aspects of children's book publishing have changed since this book was written.

1851. Duke, Judith S. *Children's Books and Magazines; A Market Study.* White Plains, New York: Knowledge Industry Publications, 1979. 236 pp.

A broad and convincing attempt to define the children's publishing scene, to draw conclusions, and to make future projections.

1852. Fitz-Randolph, Jane. *Writing for the Juvenile and Teenage Market.* New York: Funk & Wagnalls, 1969. 286 pp.

Intended as a text, complete with questions and exercises, this is a competent overview of the subject. As a step-by-step blueprint for writing, it offers a good blend of principle and technique.

1853. Hildick, Wallace. *Children and Fiction; A Critical Study of the Artistic and Psychological Factors Involved in Writing for and about Children.* New York: World, 1971. 222 pp.

Children and Fiction is a critical study of the factors in fiction that contribute to the healthy development of children. Hildick is the author of more than thirty books for children, several of which have been award winners. In addition to parents, teachers, and librarians, his book is addressed to writers, publishers, and reviewers of children's books. Though Hildick offers no step-by-step formula for writing children's fiction, he gives sound advice about technique and backs up his assertions with excerpts from sources generally recognized by children and adults as excellent. Hildick provides a balanced and lively study in an area that has been subject to much misleading theorizing.

1854. Hinds, Marjorie M. *How to Write for the Juvenile Market.* New York: Frederic Fell, 1966. 211 pp.

The working habits and techniques of an experienced story writer are revealed through advice and example, though the world of juvenile writing has turned many times since this was published.

1855. Hopkins, Lee Bennett. *Books Are by People; Interviews with 104 Authors and Illustrators of Books for Young Children.* New York: Citation Press, 1969. 349 pp.

Each interview is no more than two-to-four pages long, but those included are Marcia Brown, John Ciardi, Ingri and Edgar P. d'Aulaire, Ezra Jack Keats, Leo Lionni, Robert McCloskey, Phyllis McGinley, Leo Polti, Maurice Sendak, Dr. Seuss, Louis Slobodkin, Tomi Ungerer, Brian Wildsmith, Herbert Zim, and Charlotte Zolotow.

1856. ———. *More Books by More People; Interviews with 65 Authors of Books for Children.* New York: Citadel Press, 1974. 410 pp.

A continuation of *Books Are by People* (see entry 1855) that includes interviews with Lloyd Alexander, Madeleine L'Engle, Maia Wojciechowska, and P.L. Travers.

1857. Hunter, Mollie. *Talent Is Not Enough; Mollie Hunter on Writing for Children.* New York: Harper, 1976. 126 pp.

An established children's writer presents her views in this anthology of articles and lectures originally published during the 1970s. These are not so much technical instructions on how to write for children as they are inspirations to write truthfully and well.

1858. Karl, Jean. *From Childhood to Childhood; Children's Books and Their Creators.* New York: John Day, 1970. 175 pp.

An experienced editor in the children's book field focuses on the needs and expectations of children, as opposed to adults who write for them. While discussing a variety of techniques used by exemplary children's writers, Karl makes an extended plea for truth, honesty, originality, and superior quality in children's literature. She also reveals, in detail, many aspects of editing and publishing in this field. This is not only a book for tips on technique, but also a source of sound critical and philosophical understandings. It is a frank, sensitive, and valuable book.

1859. Klemin, Diana. *The Art of Art for Children's Books; A Contemporary Survey.* New York: C.N. Potter, 1966. 128 pp.

Surveys the revolution in children's book illustration that was underway in the mid sixties and that largely determines creative decisions today. Analyses of works include those of Edward Legrand Ardizzone, Roger Duvoisin, Edy Legrand, Maurice Sendak, Beni Montresor, Joan Walsh Anglund, and Antonio Franconi. Klemin's experience includes art direction at Doubleday, where she supervised hundreds of children's book designs.

1860. Lewis, Claudia. *Writing for Young Children.* New York: Simon & Schuster, 1954. 115 pp.

Originally the subject of many favorable reviews, this balanced work continues to offer potent advice about children's use of language and how writers must respond to it. Lewis includes chapters on rhythm, sound, form, content, and "common pitfalls" to be avoided when writing for the younger child.

Nixon, Joan L. *Writing Mysteries for Young People.* See entry 2171.

1861. Potter, Beatrix. *Beatrix Potter's Americans; Selected Letters.* Edited by Jane C. Morse. Boston: Horn Book, 1982. 232 pp.

Reveals Potter's wide range of interests, including writing children's books.

1862. Rees, David. *The Marble in the Water; Essays on Contempory Writers for Children and Young Adults.* Boston: Horn Book, 1980. 224 pp.

Outstanding critical essays on seventeen authors: Penelope Farmer, E.L. Konigsburg, Paul Zindel, Philippa Pearce, Alan Garner, Doris Buchanan Smith, Ursula K. LeGuin, Rodie Sudbery, Beverly Cleary, Mildred D. Taylor, Paula Fox, Nina Bawden, Jill Paton Walsh, Robert Cormier, Jill Chaney, Judy Blume, and Penelope Lively.

1863. Reeves, James. *How to Write Poems for Children.* Don Mills, Ontario: William Collins, 1971. 132 pp.

Reeves has written poetry for children during the twenty-five years preceding the publication of this book, and admits that there are few received ideas left about the writing of verse. Yet, he offers many perceptive opinions on what makes children's verse work. In the first part of the book he treats magic, myth, folklore, humor, nonsense, word play, riddles, and songs. Part two deals with technique and covers rhythm, meter, verse forms, diction, and figures of speech. Taken from collections published by Oxford University Press and Heinemann, his poems dance and laugh.

1864. Roberts, Ellen M. *The Children's Picture Book; How to Write It, How to Sell It.* Cincinnati: Writer's Digest, 1981. 189 pp.

For accuracy, currency, and simple good advice there is no other book that comes close to this work. Roberts brings her editorial experience with St. Martin's, Lee and Shepard, and Lothrop to bear on such questions as manuscript submission and marketing. From a discussion of the state of the art of picture books, through plot, character, place, and tone, one senses a keen and analytical mind at work. Roberts has brought a number of Caldecott, Greenaway, and Prix Graphique medal winning books to print and is currently Editor-in-Chief of children's books for Prentice-Hall.

1865. Seuling, Barbara. *How to Write a Children's Book and Get It Published.* New York: Scribner's, 1984. 191 pp.

This carefully crafted and upbeat introduction counsels both practice and patience. It discusses categories of children's literature, developing ideas, illustration, marketing strategies, and interacting with editors. Special appendices include book reviewing and organizations for writers of children's books.

1866. Turow, Joseph. *Getting Books to Children; An Exploration of Publisher-Market Relations.* Chicago: American Library Association, 1979. 137 pp.

A systematic examination of library and mass markets with regard to sales and distribution of children's books.

1867. Van Horne, Marion. *Give Children Wings; A Manual on How to Write for Children.* New York: Committee on World Literacy and Christian Literature, 1970. 109 pp.

Intended both for teachers and writers of children's literature, this work relies on Van Horne's participation in numerous writers' workshops. Robert Lawson's *Rabbit Hill,* Meindert De Jong's *The Wheel on the School,* Elizabeth Yates' *Amos Fortune Free Man,* Charles Finger's *Tales from Silver Lands,* and Elizabeth Speare's *Bronze Bow* are drawn upon to illustrate techniques for fantasy, realistic fiction, biography, and other major forms.

1868. Whitney, Phyllis A. *Writing Juvenile Stories and Novels; How to Write and Sell Fiction for Young People.* Boston: Writer, 1976. 188 pp.

A prolific author of dozens of novels and mysteries gives advice based on a lifetime of successful fiction writing. Particularly germane are her discussions of work habits, technique, and rewriting. As might be expected, special attention is given to the novel and to the juvenile mystery.

1869. Wyndham, Jane Andrews (Lee). *Writing for Children and Teenagers.* Cincinnati: Writer's Digest, 1972. 269 pp.

A prescription for learning a craft rather than a promise of success. Wyndham is a respected children's and young people's author, and her frequent dos and don'ts can be taken seriously. Much analytical thought has obviously gone into the making of her book, which is a laudable overview of markets, the elements of good story telling, and a wide range of special writing problems and situations.

1870. Yolen, Jane H. *Writing Books for Children.* Boston: Writer, 1973. 150 pp.

A children's author shares valuable perceptions about her craft, variously dealing with folktales, picture books, fiction, and creative nonfiction. Her chapters contain relevant quotations from fellow authors and from critics, as well as revelations from her own writing and experiences. Well indexed and accompanied by a supplementary reading list.

Articles

1871. Adventures in plotting; mystery stories for children. Elizabeth Honness. *Writer,* vol. 87, March 1974, pp. 17-19+.

1872. Album and the artist. N. Streatfeild. *Horn Book,* vol. 40, April 1964, pp. 159-161.

1873. All who hide too well away (poetry). H. Plotz. *Horn Book,* vol. 35, April 1959, pp. 112-119.

1874. All's grist that comes to my mill. M. Garthwaite. *Horn Book,* vol. 44, February 1968, pp. 36-39.

1875. And so it grows; excerpt from address, 1967. Leon Garfield. *Horn Book,* vol. 44, December 1968, pp. 668-672.

1876. And then what happened? M.G. Clark. *Writer,* vol. 77, December 1964, pp. 23-25.

1877. Art of Elizabeth Enright (part one). E. Cameron. *Horn Book,* vol. 45, December 1969, pp. 641-651.

1878. Art of Elizabeth Enright (part two). E. Cameron. *Horn Book,* vol. 46, February 1970, pp. 26-30.

1879. Art of M.B. Goffstein. J. Giusto-Davis. *Publishers Weekly,* vol. 218, October 24, 1980, pp. 22-23.

1880. Art of the picture book; symposium. W. Lorraine. *Wilson Library Bulletin,* vol. 52, October 1977, pp. 144-147.

1881. Art of the word; significance in stories for young people. Peter F. Neumeyer. *English Journal,* vol. 66, May 1977, pp. 62-64.

1882. As far as you can bear to see; excellence in children's literature. M.Q. Steele. *Horn Book,* vol. 51, June 1975, pp. 250-255.

1883. Assorted thoughts on creative authors and artists; excerpts from address, April 27, 1974. U. Nordstrom (Sr. Editor, Harper & Row). *Library Journal,* vol. 99, September 15, 1974, pp. 2211-2214.

1884. Authors and editors; Scott O'Dell (interview). *Publishers Weekly,* vol. 200, November 15, 1971, pp. 21-23.

1885. Barbara Harmon: magic and mastery. M.C. Nelson. *American Artist,* vol. 39, May 1975, pp. 48-53+.

1886. Barbara Wersba (interview). *English Journal,* vol. 65, November 1976, pp. 20-21.

1887. Believe what you write about. Mary Stolz. *Writer,* vol. 93, October 1980, pp. 22-23.

1888. Biographies for children, more facts, less fiction. J. Forman. *Library Journal,* vol. 97, September 15, 1972, pp. 2968-2969.

1889. Biography; the other face of the coin. R. Sprague. *Horn Book,* vol. 42, June 1966, pp. 282-289.

1890. Books; children's books that use photography. L. Kirschbrown. *Popular Photography,* vol. 77, September 1975, pp. 98+.

1891. Books for children. K. Kuskin. *Saturday Review,* vol. 55, August 19, 1972, pp. 59-61.

1892. Books that say yes. Madeleine L'Engle. *Writer,* vol. 89, June 1976, pp. 9-12.

1893. But few are chosen. Zena Sutherland. *Saturday Review,* vol. 55, May 20, 1972, p. 80.

1894. Call it a wheel. I. Southall. *Horn Book,* vol. 50, October 1974, pp. 43-49.

1895. Catching young readers' interest. L.D. Chaffin. *Writer,* vol. 88, October 1975, pp. 23-24.

1896. Changing market for juvenile books. *Writer,* vol. 94, August, 1981, pp. 25-27.

1897. Children's book by any other name just might not sell. Andrea Brown and Debra Maltzman. *Writer's Digest,* vol. 61, June 1981, pp. 34-36.

1898. Children's book markets. Ray Ory. *Writer's Digest,* vol. 58, May 1978, pp. 28+.

1899. Children's stories-in-verse; successful verse-story authors: how they do it; with a list of publishers. *Writer's Digest,* vol. 48, October 1968, pp. 42-47+, 58-59+.

1900. Clues to the juvenile mystery. Joan L. Nixon. *Writer,* vol. 90, February 1977, pp. 23-26.

1901. Coffee break book and other lies. Jane H. Yolen. *Writer,* vol. 83, November 1970, pp. 21-22.

1902. Confessions of a leprechaun. B. Turkle. *Publishers Weekly,* vol. 196, July 14, 1969, pp. 133-136.

1903. Confessions of an old story-teller, (part one). K.I. Chukovskii. *Horn Book,* vol. 46, December 1970, pp. 577-591.

1904. Confessions of an old story-teller, (part two). K.I. Chukovskii. *Horn Book,* vol. 47, February 1971, pp. 28-39.

1905. Children's book illustrators play favorites. Arnold Lobel and others. *Wilson Library Bulletin,* vol. 52, October 1977, pp. 165-173.

1906. Children's books in 1990. James Giblin. *Writer's Digest,* vol. 60, May 1980, pp. 20-25+.

1907. Cooking up the teen romance novel. Helen Cavanagh. *Writer's Digest,* vol. 62, May 1982, pp. 43-45.

1908. Coping with trends in children's books; excerpt from address. James Giblin. *Writer,* vol. 89, July 1976, pp. 15-17+.

1909. Creating a picture book. Shirley Climo. *Writer,* vol. 96, July 1983, pp. 18-20+.

1910. Creating books. Lois Lenski. *Library Journal,* vol. 88, October 15, 1963, pp. 3987-3990+.

1911. Creation of *Charlotte's Web* (E.B. White): from drafts to book. Part one. Peter F. Neumeyer. *Horn Book,* vol. 58, October 1982, pp. 489-497.

1912. Creation of *Charlotte's Web* (E.B. White): from drafts to book. Part two. Peter F. Neumeyer. *Horn Book,* vol. 58, December 1982, pp. 617-625.

1913. Creativity limited. K. Paterson. *Writer,* vol. 93, December 1980, pp. 11-14.

1914. Developing the picture book story. Mary Calhoun. *Writer,* vol. 94, July 1981, pp. 16-18+.

1915. Digging for ideas. J. Nelms. *Writer,* vol. 79, March 1966, pp. 27-28.

1916. Divorce, drugs, desertion, the draft; facing up to the realities in children's literature. N. Larrick. *Publishers Weekly,* vol. 201, February 21, 1972, pp. 90-91.

1917. Do I dare disturb the universe? Madeleine L'Engle. *Horn Book,* vol. 59, December 1983, pp. 673-682.

1918. Double image; language as the perimeter of culture; address, 1969. E.L. Konigsburg. *Library Journal,* vol. 95, February 15, 1970, pp. 731-734.

1919. Down the rabbit hole, how and why. Jane H. Yolen. *Writer,* vol. 86, February 1973, pp. 22-24+.

1920. Editors and children's book writers; two sketches. R. Burch, and A. Duff. *Horn Book,* vol. 50, June, August 1974, pp. 249-255, 409-415.

1921. Evaluative criteria to be used as guides by writers of children's literature. H.W. Lowry. *Elementary English,* vol. 48, December 1971, pp. 922-925.

1922. Exclusive interview; with Newbery award winning author. Lloyd Alexander. *Writer's Digest,* vol. 53, April 1973, pp. 32-35+.

1923. A few men and women. M.K. McElderry. *Horn Book,* vol. 38, February 1962, pp. 28-40.

1924. Fiction for teen-agers. N. Hentoff. *Atlantic,* vol. 220, December 1967, pp. 136+.

1925. Fiction for teen-agers; with reply by L.W. Warrick. N. Hentoff. *Wilson Library Bulletin,* vol. 43, November 1968, pp. 261-268.

1926. Fighter, the writer (advice from boxer turned writer and author of *Gentle Ben,* Walt Morey). Larry Leonard. *Writer's Digest,* vol. 64, September 1984, pp. 30-32.

1927. Find the child. Winifred Madison. *Writer,* vol. 86, April 1973, pp. 20-22.

1928. Flat-heeled muse. Lloyd Alexander. *Horn Book,* vol. 41, April 1965, pp. 141-146.

1929. Following one's instincts. E.B. White. *Writer,* vol. 79, July 1966, pp. 22-23.

1930. From reading to writing. F. Hightower. *Horn Book,* vol. 44, February 1968, pp. 24-29.

1931. From the ground upwards. (research) C. Harnett. *Horn Book,* vol. 37, October 1961, pp. 413-418.

1932. Gee, what a big best-seller Jean George has; interview. J.C. George. *Writer's Digest,* vol. 54, March 1974, pp. 9-11.

1933. Getting inside jazz country. N. Hentoff. *Horn Book,* vol. 42, October 1966, pp. 528-532.

1934. Great men, melodies, experiments, plots, predictability, and surprises; adaptation of address, June 6, 1975. F.N. Monjo. *Horn Book,* vol. 51, October 1975, pp. 433-441.

1935. Heroes and villains in stories for children and teenagers; excerpts from *Writing for Children and Teenagers.* Jane Andrews (Lee) Wyndham. *Writer's Digest,* vol. 50, November 1970, pp. 32-33+.

1936. Hitting the juvenile nature trail (nature stories). Elizabeth Hennefrund. *Writer's Digest,* vol. 62, February 1982, pp. 34-38.

1937. Honorable profession; writing for children. Mary Stolz. *Saturday Review,* vol. 47, November 7, 1964, pp. 45-46.

1938. How can we write children's books if we don't know anything about children? Natalie Babbitt. *Publishers Weekly,* vol. 200, July 19, 1972, pp. 64-66.

1939. How (maybe) to write a children's book; excerpts from *Turn Not Pale, Beloved Snail.* J. Jackson. *Publishers Weekly,* vol. 201, February 21, 1972, pp. 92-94.

1940. How (maybe) to write a children's book; excerpts from *Turn Not Pale, Beloved Snail.* J. Jackson. *Writer,* vol. 87, April 1974, pp. 22-25.

1941. How publishers promote children's books. C.W. Dorsey. *Writer's Digest,* vol. 53, January 1973, pp. 22-24.

1942. How to create live characters in a juvenile short story. N.R. Ainsworth. *Writer's Digest,* vol. 49, December 1969, pp. 36-39+.

1943. I would not coddle the child. J. Beatty and P. Beatty. *Horn Book,* vol. 40, April 1964, pp. 149-152.

1944. I'd like to know; writing and publishing children's books. Maia Wojciechowska. *Horn Book,* vol. 49, October 1973, pp. 419+.

1945. Ideas for books. M. Crary. *Elementary English,* vol. 43, December 1966, pp. 902-904.

1946. If there is no happy ending: children's book publishing—past, present and future: Part I. Ann Durell. *Horn Book,* vol. 58, February 1982, pp. 23-30.

1947. If there is no happy ending: children's book publishing—past, present and future: Part II. Ann Durell. *Horn Book,* vol. 58, April 1982, pp. 145-150.

1948. Illustrating science books for children. L. Bendick. *Science and Children,* vol. 10, April 1973, pp. 20-21.

1949. Imaginary correspondence; B. Potter and a present day children's book editor. R. Godden. *Horn Book,* vol. 39, August 1963, pp. 369-375.

1950. In search of the perfect picture book definition. Zena Sutherland and Betsy Hearn. *Wilson Library Bulletin,* vol. 52, October 1977, pp. 158-160.

1951. In tune with tomorrow. C. Harris. *Canadian Literature,* vol. 78, Autumn 1978, pp. 26-30.

1952. It's not all Peter Rabbit; realism in children's books. Jane H. Yolen. *Writer,* vol. 88, April 1975, pp. 12-15.

1953. Jay Bennet (interview). *English Journal,* vol. 65, May 1976, pp. 86-88.

1954. Judy Blume (interview). *Teen,* vol. 26, October 1982, pp. 30+.

1955. Judy Blume as herself. Paula Saunders. *Writer's Digest,* vol. 59, February 1979, pp. 18-24.

1956. Juvenile characters must grow. Dorothy Francis. *Writer,* vol. 91, September 1978, pp. 21-22+.

1957. Kids rule for writing. B. Boshinski. *Writer's Digest,* vol. 50, July 1970, pp. 31-32.

1958. Last buffalo killed in Tennessee; excerpt from address, 1967. W.O. Steele. *Horn Book,* vol. 45, April 1969, pp. 196-199.

1959. Letter from C.S. Lewis. J.E. Higgins. *Horn Book,* vol. 42, October 1966, pp. 533-539.

1960. Life ain't been no crystal stair; address, 1968. N. Larrick. *Library Journal,* vol. 94, February 15, 1969, pp. 843-845.

1961. Literature, creativity, and imagination. Lloyd Alexander. *Childhood Education,* vol. 47, March 1971, pp. 307-310.

1962. Literature written for young children. Leland B. Jacobs. *Elementary English,* vol. 47, October 1970, pp. 781-783.

1963. Lively, profitable world of kid lit. S. Kanfer. *Time,* vol. 116, December 29, 1980, pp. 62-65.

1964. Lloyd Alexander (interview). *Library Journal,* vol. 96, April 15, 1971, pp. 1421-1423.

1965. M.E. Kerr (interview). *English Journal,* vol. 64, December 1975, pp. 75-77.

1966. Magic, craft, and the making of children's books. Nancy Willard. *Writer,* vol. 94, April 1981, pp. 17-19.

1967. Make room for the eighteenth century; American History for children. J. Fritz. *Horn Book,* vol. 50, October 1974, pp. 177-181.

1968. Makers of modern myths. Jane H. Yolen. *Horn Book,* vol. 51, October 1975, pp. 496-497.

1969. Many worlds of children's books. Arnold Dobrin. *Writer's Digest,* vol. 58, May 1978, pp. 24-27.

1970. Market for children's books today. M. Chaikin. *Writer,* vol. 95, February 1982, pp. 24-25.

1971. Maurice Sendak (interview). *Wilson Library Bulletin,* vol. 52, October 1977, pp. 152-157.

1972. Maybe Johnny's not reading because you're not writing well enough; excerpt from *Writing for the Juvenile and Teenage Market.* Jane Fitz-Randolph. *Writer's Digest,* vol. 54, March 1974, pp. 14-18.

1973. Mildred D. Taylor. P.J. Fogelman. *Horn Book,* vol. 53, August 1977, pp. 410-414.

1974. Milton Glaser asks: do we know what we are doing in children's books? *Publishers Weekly,* vol. 205, April 1, 1974, p. 46.

1975. My heroine helped me. C. Harris. *Horn Book,* vol. 40, August 1964, pp. 361-363.

1976. My struggle with facts (biography). O. Coolidge. *Wilson Library Bulletin,* vol. 49, October 1974, pp. 146-151.

1977. Nathaniel Benchley (interview). *English Journal,* vol. 65, September 1976, pp. 23-25.

1978. New generation of writers and artists brings fresh vision to children's books. J.F. Mercier. *Publishers Weekly,* vol. 211, February 28, 1977, pp. 99-100.

1979. New kind of fiction; writing for the reluctant reader. N.R. Ainsworth. *Writer,* vol. 78, January 1965, pp. 26-29.

1980. New realism. R. Burch. *Horn Book,* vol. 47, June 1971, pp. 257-264.

1981. New realism; traditional cultural values in recent young-adult fiction. M.P. Mertz. *Phi Delta Kappan,* vol. 60, October 1978, pp. 101-105.

1982. Notes on the children's book trade. J. Goldthwaite. *Harper's Magazine,* vol. 254, January 1977, pp. 76+; discussion, March 1977, pp. 6-7.

1983. Notes on the children's book trade; discussion. J. Goldthwaite. *SLJ/ School Library Journal,* vol. 23, February 1977, p. 7.

1984. Novels for teen-agers. H.G. Jordan. *Writer,* vol. 88, December 1975, pp. 16-18.

1985. Obligations of a children's book writer. R. Burch. *Indiana University, School of Education, Bulletin,* vol. 45, November 1969, pp. 1-14.

1986. Of style and the stylist. E. Cameron. *Horn Book,* vol. 40, February 1964, pp. 25-32.

1987. On spies and applesauce and such. R.H. Viguers. *Horn Book,* vol. 41, February 1965, pp. 74-76.

1988. On three ways of writing for children; reprint. C.S. Lewis. *Horn Book,* vol. 39, October 1963, pp. 459-469.

1989. One world. Mollie Hunter. *Horn Book,* vol. 51, December 1975, pp. 557-563.

1990. Our dreams are tales. R. Manning. *Horn Book,* vol. 41, February 1965, pp. 25-27.

1991. Out of experience; background for the writing of *The Son of the Gondolier.* E. Steinmann. *Horn Book,* vol. 35, October 1959, pp. 408-411.

1992. Patterns on a wall; address, August 3, 1973. Penelope Farmer. *Horn Book,* vol. 50, October 1974, pp. 169-176.

1993. Peculiar understanding: recreating the literary fairy tale. Ellin Greene. *Horn Book,* vol. 59, June 1983, pp. 270-286.

1994. Perhaps we need to return to basics (teen fiction). Corinne Bergstrom. *Writer's Digest,* vol. 58, May 1978, p. 26.

1995. Persuaded muse; writing for children. Zena Sutherland. *Saturday Review,* vol. 52, February 22, 1969, p. 46.

1996. Picture book as art object: a call for balanced reviewing. Kenneth Marantz. *Wilson Library Bulletin,* vol. 52, October 1977, pp. 148-151.

1997. Picture books for children who are masters of few words. B. Lucas. *Library Journal,* vol. 98, May 15, 1973, pp. 1641-1645.

1998. Pied Pipers. J. Wintle and E. Fisher. *Psychology Today,* vol. 9, July 1975, pp. 9+.

1999. Place for poetry. R. Lewis. *Publishers Weekly.* vol. 192, July 10, 1967, pp. 119-120.

2000. Plotting the children's novel. Joan Aiken. *Writer,* vol. 95, April 1982, pp. 14-17; May 1982, pp. 15-17.

2001. Poems for children. M. Ponsot. *Poetry,* vol. 101, December 1962, pp. 208-209.

2002. Poet in the playpen. X.J. Kennedy. *Poetry,* vol. 105, December 1964, pp. 190-193.

2003. Poetry for children. H. Behn. *Horn Book,* vol. 42, April 1966, pp. 163-175.

2004. Poetry for children; a neglected art. M. Benton. *Children's Literature in Education,* vol. 9, Autumn 1978, pp. 111-126.

2005. Poetry for the youngest. L. Clark. *Horn Book,* vol. 38, December 1962, pp. 582-585.

2006. Poetry is the natural language of children. N. Larrick. *Parent's Magazine,* vol. 44, August 1969, pp. 46-47+.

2007. Poetry—stepchild of children's literature; searching CSD's notable book lists 1940-1955. M.C. Livingston. *Library Journal,* vol. 99, May 15, 1974, pp. 1446-1449.

2008. Promotions that help sell children's books in the stores. *Publishers Weekly,* vol. 187, February 22, 1965, pp. 160-162.

2009. Psyching out kid's writers (psychological aspects of children's writers). *Human Behavior,* vol. 2, no. 73, p. 38.

2010. Publishers record their best in-store sellers among children's books. *Publishers Weekly,* vol. 209, February 23, 1976, pp. 72-73.

2011. Publishers report top-selling juveniles. *Publishers Weekly,* vol. 210, July 19, 1976, pp. 80-81.

2012. Publishers report top-selling juveniles. *Publishers Weekly,* vol. 211, February 28, 1977, pp. 97-98.

2013. Putting words into wordless books. L.S. Degler. *The Reading Teacher,* vol. 32, January 1979, pp. 399-402.

2014. PW interviews: David Macauley. *Publishers Weekly,* vol. 213, April 10, 1978, pp. 6-7.

2015. PW interviews: Harper and Row's children's books editor; Charlotte Zolotow. *Publishers Weekly,* vol. 205, June 10, 1974, pp. 8-9.

2016. PW interviews: R. Isadora and R. Maiorano. *Publishers Weekly,* vol. 219, February 27, 1981, p. 66.

2017. Reaching the teenage market. D. Stanford. *Writer,* vol. 72, August 1959, pp. 14-15.

2018. Realism in children's books. R. Burch. *Claremont Reading Conference Yearbook,* vol. 38, 1974, pp. 56-62.

2019. Realism in children's literature. E. Enright. *Horn Book,* vol. 43, April 1967, pp. 165-170.

2020. Realism in children's literature. E. Enright. *Writer,* vol. 81, April 1968, pp. 19-22.

2021. Realism, truth, and honesty; address, July 1970. M.Q. Steele. *Horn Book,* vol. 47, February 1971, pp. 17-27.

2022. Recipes for writing from children's books. C.J. Fisher. *Instructor,* vol. 87, February 1978, pp. 138-40.

2023. Report of a journey (address). Elizabeth Speare. *Horn Book,* vol. 38, August 1962, pp. 336-341.

2024. Resurrection of the pop-up book (W.H. Hunt's Intervisual Communications, Inc.). P. Seymour. *Publishers Weekly,* vol. 219, February 27, 1981, pp. 97-99.

2025. Rewards of writing. Zena Sutherland. *Saturday Review,* vol. 54, October 16, 1971, p. 56.

2026. Richard Peck (interview). *English Journal,* vol. 65, February 1976, pp. 97-99.

2027. RLS factor; Children's garden of verses. R.S. Baker. *Nation,* vol. 189, November 14, 1959, pp. 364-366.

2028. Root and measure of realism; modern stories for children. V.L. Wolf. *Wilson Library Bulletin,* vol. 44, December 1969, pp. 409-415.

2029. Science fiction for young readers. Douglas Hill. *Writer,* vol. 97, January 1984, pp. 15-18.

2030. Scott O'Dell: immortal writer (interview). *American Libraries,* vol. 4, June 1973, pp. 356-357.

2031. Selecting a manuscript for publication. J.D. Chenery. *Writer,* vol. 84, October 1971, pp. 24-25.

2032. Selling the young adult novel; with list of publishers. H. Schellenberg. *Writer's Digest,* vol. 48, April 1968, pp. 59-61.

2033. Selling to juvenile publications. E.P. Johnson. *Writer,* vol. 79, February 1966, pp. 30-31.

2034. Short talk with a prospective children's writer. A. Lindgren. *Horn Book,* vol. 49, June 1973, pp. 248-252.

2035. Slake's limbo; in which a book switches authors. F. Holman. *Horn Book,* vol. 52, October 1976, pp. 479-485.

2036. Some more advice on how to reach children from people who do it for a living. M. Lasky and R. Kramer. *Writer's Digest,* vol. 54, March 1974, pp. 12-13.

2037. Some thoughts about picture books. Mae Durham. *Horn Book,* vol. 39, October 1963, pp. 476-484.

2038. Speaking to the imagination. S.F. Morse. *Horn Book,* vol. 41, June 1965, pp. 255-259.

2039. Spirit of '76; some revolutionary work by children's authors. J.F. Mercier. *Publishers Weekly,* vol. 210, July 19, 1976, p. 82.

2040. Sprezzatura; a kind of excellence; excerpts from address, April 12, 1975. E.L. Konigsburg. *Horn Book,* vol. 52, June 1976, pp. 253-261.

2041. Stanley the Fierce and other poems. J. Viorst. *Redbook,* vol. 156, November 1980, p. 96.

2042. Still playing it safe; restricted realism in teen novels. J. Abramson. *SLJ/Scholastic Library Journal,* vol. 22, May 1976, pp. 38-39.

2043. Stories we tell ourselves; writing for children. G. Swarthout. *Writer,* vol. 86, January 1973, pp. 16-17+.

2044. Tale of a story. E. Hopkins. *Canadian Literature,* vol. 78, Autumn 1978, pp. 22-24.

2045. Talk with Natalie Babbitt. S.G. Lanes. *New York Times Book Review,* vol. 87, November 14, 1982, pp. 44+.

2046. Teacher writes a book. R. Shields. *Writer,* vol. 87, September 1974, pp. 25-26.

2047. Tent of green. William J. Smith. *Horn Book,* vol. 38, April 1962, pp. 137-140.

2048. There's more to the picture than meets the eye. Blair Lent. *Wilson Library Bulletin,* vol. 52, October 1977, pp. 161-164.

2049. Things they write me; an author's-eye-view of young readers. L.G. Erdman. *Education Digest,* vol. 40, January 1975, pp. 51-53.

2050. Three remarkable editors of children's books. B. Huerlimann. *Horn Book,* vol. 50, February 1974, pp. 17-23.

2051. Timely and timeless young adult novel. Laurie Glieco. *Writer,* vol. 97, March 1984, pp. 22-23.

2052. To make a child laugh. Jane H. Yolen. *Writer,* vol. 96, August 1983, pp. 15-16+.

2053. Today's best-selling children's books. J.F. Mercier. *Publishers Weekly,* vol. 207, February 24, 1975, pp. 68-69.

2054. Top-selling children's books. *Publishers Weekly,* vol. 212, July 18, 1977, pp. 85-87.

2055. Transformation of a poet; John Ciardi. P.J. Groff. *Horn Book,* vol. 40, April 1964, pp. 153-158.

2056. Transition years. J.L. Oppenheimer. *Writer,* vol. 89, October 1976, pp. 25-27+.

2057. Trends in juvenile fiction today. James Giblin. *Writer's Digest,* vol. 62, April 1982, pp. 41-44.

2058. Tune beyond us; the bases of choice. M.C. Livingston. *Wilson Library Bulletin,* vol. 44, December 1969, pp. 448-455.

2059. Two most popular types of picture book ideas. W. Yeo. *Writer's Digest,* vol. 52, April 1972, pp. 28-30+.

2060. Unauthorized juvenile biography. Gloria Miklowitz. *Writer,* vol. 92, October 1979, pp. 15-17+.

2061. Use of literary epiphany in children's literature. J. Buyze. *Elementary English,* vol. 49, November 1972, pp. 986-988.

2062. Weaving the web of story; archetype and image as the bearers of the tale. M. Lasser. *Children's Literature in Education.* vol. 10, Spring 1979, pp. 4-10.

2063. What is real? Asked the rabbit one day; realism vs. fantasy in the children's and adult literature. P. Merla. *Saturday Review,* vol. 55, November 4, 1972, pp. 43-50.

2064. What makes a funny children's book? S.S. Steinberg. *Publishers Weekly,* vol. 213, February 27, 1978, pp. 87-90.

2065. What story-book pictures convey—an experiment with Japanese picture-story books. Bernice W. Carlson. *Horn Book,* vol. 36, June 1960, p. 184.

2066. What to read and how to write it. A. Prince. *Times Educational Supplement,* vol. 2979, June 23, 1972, p. 40.

2067. What you can make live. C.C. Greene. *Writer,* vol. 95, August 1982, pp. 23-26.

2068. What's new in children's books? Eve Bunting. *Writer,* vol. 97, April 1984, pp. 12-14+.

2069. When the magic has to stop. J. McNeill. *Horn Book,* vol. 48, August 1972, pp. 337-342.

2070. Where do you get your ideas? An interview with Winifred Madison. *Writer,* vol. 88, November 1975, pp. 17-19+.

2071. Who wants to throw a cannonball? The young adult field. E. Allen. *Writer,* vol. 83, October 1970, pp. 25-26+.

2072. Who'll kill the mockingbirds? David C. Davis. *Horn Book,* vol. 39, June 1963, pp. 265-271.

2073. Why children don't like to read. Bruno Bettelheim and Karen Zelan. *Atlantic,* vol. 248, November 1981, pp. 25-31.

2074. Why did you end your story that way? Elizabeth Yates. *Horn Book,* vol. 43, December 1967, pp. 709-714.

2075. William Armstrong (address). *Horn Book,* vol. 46, August 1970, pp. 352-355.

2076. Winners and losers; what makes the difference (young adult). Bebe Willoughby Slappey. *Writer,* vol. 97, October 1984, pp. 19-22.

2077. Wishful thinking or hopeful dreaming? (address). Lloyd Alexander. *Horn Book,* vol. 44, August 1968, pp. 382-390.

2078. Witchcraft for kids. T.G. Aylesworth. *Publishers Weekly,* vol. 221, February 26, 1982, pp. 80-81.

2079. Writing a book; excerpt from address. Philippa Pearce. *Horn Book,* vol. 43, June 1967, pp. 317-322.

2080. Writing a first juvenile. B. Conrad. *Writer,* vol. 85, April 1972, pp. 29-30+.

2081. Writing about Abraham Lincoln; address November 9, 1974. O. Coolidge. *Horn Book,* vol. 51, February 1975, pp. 31-35.

2082. Writing animal stories for children. Patsey Gray. *Writer,* vol. 91, February 1978, pp. 20-22.

2083. Writing biographies for young readers. O.W. Burt. *Writer,* vol. 85, February 1972, pp. 18-21.

2084. Writing biography for young people. F. Cavanah. *Writer's Digest,* vol. 48, January 1968, pp. 36-38+.

2085. Writing books for children. R. Caudill. *Conference on Reading, University of Pittsburg, Report,* vol. 1959, pp. 177-179.

2086. Writing books for young people. *Writer,* vol. 95, March 1982, pp. 18-20+.

2087. Writing children's books. M.R. Carafoli. *Writer,* vol. 87, February 1974, pp. 25-26.

2088. Writing children's books. R. Dahl. *Writer,* vol. 89, August 1976, pp. 18-19.

2089. Writing children's theatre is no child's play. William Brohaugh and Dennis Chaptman. *Writer's Digest,* vol. 59, August 1979, pp. 29-32.

2090. Writing children's verse. A. Fisher. *Writer,* vol. 76, April 1963, pp. 21-24.

2091. Writing for children. Charlotte Zolotow. *Writer,* vol. 80, April 1967, pp. 36-38.

2092. Writing for children. I. Hunt. *Writer,* vol. 83, March 1970, pp. 17-20.

2093. Writing for children. M. Grenier. *Writer's Digest,* vol. 52, October 1972, pp. 30-31+.

2094. Writing for children; a joy and a responsibility. E. Greenfield. *Interracial Books for Children.* Bulletin 10, no. 3, 1979, pp. 3-4.

2095. Writing for children; excerpts from address. R. Godden. *Writer,* vol. 90, July 1977, pp. 18-19.

2096. Writing for children in a fragmented society. E.K. Cooper. *Claremont Reading Conference Yearbook,* vol. 36, 1972, pp. 85-89.

2097. Writing for children is no child's play. M. Tournier. *UNESCO Courier,* vol. 35, June 1982, pp. 33-34.

2098. Writing for children vs. writing for adults. S. Shreve. *Publishers Weekly,* vol. 222, July 23, 1982, pp. 78-79.

2099. Writing for children—with respect. A. Bach. *Publishers Weekly,* vol. 207, February 24, 1975, pp. 66-67.

2100. Writing for children's publications (magazines). Ray Ory and William Brohaugh. *Writer's Digest,* vol. 58, June 1978, pp. 44-47.

2101. Writing for Saturday morning television. Ted Pedersen and Martha Humpherys. *Writer's Digest,* vol. 60, February 1980, pp. 26-31.

2102. Writing for teenagers. Gloria Miklowitz. *Writer,* vol. 91, March 1978, pp. 22-24+.

2103. Writing for the reluctant reader. Elizabeth Hennefrund. *Writer's Digest,* vol. 58, August 1978, pp. 30-35.

2104. Writing juvenile biography. C.O. Peare. *Writer,* vol. 79, April 1966, pp. 23-24+.

2105. Writing juvenile mysteries. Arnold Madison. *Writer,* vol. 85, August 1972, pp. 21-23.

2106. Writing non-fiction books for children. R.S. Radlauer. *Writer's Digest,* vol. 52, March 1972, pp. 28-31.

2107. Writing nonfiction for young people. Karen O'Connor. *Writer,* vol. 96, October 1983, pp. 27-28+.

2108. Writing novels for children. C. Aaron. *Writer,* vol. 86, July 1973, pp. 21-22+.

2109. Writing science books for children. M.E. Selsam. *Science and Children,* vol. 10, April 1973, p. 19.

2110. Writing teen romances. J.C. Miner. *Writer,* vol. 95, July 1982, pp. 18-20.

2111. Writing; the sound of one hand clapping. M. Ho. *Interracial Books for Children.* Bulletin 8, no. 8, 1977, pp. 5+.

2112. Writing the teen-age soap opera. A.B. Eaglen. *School Library Journal,* vol. 25, April 1979, pp. 24-27.

2113. Writing the two-level juvenile story. Arnold Madison. *Writer,* vol. 94, March 1981, pp. 15-17+.

2114. You can't animate a plaid shirt (Berenstain Bears). S. Berenstain and J. Berenstain. *Publishers Weekly,* vol. 219, February 27, 1981, pp. 99-100.

2115. Young people: victims of realism in books and in life; adaptation of address, June 1973. J. Jordan. *Wilson Library Bulletin,* vol. 48, October 1973, pp. 140-145.

Confessions

"Confess your sins to one another."

—Venerable Bede

Books

2116. Collett, Dorothy. *Writing the Modern Confession Story.* Boston: Writer, 1971. 185 pp.

Dividing her analysis into ten elements and discussing each in detail, Collett then reproduces two of her published stories to show how these elements apply. She offers reasoned advice for those interested in the confession field.

Duncan, Lois. *How to Write and Sell Your Personal Experiences.* See entry 2818.

2117. Feldhake, Susan C. *How to Write and Sell Confessions.* Boston: Writer, 1980. 105 pp.

A short but practical guide which describes current markets and editorial policies in three major categories of confession magazines: wholesome, racy, and erotic. Emphasis is placed on the changes that have taken place since the time when sin-suffer-and-repent formulas dominated the field. Viewpoint, characterization, and producing the final draft are also covered in detail.

2118. Palmer, Florence K. *Confession Writer's Handbook.* Cincinnati: Writer's Digest, 1980. 173 pp.

Palmer provides a well-rounded introduction to what many disparage as the lowest level of formula fiction. She divides the confession story into easy-to-identify categories and provides expert advice on plot, characterization and general craftsmanship. Marketing details, so vital to confession writers, are covered in depth. Generally one of the most competent works on the subject.

2119. Williams, Nan Schram. *Confess for Profit; Writing and Selling the Personal Story. A Comprehensive Guide.* Los Angeles: Douglas-West Publishers, 1973. 225 pp.

A large part of this book is given over to examples from confession stories written by the author. These tend to pad the text to the point of virtually turning the book into an anthology. Overall, this is a middling effort when compared with the previously cited Palmer.

Articles

2120. Changing confession market. J. Jackson. *Writer,* vol. 88, May 1975, pp. 15-17+.

2121. Choose your title—then confess. E.M. Rogers. *Writer,* vol. 93, February 1980, pp. 25-27.

2122. Confessing on the confessions. Hayes B. Jacobs. *Writer's Digest,* vol. 59, August 1979, pp. 18-21+.

2123. Confession is good for the pocketbook. V.C. Munn. *Writer,* vol. 89, May 1976, pp. 18-20.

2124. Confessions. F.A. Rockwell. *Writer,* vol. 75, October 1962, pp. 24-27.

2125. Confessions are easy, but—. E. Oliphant. *Writer,* vol. 73, May 1960, pp. 15-17.

2126. Confessions buy articles, too! B.Y. O'Dell. *Writer's Digest,* vol. 48, May 1968, pp. 64-65+.

2127. How to write a selling confession story. L. Robins. *Writer's Digest,* vol. 54, July 1974, pp. 17-19.

2128. In-depth market report: the lucrative confessions. L. Ellinwood. *Writer's Digest,* vol. 51, January 1971, pp. 28-30+.

2129. It pays to write confession stories. H. Withrow. *Writer's Digest,* vol. 77, February 1964, pp. 17-21.

2130. Let's confess. Colan Francis. *Writer,* vol. 91, May 1978, pp. 24-27.

2131. Men sell confessions too! P.K. Brown. *Writer's Digest,* vol. 50, August 1970, pp. 26-28+.

2132. Nine points to confession. G. Burk. *Writer,* vol. 93, May 1980, pp. 16-18+.

2133. Sex-less confessions. P. Kehret. *Writer,* vol. 91, October 1978, pp. 18-19+.

2134. Short story market that's always ready for more; confession story writing. P. McQuinn. *Writer's Digest,* vol. 49, June 1969, pp. 53-55.

2135. Six ways to successful confessions. Florence K. Palmer. *Writer,* vol. 82, May 1969, pp. 15-18.

2136. Sixteen tips for confession writers. D. Brookins. *Writer's Digest,* vol. 48, May 1968, pp. 61-63.

2137. Stories for modern romances. H.P. Malmgreen. *Writer,* vol. 79, December 1966, pp. 26-29.

2138. Ten guidelines for salable confessions. Elvira Weaver. *Writer,* vol. 96, June 1983, pp. 16-18+.

2139. Twelve don'ts for confession writers. L. Robins. *Writer,* vol. 87, May 1974, pp. 16-18.

2140. Using the "suppose" technique in confessions. R. Sandler. *Writer,* vol. 95, June 1982, pp. 21-23+.

2141. We eat confessions. Lois Duncan. *Writer,* vol. 79, October 1966, pp. 25-27.

2142. What makes a salable confession? Sin, suffer, and repent formula. J. Jackson. *Writer,* vol. 78, March 1965, pp. 17-22.

2143. Why write confessions? A. Myers, and E. Jones. *Writer,* vol. 83, June 1970, pp. 14-17.

2144. Wringing a good confession out of your writing. J. Grice. *Writer's Digest,* vol. 54, February 1974, p. 9.

2145. Writing confessions. Hayes B. Jacobs. *Writer's Digest,* vol. 59, August 1979, pp. 18-21+.

2146. Writing confessions. P.A. Warady. *Writer,* vol. 86, May 1973, pp. 20-22+.

2147. Writing for the confessions market. R. Beck. *Writer,* vol. 81, May 1968, p. 19.

2148. Writing the confession story today. N. Stoyenoff. *Writer,* vol. 90, October 1977, pp. 26-30.

2149. Writing the male confession. J.D. Harsh. *Writer,* vol. 84, May 1971, pp. 18-19.

Detective, Mystery, and Spy Fiction

"The best time for planning a book is while you're doing the dishes."

—Agatha Christie

Books

2150. Ball, John, editor. *Mystery Story.* San Diego: University of California, 1976. 390 pp.

The history and development of the genre are explored, in general and with regard to categories such as gothic, mystery, the police procedural, and the private-eye mystery, by eighteen seasoned writers, critics, and editors of mystery fiction. Though not intended as a text on writing, this collection makes for productive background reading.

2151. Barzun, Jacques, and Wendell Hertig Taylor. *Catalogue of Crime.* New York: Harper & Row, 1971. 831 pp.

Provides critical annotations for over 7,500 novels, short story collections, studies, biographies, and other books relating to crime and detection. Tells not how to write in this genre, but what has been written in it and about it.

2152. Brabazon, James. *Dorothy L. Sayers; A Biography.* Foreword by P.D. James. Preface by Anthony Fleming. New York: Scribner, 1981. 308 pp.

The life story of the creator of Lord Peter Wimsey is revealed not only by Brabazon's analysis, but through ample quotations from Sayers's letters and other writings which tell of her progress as a mystery writer, playwright, and theologian.

2153. Burack, Abraham Saul. *Writing Suspense and Mystery Fiction.* Boston: Writer, 1977. 341 pp.

More than thirty mystery and suspense authors discuss their craft in this anthology of expert opinions on plot, irony, surprise, pace, setting, characterization, and other elements. Ngaio Marsh, A.A. Fair, Dorothy Sayers, Mary Stewart, and Raymond Chandler are among those included. S.S. Van Dine's "Twenty Rules for Writing Detective Stories" appears also. Two valuable supplements prepared by the American Bar Association, "A Layman's Guide to Law and the Courts" and a "Glossary of Legal Terms," complete the work. This is a revision of Burack's earlier *Writing Detective and Mystery Fiction,* 1945, revised edition, 1967. Several contributors to these earlier anthologies have not been carried over into the present edition.

2154. Cawelti, John George. *Adventure, Mystery, and Romance; Formula Stories as Art and Popular Culture.* Chicago: University of Chicago Press, 1976. 336 pp.

A highly valuable critical analysis which takes into account the cultural importance of formula writing. Contains a wealth of examples.

2155. Champigny, Robert. *What Will Have Happened; A Philosophical and Technical Essay on Mystery Stories.* Bloomington: University of Indiana Press, 1977. 183 pp.

This is a skillful critical study which offers the mystery writer a number of useful technical insights. Citing both recent and classic mystery novels and stories, Champigny defines the limits and possibilities of story, narration, and cryptic elements.

2156. Chandler, Raymond. *Raymond Chandler Speaking.* Boston: Houghton Mifflin, 1962. 271 pp.

These lucid letters and other pieces address the problems and rewards facing the crime fiction writer. They show Chandler's debt to Dashiell Hammet and reflect the concerns of a true literary professional.

2157. Cooper-Clark, Diana. *Designs of Darkness; Interviews with Detective Novelists.* Bowling Green, Ohio: Bowling Green University Press, 1983. 239 pp.

These perceptive interviews were conducted with P.D. James, Peter Lovesey, Margaret Millar, Ross MacDonald, Patricia Highsmith, Janwillem van de Wetering, Julian Symons, Amanda Cross, Dick Francis, Jean Stubbs, Howard Engel, and Anne Perry.

2158. Creasey, John. *John Creasey; Fact or Fiction? A Candid Commentary in Third Person.* With a John Creasey bibliography by R.E. Briney and John Creasey. White Bear Lake, Minnesota: 1969. (Offprint from *The Armchair Detective,* vol. 2, no. 1.)

2159. Dove, George N. *The Police Procedural.* Bowling Green, Ohio: Bowling Green University Popular Press, 1982. 274 pp.

Provides a short history of the genre and then discusses such authors as John Creasey, Ed McBain, and Nicholas Freeling. Though this is a critical work, the treatment of technique will be of immediate value to the working writer.

2160. Freeman, Lucy. *Murder Mystique; Crime Writers on Their Art.* New York: Ungar, 1982. 140 pp.

This uneven potpourri of opinion consists of eleven essays authored by Edward Hoch, D.R. Bensen, and Hillary Waugh, to name a few.

2161. Fugate, Francis L., and Roberta B. Fugate. *Secrets of the World's Best Selling Writer; The Storytelling Techniques of Erle Stanley Gardner.* New York: Morrow, 1980. 352 pp.

The Fugates explore the themes, plots, conflicts, and other techniques that sold over three hundred million copies of Gardner's books.

2162. Gilbert, Michael Francis, and others. *Crime in Good Company; Essays on Criminals and Crime Writing.* Collected on behalf of the Crime Writers' Association. London: Constable, 1959. 242 pp.

Raymond Chandler writes on "The Simple Art of Murder," Eric Ambler on "The Novelist and Films," and so on. These are speculative and thought-provoking selections.

2163. Highsmith, Patricia. *Plotting and Writing Suspense Fiction.* Boston: Writer, 1972. 149 pp.

Highsmith, a widely reviewed crime and suspense novelist, relates in anecdotal and informal style how she gets her ideas for both novels and short stories, how she plots, and how she revises. She relies mainly on her own work for examples, with all the advantages and disadvantages that implies.

Hubert, Karen M. *Teaching and Writing Popular Fiction; Horror, Adventure, Mystery and Romance in the American Classroom.* See entry 1126.

2164. Johnston, Alva. *Case of Erle Stanley Gardner.* New York: William Morrow & Company, 1947. 87 pp.

Originally published in *The Saturday Evening Post,* this is a biographical sketch of a master detective fiction writer. But most important is a revealing account of Gardner's day-to-day living and work habits. Short but essential.

2165. Keating, Henry Reymond Fitzwalter. *Whodunit; A Guide to Crime, Suspense, and Spy Fiction.* New York: Van Nostrand, 1982. 320 pp.

Includes biographical sketches of noteworthy crime fiction authors and essays discussing their work. In addition, a number of crime and suspense masters reveal their own techniques. Among these are P.D. James, Patricia Highsmith, Gregory McDonald, and Len Deighton.

2166. Lambert, Gavin. *The Dangerous Edge.* New York: Grossman, 1975. 272 pp.

> The lives of nine masters of suspense are examined for clues to what shaped their writing, particularly crises that brought them to a "dangerous edge." The lives examined are those of Wilkie Collins, Sir Arthur Conan Doyle, G.K. Chesterton, John Buchan, Eric Ambler, Graham Greene, Georges Simenon, Raymond Chandler, and Alfred Hitchcock.

2167. McAleer, John. *Rex Stout, A Biography.* Boston: Little, Brown, 1977. 621 pp.

> An extended treatment of the literary career of a major American mystery writer. Stout's personality is compared with his detective character Nero Wolfe.

2168. MacDonald, Ross (pseud. of Kenneth Millar). *On Crime Writing; The Writer as Detective Hero. Writing "The Galton Case."* Santa Barbara, California: Capra Press, 1973. 45 pp.

> A modern master of detective fiction places his genre in historical perspective by relating the personalities of fictional detectives to those of their creators. He then discusses his own methods in the context of writing one of his novels, *The Galton Case.*

2169. Mystery Writers of America. *Mystery Writer's Handbook, Newly Revised Edition.* Preface by Lawrence Treat. Cincinnati: Writer's Digest, 1976. 275 pp.

> This anthology gives practical advice on how to plot, how to develop ideas, how to create suspense, how to write good dialogue, and how to revise mystery fiction. Specific types of mysteries are individually discussed under such topics as gothics, soft-cover originals, and true crime stories. A final section deals with agents, legal aspects of writing, and "tricks of the trade." This edition contains twenty new articles plus eight taken from the first edition. Contributors include Rex Stout, John MacDonald, and Hillary Waugh.

2170. Nevins, Francis M., Jr., editor. *Mystery Writer's Art.* Bowling Green, Ohio: Bowling Green University, Popular Press, 1970. 338 pp.

> This anthology, in the words of its editor, "...brings together some of the best writing in recent years on the...subject of crime fiction." Of particular interest to the writer are "The Janus Resolution" by Frank McSherry and "The Writer as Detective Hero" by Ross MacDonald.

2171. Nixon, Joan L. *Writing Mysteries for Young People.* Boston: Writer, 1977. 123 pp.

> Nixon explores, though not in-depth, a variety of techniques that she has used in writing salable mysteries in

such categories as short picture books for preschoolers, mystery short stories for juvenile magazines, novels for 8-to 12-year olds, and young adult mystery novels. An entire chapter is devoted to the problems of beginnings and endings. A discussion of markets, and manuscript lengths for specific markets, completes this serviceable guide.

2172. Rodell, Marie F. *Mystery Fiction; Theory and Technique.* New York: Duell, Sloan, and Pearce, 1943. 320 pp. (Revised edition published by Hermitage House, 1952.)

This early text on the subject retains considerable value as a source of analysis and practical guidance, drawing as it does on examples set by such great mystery writers as Dorothy Sayers and Dashiell Hammett. From a suggestion on developing a basic plot to a discussion of the traits of the typical reader of mysteries, this is a sound and informed approach to writing mystery novels. Users will be aware that attitudes toward sex and violence have changed since it was written.

2173. Winn, Dilys. *Murder Ink; The Mystery Reader's Companion.* New York: Workman Publishing, 1977. 522 pp.

This is a loosely arranged encyclopedia of mystery fiction and fact. The latter covers information about fake passports, laundering money, and techniques of wiretapping. Though sometimes shallow, this work contains valuable background material.

2174. Zeiger, Henry A. *Ian Fleming; The Spy Who Came in with the Gold.* New York: Duell, Sloan, and Pearce, 1966. 150 pp.

This otherwise undistinguished biography contains information about how Fleming came to write the James Bond series, and the chapter "Author at Work" reveals Fleming's day-to-day creative routines. Central to his method was the isolation of his Jamaican retreat, where he wrote the first drafts of most of his novels, free from the social and business distractions of London.

Articles

2175. Advice to crime writers. Lee Wright. *Writer,* vol. 92, May 1979, p. 14.

2176. Agatha Christie on mystery fiction; interview. *Writer,* vol. 79, August 1966, pp. 27-28.

2177. And then the queen died. A.M. Wells. *Writer,* vol. 79, September 1966, pp. 12-14.

2178. Another spring, another murder. M. Rippon. *Writer,* vol. 88, May 1975, pp. 12-14.

2179. Awesome beige typewriter; calling on John D. MacDonald. *Esquire,* vol. 84, August 1975, pp. 68+.

2180. Becoming a novelist. Peter Lovesey. *Writer,* vol. 88, August 1975, pp. 21-23.

2181. Behind the best sellers: Joseph Wambaugh. J. Dunning. *New York Times Book Review,* vol. 83, January 15, 1978, p. 25.

2182. Bill Pronzini (interview). *Armchair Detective,* vol. 11, no. 1, January 1978, pp. 46-48.

2183. Birth of a sleuth. Ngaio Marsh. *Writer,* vol. 90, April 1977, pp. 23-25.

2184. Bond and I; techniques of Ian Fleming; Len Deighton; John Le Carre. S. Eimer. *The Reporter,* vol. 37, July 13, 1967, pp. 55-58.

2185. Breaking and entering. Sue Grafton. *Writer,* vol. 96, January 1983, pp. 16-18+.

2186. Case history of a first novel: writing *The Hand of Solange;* with editoral comment by L.P. Ashmead. M. Rippon. *Writer,* vol. 83, March 1970, pp. 12-16.

2187. Case of Raymond Chandler. Julian Symons. *New York Times Magazine,* December 23, 1973, pp. 12-13+.

2188. Casual notes on the mystery novel. Raymond Chandler. *Writer,* vol. 76, July 1963, pp. 13-16+.

2189. Challenge of detective story conventions. Jonathan Valin. *Writer,* vol. 94, August 1981, pp. 19-21.

2190. Characters for mystery fiction. G.H. Coxe. *Writer,* vol. 72, September 1959, pp. 5-7.

2191. Close-up: Georges Simenon, excuse me, I think I'm about to have a novel; with report. M. Mok. *Life,* vol. 66, May 9, 1969, pp. 43-44+.

2192. Clues to a medal mystery. S. Hacker. *Writer,* vol. 79, November 1966, p. 34.

2193. Clues to writing for the Mysterious Press (from its editor). Michael Seidman. *Writer,* vol. 97, February 1984, pp. 24+.

2194. Conversation wth Rex Stout. *Holiday,* vol. 46, November 1969, pp. 38-39+.

2195. *Created, The Destroyer:* an interview with Warren Murphy. *Armchair Detective,* vol. 11, no. 3, July 1978, pp. 284-286.

2196. Creating a female sleuth. M. Muller. *Writer,* vol. 91, October 1978, pp. 20-22+.

2197. Creating a series character (detective novel character Spencer). R.B. Parker. *Writer,* vol. 94, January 1981, pp. 15-17.

2198. Crime writers convene. R.R. Lingeman. *New York Times Book Review,* vol. 83, April 2, 1978, p. 47.

2199. Death as game. M. Innes. *Esquire,* vol. 63, January 1965, pp. 55-56.

2200. Defense of the bedside pad. W. Brown. *Writer,* vol. 78, september 1965, pp. 15-17.

2201. Detection and the literary art. Jacques Barzun. *New Republic,* vol. 144, April 24, 1961, pp. 17-20.

2202. Detective detected: from Sophocles to Ross MacDonald. Max Byrd. *Yale Review,* vol. 64, October 1974, pp. 72-83.

2203. Detective novel. Catherine Aird. *Writer,* vol. 82, August 1969, pp. 11-14.

2204. Detective novel; tricks and facts. Robert Martin. *Writer,* vol. 75, March 1962, pp. 7-9+.

2205. Dinner with Dorothy Sayers; or, As my whimsy feeds me. *Journal of Popular Culture,* vol. 13, Winter 1979, pp. 434-436.

2206. Do-it-yourself homicide; rules for crime writing. J. Webb. *Writer,* vol. 76, October 1963, pp. 17-20+.

2207. Dorothy L. Sayers and the tidy art of detective fiction. B. G. Harrison. *Ms.,* vol. 3, November 1974, pp. 66-69+.

2208. Editing the mystery and suspense novel. J. Kahn. *Writer,* vol. 79, July 1966, pp. 18-21.

2209. Elements of suspense. Bill Pronzini. *Writer,* vol. 89, February 1976, pp. 14-17.

2210. Elements of the police procedural novel. Rex Burns. *Writer,* vol. 90, July 1977, pp. 14-17.

2211. End game. D.R. Bensen. *Writer,* vol. 85, February 1972, pp. 22-23.

2212. Endless quest for Supermole. Bruce Page. *New Statesman,* vol. 98, September 21, 1979, pp. 414-416.

2213. Essence of suspense. J. McKimmey. *Writer,* vol. 86, June 1973, pp. 14-16+.

2214. Eternal world of mystery and suspense; symposium. Edited by T. Chastain, with introduction by B.A. Bannon. *Publishers Weekly,* vol. 213, March 13, 1978, p. 45.

2215. Excitement for sale. Mildred Gordon and Gordon Gordon. *Writer,* vol. 86, November 1973, pp. 13-15.

2216. Eye spy. O. Ruhen. *Writer,* vol. 76, January 1963, pp. 9-11+.

2217. From puzzles to people: suspense novels. J. Kahn. *Writer,* vol. 82, February 1969, pp. 19-20.

2218. Getting away with murder. Erle Stanley Gardner. *Atlantic,* vol. 215, January 1965, pp. 72-75.

2219. Getting started on mysteries. Janice Law. *Writer,* vol. 93, March 1980, pp. 17-19.

2220. Gregory McDonald (interview). *Armchair Detective,* vol. 12, no. 2, Spring 1979, pp. 134-135.

2221. Have typewriter, should travel. E. Lacy. *Writer,* vol. 77, April 1964, pp. 16-17+.

2222. Have you tried murder? Peter Lovesey. *Writer,* vol. 96, April 1983, pp. 9-11+.

2223. How I began; excerpt from *An Autobiography.* Agatha Christie. *Writer,* vol. 91, June 1978, pp. 18-21.

2224. How I sold a series of paperback mystery novels. M.A. Avallone, Jr. *Writer's Digest,* vol. 51, January 1971, pp. 24-25+.

2225. How to devise an ingenius plot. R. Gatenby. *Writer,* vol. 88, October 1975, pp. 11-14.

2226. How to keep the reader on the edge of the chair. Joan Aiken. *Writer,* vol. 86, March 1973, pp. 9-13.

2227. How to tell Sam Spade from Philip Marlowe from Lew Archer. R.R. Lingeman. *Esquire,* vol. 84, August 1975, pp. 62-65.

2228. How to write a good suspense novel: beginnings and endings. J. Kahn. *Writer,* vol. 86, January 1973, pp. 18-21.

2229. Humor in the mystery novel. D. Gilman. *Writer,* vol. 91, July 1978, pp. 13-15.

2230. I-can't-put-it-down factor. B.H. Deal. *Writer,* vol. 89, May 1976, pp. 9-11.

2231. I care who killed Roger Ackroyd. J. Leonard. *Esquire,* vol. 84, August 1975, pp. 60-61.

2232. I couldn't put it down. Phyllis A. Whitney. *Writer,* vol. 86, April 1973, pp. 11-14+.

2233. I spy, you spy, he spies. J.B. Breslin. *America,* vol. 131, September 7, 1974, pp. 100+.

2234. Ideas for mystery fiction. Stanley Ellin. *Writer,* vol. 80, December 1967, pp. 11-13.

2235. I'm old-fashioned (mysteries). Isaac Asimov. *Writer,* vol. 91, April 1978, pp. 20-21.

2236. Inner suspense story. Marcia Muller. *Writer,* vol. 96, December 1983, pp. 23-25+.

2237. Inside the mystery novel. Stanley Ellin. *Writer,* vol. 92, December 1979, pp. 9-11+.

2238. Invention, imagination, and reality; excerpt from introduction to *Passenger to Frankfurt.* Agatha Christie. *Writer,* vol. 85, June 1972, pp. 22-23.

2239. Is there gold in your reject pile? (detective stories). Patricia McGerr. *Writer,* vol. 89, March 1976, pp. 15-17+.

2240. Issue is murder; symposium. *New Republic,* vol. 175, July 31, 1976, pp. 21-32.

2241. Issue is murder; symposium. *New Republic,* vol. 179, July 22, 1978, pp. 26-39.

2242. It came as no mystery: crime writers want publishers to sell more books; international Congress of Crime Writers; symposioum. *Publishers Weekly,* vol. 213, March 27, 1978, pp. 32+.

2243. It's a mystery. J. Thompson. *Harper's Magazine,* vol. 243, October 1971, pp. 120-125.

2244. It's Mickey Spillane, all right! interview. *Writer's Digest,* vol. 56, September 1976, pp. 18-20.

2245. It's the police, not the procedure. Gerald Petievich. *Writer,* vol. 94, September 1981, pp. 13-14+.

2246. Jay Bennett (interview). *Armchair Detective,* vol. 10, no. 4, October 1977, pp. 342-346.

2247. Jay Bennett (interview). *English Journal,* vol. 65, May 1976, pp. 86-88.

2248. Keeping the reader breathless. A. Chamberlain. *Writer,* vol. 90, August 1977, pp. 20-22+.

2249. Labyrinth of espionage (interview). John Le Carre. *World Press Review,* vol. 27, May 1980, p. 62.

2250. Le Carre's circus: lamplighters, moles, and others of that ilk (interview). John Le Carre. *Listener,* vol. 102, September 13, 1979, pp. 339-340.

2251. Lure of the adventure novel. Gordon Gordon. *Writer,* vol. 97, March 1984, pp. 7-9+.

2252. Madame Sleuth confesses; D. Uhnak, creator of Christie Opara. M. Meade. *McCalls,* vol. 98, July 1971, p. 43.

2253. Make your reader wonder. N.A. Hintze. writer, vol. 85, November 1972, pp. 18-20.

2254. Making crime pay. C.W. Sasser. *Writer's Digest,* vol. 57, September 1977, pp. 29-32.

2255. Making crime pay. John B. Hilton. *Writer,* vol 97. November 1984, pp. 13-14+.

2256. Mastering the mystery story. Lawrence Treat. *Writer's Digest,* vol. 48, January 1968, pp. 17-21+.

2257. Masters of the white-collar homicide; co-authors of Emma Lathan and R.B. Dominic mysteries. *Forbes,* vol. 120, December 1, 1977, p. 89.

2258. Moonstone and mousetrap. Herbert R. Mayes. *Saturday Review,* vol. 53, October 17, 1970, pp. 4+.

2259. Murder is my business, sort of; ladies who write of murder. Lee Wright. *McCalls,* vol. 96, April 1969, pp. 97-98.

2260. Mysteries within mysteries. P. Moyes. *Writer,* vol. 89, October 1976, pp. 20-22.

2261. Mystery. E. Fenton. *Horn Book,* vol. 44, June 1968, pp. 277-280.

2262. Mystery novel or crime novel? Stanley Ellin. *Writer,* vol. 86, January 1973, pp. 22-24.

2263. Mystery revisited. J. Davey. *The Reporter,* vol. 20, April 16, 1959, pp. 37-38.

2264. Mystery writers' organizations. Edward Hoch. *Publishers Weekly,* vol. 213, March 13, 1978, p. 55.

2265. Nancy Drew and the secret fort. L. Conger. *Writer,* vol. 89, February 1976, pp. 9-10.

2266. Narrative murder. L. Bersani. *Yale Review,* vol. 59, March 1970, pp. 376-390.

2267. New Mystery. Joseph Hansen. *Writer,* vol. 86, September 1973, pp. 15-17+.

2268. Nine most devilish murders. S. Edmiston. *Esquire,* vol. 84, August 1975, pp. 66-67+.

2269. No mirrors, please! D. Gardiner. *Writer,* vol. 77, January 1964, pp. 16-19.

2270. Not to be overlooked. Distinguished writers in the field of crime fiction nominate authors and individual works which they feel have been underrated or unjustly neglected. Eric Ambler and others. *Times Literary Supplement,* June 5, 1981, pp. 632-633.

2271. Notes on the suspense novel. H.Q. Masur. *Writer,* vol. 88, September 1975, pp. 12-14+.

2272. Of spies and stories. P. Henissart. *Writer,* vol. 91, May 1978, pp. 15-18.

2273. On the track of *Murder Ink.* Sue Arnold. *Observer Magazine,* September 12, 1976, pp. 25-26.

2274. One clue at a time. P.D. James. *Writer,* vol. 97, February 1984, pp. 9-11.

2275. Pen to paper. Catherine Aird. *Writer,* vol. 84, October 1971, pp. 14-16.

2276. Planning a mystery back to front. Stanley Ellin. *Writer,* vol. 79, December 1966, pp. 11-13+.

2277. Planning and plotting the detective story. Catherine Aird. *Writer,* vol. 96, March 1983, pp. 15-17.

2278. Plot and life in the police procedural. Rex Burns. *Writer,* vol. 94, March 1981, pp. 11-14.

2279. Plots and people. Hillary Waugh. *Writer,* vol. 82, December 1969, pp. 9-11+.

2280. Plots in crime fiction. M. Underwood. *Writer,* vol. 87, December 1974, pp. 17-19+.

2281. Plotting a murder. Joseph Hansen. *Writer,* vol. 93, April 1980, pp. 16-19.

2282. Plotting the mystery short story. Edward Hoch. *Writer,* vol. 93, May 1980, pp. 13-15.

2283. Plotting the short mystery story. M. Maron. *Writer,* vol. 89, June 1976, pp. 26-28+.

2284. Poirot's first case; excerpt from *An Autobiography.* Agatha Christie. *New York Times Magazine,* September 18, 1977, pp. 41-42+.

2285. Private eye as illegal hero. G.V. Higgins. *Esquire,* vol. 78, December 1972, pp. 348+.

2286. Psychology of mystery story writing. M.A. DeFord. *Writer,* vol. 77, June 1964, pp. 12-14.

2287. PW interviews: D.B. Hughes. *Publishers Weekly,* vol. 213, March 13, 1978, pp. 6-7.

2288. PW interviews: D.M. Disney and I. Taylor. *Publishers Weekly,* vol. 204, August 13, 1973, pp. 24-25.

2289. PW interviews: John Le Carre. *Publishers Weekly,* vol. 212, September 19, 1977, pp. 56-58.

2290. PW interviews: P.D. James. *Publishers Weekly,* vol. 209, January 5, 1976, pp. 8-9.

2291. Research for the mystery writer. F. Crane. *Writer,* vol. 78, February 1965, pp. 15-17.

2292. Researching and writing the fact-crime book. Clark Howard. *Writer,* vol. 97, June 1984, pp. 16-18+.

2293. Richard Lockridge (interview). *Armchair Detective,* vol. 11, no. 4, October 1978, pp. 382-393.

2294. Road to a best seller. S. Howatch. *Writer,* vol. 84, December 1971, pp. 11-12.

2295. Ross MacDonald; the prince in the poorhouse. B. Cook. *Catholic World,* vol. 214, October 1971, pp. 27-30.

2296. Routines and rules for the police procedural. L. O'Donnell. *Writer,* vol. 91, February 1978, pp. 17-19+.

2297. *Saint* on T.V. L. Charteris. *Writer,* vol. 79, February 1966, pp. 19-21+.

2298. Sayers, Lord Peter, and God. C. Heilbrun. *American Scholar,* vol. 37, Spring 1968, pp. 324-330+.

2299. Sociology and the thriller: the case of Dashiell Hammett. D. Glover. *Sociological Review,* vol. 27, February 1979, pp. 21-40.

2300. Sociology of sudden death. Julian Symons. *Times Literary Supplement,* January 9, 1981, p. 30.

2301. Some like it crude; some like it subtle. Richard Lockridge. *Writer,* vol. 74, October 1961, pp. 10-11+.

2302. Spy story; excerpt from introduction to *The Spy Who Came in from the Cold.* John Le Carre. *New York Times Book Review,* vol. 83, March 12, 1978, pp. 3+.

2303. Start with an answer. Patricia McGerr. *Writer,* vol. 96, June 1983, pp. 13-15.

2304. Story behind the book: *The Day of the Jackal* (Frederick Forsyth). *Publishers Weekly,* vol. 200, August 9, 1971, pp. 34-35.

2305. Story that goes some place. Mildred Gordon and Gordon Gordon. *Writer,* vol. 79, November 1966, pp. 11-14.

2306. Strike a note, and hold it! D.J. Marlowe. *Writer,* vol. 76, August 1963, pp. 20-21.

2307. Suspense and a sense of place. E. Ogilvie. *Writer,* vol. 89, September 1976, pp. 14-16+.

2308. Suspense in fiction. E. Ogilvie. *Writer,* vol. 83, January 1970, pp. 11-14.

2309. Suspense is where the action is. B. Garfield. *Writer,* vol. 89, December 1976, pp. 27-31.

2310. Suspense: rules and non-rules. Patricia Highsmith. *Writer,* vol. 77, November 1964, pp. 9-12.

2311. Suspense short story. Patricia Highsmith. *Writer,* vol. 79, March 1966, pp. 9-12.

2312. Suspense, suspense, suspense. R.M. Stern. *Writer,* vol. 88, March 1975, pp. 11-13.

2313. Suspense writing. Mary Higgins Clark. *Writer,* vol. 93, September 1980, pp. 9-12.

2314. Take it seriesly! (sic) Honey West, lady private investigator. S. Fickling. *Writer,* vol. 79, May 1966, pp. 18-20.

2315. Taking the mystery out of writing mysteries. Jean Hager. *Writer's Digest,* vol. 60, October 1980, pp. 44-47.

2316. Talk with John Le Carre. *New York Times Book Review,* vol. 88, March 13, 1983, pp. 1+.

2317. Ten rules for suspense fiction. B. Garfield. *Writer's Digest,* vol. 53, February 1973, pp. 24-25+.

2318. There's a dividend in mysteries. Patricia McGerr. *Writer,* vol. 78, April 1965, pp. 9-11.

2319. Thriller is a novel. Ellis Peters. *Writer,* vol. 85, March 1972, pp. 9-11.

2320. Thriller writing. Andrew York. *Writer,* vol. 92, February 1979, pp. 20+.

2321. To a would-be detective story writer; an open letter. J. Porter. *Writer,* vol. 87, August 1974, pp. 14-16.

2322. Today's short suspense fiction. D. Olson. *Writer,* vol. 87, October 1974, pp. 20-23.

2323. Travels with Le Carre; writing spy thriller, *The Honourable Schoolboy. Newsweek,* vol. 90, Octobber 10, 1977, p. 102.

2324. Tricks and traps in writing suspense fiction. Jean L. Backus. *Writer,* vol. 90, March 1977, pp. 11-14.

2325. Using technology in mysteries. J. Lutz. *Writer,* vol. 91, August 1978, pp. 16-18.

2326. Verisimilitude in the crime story. A.F. Nussbaum. *Writer,* vol. 84, January 1971, pp. 13-15+.

2327. View from the middle window. Dorothy S. Davis. *Publishers Weekly,* vol. 213, March 13, 1978, pp. 46-47.

2328. Viewpoint and the mystery short story. Stanley Ellin. *Writer,* vol. 76, May 1963, pp. 7-9.

2329. Viewpoint: crime stories. Russell Davies. *Times Literary Supplement,* June 5, 1981, p. 631.

2330. W.T. Ballard: an interview. *Armchair Detective,* vol. 12, Winter 1979, no. 1, pp. 14-19.

2331. Way to maintain success. D. Wheatley. *Writer,* vol. 82, October 1969, pp. 22-24.

2332. We care. Roger N. Callendar. *New York Times Book Review,* vol. 83, July 23, 1978, pp. 3+.

2333. Whatever happened to Sam Spade? The private eye in fact and fiction. C.D. May. *Atlantic,* vol. 236, August 1975, pp. 27-35.

2334. Who is your hero? D. MacKenzie. *Writer,* vol. 81, January 1968, pp. 18-19.

2335. Why *Mousetrap* catches us all. Christopher Booker. *Daily Telegraph,* December 3, 1977, p. 8.

2336. Without bent wire or stethoscope. D. MacKenzie. *Writer,* vol. 74, August 1961, pp. 20+.

2337. World of action; suspense novel. James Lowry Clifford. *Writer,* vol. 80, November 1967, pp. 17-18.

2338. Write me an adventure novel. B. Cassiday. *Writer,* vol. 82, March 1969, pp. 11-14.

2339. Writing a first mystery novel. M.R. Reno. *Writer,* vol. 89, July 1976, pp. 18-20.

2340. Writing a mystery. P. Moyes. *Writer,* vol. 83, April 1970, pp. 11-14.

2341. Writing a mystery novel. Stanley Ellin. *Writer,* vol. 73, November 1960, pp. 7-10.

2342. Writing a thriller. Bill Granger. *Writer,* vol. 97, April 1984, pp. 9-11+.

2343. Writing action fiction. Desmond Bagley. *Writer,* vol. 86, May 1973, pp. 11-13.

2344. Writing and selling the police procedural novel. C. Wilcox. *Writer,* vol. 89, January 1976, pp. 20-22+.

2345. Writing mystery novels. Dick Francis. *Writer,* vol. 96, August 1983, pp. 11-12.

2346. Writing suspense. Robert Fish. *Writer,* vol. 92, September 1979, pp. 14-15.

2347. Writing the juvenile mystery. Phyllis A. Whitney. *Writer,* vol. 76, April 1963, pp. 14-18.

2348. Writing the library whodunit; *Dewey Decimated.* C.A. Goodrum. *American Libraries,* vol. 8, April 1977, pp. 194-196.

2349. Writing the mystery short-short. Bill Pronzini. *Writer,* vol. 90, December 1977, pp. 19-23.

2350. Writing the mystery short story. J. Gores. *Writer,* vol. 84, August 1971, pp. 13-16+.

2351. Writing the mystery short story. Edward Hoch. *Writer,* vol. 87, April 1974, pp. 16-18.

2352. Writing the police-routine novel. D. Shannon. *Writer,* vol. 80, March 1967, pp. 11-13+.

2353. Writing the suspense-adventure novel. Clive Cussler. *Writer,* vol. 91, February 1978, pp. 11-14.

Gothic and Horror Literature

"It is far harder to kill a phantom than a reality."
—Virginia Woolf

Books

2354. Bayer-Berenbaum, Linda. *The Gothic Imagination; Expansion in Gothic Literature and Art.* Madison, New Jersey: Fairleigh Dickinson University Press, 1982. 155 pp.

Provides a detailed analysis of several Gothic works, including Mary Shelley's *Frankenstein* and Victoria Holt's *On the Night of the Seventh Moon.*

See also the chapter on Detective, Mystery, and Spy Fiction (page 181) for book annotations containing references to Gothic and horror literature.

Articles

2355. Character and humor in gothics. Elizabeth Peters. *Writer,* vol. 89, November 1976, pp. 15-17.

2356. From Jane to Germaine, with love; the gothic novel. R. Minudri. *Library Journal,* vol. 98, February 15, 1973, pp. 658-659.

2357. Gothic fiction and the grotesque. E.M. Novak. *Novel,* vol. 13, Fall 1979, pp. 50-67.

2358. Gothic possibilities. N.N. Holland and L.F. Sherman. *New Literary History,* vol. 8, Winter 1977, pp. 279-294.

2359. Help! Alicia is caught in the arms of the headstrong lord of Stonecliffe Manor and I can't stop reading.... A. Barry. *Glamour,* vol. 76, July 1978, pp. 136-137+.

2360. Heroine doesn't have to be an idiot. W.D. Roberts. *Writer,* vol. 88, January 1975, pp. 12-14.

2361. Horror market writer and the ten bears. Stephen King. *Writer's Digest,* vol. 53, November 1973, pp. 10-13.

2362. How to write a gothic novel. H. Rogan. *Harper's,* vol. 250, May 1975, pp. 45-47.

2363. Imagery and the third eye. Stephen King. *Writer,* vol. 93, October 1980, pp. 11-14+.

2364. Jay Anson, the man who wrote *The Amityville Horror. Writer's Digest,* vol. 59, March 1979, pp. 23-26.

2365. Monk as criminal; Italian villains in the gothic novel. J.J. Navone. *Commonweal,* vol. 98, July 27, 1973, pp. 407-410.

2366. Narrative distance in *Frankenstein.* Richard Dunn. *Studies in the Novel,* vol. 6, 1974, pp. 408-417.

2367. Northern gothic. F. Baldanza. *Southern Review,* vol. 10, July 1974, pp. 566-582.

2368. On the writing of ghost stories; excerpt from address, November, 1967. M.A. Polland. *Horn Book,* vol. 44, April 1968, pp. 147-150.

2369. Plotting the gothic novel. Elizabeth Peters. *Writer,* vol. 93, October 1980, pp. 18-21+.

2370. Realism in modern gothics. S. Howatch. *Writer,* vol. 87, May 1974, pp. 11-13.

2371. Recommended ghost stories. R. Rosenblatt. *New Republic,* vol. 173, November 1, 1975, pp. 39-40.

2372. Scaring yourself silly. Phyllis Naylor. *Writer,* vol. 92, May 1979, pp. 11-14.

2373. Selling ghost stories. Pauline Saltzman. *Writer's Digest,* vol. 58, September 1978, p. 24.

2374. Survival of the gothic response. J.M. Keech. *Studies in the Novel,* vol. 6, Summer 1974, pp. 130-144.

2375. Ultimate in horror. J.N. Williamson. *Writer,* vol. 96, May 1983, pp. 7-9+.

2376. When you write a gothic. E. Lee. *Writer,* vol. 86, May 1973, pp. 17-19+.

2377. Willing suspension of disbelief. Elizabeth Peters. *Writer,* vol. 87, February 1974, pp. 15-17.

2378. Witches and aspirin; Stephen King (interview). *Writer's Digest,* vol. 57, June 1977, pp. 26-27.

2379. Writing and selling the gothic novel. J.L. Roberts. *Writer's Digest,* vol. 53, January 1973, pp. 25-27.

2380. Writing from the dark side. The horror short story. Steve Rasnic Tem. *Writer,* vol. 97, May 1984, pp. 16-19+.

2381. Writing the gothic novel. Phyllis A. Whitney. *Writer,* vol. 80, February 1967, pp. 9-13+.

Romance

"Love—the quest
Marriage—the conquest
Divorce—the inquest."

— Helen Rowland

Books

2382. Barnhart, Helene. *Writing Romance Fiction—For Love and Money.* Cincinnati: Writer's Digest, 1983. 272 pp.

Stresses plot development, character appeal, conflict, research for authenticity, and marketing. In addition, this serviceable introduction provides reading lists, exercises, and advice from "name authors in the field." Barnhart is a veteran romance novelist and teacher.

2383. Biederman, Jerry, and Tom Silberkeit, editors. *Your First Romance.* By Jennifer Blake, Norah Lofts, Johanna Lindsey, Alice Morgan, Barbara Michaels, Nora Roberts, and others. Introduction by Kathryn Falk. New York: St. Martin's Press, 1984. 154 pp.

This workbook approach offers beginning ideas for twenty separate romance mini-works from twenty romance novel authors with the expectation that the user will be stimulated to complete them. Also included are sample publishers' tip sheets and a directory of romantic novel publishers.

2384. Falk, Kathryn, editor. *How to Write a Romance and Get It Published; With Intimate Advice from the World's Most Popular Romance Writers.* New York: Crown, 1983. 380 pp.

Draws on what Falk considers the "best" writing about romance fiction. Janet Dailey explains her filmstrip method, Jayne Castle writes on the subject of beginnings, and Alice Morgan and Donna Vitek discuss sexuality and sensuality.

Hubert, Karen M. *Teaching and Writing Popular Fiction: Horror, Adventure, Mystery, and Romance in the American Classroom.* See entry 1126.

2385. Kent, Jean, and Candace Shelton. *The Romance Writers' Phrase Book.* New York: Putnam, 1984. 144 pp.

On the assumption that the correct descriptive phrase can add what is called "romantic tension," the authors have provided over 3,000 short phrases that can be used to describe everything from body movements, "he came close, looking down at her intensely," to voices, "her voice rose an octave." An appendix covers a variety of color terms: twenty for green, twenty-three for blue, and so on. Perhaps a suitable subtitle would be Cliches; break glass in case of mental brownout.

2386. Lowery, Marilyn M. *How to Write Romance Novels That Sell.* New York: Rawson Wade, 1983. 256 pp.

A successful romance novelist who writes under the name of Philippa Castle quotes from and comments upon the works of other authors in this genre to illustrate a variety of techniques. Other features include lists of publishers, reference materials, and organizations of interest to romance writers. Considered by several reviewers to be the best available introduction to the subject.

2387. MacManus, Yvonne. *You Can Write a Romance and Get It Published.* New York: Pocket Books, 1983. 122 pp.

As the title would suggest this "how-to" approach addresses such basics as manuscript preparation, dealing with publishers, and the fundamental aspects of the romance novel.

Articles

2388. Characterization in the romance novel. Laurie McBain. *Writer,* vol. 96, May 1983, pp. 10-12.

2389. Cooking up the teen romance novel. Helen Cavanagh. *Writer's Digest,* vol. 62, May 1982, pp. 43-45.

2390. Guess who writes 70,000 words a week, publishes 24 books a year, and says "Me Tarzan, you Jane" works best in sex scenes (Barbara Cartland). Arturo F. Gonzalez, Jr. *Writer's Digest,* vol. 59, June 1979, pp. 22-24.

2391. "Had-I-but-known:" how to use it in plotting romantic suspense (part 1). Elizabeth Peters. *Writer,* vol. 96, September 1983, pp. 9-12+.

2392. "Had-I-but-known:" how to use it in plotting romantic suspense (part 2). Elizabeth Peters. *Writer,* vol. 96, October 1983, pp. 24-26+.

2393. Historical romances. D. Winston. *Writer,* vol. 91, November 1978, pp. 11-14.

2394. Innocence of Eden—almost; writing the light romance. Linda Jacobs. *Writer,* vol. 87, June 1974, pp. 15-18.

2395. Love stories that solve problems. H.L. Coffer. *Writer,* vol. 89, April 1976, pp. 14-16+.

2396. Paperback historical romance (views of editors and publishers). J.A. Glass and others. *Writer,* vol. 90, April 1977, pp. 33-35, May 1977, p. 18.

2397. Paperbacks: romance for sale. Elizabeth Jenkins. *Sunday Times Magazine,* June 5, 1977, pp. 14-15.

2398. Romance book publishers. *Writer,* vol. 97, July 1984, pp. 43-44.

2399. Romance market. *Writer's Digest,* vol. 64, January 1984, p. 33.

2400. Romance roundup: how and where to sell romance novels. Jean M. Fredette. *Writer's Digest,* vol. 64, January 1984, pp. 31-32+.

2401. Selling the regency romance. Donna Meyer. *Writer,* vol. 97, August 1984, pp. 18-21.

2402. Story is a love affair. N.B. Owen. *Writer,* vol. 75, October 1962, pp. 22-23.

2403. Writing romantic short stories. R. Pilcher. *Writer,* vol. 93, November 1980, pp. 16-17+.

2404. Writing teen romances. J.C. Miner. *Writer,* vol. 95, July 1982, pp. 18-20.

2405. Writing the category romance. Barbara Delinsky. *Writer,* vol. 96, December 1983, pp. 16-19+.

2406. Writing the historical romance. Robyn Carr. *Writer's Digest,* vol. 63, July 1983, pp. 38-40.

2407. Writing the romantic saga. Douglas K. Hall. *Writer,* vol. 91, August 1978, pp. 13-15.

Historical Fiction

"Gone today, here tomorrow."

—Alfred Knopf

Books

Marston, Doris K. *A Guide to Writing History.* See entry 4256.

Articles

2408. Anyone for history? J. Potter. *Writer,* vol. 85, September 1972, pp. 16-17+.

2409. Choosing an historical character. Norah Lofts. *Writer,* vol. 85, December 1972, pp. 21-22+.

2410. Creating a sense of immediacy. Marilyn Durham. *Writer,* vol. 97, January 1984, pp. 12-14+.

2411. Dimensions in time. C. Horovitz. *Horn Book,* vol. 38, June 1962, pp. 255-267.

2412. Exclusive interview with Frances Parkinson Keyes. *Writer's Digest,* vol. 49, October 1969, pp. 56-59.

2413. Fiction of history. Mary Renault. *London Magazine,* vol. 18, March 1979, pp. 52-57.

2414. Fictional history. *Times Literary Supplement,* vol. 3114, November 3, 1961, p. 789.

2415. Finding the straw for the bricks. Norah Lofts. *Writer,* vol. 75, July 1962, pp. 17-19.

2416. Getting into historical fiction. J. Sanders. *Writer,* vol. 79, August 1966, pp. 18-22.

2417. Gold in history. F.A. Seward. *Writer,* vol. 75, September 1962, pp. 22-23.

2418. Growth of a saga. J.A. Hodge. *Writer,* vol. 91, April 1978, pp. 22-25.

2419. Historian as artist. Barbara Tuchman. *Writer,* vol. 81, February 1968, pp. 15-17+.

2420. Historical fiction, its infinite variety. Dee Brown. *Writer,* vol. 96, October 1983, pp. 11-14.

2421. Historical novel: violent inventions... Robert Hewison. *Times Literary Supplement,* August 28, 1981, p. 991.

2422. Historical novels. S. Marcus. *Harper's Magazine,* vol. 248, March 1974, pp. 85-90.

2423. Historical romances. D. Winston. *Writer,* vol. 91, November 1978, pp. 11-14.

2424. History and fiction. C. Gavin. *Writer,* vol. 86, February 1973, pp. 16-18+.

2425. History as fiction. Leah Lenerman. *History Today,* vol. 30, January 1980, pp. 52-55.

2426. History in fiction. Mary Renault. *Times Literary Supplement,* March 23, 1973, pp. 315-316.

2427. History is fiction. Jill Paton Walsh. *Horn Book,* vol. 48, February 1972, pp. 17-23.

2428. Imagining the past. M. Renault. *Times Literary Supplement,* no. 3781, August 23, 1974, pp. 893-894.

2429. Making history come alive in fiction. Parris Afton Bonds. *Writer,* vol. 96, August 1983, pp. 17-19.

2430. On writing historical fiction. J. Fritz. *Horn Book,* vol. 43, October 1967, pp. 565-570.

2431. Paperback historical romance (views of editors and publishers). J.A. Glass and others. *Writer,* vol. 90, April 1977, pp. 33-35; May 1977, p. 18.

2432. Paperbacks: romance for sale. Elizabeth Jenkins. *Sunday Times Magazine,* June 5, 1977, pp. 14-15.

2433. Present uses for the past: the novelist as historian. James C. Simmons and Robert Lee Wolff. *Times Literary Supplement,* December 13, 1974, p. 1404.

2434. Reader as eye-witness of the past. W.O. Steele. *Writer,* vol. 78, March 1965, pp. 15-16+.

2435. Revising a historical novel. C. Holland. *Writer,* vol. 82, October 1969, pp. 17-19+.

2436. Setting in the historical novel. Jane Gilmore Rushing. *Writer,* vol. 97, September 1984, pp. 13-15.

2437. Versions of the past. H.B. Henderson. 3rd Review. *New Republic,* vol. 171, October 19, 1974, pp. 20-22.

2438. Vidal to Vidal: on misusing the past. Gore Vidal. *Harper's,* vol. 231, October 1965, pp. 162-164.

2439. What shall we tell the children? Mark Cohen. *History Today,* vol. 29, December 1979, pp. 845-846.

2440. With the help of my reader. J.L. Latham. *Writer,* vol. 75, December 1962, pp. 19-20+.

2441. Writers and history: my own case. R. Drake. *Christian Century,* vol. 90, December 26, 1973, pp. 1275-1276.

2442. Writing historical novels. J.A. Hodge. *Writer,* vol. 85, June 1972, pp. 15-18.

2443. Writing of historical novels; excerpt from address, August 1968. H. Burton. *Horn Book,* vol. 45, June 1969, pp. 271-277.

2444. Writing the historical romance. Robyn Carr. *Writer's Digest,* vol. 63, July 1983, pp. 38-40.

2445. Writing the romantic saga. Douglas K. Hall. *Writer,* vol. 91, August 1978, pp. 13-15.

2446. You-are-thereness. G. Bristow. *Writer,* vol. 72, October 1959, pp. 8-9+.

Humor, Including Light Verse and Greeting Cards

"Poets aren't very useful. Because they aren't consumeful or very produceful."

—Ogden Nash

Books

2447. Armour, Richard. *Writing Light Verse and Prose Humor.* Boston: Writer, 1980. 141 pp.

A master humorist and mirthful verse writer reveals his craft. From getting ideas, mastering meter, and developing marketable rhyme to beginnings and endings, this short authoritative text by the dean of humorous poetry will inform and reward.

2448. Barr, June. *Writing and Selling Greeting Card Verse.* Boston: Writer, 1969. 114 pp.

Covers the generation of ideas, writing methods, taboos, and marketing strategies.

2449. Berger, Phil. *The Last Laugh; The World of Stand-Up Comics.* New York: Morrow, 1975. 377 pp.

A collection of interviews and comic routines intended to shed light on the efforts of Adam Keefe, Robert Klein, Shelly Berman, Dick Gregory, and others.

2450. Blistein, Elmer M. *Comedy in Action.* Durham, North Carolina: Duke University Press, 1964. 146 pp.

Defines types of humor and comedic characters and provides examples for each.

Burack, Sylvia K., editor. *How to Write and Sell Short Fillers, Light Verse, and Short Humor.* See entry 2813.

2451. Chadwick, H. Joseph. *Greeting Card Writer's Handbook.* Cincinnati: Writer's Digest, 1975. 268 pp.

Chadwick and eight other greeting card experts survey markets, sources of ideas, humor, and editorial inside information. Containing hundreds of examples of top-rated greeting cards, this well-organized introduction covers inspiration, humor, rhyme and meter, editorial viewpoints, juveniles, and marketing. Chadwick was editor of Barker Greeting Cards as well as having been a freelance greeting card writer.

2452. Esar, Evan. *Twenty Thousand Quips and Quotes.* New York: Doubleday, 1968. 908 pp.

These wisecracks and witticisms will serve as references and will provide inspiration for humorous writers of all kinds.

2453. Fisher, Seymour, and Rhoda Fisher. *Pretend the World Is Funny and Forever; A Psychological Analysis of Comedians, Clowns, and Actors.* Hillsdale, New Jersey: Erlbaum, 1981. 252 pp.

Considered by *Choice* to be "...a major contribution in the study of humor," this work provides a detailed inquiry about actors, stage comedians, and other "humor producers." It not only discusses the methods and personalities of those who make us laugh, but also provides much valuable information about those of us who do the laughing and why.

2454. Goeller, Carl G. *Writing and Selling Greeting Cards.* Boston: Writer, 1980. 151 pp.

Written by the director of the American Greeting Cards Corporation, this work addresses themes, variety, and detailed marketing considerations. "Sound advice and specific inside information on the demands of the greeting-card industry for prospective free-lancers," *Booklist.*

2455. Hardt, Lorraine. *How to Make Money Writing Greeting Cards.* New York: Frederick Fell, 1968. 180 pp.

This analysis of verse forms, types of greetings, unmentionable subjects, and dealing with greeting card company editors is filled with anecdotes about approaches that failed and succeeded.

2456. Hohman, E.J., and Norma Leary. *The Greeting Card Handbook; What to Write, How to Write It, Where to Sell It.* New York: Barnes & Noble, 1981. 124 pp.

2457. Lax, Eric. *On Being Funny; Woody Allen and Comedy.* New York: McKay, 1975. 243 pp.

The techniques of Allen's stand-up routines, his working habits, and his filmscripts are analyzed for comic success by Lax, who spent two years observing and interviewing Allen.

Leacock, Stephen B. *How to Write.* See entry 3970.

2458. Markow, Jack. *Cartoonist's and Gag Writer's Handbook.* Cincinnati: Writer's Digest, 1967. 157 pp.

A successful cartoonist and gag writer discusses and illustrates techniques and sources of inspiration.

2459. Perret, Gene. *How to Hold Your Audience with Humor; A Guide to More Effective Speaking.* Cincinnati: Writer's Digest, 1982. 280 pp.

A veteran comedy writer (for Bob Hope and others) shows how to keep your audience laughing, learning, and listening, how a touch of wit increases your audience's listening power and brings you recognition and respect, why a serious theme doesn't rule out humor, adapting your material to fit your audience, and types of humor to avoid.

2460. ————. *How to Write and Sell (Your Sense of) Humor.* Cincinnati: Writer's Digest, 1982. 264 pp.

Written by a producer and writer who has worked with Carol Burnett and Bob Hope, this lively and comprehensive work addresses a wide variety of comedy situations from one-liners to sit-com scripts. It tells how to stimulate ideas, how to build routines, and finally how to be funny. It is filled with humorous anecdotes and instructive script examples.

2461. Sandman, Larry. *Guide to Greeting Card Writing.* Cincinnati: Writer's Digest, 1980. 242 pp.

These essays by Larry Sandman, Laurie Kohl, Bernice Gourse, Patricia Emme, Dick Lorenz, and other greeting card writers and editorial professionals zero in on specific kinds of card writing, such as personal relationship, inspirational, juvenile, humorous, and studio. Four of the essays deal with humor and humorous verse writing, while four others cover business aspects, marketing, and author-editor relationships. This is an indispensable work for those who would know the techniques and markets for such writing.

2462. Schaeffer, Neil. *The Art of Laughter.* New York: Columbia, 1981. 166 pp.

Called by *Choice,* "...one of the more pleasant and sensible attempts..." at a definition of humor, this work is supported by examples from Shakespeare to Lenny Bruce. Cues and contexts are examined, but the ultimate question of human laughter remains a mystery.

Articles

2463. Anyone for light verse?. Richard Armour. *Writer,* vol. 85, April 1972, pp. 22-24.

2464. Art of humor (reprint). Luigi Pirandello. *Massachusetts Review,* vol. 6, Spring 1965, pp. 515-520.

2465. Beating the odds in the "card game." E.J. Hohman. *Writer,* vol. 96, June 1983, pp. 22-24.

2466. Comic compulsion. J. Moses. *Sewanee Review,* vol. 86, Winter 1978, pp. 84-100.

2467. Five thousand poems ago; writing light verse. Richard Armour. *Writer,* vol. 74, October 1961, pp. 15-17.

2468. Gag writing for stand-up comics. D. Holmberg. *Writer,* vol. 91, February 1978, pp. 28-29.

2469. Glad tidings from the greeting card market. Patricia Ann Emme. *Writer's Digest,* vol. 60, March 1980, pp. 28-31.

2470. Greeting card markets. *Writer,* vol. 97, September 1984, pp. 41-44.

2471. How to be funny for money. Agnes W. Thomas. *Writer,* vol. 95, November 1982, pp. 20-22.

2472. How to build humor, one chuckle at a time. Gene Peret. *Writer's Digest,* vol. 64, July 1984, pp. 30-32.

2473. How to put funny ideas into somebody's head: from *Cartoonist's and Gag Writer's Handbook.* Jack Markow. *Writer's Digest,* vol. 55, April 1975, pp. 23-24.

2474. How-to's of humor. Shirley Climo. *Writer,* vol. 92, December 1979, pp. 21-23.

2475. Humor magazine markets. *Writer's Digest,* vol. 55, April 1975, p. 22.

2476. Humor markets. William Brohaugh. *Writer's Digest,* vol. 57, October 1977, pp. 31-34.

2477. Humorous Rex May: king of the gagwriters. Dennis E. Hensley. *Writer's Digest,* vol. 63, July 1983, pp. 22-23.

2478. Last laughs (markets). *Writer's Digest,* vol. 57, November 1977, p. 39.

2479. Light verse from everyday experiences. R. Williamson. *Writer,* vol. 94, June 1981, pp. 26-27.

2480. Light verse: questions and answers. Richard Armour. *Writer,* vol. 78, September 1965, pp. 26-28.

2481. Little light on lighthearted writing. Richard Armour. *Writer,* vol. 88, February 1975, pp. 19-21.

2482. Make 'em laugh (interview). Neil Simon. *Plays and Players,* vol. 24, September 1977, pp. 12-15.

2483. Markets for gagmen. Jack Markow. *Writer's Digest,* vol. 51, August 1971, pp. 38-41.

2484. Martin Levin: the good humor man (interview). *Writer's Digest,* vol. 57, October 1977, p. 29.

2485. Now that's a laugh; with list of markets. R.S. Aldrich. *Writer's Digest,* vol. 57, October 1977, pp. 27-31.

2486. Peg Bracken: an exclusive interview. *Writer's Digest,* vol. 50, May 1970, pp. 24-26.

2487. Reading between the lines (greeting cards). Ronald Porep. *Writer's Digest,* vol. 60, March 1980, p. 30.

2488. Rod McKuen's *Sounds of Solitude* (interview). *Writer's Digest,* vol. 64, February 1984, pp. 24-30.

2489. Serious look at light verse. J.D. Engle, Jr. *Writer's Digest,* vol. 49, July 1969, pp. 47-49+.

2490. Sharpening the one-lners; ideas of Robert Orben. D. Link. *Writer's Digest,* vol. 57, October 1977, p. 30.

2491. Some funny markets for humor. Richard Armour. *Writer,* vol. 86, November 1973, pp. 19-20+.

2492. Successful light verse writing. Richard Armour. *Writer,* vol. 86, February 1973, pp. 19-21.

2493. Throwing some light on light verse. Richard Armour. *Writer,* vol. 90, October 1977, pp. 15-18.

2494. Title-author jokes, now and long ago. C.C. Doyle. *Journal of American Folklore,* vol. 86, January 1973, pp. 52-54.

2495. Uses of incongruity. W. Gray. *Educational Theatre Journal,* vol. 15, December 1963, pp. 343-347.

2496. Variety is the spice of writing. Richard Armour. *Writer,* vol. 76, November 1963, pp. 18-19.

2497. Wacky writing world of Joan Rivers. Ronald L. Smith. *Writer's Digest,* vol. 58, September 1978, pp. 26-27.

2498. What can you be funny about? Richard Armour. *Writer,* vol. 83, December 1970, pp. 21-23.

2499. What makes a good sentimental greeting? D.K. Quinn. *Writer,* vol. 77, October 1964, pp. 21-24+.

2500. Writing for the greeting card market. Lorraine Hardt. *Writer,* vol. 80, March 1967, pp. 28-29.

2501. Writing greeting cards (with list of companies). Selma Glasser. *Writer,* vol. 91, October 1978, pp. 23-25+.

2502. Writing humor—but seriously folks. Esther Blumenfeld and Lynne Alpern. *Writer's Digest,* vol. 62, January 1982, pp. 32+.

2503. Writing light verse is heavy. C. Bare. *Writer's Digest,* vol. 52, June 1972, pp. 33+.

2504. Writing short prose humor. K. Nelson. *Writer,* vol. 73, July 1960, pp. 9-12.

Religious and Devotional Literature

"God will forgive me; it is his trade."
—Heinrich Heine

Books

2505. Anderson, Margaret J. *The Christian Writer's Handbook.* New York: Harper & Row, 1974. 270 pp.

This competent overview addresses feature-length nonfiction, interviews, how-to articles, columns, fiction, and poetry. In addition, each step of the publishing process is carefully outlined. Anderson is credited with many books and hundreds of articles in this specialized field.

2506. Gentz, William H., Lee Roddy, and others. *Writing to Inspire; A Guide to Writing and Publishing for the Expanding Religious Market.* Cincinnati: Writer's Digest, 1982. 319 pp.

Ranging from film scripts to greeting cards, here is the advice of twenty-eight Christian writers on creating inspirational literature.

2507. McCarthy, David S. *Practical Guide for the Christian Writer.* Valley Forge, Pennsylvania: Judson, 1983. 112 pp.

Offers technical tips on writing and marketing religious fiction and non-fiction. The author has published numerous books and thousands of articles.

2508. Moore, John. *Write for the Religion Market.* Palm Springs, California: ETC Publications, 1981. 128 pp.

Sound advice to the inexperienced from a thirty-year veteran.

2509. Osteyee, Edith Tiller. *Writing for Christian Publications.* Philadelphia: Judson Press, 1953. (Reprinted by Greenwood Press, 1969.)

This is an increasingly dated how-to approach to religious journalism, but it contains useful information on both religious fiction and article writing for beginners.

Shedd, Charlie. *If I Can Write, You Can Write.* See entry 4259.

2510. Unger, Henry E. *Writers in Roman Collars; Freelancing for Catholics.* Fresno, California: Academy Guild Press, 1959. 193 pp.

Addressed to members of the priesthood and other Catholics. The bulk of the book consists of general and rather sketchy advice on writing, with only a smattering of the specialized information implied by the title. Dated and of marginal usefulness, to Catholics or anyone else.

2511. Yost, Donald F. *Writing for Adventist Magazines.* Nashville: Southern, 1968. 144 pp.

Specifically tailored for materials suitable for Seventh-Day Adventist magazines, this book sees religious writing as a ministry. It contains an analysis of what Yost feels the editors of Adventist magazines want from writers and also describes the major magazines in this field.

2512. Youngberg, Norma R. *Creative Techniques for Christian Writers.* Mountain View, California: Pacific, 1968. 262 pp.

This elementary introduction to fiction, poetry, and article writing will appeal to hopeful novices. It provides basic definitions of writing terms and discusses techniques such as plot, characterization, viewpoint, and dialogue, as well as marketing techniques. The frequent prose and poetry examples are taken from standard religious magazines and books.

Articles

2513. Are you that special person who can write inspirational articles? R. Peterman. *Writer's Digest,* vol. 51, December 1971, pp. 31-32+.

2514. Continuing phenomenon of the religious best seller. G.C. Wharton. *Publishers Weekly,* vol. 211, March 14, 1977, pp. 82-83.

2515. Devotional books: assessing the state of the genre. M. Boyd. *Christian Century,* vol. 91, April 3, 1974, pp. 373-376.

2516. Down to earth guide to writing religious fiction. T.A. Noton, *Writer's Digest,* vol. 62, February 1982, pp. 40-42+.

2517. Ducking the mailed fist; religion editing. J.D. Douglas. *Christianity Today,* vol. 16, September 15, 1972, pp. 63-64.

2518. Gospel truths of religious writing. Sister Marie Emanuel. *Writer's Digest,* vol. 57, December 1977, pp. 20-23.

2519. Hallelujah for the Christian how to book. Edith Kilgo. *Writer's Digest,* vol. 61, August 1981, pp. 20-26.

2520. *Harpers'* "Bishop" reflects on 50+ years of religious bookselling. Jerome P. Frank. *Publishers Weekly,* vol. 223, March 4, 1983, pp. 65-66+.

2521. Hidden best sellers among religious books. Chandler Grannis. *Publishers Weekly,* vol. 201, February 28, 1972, p. 45.

2522. How religious are religion editors? R.L. Peck. *Christianity Today,* vol. 15, April 9, 1971, pp. 36-37.

2523. How to sell to the top religious magazines. E.H. Pitts. *Writer,* vol. 80, June 1967, pp. 31-33.

2524. "I hate you!...love, Jeff." Joan Martin. *Writer's Digest,* vol. 57, December 1977, p. 22.

2525. Inspiration for; symposium. *Writer's Digest,* vol. 54, December 1974, pp. 10-17.

2526. Literary style in religious writing. C.D. Linton. *Christianity Today,* vol. 15, June 18, 1971, pp. 5-6+; July 2, 1971, pp. 8-12.

2527. Making of many books. C.F.H. Henry. *Christianity Today,* vol. 21, December 3, 1976, pp. 40-41.

2528. Outlines for success in the religious market. Wesley Tracy. *Writer's Market,* vol. 61, March 1981, pp. 30-34.

2529. Path to the Evangelicals is straight and narrow—but easy to follow. Elsa Houtz. *Writer's Digest,* vol. 57, December 1977, pp. 24-25.

2530. Phenomenon of the religious best seller. *Publishers Weekly,* vol. 208, July 14, 1975, pp. 45-47.

2531. Problems of overstatement in religious fiction and criticism. P.S. Hawkins. *Renascence,* vol. 33, Autumn 1980, pp. 36-46.

2532. Religious book markets. *Writer's Digest,* vol. 58, February 1978, pp. 42-46+.

2533. Religious markets (magazines). William Brohaugh. *Writer's Digest,* vol. 57, December 1977, pp. 25-30+.

2534. Robert Schuller (interview). *Publishers Weekly,* vol. 223, March 4, 1983, pp. 38-39.

2535. Selling to religious publications. Virginia Westervelt. *Writer,* vol. 96, December 1983, pp. 26-27.

2536. Their utmost for His Highest; O. Chambers. S.E. Wirt. *Christianity Today,* vol. 18, June 21, 1974, pp. 16-17.

2537. Today's changing religious market. Steve Lawhead. *Writer,* vol. 94, December 1981, pp. 27-28.

2538. Total writer; Marabel Morgan (interview). *Writer's Digest,* vol. 61, August 1981, pp. 24-25.

2539. Unlisted bestsellers. C.A. Forbes. *Christianity Today,* vol. 16, June 23, 1972, pp. 40+.

2540. Welcome to a new breed of religious writers (and about time, too). Floyd Thatcher. *Publishers Weekly,* vol. 223, March 4, 1983, p. 46.

2541. Where to sell manuscripts: religious and denominational magazines and syndicates. *Writer,* vol. 94, December 1981, pp. 29-31.

2542. Who or what is a religious poet? J. Moffitt. *America,* vol. 133, December 6, 1975, pp. 396-399.

2543. William Law: a devout and holy life. M.W. Hess. *Christianity Today,* vol. 19, January 31, 1975, pp. 4-6.

2544. Writing for the Catholic markets. Some shalts and shalt nots. Lucy Fuchs. *Writer's Digest,* vol. 58, December 1978, pp. 28-32.

2545. Writing for the inspirational market: with list of periodicals. Dina Donohue. *Writer,* vol. 88, June 1975, pp. 13-17.

Science Fiction and Fantasy

"Imagination is the eye of the soul."

—Joseph Jourbert

Books

Asimov, Isaac. *In Joy Still Felt.* See entry 3930.

2546. Bova, Ben W., editor. *Notes to a Science Fiction Writer.* New York: Scribners, 1975. 178 pp.

Bova, editor of *Analog,* gives an expert's advice to beginning writers wishing to break into the field. Using a conversational tone, he discusses craftsmanship and the basic elements of telling a good story. Four of his own stories are included as models for discussion. Though character, background, conflict, and plot are discussed at length, this is not a text on writing. It is, however, a practical set of suggestions from an award-winning editor and author of science fiction.

Bradbury, Ray. *Zen and the Art of Writing and the Joy of Writing; Two Essays.* See entry 3935.

2547. Bretnor, Reginald. *Craft of Science Fiction; A Symposium on Writing Science Fiction.* New York: Harper, 1976. 321 pp.

These fifteen essays by Poul Anderson, Norman Spinrad, Frederik Pohl, and others give detailed advice to writers about sources and creativity as well as professional writing "secrets." This book abounds in both theory and practical application. Topics such as "Alien Minds and Nonhuman Intelligences" and "The Science Fiction Professional" are well written and convincing. A section on television writing is also included.

2548. Bretnor, Reginald, and others. *Science Fiction, Today and Tomorrow; A Discursive Symposium.* New York: Harper, 1974. 342 pp.

Though not intended as an approach to the technical aspects of writing science fiction, several of the essays in this collection bear directly on such considerations. Poul Anderson's "The Creation of Imaginary Worlds" and Gordon Dickson's "Plausibility in Science Fiction" should please and inform creative writers. Frederik Pohl's "The

Publishing of Science Fiction" gives a sobering account of
the realities of the science fiction marketplace.

2549. Carroll, Lewis. *The Annotated Alice. Alice's Adventures in
Wonderland and Through the Looking Glass.* Introduction and
notes by Martin Gardner. New York: Potter, 1960. 351 pp.

2550. De Camp, L. Sprague, and Catherine Crook De Camp. *Science
Fiction Handbook, Revised; A Guide to Writing Imaginative
Literature.* Philadelphia: Owlswick Press, 1975. 220 pp.

This collection of essays by authors, editors, and publishers
associated with imaginative fiction covers a broad range of
topics within that genre, such as ideas, plotting, marketing,
and nine other topics, including a survey of the history and
recent developments in the genre. The De Camps are
respected members of their profession who have updated
what was already considered by many to be a standard
resource. Contains a comprehensive index and
bibliography.

2551. Elrick, George S. *Science Fiction Handbook for Readers and Writers.*
Chicago: Chicago Review Press, 1978. 315 pp.

A dictionary of science fiction terms from "ablating
materials" to "zodiacal light."

2552. Eshbach, Lyod Arthur, editor. *Of Worlds Beyond; The Science of
Science Fiction Writing; A Symposium by Robert A. Heinlein (and
Others).* Chicago: Advent Publishers, 1964. 104 pp.

Each of the "name" contributors to this slim volume
presents a separate view of writing science fiction.
Originally published in 1947, these essays lack some of the
freshness they once had, and on the whole the book is far
too fragmented to offer much more than a set of
philosophical introductions to the subject.

2553. Kocher, Paul H. *Master of Middle-Earth; The Fiction of J.R.R.
Tolkien.* Boston: Houghton Mifflin, 1972. 247 pp.

Considered by many to be the best book-length study of
Tolkien's writings.

2554. LeGuin, Ursula K. *From Elfland to Poughkeepsie.* Portland, Oregon:
Pendragon Press, 1975. 31 pp.

Based upon a speech about fantasy delivered at the
University of Washington in 1972.

2555. ———. *Language of the Night; Essays on Fantasy and Science
Fiction.* New York: Berkley, 1979. 288 pp.

As seen by *Booklist,* this is "an indispensable book for those
who study science fiction seriously as a genre in transition
toward conscious literary excellence. Gathered from a

number of sources, many of them not accessible to most scholars, this collection of critical writing and expository essays reveals the precepts on which LeGuin's work is founded. It also houses her observations on various other prominent aspects of the science fiction landscape. Casual LeGuin readers might be agreeably surprised by her wit and literacy as an essayist; scholars will be impressed by the depth of organization in her thinking."

2556. Lewis, C.S. *Of Other Worlds; Essays and Stories.* Edited by Walter Hooper. New York: Harcourt, 1966. 148 pp.

Contains several important Lewis essays on the subject of science fiction writing, including the now well-known "On Science Fiction." The essays are more critical than technical in tone.

2557. Longyear, Barry B. *Science Fiction Writer's Workshop; An Introduction to Fiction Mechanics.* Philadelphia: Owlswick, 1980. 161 pp.

Written by an award-winning science fiction writer, this clear text covers such basic points as the peculiarities of science fiction and how to prepare and market manuscripts. Covers some of the same ground as Ben Bova's *Notes to a Science Fiction Writer* (see entry 2546), but with greater detail. According to *Analog,* "If you have any hope of becoming a SF or other writer, buy *Workshop.* It will help you more than any three texts." A glossary is included.

2558. Lowndes, Robert A.W. *Three Faces of Science Fiction.* Boston: NESDA Press, 1973. 96 pp.

A survey of the works of Heinlein, Verne, and Wells, among others.

2559. Science Fiction Writers of America. *Writing and Selling Science Fiction.* Cincinnati: Writer's Digest, 1976. 191 pp.

Less balanced than either the *Craft of Science Fiction* (see entry 2547) or the *Science Fiction Handbook, Revised* (see entry 2550). But with contributions like Poul Anderson's "Nomenclature in Science Fiction" and Tom Purdom's "Who's Going to Run Things in Twenty Three Hundred?," there remains much useful information for the hopeful writer and student of the genre.

2560. Wymer, Thomas, and others. *Intersections; The Elements of Fiction in Science Fiction.* Bowling Green, Ohio: Popular Press, 1978. 130 pp.

Contains chapters on plot, character, setting, point of view, language, tone, theme and value, and symbol and mythology.

Articles

2561. Anne McCaffrey (interview). *Luna Monthly,* no. 56, 1974, pp. 1-5.

2562. Approach to the structure of LeGuin's SF. Rafail Nudleman. *Science Fiction Studies,* vol. 2, 1975, pp. 210-220.

2563. Archetypal patterns in science fiction. Willis E. McNelly. *CEA Critic,* vol. 35, May 1973, pp. 15-19.

2564. Building four-dimensional people in science fiction. J. Brunner. *Writer,* vol. 84, December 1971, pp. 21-24.

2565. Challenge of science fiction writing. B. Bova. *Writer,* vol. 95, September 1982, pp. 9-12.

2566. Character in science fiction; excerpt from *Notes to a Science Fiction Writer.* Ben Bova. *Writer,* vol. 90, April 1977, pp. 17-19+.

2567. Confessions of a wage slave. David M. Harris. *Science Fiction Review,* vol. 4, no. 1, 1975, pp. 26-28.

2568. Conflict in science fiction stories. Ben Bova. *Writer,* vol. 89, August 1976, pp. 15-17+.

2569. Constructing a science fiction novel. Roger Zelany. *Writer,* vol. 97, October 1984, pp. 9-12+.

2570. Do I dare disturb the universe? Madeleine L'Engle. *Horn Book,* vol. 59, December 1983, pp. 673-682.

2571. Early novels; Arthur C. Clarke. Thomas D. Clareson. *Algol,* vol. 12, no. 1, 1974, pp. 7-10.

2572. Economic scofflaws (SF writers should not ignore the laws of economics). R.S. Potts. *Analog Science Fiction,* vol. 96, November 1976, p. 5+.

2573. Evening with Walter Hooper. *CSL: The Bulletin of the New York C. S. Lewis Society,* vol. 6, no. 9, 1975, pp. 1-7.

2574. Fantasy as technique. R.B. Schmerl. *Virginia Quarterly Review,* vol. 43, Autumn 1967, pp. 644-656.

2575. Finding science fiction ideas. Kathleen Sky. *Writer,* vol. 94, May 1981, pp. 17-18.

2576. Flying nonesuch (Martin Caidin). D.R. Branch. *Writer's Digest,* vol. 57, August 1977, pp. 41-43.

2577. From mad professors to brilliant scientists: the evolution of a genre. Ben Bova. *Library Journal,* vol. 98, 1973, pp. 1646-1649.

2578. Function of time travel in Vonnegut's *Slaughterhouse Five.* Gerard W. O'Connor. *Riverside Quarterly,* vol. 5, 1972, pp. 206-207.

2579. Heroism in *The Lord of the Rings*. Charles W. Moorman. *Southern Quarterly,* vol. 11, 1972, pp. 29-39.

2580. High fantasy versus low comedy: humor in J.R.R. Tolkien. C.D. Stevens. *Extrapolation,* vol. 21, Summer 1980, pp. 122-129.

2581. How to build a science fiction story. Reginald Bretnor. *Writer's Digest,* vol. 56, July 1976, pp. 24-25.

2582. How to write for *Omni*. Ben W. Bova. *Writer,* vol. 94, July 1981, pp. 26-27.

2583. Idea and imagery in Herbert's *Dune*. John B. Ower. *Extrapolation,* vol. 15, 1974, pp. 129-139.

2584. Interviews with two German science fiction writers; C. Rasch and H. Franke. P.W. Koenig. *Extrapolation,* vol. 18, May 1977, pp. 150-154.

2585. J.R. Tolkien and the fairy tale truth. Mary Sirridge. *The British Journal of Aesthetics,* vol. 15, 1975, pp. 81-92.

2586. Man from minehead; Arthur C. Clarke. Walter Gillings. *Algol,* vol. 12, no. 1, 1974, pp. 12-14.

2587. Manacle-forged minds: two images of the computer in science fiction. John B. Ower. *Diogenes,* no. 85, Spring 1974, pp. 47-61.

2588. Mandalic activism: an approach to structure, theme, and tone in four novels by Philip K. Dick. Mary Kay Bray. *Extrapolation,* vol. 21, Summer 1980, pp. 146-157.

2589. Masterpiece in science fiction: power or parody? J. Bier. *Journal of Popular Culture,* vol. 12, Spring 1979, pp. 604-610.

2590. Metaphysician as fiction writer: G.K. Chesterton's narrative techniques. David Jago. *Antigonish Review,* vol. 22, 1975, pp. 85-99.

2591. Michael Moorcock (interview). *Luna Monthly,* no. 59, 1975, pp. 1-9.

2592. Names and roles of characters in science fiction. Robert Plank. *Names,* vol. 9, September 1961, pp. 151-159.

2593. Of other worlds: worldly wisdom as it grows in science fiction. J. Neuleib. *Extrapolation,* vol. 19, May 1978, pp. 108-111.

2594. On science fiction. Boris Eizykman. *Science Fiction Studies,* vol. 2, 1975, pp. 164-166.

2595. On the poetic of the science fiction genre. D. Suvin. *College English,* vol. 34, December 1972, pp. 372-382.

2596. On the structural analysis of science fiction. Stanislaw Lem. *Science Fiction Studies,* vol. 1, 1973, pp. 26-33.

2597. On writing science fiction. Ursula K. LeGuin. *Writer,* vol. 94, February 1981, pp. 11-14.

2598. Other worlds to conjure. M.R. Hillegas. *Saturday Review,* vol. 49, March 26, 1966, pp. 33-34.

2599. Participant past imperfect. A.B. Malec. *Writer,* vol. 82, August 1969, pp. 19-21.

2600. Perception and value in science fiction. Thomas Wymer. *Extrapolation,* vol. 16, May 1975, pp. 103-112.

2601. Place of evil in science fiction. Robert Plank. *Extrapolation,* vol. 14, 1973, pp. 100-111.

2602. Plot in science fiction; excerpt from *Notes to a Science Fiction Writer.* Ben Bova. *Writer,* vol. 88, August 1975, pp. 17-20+.

2603. Presidency in science fiction. Robert Plank. *Extrapolation,* vol. 16, May 1975, pp. 173-192.

2604. Putting science into science fiction. G. Benford. *Writer,* vol. 96, July 1983, pp. 7-10.

2605. Realistic guide to writing fantasy fiction. Joel Rosenberg. *Writer's Digest,* vol. 64, July 1984, pp. 22-25.

2606. Robert Silverberg: the complete writer. Thomas D. Clareson. *Fantasy and Science Fiction,* vol. 46, April 1974, pp. 73-80.

2607. Science and conscience in Huxley's *Brave New World.* Peter Firchow. *Contemporary Literature,* vol. 16, no. 3, 1975, pp. 301-316.

2608. Science and sensibility; science fiction. M. Green. *Kenyon Review,* vol. 25, Autumn 1963, pp. 713-728.

2609. Science fiction and reality. Ben W. Bova. *Writer,* vol. 92, May 1979, pp. 7-10+.

2610. Science fiction and the fallacy of hope. J.C. Wolf. *Extrapolation,* vol. 17, May 1976, pp. 151-152.

2611. Science fiction as fictive history. R.H. Canary. *Extrapolation,* vol. 16, December 1974, pp. 81-95.

2612. Science fiction for young readers. Douglas Hill. *Writer,* vol. 97, January 1984, pp. 15-18.

2613. Science fiction futures. Irving H. Buchen. *Intellect,* vol. 103, 1975, p. 459.

2614. Science of writing the science editor. S. Schmidt (editor of *Analog*). *Writer's Digest,* vol. 63, February 1983, pp. 28-31+.

2615. SF as structural fabulation. T. Remington. *North American Review,* vol. 260, Winter 1975, pp. 53-55.

2616. Simplicity in scientific writing. L. DeBakey. *Writer,* vol. 79, September 1966, pp. 25-26.

2617. Special demands of point of view in science fiction. H.P. Kroitor. *Extrapolation,* vol. 17, May 1976, pp. 153-159.

2618. Special problems of science fiction. Gene Wolfe. *Writer,* vol. 89, May 1976, pp. 12-14.

2619. Spinning galaxy: a shift in perspective on magazine science fiction. D.N. Samuelson. *Extrapolation,* vol. 17, December 1975, pp. 44-48.

2620. Stanislaw Lem (interview). *The Alien Critic,* vol. 3, no. 3, 1974, pp. 4-14.

2621. Stanislaw Lem on men and rockets. Michael Kandel. *Extrapolation,* vol. 14, 1972, pp. 13-24.

2622. Symbolic fantasy. Gene Wolfe. *Genre,* vol. 8, no. 3, 1975, pp. 194-209.

2623. Symbolism in science fiction. Ben W. Bova. *Writer,* vol. 97, June 1984, pp. 7-9.

2624. Telling lives. Edmund Morris (prize-winning author of *The Rise of Theodore Roosevelt). Wilson Quarterly,* vol. 7, Summer 1983, pp. 165-169.

2625. Theme for SF: aesthetics and overpopulation. Mary S. Weinkauf. *Extrapolation,* vol. 13, 1972, pp. 152-164.

2626. Time travel story and related matters of SF structuring. Stanislaw Lem. *Science Fiction Studies,* vol. 1, 1974, pp. 143-154.

2627. Toward a definition of fantasy fiction. *Extrapolation,* vol. 15, 1974, pp. 117-128.

2628. Unreal estates; on science fiction. C.S. Lewis, K. Amis, and B. Aldiss. *Encounter,* vol. 24, March 1965, pp. 61-65.

2629. Ursula K. LeGuin (interview). *Algol,* vol. 12, no. 2, 1975, pp. 7-10.

2630. Utopia: the problem of definition. L.T. Sargent. *Extrapolation,* vol. 16, May 1975, pp. 137-148.

2631. Visit with Arthur C. Clarke. Billye Cutchen. *Writer's Digest,* vol. 59, January 1979, pp. 24-25.

2632. What do they mean, SF? Gene Wolfe. *Writer,* vol. 93, August 1980, pp. 11-13+.

2633. What is time? more theological aspects of science fiction. E.H. Lantero. *Religion in Life,* vol. 40, Autumn 1971, pp. 423-435.

2634. Writer and SF. B.A. Bannon. *Publishers Weekly,* vol. 209, June 14, 1976, pp. 46-48.

2635. Writer's Digest interview, Ray Bradbury. *Writer's Digest,* vol. 56, February 1976, pp. 18-25.

2636. Writing science fiction: think like an alien, write like an angel; excerpt from *Writing and Selling Fiction.* G. Dozois. *Writer's Digest,* vol. 56, February 1976, pp. 26-28+.

2637. Writing science fiction today. M. Leinster. *Writer,* vol. 81, May 1968, pp. 16-18.

2638. Zenna Henderson (interview). Paul Walker. *Luna Monthly,* no. 52, 1974, pp. 1-5+.

Biography and Autobiography, Including Diaries, Journals, Ghostwriting, and Collaboration

"A well written life is almost as rare as a well spent one."
—Thomas Carlyle

Books

2639. Bowen, Catherine Drinker. *Adventures of a Biographer.* Boston: Little, Brown, 1959. 235 pp.

Anecdotal in style, Bowen's accounts take us to the Soviet Union for research on Anton and Nicholas Rubinstein, through a mass of legal opinion for work on Justice Holmes, and into a variety of research libraries for experiences both pleasurable and otherwise. This book tells little about how to write biography, but broadly reveals the difficulties and the rewards of being a biographer.

2640. ———. *Biography; The Craft and the Calling.* Boston: Little, Brown, 1969. 174 pp.

This valuable and systematic text adds to and reassesses Bowen's previously published views on biographical writing. Among the major topics covered are plotting, openings, endings, research, descriptions, quotations, and the question of talent.

2641. ———. *Writing of Biography.* Boston: Writer, 1951. 31 pp.

Based on a lecture given at Scripps College, this is a discussion of Bowen's methods and philosophy for avoiding conventional knowledge and for uncovering the "facts" about the past.

2642. Clifford, James Lowry. *From Puzzles to Portraits; Problems of a Literary Biographer.* Chapel Hill: University of North Carolina Press, 1970. 151 pp.

Clifford discusses research methods and writing considerations in ways that should interest anyone attempting to write a biography of whatever type. He stresses his distrust of secondary sources and, by way of anecdote, demonstrates how difficult the finding of certain primary sources can be. He also discusses several types of biographical styles and when to use each, as well as that most difficult of biographical questions: how much should be told and how much not. The question of insignificant detail is not entirely answered, but it is thoroughly aired.

2643. Cockshut, A.O.J. *Truth to Life; The Art of Biography in the 19th Century.* New York: Harcourt, 1974. 220 pp.

Taking the position that for nearly two centuries we have been living in a golden age of biographical writing, Cockshut goes on to explore a number of noted biographers and their backgrounds. Though this is in no sense a "how-to" guide to modern biographical writing, it does serve to place biography, as a form, in some perspective. Those who seek a detailed account of the methods employed by the biographers included will go wanting. Those ready to learn about the traditions of English language biography will be pleased. To quote *Library Journal:* "Cockshut's book might well serve as a little bible for biographers...."

2644. Daniel, Lois. *How To Write Your Own Life Story; A Step by Step Guide for the Non-professional Writer.* Chicago: Chicago Review Press, 1980. 216 pp.

A competent approach to autobiography which will both inspire and instruct.

2645. Dixon, Janice, and Dora D. Flack. *Preserving Your Past; A Painless Guide to Writing Your Autobiography and Family History.* New York: Doubleday, 1977. 334 pp.

A full discussion, on a popular level, of the writing of diaries and extended personal and family chronicles. Section four covers research and records, as well as oral accounts.

2646. Gittings, Robert. *The Nature of Biography.* Seattle: University of Washington Press, 1978. 96 pp.

An established biographer in his own right, Gittings struggles with the question of balance in the attempt to portray another person's life. In the end, he feels, it is a matter of combining careful observation with a kind of artistic intuition and a keen sense of what to leave out. He also provides an overview of his favorite biographers from Plutarch to the present.

2647. Kanin, Ruth. *Write the Story of Your Life.* New York: Dutton, 1981. 219 pp.

Taking the position that every life is worth recording, Kanin provides advice about drawing on one's own memory, locating facts, literary style, revision, and even finding a publisher. Through systematic analysis and frequent exercises, the user is guided and encouraged toward honesty and artful catharsis.

2648. Kendall, Paul Murray. *Art of Biography.* New York: Norton, 1965. 158 pp.

Kendall discusses the sorting out of the paper trail left by one's subject, the recollections of the subject's friends and enemies, and the interpretations of later observers. He views biography as the "craft-science-art of the impossible," which can never be science nor quite be literature. In this useful summary, he chronicles the history of biographical writing and then succeeds in categorizing modern biography.

2649. Olney, James, editor. *Autobiography; Essays Theoretical and Critical.* Princeton, New Jersey: Princeton University Press, 1980. 360 pp.

In these sixteen essays we find discussions of style, principles, limiting of voice, imagination, and the self as fiction.

2650. Pachter, Mare, editor. *Telling Lives, The Biographer's Art.* Washington, D.C.: New Republic Books, 1979. 151 pp.

On the occasion of the tenth anniversary of The National Portrait Gallery, such distinguished biographers as Leon Edel, Barbara Tuchman, and Justin Kaplan gathered there to discuss the art of telling lives. This book expands on those remarks and adds other voices in a way that makes for compelling reading.

2651. Reynolds, Frank E., and Donald Capps. *Biographical Process; Studies in the History and Psychology of Religion.* The Hague: Moulton, 1976. 436 pp.

A specialized series of essays which treats, among other things, the subject of psychobiography in popular culture. Of particular interest to religious biographers.

2652. Salaman, Esther. *The Great Confession.* London: Penguin, 1973. 312 pp.

The autobiographical writings of S.T. Aksakov, Leo N. Tolstoy, Thomas DeQuincey, and Marcel Proust are studied for their success in decoding the book Proust called "...more laborious to decipher than any other—the only one dictated to us by reality."

2653. Veninga, James F., editor. *The Biographer's Gift; Life Histories and Humanism.* Galveston, Texas: A & M Press, 1984. 129 pp.

This seminar approach begins with a keynote essay on the relationship between biography and humanism. The essays which follow extend and amplify the issues raised in the keynote essay. These are followed by interviews with the seminar members.

Articles

2654. Alternative accounts of lives: an argument for epistemological relativism. William McKinley Runyan. *Biography,* vol. 3, Summer 1980, pp. 209-224.

2655. And then the queen died. A.M. Wells. *Writer,* vol. 79, September 1966, pp. 12-14.

2656. Anecdotal autobiographies. R. Lambert and D. Mack. *English Journal,* vol. 48, December 1959, pp. 528+.

2657. Another love affair! L. Conger. *Writer,* vol. 89, May 1976, pp. 7-8.

2658. Art of autobiography. R. Church. *Cornhill Magazine,* vol. 171, Winter 1960-61, pp. 469-480.

2659. Art of biography. Mary Purcell. *Studies,* vol. 48, Autumn 1959, pp. 305-317.

2660. Art of keeping a diary. N. Nicolson. *Esquire,* vol. 66, December 1966, p. 28+.

2661. As-told-to article (collaboration). J. Stocker. *Writer's Digest,* vol. 50, April 1970, pp. 20-22.

2662. Autobiography and the dialectic of consciousness. J.C. Curtin. *International Philosophical Quarterly,* vol. 14, September 1974, pp. 343-346.

2663. Autobiography as an art. Elizabeth Bowen. *Saturday Review,* vol. 24, March 17, 1951, pp. 9-10.

2664. Autobiography as the presentation of self for social immortality. I.L. Horowitz. *New Literary History,* vol. 9, Autumn 1977, pp. 173-179.

2665. Autobiography in the third person; translation. P. Lejeune. *New Literary History,* vol. 9, Autumn 1977, pp. 27-50.

2666. Autobiography: the gold of writing power. D.M. Wolfe. *English Journal,* vol. 60, October 1971, pp. 937-946.

2667. Basic assumptions of literary biography. Peter Nagourney. *Biography,* vol. 1, Spring 1978, pp. 86-104.

2668. Bibliographical problem of biography: identification of names. Robert Collison. *Biography,* vol. 4, Fall 1978, pp. 69-75.

2669. Biographer and his hero; excerpt from *Biography: The Craft and The Calling.* Catherine Drinker Bowen. *American Heritage,* vol. 20, December 1968, pp. 16-17.

2670. Biographer and psycho-analysis. *New World Writing,* no. 18, Winter 1961, pp. 50-64.

2671. Biographer as a center of reference. William Snipes. *Biography,* vol. 5, Summer 1982, pp. 215-225.

2672. Biographers craft. F.B. Tolles. *South Atlantic Quarterly,* vol. 53, October 1954, pp. 508-520.

2673. Biographical images: effects of formal features on the way we see a life. J.W. Halpern. *Biography,* vol. 1, Fall 1978, pp. 1-14.

2674. Biographical novel. Irving Stone. *Writer,* vol. 75, January 1962, pp. 9-13.

2675. Biographies for children, more facts, less fiction. J. Forman. *Library Journal,* vol. 97, September 15, 1972, pp. 2968-2969.

2676. Biographies of women. Margot Peters. *Biography,* vol. 2, Summer 1979, pp. 201-217.

2677. Biography. Frank Brady. *Yale Review,* vol. 69, Autumn 1979, pp. 118-124.

2678. Biography: a manifesto. Leon Edel. *Biography,* vol. 1, Winter 1978, pp. 1-3.

2679. Biography is... Leon Edel. *Today's Education,* vol. 61, December 1972, pp. 16-19.

2680. Biography; the other face of the coin. R. Sprague. *Horn Book,* vol. 42, June 1966, pp. 282-289.

2681. Biography—the 'scarlet experiment.' Antony Alpers. *Times Literary Supplement,* March 28, 1980, pp. 369-370.

2682. Biography, true and false. I. Origo. *Atlantic,* vol. 203, February 1959, pp. 37-42.

2683. Biography, true and false. I. Origo. *Cornhill Magazine,* vol. 171, Fall 1960, pp. 379-394.

2684. Black autobiography: life as the death weapon. R. Rosenblatt. *Yale Review,* vol. 65, Summer 1976, pp. 515-527.

2685. Book worth writing. L. Conger. *Writer,* vol. 92, January 1979, pp. 9-10.

2686. Business of a biographer. Catherine Drinker Bowen. *Atlantic Monthly,* vol. 187, May 1951, pp. 50-56.

2687. Current bibliography on life writing. Donald J. Winslow and Kathleen A. Bennett. *Biography,* vol. 3, Fall 1980, pp. 348-356.

2688. Dialogue weekend; intensive journal workshop. R.A. Blake. *America,* vol. 136, February 5, 1977, pp. 105-106.

2689. Do women make the best biographers? D. Cox. *Saturday Review*, vol. 43, July 9, 1960, pp. 8-10+.

2690. Doctor and the biographer. Hector Bolitho. *Texas Quarterly*, vol. 11, Winter 1968, pp. 52-60.

2691. Doing life histories. Annabel Farraday and Kenneth Plummer. *Sociological Review*, vol. 27, November 1979, pp. 773-798.

2692. Double in the autobiography of the elder Henry James. H. Feinstein. *American Imago*, vol. 31, Fall 1974, pp. 293-315.

2693. Electronic diary; tape recorder technique of D. Schaap. P.D. Zimmerman. *Newsweek*, vol. 73, February 3, 1969, pp. 88+.

2694. Equal credit for ghosts. R. Reeves. *Esquire*, vol. 88, August 1977, pp. 40-41.

2695. Eunuchs in the harem. John O'Hara. *Holiday*, vol. 40, September 1966, pp. 16+.

2696. Experiment in collaboration. L. Bergson and R. McMahon. *Writer*, vol. 81, October 1968, pp. 14-16+.

2697. Facts about co-writing fiction. Laurie Lawlor. *Writer's Digest*, vol. 60, July 1980, p. 24.

2698. Fictional biography, factual biography, and their contaminations. Ina Schabert. *Biography*, vol. 5, Winter 1982, pp. 1-16.

2699. Figure of autobiography. J. Leigh. *MLN*, vol. 93, May 1978, pp. 733-749.

2700. Franklin's *Autobiography*, important lessons in tone, syntax, and persona. Elizabeth Tebeaux. *Journal of Technical Writing and Communication*, vol. 11, no. 4, 1981, pp. 341-349.

2701. Freelance job idea: political ghostwriting. J.C. Behrens. *Writer's Digest*, vol. 49, November 1969, pp. 48-50+.

2702. From the working notebooks. G.M. Kozintsev. *Soviet Literature*, no. 8, 1974, pp. 119-125.

2703. Genesis of the diary. Anais Nin. *Voyages*, vol. 2, Fall 1968, pp. 5-13.

2704. Getting at the truth. Marchette Chute. *Saturday Review*, vol. 36, September 19, 1953, pp. 11-12, 43-44.

2705. Getting the most out of a short interview. Dennis Chaptman. *Writer's Digest*, vol. 62, July 1982, pp. 30-34.

2706. Ghost's story. S. Dworkin. *Ms.*, vol. 3, October 1974, pp. 12+.

2707. Ghostwriting. B. Cook. *Commonweal*, vol. 102, May 9, 1975, pp. 105-108.

2708. Glossary of terms in life writing: part 1. Donald J. Winslow. *Biography*, vol. 1, Winter 1978, pp. 61-78.

2709. Glossary of terms in life writing: part 2. Donald J. Winslow. *Biography,* vol. 1, Spring 1978, pp. 61-85.

2710. Goodbye, Dolly (unauthorized biography of a living celebrity). Alanna Nash. *Writer's Digest,* vol. 59, July 1979, pp. 18-24.

2711. Grammatical autobiography. D.M. Wolfe. *English Journal,* vol. 49, January 1960, pp. 16-21.

2712. Hidden Presidents: looking through their memoirs for involuntary truth. F.M. Brodie. *Harper's,* vol. 254, April 1977, pp. 61-66+; discussion, June 1977, pp. 4+.

2713. History and the biographer. Wallace Notestein. *Yale Review,* vol. 22, March 1933, pp. 549-558.

2714. History's 50-minute hour; psychobiography. K.L. Woodward and others. *Newsweek,* vol. 89, April 18, 1977, pp. 96+.

2715. How and where to find biographical information. C. MacLeod. *Writer's Digest,* vol. 52, January 1972, pp. 28-30.

2716. How lives are written. R.D. Altick. *Nation,* vol. 189, December 19, 1959, pp. 470-471.

2717. How much should a biographer tell? Stephen Spender. *Saturday Review,* vol. 47, January 25, 1964, pp. 16-19; discussion, March 28, 1964, p. 19; April 18, 1964, p. 28.

2718. How to make pay while politicians make hay (ghostwriting speeches). Mike McCarville. *Writer's Digest,* vol. 59, September 1979, pp. 28-34.

2719. How to write a biography. J.A. Garraty. *South Atlantic Quarterly,* vol. 55, January 1956, pp. 73-86.

2720. I'm a fiction ghost. J. Pearl. *Writer's Digest,* vol. 50, June 1970, pp. 30-32.

2721. Impossible assignment: finding personalities and writing their stories. F. Marks. *Writer's Digest,* vol. 53, April 1973, pp. 29+.

2722. In loneliness, in separate rooms. L. Conger. *Writer,* vol. 88, August 1975, pp. 7-8.

2723. Innocent art of confession and reverie. L. Gossman. *Daedalus,* vol. 107, Summer 1978, pp. 59-77.

2724. Interrelations of psychology and biography. J.A. Garraty. *Psychological Bulletin,* vol. 51, November 1954, pp. 569-582.

2725. Intuitions and interactions. N. Phillipson. *Times Literary Supplement,* no. 3803, January 24, 1975, p. 90.

2726. Keep a diary. A.W. Lyons. *Writer,* vol. 81, December 1968, pp. 14-15+.

2727. Keys to the as-told-to article, or book; adaptation of address. B. Day. *Writer's Digest,* vol. 51 March 1971, pp. 30-32+.

2728. Kinds of literary collaboration. Roy Paul Nelson. *Writer's Digest,* vol. 48, October 1968, p. 53.

2729. Lady political ghost speaks up. B. Bridgman. *Writer's Digest,* vol. 49, November 1969, p. 51.

2730. Literary biography. James Atlas. *American Scholar,* vol. 45, Summer 1976, pp. 448+.

2731. Literary biography: art or archaeology? Louis Kronenberger. *Atlantic,* vol. 218, September 1966, pp. 111-114.

2732. Literary detection. R. Arnold. *Blackwood's Magazine,* vol. 289, February 1961, pp. 109-116.

2733. Lives of the thinkers. A. Quinton. *Times Literary Supplement,* no. 3803, January 24, 1975, pp. 87-88.

2734. Living documents: oral history and biography. David J. Mitchell. *Biography,* vol. 3, Fall 1980, pp. 283-296.

2735. Locating belief in biography. David E. Schwalm. *Biography,* vol. 3, Winter 1980, pp. 14-27.

2736. Marilyn: Mailer's novel biography. Carl E. Rollyson, Jr. *Biography,* vol. 1, Fall 1978, pp. 49-67.

2737. Men behind Nixon's speeches. W.H. Honan. *New York Times Magazine,* January 19, 1969, pp. 20-21+.

2738. Metamorphoses of spiritual autobiography. R. Bell. *ELH,* vol. 44 Spring 1977, pp. 108-126.

2739. My lives. M. Holroyd. *Harper's Magazine,* vol. 253, October 1976, pp. 80-84.

2740. My magic box. Leo Rosten. *Look,* vol. 31, March 7, 1967, pp. 22-23.

2741. My struggle with facts. O. Coolidge. *Wilson Library Bulletin,* vol. 49, October 1974, pp. 146-151.

2742. New model autobiographer. J. Sturrock. *New Literary History,* vol. 9, Autumn 1977, pp. 51-63.

2743. Of cannibalism and autobiography. J.M. Blanchard. *MLN,* vol. 93, May 1978, pp. 654-676.

2744. On the *Playboy* interview: Larry Grobel. *Writer's Digest,* vol. 58, January 1978, p. 21.

2745. Out of the pages: ghost writers. *People,* vol. 10, December 18, 1978, pp. 15-16.

2746. Participants as historians; do war memoirs make good history. V. Dedijer. *Times Literary Supplement,* no. 3457, May 30, 1968, pp. 555-556.

2747. Perfect interview. Joni Winn. *Writer,* vol. 97, August 1984, pp. 15-17+.

2748. Perils and paradoxes of writing biography. Paul Murray Kendall. *Saturday Review,* vol. 48, March 27, 1965, pp. 14-16+.

2749. Permission to quote; use of original documents, letters, etc. E.L. Bernays. *Writer,* vol. 79, April 1966, pp. 20-22.

2750. Personal point of view in orally communicated history. Barbara Allen. *Western Folklore,* vol. 38, April 1979, pp. 110-118.

2751. Plotting the biography; excerpts from *Biography: The Craft and The Calling.* Catherine Drinker Bowen. *Writer,* vol. 82, February 1969, pp. 16-18.

2752. Popular and super-pop biographies: definitions and distinctions. Lynn Z. Bloom. *Biography,* vol. 3, Summer 1980, pp. 225-239.

2753. Popular topical autobiography. Beverly Seaton. *Biography,* vol. 5, Summer 1982, pp. 253-266.

2754. Portrait of the artist as an old man. Leon Edel. *American Scholar,* vol. 47, Winter 1977, pp. 52-68.

2755. Practical biography. B.L. Reid. *Sewanee Review,* vol. 83, Spring 1975, pp. 357-363.

2756. Prison diarist's coming of age. N. Di Spoldo. *America,* vol. 132, January 18, 1975, pp. 30-32.

2757. Private lives and public accounts. Thomas J. Cottle. *Biography,* vol. 1, Winter 1978, pp. 23-39.

2758. Private lives and public faces: ethnic American autobiography. (Panunzo, Covello, and Carnevali). J.C. Holte. *Ethnic Groups,* vol. 4, 1982, pp. 61-83.

2759. Problems of a biographer. Reginald Pound. *Author,* vol. 87, Spring 1976, pp. 24-25.

2760. Psychobiography: case history or life history? R.W. Noland. *Midwest Quarterly,* vol. 20, Autumn 1978, pp. 7-17.

2761. Psychobiography of everyday life. R.W. Noland. *Nation,* vol. 224, May 7, 1977, pp. 570-572.

2762. Psychohistory and its discontents. Donna Arzt. *Biography,* vol. 1, Summer 1978, pp. 1-36.

2763. Reading other people's mail: a sampler of great letters. Alden Whitman. *Harvard Magazine,* vol. 82, March/April 1980, pp. 57-59.

2764. Reality of real people. A. Pryce-Jones. *Commonweal,* vol. 83, October 22, 1965, pp. 88-89+.

2765. Reflecting women. Patricia Spacks. *Yale Review,* vol. 63, Autumn 1973, pp. 26-42.

2766. Researching and writing the biography. W.C. Roper. *Writer's Digest,* vol. 52, May 1972, pp. 30-32+.

2767. Rosamond ravished, but Rose rose. Rebecca West. *Vogue,* vol. 161, January, 1973, p. 113.

2768. Santayana on autobiography. J. Ballowe. *American Literature,* vol. 41, May 1969, pp. 219-230.

2769. Scientist in biography. H.I. Sharlin. *Bulletin of Atomic Scientists,* vol. 19, November 1963, pp. 27-28.

2770. Second thoughts about notebooks. A.B. Holland. *Writer's Digest,* vol. 49, March 1969, p. 18.

2771. Some considerations on psycho-history. J.M. Woods. *Historian,* vol. 36, August 1974, pp. 722-735.

2772. Some principals of autobiography. William L. Howarth. *New Literary History,* vol. 5, Winter 1974, pp. 363-381.

2773. Sound of Justin Kaplan's *Brainwaves* (popular biographer of Twain and Whitman). Gary Provost. *Writer's Digest,* vol. 62, January 1982, pp. 46-49.

2774. Spirit of the ghostwriter. Nan Schram Williams. *Writer's Digest,* vol. 56, December 1976, pp. 38-40+.

2775. Stalking the science interview. Dean R. Lambe. *Writer's Digest,* vol. 58, February 1978, p. 20.

2776. Star interview is born. Larry Grobel. *Writer's Digest,* vol. 58, January 1978, pp. 19-23.

2777. Stars are easier to reach than you think; writing and selling the celebrity interview. J.P. Kowal. *Writer's Digest,* vol. 54, November 1974, pp. 30-33.

2778. Stephen Birmingham; master of the unauthorized biography. Jane Heimlich. *Writer's Digest,* vol. 60, April 1980, pp. 26-27.

2779. Stop watering down biographies: biography for children. F. Martin. *Library Journal,* vol. 84, December 15, 1959, pp. 3887-3888.

2780. Stories of real life. David Gervais. *Cambridge Quarterly,* vol. 9, no. 1, pp. 56-64.

2781. Successful collaboration. D.T. Streib. *Writer's Digest,* vol. 49, November 1969, pp. 63-65+.

2782. Successful collaboration; when two pens are better than one. Leonard Fedler. *Writer,* vol. 96, December 1983, pp. 20-22.

2783. Talk with the biographers. *New York Times Book Review,* April 20, 1980, pp. 29-31.

2784. That one may say this was the man: the biographer must blow the breath of life into inert bits of the past. Leon Edel. *New York Times Book Review,* June 24, 1956, pp. 1, 12.

2785. Thinking about biography. P. Stansky. *New Republic,* vol. 172, April 19, 1975, pp. 25-27.

2786. Time in autobiography. B. Pike. *Comparative Literature,* vol. 28, Fall 1976, pp. 326-342.

2787. Tips on how and why—to write your autobiography. George Moberg. *Writer's Digest,* vol. 63, May 1983, pp. 32-33.

2788. Trade winds; ghostwriters. J. Beatty. *Saturday Review,* vol. 51, September 14, 1968, p. 21.

2789. Two pens are better than one (collaboration). Julie Raskin and Carolyn Males. *Writer's Digest,* vol. 60, July 1980, pp. 20-24.

2790. Unfulfilled promise of life histories. James M. Freeman and David L. Krantz. *Biography,* vol. 3, Winter 1980, pp. 1-13.

2791. Use of court records in biographical research. Robert J. Brink. *Biography,* vol. 1, Winter 1978, pp. 79-89.

2792. Uses of autobiography. P. Shaw. *American Scholar,* vol. 38, Winter 1968, pp. 136+.

2793. Veto of the imagination: a theory of autobiography. L.A. Renza. *New Literary History,* vol. 9, Autumn 1977, pp. 1-26.

2794. When sports figures turn author: jocks and their ghosts. H. Higdon. *Saturday Review,* vol. 54, August 14, 1971, pp. 48-49+.

2795. Why I? Herbert Gold. *Saturday Review,* vol. 2, February 8, 1975, pp. 18-21.

2796. Women's stories, women's selves. Patricia Spacks. *Hudson Review,* vol. 30, Spring 1977, pp. 29-46.

2797. Write your own history. J.A. McCracken. *Reader's Digest,* vol. 111, August 1977, pp. 7-9+.

2798. Writing about Abraham Lincoln; address November 9, 1974. O. Coolidge. *Horn Book,* vol. 51, February 1975, pp. 31-35.

2799. Writing about the superstar. J.W. Steen. *Writer's Digest,* vol. 53, March 1973, pp. 27-28+.

2800. Writing and selling the personality profile. Gary Provost. *Writer's Digest,* vol. 61, November 1981, pp. 21-23+.

2801. Writing biographies for young readers. O.W. Burt. *Writer,* vol. 85, February 1972, pp. 18-21.

2802. Writing biography for young people. F. Cavanah. *Writer's Digest,* vol. 48, January 1968, pp. 36-38+.

2803. Writing juvenile biography. C.O. Peare. *Writer,* vol. 79, April 1966, pp. 23-24+.

2804. Writing of biography. Elisabeth Young-Bruehl. *Partisan Review,* vol. 50, no. 3, 1983, pp. 413-427.

2805. Writing the unauthorized biography. Gloria Miklowitz. *Writer's Digest,* vol. 60, April 1980, pp. 22-25.

Freelancing, Including Magazine Article Writing

"No man but a blockhead ever wrote except for money."
—Samuel Johnson

Books

2806. Alexander, Louis. *Beyond the Facts; A Guide to the Art of Feature Writing.* Houston: Gulf, 1975. 263 pp.

With newspapers, magazines, and broadcasting in mind, Alexander has created a serviceable guide to ideas, interviewing, researching, illustration, captions, and achievement features. The latter part of this well-organized effort deals with the types and inner workings of magazines.

2807. American Society of Magazine Editors. *Making Magazines.* New York: ASME, 1978. 95 pp.

This slim volume has been called "... a cram course on the fundamentals of the magazine business." It covers circulation, editorial philosophy, and production concepts.

Barnhart, Helene. *How to Write and Sell the Eight Easiest Article Types.* See entry 4247.

2808. Behrens, John. *The Magazine Writer's Workbook; A Worktext of Instructions and Exercises for the Beginning Magazine Article Writer.* Introduction by Alex Haley. Revised edition. Columbus, Ohio: Grid, 1972. 162 pp.

Seven chapters take the user through such fundamentals of magazine writing as interviewing, query letters, and marketing finished products. These are followed by nineteen lengthy exercises which allow the user to write a wide variety of short articles suggested by interview accounts and other resource materials.

2809. Biagi, Shirley. *How to Write and Sell Magazine Articles.* Englewood Cliffs, New Jersey: Prentice-Hall, 1981. 156 pp.

A crisp and informed analysis of writing free-lance magazine articles which received a good critical reception.

2810. Boeschen, John. *How to Make Money Freelancing; A Guide to Writing and Selling Nonfiction Articles.* Richmond, California: Wordworks, 1979. 141 pp.

This short conversational approach provides tips on developing publishable article ideas, locating markets, convincing editors of the value of one's ideas, researching and finding facts, and writing readable and entertaining prose. The final chapter, "Saving at tax time," offers brief but useful advice.

2811. Boggess, Louise. *How to Write Fillers and Short Features that Sell.* 2nd edition. New York: Harper & Row, 1981. 256 pp.

A practical and informative guide written by an established free-lance writer which discusses motivation, methods, and markets.

2812. Borland, Hal G. *How to Write and Sell Non-fiction.* Westport, Connecticut: Greenwood Press, 1973. 223 pp. Reprint of the 1956 edition.

While the information about earnings and markets is hopelessly dated, the chapters dealing with writing discipline, interviewing, and sources of ideas remain valid. Borland is the author of the widely praised *When the Legends Die.*

2813. Burack, Sylvia K., editor. *How to Write and Sell Short Fillers, Light Verse, and Short Humor.* Boston: Writer, 1977. 143 pp.

This lively anthology by experienced authors and editors covers topics that range from how to be funny and preparing and selling copy to writing light verse. Part 2 contains a list of publications, along with addresses and market information about each, including rates of pay.

2814. Burgett, Gordon. *Ten Sales from One Article Idea.* Carpentina, California: Write to Sell, 1982. 101 pp.

Tells how to rewrite a sound set of ideas and how to walk the resulting editorial tightropes.

2815. Casewit, Curtis. *Freelance Writing, Advice from the Pros.* New York: Collier Macmillan, 1974. 272 pp.

Casewit says that he draws on interviews with writers such as Irving Wallace, James Jones, James Baldwin, Francois Sagan, and Lawrence Durrell to produce a beginning text on both magazine and book freelancing. Despite such name dropping, this is a middling effort.

2816. Cassill, Kay. *The Complete Handbook for Freelance Writers.* Cincinnati: Writer's Digest, 1981. 400 pp.

This better than average manual addresses nonfiction freelancing as a prospective business and calls for disciplined market analysis, research, and self organization. Less a "how-to write" book than a work on "how-to organize your resources," it challenges the reader to think in terms of reasonable cash flow, taxes, and promotion.

Delton, Judy. *The Twenty-nine Most Common Writing Mistakes and How to Avoid Them.* See entry 4251.

2817. Dickson, Frank A. *One Thousand One Article Ideas.* Cincinnati: Writer's Digest, 1979. 270 pp.

To quote the book's jacket, "a treasure trove of salable article ideas, plus ... formulas for developing your own." If this sounds like a gimmick book, it is just that, but one which works.

2818. Duncan, Lois. *How to Write and Sell Your Personal Experiences.* Cincinnati: Writer's Digest, 1979. 226 pp.

Tells how to turn mundane experiences, such as recollections from adolescence or current family problems, into salable articles and books. Written by one who has done just that with over three hundred articles and stories and more than twenty-two books, this is an up-to-date discussion of markets and technique for one of the most reliable of the freelance writing areas: confessions and women's slicks.

2819. Emerson, Connie. *How to Make Money Writing Fillers.* Cincinnati: Writer's Digest, 1983. 266 pp.

Emerson offers advice and instruction on short articles, one-liners, greeting cards, recipes, and the like.

2820. ———. *Write on Target.* Cincinnati: Writer's Digest, 1981. 234 pp.

Style, title, article tone, point of view, editorial references, and taboos are examined for antidotes to rejection. This practical book can be recommended to the beginner both for its advice and its wealth of examples.

2821. Evans, G., editor. American Society of Journalists and Authors. *The Complete Guide to Writing Non-Fiction.* Cincinnati: Writer's Digest, 1983. 800 pp.

Over one hundred professional writers draw on their experiences relating to manuscript mechanics, research, interviewing, work habits, contracts, and collaboration. Section two reveals fifteen "hot" writing specialities and how to break into them.

2822. Freedman, Helen R., and Karen Krieger. *The Writer's Guide to Magazine Markets; Non-fiction.* New York: New American Library, 1983. 384 pp.

Provides marketing information about 125 well-established magazines that publish nonfiction articles. The entries, based on editor responses, tell who to contact, what they are buying, how much they pay, and so on. Added information covers queries, manuscript submissions, and a glossary of terms.

2823. Faux, Marian. *Successful Freelancing; The Complete Guide to Establishing and Running Any Kind of Freelance Business.* New York: St. Martins, 1982. 256 pp.

Written mainly for the literary freelancer, this well-planned work offers valuable advice on insurance and retirement plans, tax considerations, time management, and marketing.

2824. Gehman, Richard. *How to Write and Sell Magazine Articles.* New York: Harper, 1959. 348 pp.

Each of fourteen articles that appeared in ranking national magazines is analyzed according to the writing problem it illustrates. Useful chapters on the lead, researching, revision, and outlining, all examined from Gehman's perspective as an experienced article writer.

Gordon, Barbara, and Elliot Gordon. *How to Survive in the Freelance Jungle—A Realistic Plan for Success in Commercial Art and Photography.* See entry 3714.

2825. Goulart, Frances S. *How to Write A Cookbook—and Sell It.* Port Washington, New York: Ashley Books, 1980. 117 pp.

Goulart tells us first that over 500 new cookbooks are published each year and then goes on to tell not only how to write one, but how to publish and promote it. Among the specific issues she addresses are agents, rejections, revisions, establishing credentials, and creating reader appeal.

2826. Gundell, Glenn. *Writing; From Idea to Printed Page. Case Histories of Stories and Articles Published in the "Saturday Evening Post."* New York: Greenwood Press, 1969. 374 pp.

Originally published in 1949, during the golden era of slick popular magazines, this book nevertheless offers a revealing analysis. For each of six stories and articles, which originally appeared in the *Post,* letters between author and editor, the rough manuscript with corrections, and the finished article itself are provided to document the development of an idea into the finished product.

2827. Gunther, Max. *Writing the Modern Magazine Article.* Boston: Writer, 1973. 185 pp.

Covers article ideas, article types, mail research, library research, interviewing, leads, anecdotes, quotes, transitions, choosing a title, endings, and style. A final section called "Anatomy of Three Articles" shows how these principles are applied in actual writing situations.

2828. Hanson, Nancy E. *How You Can Make $20,000 a Year Writing (No Matter Where You Live).* Cincinnati: Writer's Digest, 1980. 270 pp.

An experienced freelancer provides informal advice on how to go about it. As for the title: well maybe, and maybe not, even if you live on Publisher's Row.

2829. Hinds, Marjorie M. *How to Make Money Writing Short Articles and Fillers.* New York: Frederick Fell, 1968. 127 pp.

This concise and practical guide tells how to "break into" the non-fiction short article and filler segment of the newspaper and magazine field. It covers short fillers by type, under hobbies, puzzles, recipes, quizzes, jokes, anecdotes, epigrams, and the like. The do's and don'ts of writing effectively and selling what one writes are also outlined in this simple survey for beginners and younger readers.

2830. Holmes, Marjorie M. *Writing the Creative Article.* Boston: Writer, 1976. 143 pp.

Holmes defines creative articles as being concerned with advice, personal experience, vigorous protest, some phase of life, nostalgia, humor, or inspiration. For such writing, she considers ideas more important than facts. She goes on to explain how to develop ideas and how to express them in various styles. She also discusses the use of anecdotes, article lengths, and marketing. Holmes is the author of many articles and books on self-help and inspirational themes.

2831. Hull, Raymond. *How to Write "How-to" Books and Articles.* Cincinnati: Writer's Digest, 1981. 202 pp.

Takes the prospective writer into the vast arena of instructing practical skills, which is seen as "accessible and lucrative."

2832. ———. *Writing for Money in Canada.* Don Mills, Ontario: Longmans, 1969. 211 pp.

Billed as a text for Canadian writers, much of this work will apply to any number of English-speaking nations, but those sections on legal aspects and copyright have more specific application, as do the marketing suggestions. Beyond this, Hull discusses the generation of ideas, writing sidelines, and brief information about writing for markets such as book, magazine, play, film, television, radio, short story, and poetry.

2833. Jacobs, Hayes B. *Writing and Selling Non-fiction.* Cincinnati: Writer's Digest, 1975. 317 pp.

Covers brainstorming for ideas, research methods, style variations, general organization, rights, and marketing techniques.

2834. Kelley, Jerome E. *Magazine Writing Today.* Cincinnati: Writer's Digest, 1978. 220 pp.

A seasoned reporter, article writer, and editor shares his experiences and insight into matters of composition and marketing. Emphasis is on common mistakes, leads, research, queries, and interviews.

2835. Kevles, Barbara. *Basic Magazine Writing; How to Master the Five Most Important Article Forms and Sell Them to the Leading National Magazines.* Cincinnati: Writer's Digest, 1981. 252 pp.

Provides both how and how-not-to examples plus marketing strategies for the biographical profile, the service article, the single issue article, the question and answer interview, and the multiple viewpoint article.

2836. Knott, William C. *The Craft of Non-Fiction.* Reston, Virginia: Reston Publishers, 1974. 126 pp.

With suggestions for local as well as national markets, Knott succinctly outlines paths, pitfalls, and techniques connected with article writing. He tells how to conduct interviews, do research, give stories significance, and sharpen one's writing style. Chapters on outlining, hooking the reader, rewriting, and daily schedules complete this short but well-written text for beginners.

2837. Krieger, Karen, and Helen R. Freedman. *The Writer's Guide to Magazine Markets: Fiction.* New York: New American Library, 1983. 336 pp.

Provides information about 125 well-established magazines that publish short fiction. Based on editor responses, the entries tell exactly whom to contact, what will sell, what they pay, and rights information. Additional information includes queries, manuscripts, and a glossary of terms.

2838. Lieberman Research, Inc. *How and Why People Buy Magazines; A National Study of the Consumer Market for Magazines.* Port Washington, New York: Publishers Clearing House, 1977. 131 pp.

This study, which reflects interviews with magazine consumers on the effects of age, leisure time, educational level, occupation, and costs on subscription and single issue purchase decisions, provides an excellent understanding of the world of which freelance writers are a part.

2839. Long, Joan, and Ronald Long. *Writer's and Photographer's Guide to Newspaper Markets.* 2nd edition. Costa Mesa, California: Helm, 1981. 175 pp.

2840. Mau, Ernest E. *The Free-lance Writer's Survival Manual.* Chicago: Contemporary Books, 1981. 224 pp.

Offers a valuable set of tips on soliciting work from company brochures and technical manuals to magazine assignments. Also discusses fees, tax angles, and other business-keeping problems.

2841. Mayes, Herbert R. *The Magazine Maze.* Garden City, New York: Doubleday, 1980. 378 pp.

Reminiscences of a Hearst Corporation executive with editing experience that included *McCall's, Good Housekeeping* and *Cosmopolitan.*

2842. Milton, John. *The Writer Photographer.* Philadelphia: Chilton Book Company, 1972. 196 pp.

Drawing on his experiences as a freelance writer-photographer the popular magazine market, Milton presents a balanced informative overview.

2843. Mitford, Jessica. *Poison Penmanship; The Gentle Art of Muckraking.* New York: Knopf, 1979. 277 pp.

Essays by one of the great investigative article and book writers of our time. Her techniques in both writing and information extraction are "shamelessly" revealed.

2844. Nelson, Roy Paul. *Articles and Features.* Boston: Houghton Mifflin, 1978. 434 pp.

Called "fuzzy" by reviewers, this text offers a number of useful insights that somewhat compensate for that designation.

2845. Peterson, Franklynn, and Judi Kesselman-Turkel. *Magazine Writer's Handbook.* Englewood Cliffs, New Jersey: Prentice Hall, 1983. 256 pp.

The authors combine experience as freelancers and editors to show how articles are taken from the idea stage, through development, to marketing. This work does a better than average job of explaining interviewing, focus, the use of anecdotes, slanting, and article research.

2846. Pickens, Judy E. *The Freelancer's Handbook; A Comprehensive Guide to Selling Your Freelance Services.* Englewood Cliffs, New Jersey: Prentice-Hall, 1981. 135 pp.

Called comprehensive by its author, this is actuallly a brief introduction to the subject. It contains valuable marketing, budgeting, and fee-setting suggestions as well as an excellent section on setting goals.

2847. Pitzer, Sara. *How to Write a Cookbook and Get It Published.* Cincinnati: Writer's Digest, 1984. 256 pp.

This well-organized and informative effort comes "highly recommended" by *Booklist* and includes chapters on the idea stage, collecting and testing recipes, overcoming writer's block, and developing marketing appeal.

2848. Polking, Kirk. *Jobs for Writers.* Cincinnati: Writer's Digest, 1980. 281 pp.

Over forty alternative freelance "writing-related" job situations are described by as many expert contributors. The writing opportunities covered in this collection range from advertising, anthology editing, indexing, reviewing, comedy writing, business freelancing, and speech writing to convention and association writing.

2849. Provost, Gary. *The Freelance Writer's Handbook.* New York: New American Library, 1982. 230 pp.

A prolific freelancer discusses article sales, the short story, reviews, ghostwriting, agents, contracts, and a wide variety of topics relating to the writing life. This work represents a good introductory guide to the business of freelancing without saying much about technique.

2850. Rees, Clair. *Profitable Part-Time/Full-Time Freelancing; A Step-By-Step Guide to Writing Your Way to Freedom and Financial Success.* Cincinnati: Writer's Digest, 1980. 195 pp.

With an emphasis on the business aspects of freelancing, this encouraging work discusses financial rewards, dry periods, marketing, and transition from part-time to full-time writing.

2851. Rivers, William L. *Free-lance and Staff Writer; Writing Magazine Articles.* Belmont, California: Wadsworth, 1976. 294 pp.

This book gives detailed advice on article writing, as well as tips on the inner workings of various kinds of magazine publishing houses. It includes sample articles, letters from editors, and instructions to the young journalist on how to break into the field. All-in-all, a highly useful source, both for understanding the world of magazine journalism and writing for it.

2852. Rivers, William L., and Shelley Smolkin. *Free-lancer and Staff Writer; Newspaper Features and Magazine Articles.* 3rd edition. Belmont, California: Wadsworth, 1980. 346 pp.

Continues as a standard source for freelancers, particularly in the magazine sector. Chapters include working with a photographer and writing humorous articles.

2853. Rose, Camille D. *How to Write Successful Magazine Articles.* Boston: Writer, 1967. 226 pp.

Rose, a former executive editor of *McCall's*, gives an informed and straightforward account of writing magazine articles. She treats not only the expected essentials, such as research, interviewing and the lead, but also a variety of ways dialogue and characterization can be used to enliven nonfiction.

2854. Ruehlmann, William. *Stalking the Feature Story; How to Get and Write the Facts on the People, Places, and Events that Make the News.* Cincinnati: Writer's Digest, 1978. 314 pp.

With an emphasis on good writing and with examples from writers such as Charles Dickens, Ernest Hemingway, and Raymond Chandler, this work suggests how to develop ideas, find leads, add color, and develop critical judgment. Journalists have called this work "inspiring" and "irresistible," and though it is mainly concerned with newspaper work it contains too much valuable advice to be ignored by freelancers. Nineteen feature articles are used to illustrate nineteen separate concepts.

2855. Samson, Jack. *How to Be a Successful Outdoor Writer.* Cincinnati: Writer's Digest, 1979. 288 pp.

Taking full account of trends such as the new environmental awareness, this work has a sharpness and variety to it that should fully benefit its readers.

2856. Schapper, Beatrice. *Writing the Magazine Article; From Idea to Printed Page.* Cincinnati: Writer's Digest, 1970. 198 pp.

Case histories of how each of eight writers developed an idea into an article that was eventually accepted by a major magazine. This book provides copies of letters between writer and editor, first drafts along with corrections, and significant research items which influenced the ultimate direction and the tone of each article. Though writing and editorial styles have changed since the mid-1960s, this is nonetheless a rare opportunity to "look over the shoulders" of professional writers as they work.

2857. Society of Magazine Writers. *A Treasury of Tips for Writers.* Edited by Marvin Weisbord. Cincinnati: Writer's Digest, 1965. 174 pp.

According to its introduction, this ".. is a compendium of habits, tricks, devices, tips, and gimmicks..." used by the contributing eighty-six professional writers. Idea formulation and time budgeting are among the host of topics covered.

2858. Spikol, Art. *Magazine Writing; The Inside Angle.* Cincinnati: Writer's Digest, 1979. 256 pp.

Spikol brings the full force of his broad experience to give his readers a tightly organized and first-rate analysis of the subject. Conversational in style and informal in tone, his work is an up-to-date account of magazine freelancing in the 1980s which realistically assesses the limits of economic reward. It also suggests the risks of libel and cites major mistakes to avoid when marketing one's work.

2859. Tarshis, Barry. *How to Write Like a Pro; The Techniques of Writing Nonfiction for Magazines, Newspapers, Technical Journals, and More.* Foreword by Dan McKinney, managing editor of *McCall's.* New York: New American Library, 1982. 192 pp.

Discusses and illustrates proven techniques for gaining reader attention and holding it, as well as for directing reader interest.

2860. Vachon, Brian. *Writing for Regional Publications.* Cincinnati: Writer's Digest, 1979. 203 pp.

Tells how to size up regional markets and describes how regional publications differ. Contains a chapter on converting article ideas into books. Plausible article ideas and convincing suggestions abound.

2861. Whittlesey, Marietta. *Freelance Forever; Successful Self Employment.* New York: Avon, 1982. 416 pp.

Though not specifically designed for writers, this well-oganized guide discusses time management, answering machines, record keeping, taxes, debt management, and general health tips.

2862. Wilbur, L. Perry. *How to Write Articles That Sell.* New York: Wiley, 1981. 217 pp.

This work received a lukewarm reception upon publication, due to its repetitiveness and poor examples.

2863. Williams, W.P., and Joseph Van Zandt. *How to Write Magazine Articles That Sell.* Chicago: Contemporary Books, 1979. 98 pp.

In three major sections, planning the article, writing the article, and selling the article, this short work discusses audience, use of newspaper techniques, photojournalism, and payments. It will supplement but hardly replace more in-depth efforts.

2864. Zobel, L. *Travel Writer's Handbook.* Cincinnati: Writer's Digest, 1980. 346 pp.

Zobel stresses such factors as research and market analysis prior to the travel writing trip, sharpening one's powers of observation when traveling, specific travel writing techniques such as viewpoint and transition, the art of interviewing, and the use of photography. She also discusses tax considerations and even what to pack for a travel writing adventure.

See also the chapter on Marketing (page 323) for book annotations containing references to freelancing.

Articles

2865. Adapting to success: writing the adaptation. Tim Kelly. *Writer's Digest,* vol. 63, March 1983, pp. 32-37.

2866. Ankle deep in warm tears: how to make nostalgia pay. Colleen Reece. *Writer's Digest,* vol. 60, October 1980, pp. 31-34.

2867. Another specialty: freelance textbook copyediting. B. Balfour. *Writer's Digest,* vol. 49, January 1969, p. 53.

2868. Arrest that reader! E. Shepherd. *Writer's Digest,* vol. 56, September 1976, pp. 50-51.

2869. Article ideas: from manuscript to magazine. J.P. Fried and H. Kurtz. *Writer,* vol. 77, December 1964, pp. 16-19+.

2870. Article: nonfiction story. M.T. Dillon. *Writer,* vol. 88, May 1975, pp. 9-11.

2871. Articles anyone can write. Don McKinney. *Writer,* vol. 94, December 1981, pp. 23-24+.

2872. Articles you can write and sell. L. Perry Wilbur. *Writer,* vol. 95, September 1982, pp. 18-20+.

2873. At your service; selling service pieces. Art Spikol. *Writer's Digest,* vol. 56, July 1976, pp. 10+.

2874. Become a self-help expert and sell. Samm S. Baker. *Writer,* vol. 96, June 1983, pp. 9-12.

2875. Begetting of *The Begatting;* How three freelancers parleyed a book idea into a book sale, movie option, and Orson Welles record. L. Haynes. *Writer's Digest,* vol. 50, August 1970, pp. 30-31.

2876. Big opportunities in the small press. Judson Jerome. *Writer's Digest,* vol. 64, June 1984, pp. 24-28.

2877. Break into print with a how-to article. K.O. Sweeney. *Writer,* vol. 89, October 1976, pp. 28-29.

2878. Building a framework for an article. Max Gunther. *Writer,* vol. 80, August 1967, pp. 14-16+.

2879. But can you break in? writing for *Esquire.* M. Lasky. *Writer's Digest,* vol. 54, October 1974, pp. 26-27.

2880. Can you cover? Art Spikol. *Writer's Digest,* vol. 56, May 1976, pp. 10+.

2881. Checklist for a salable article. Louise Boggess. *Writer,* vol. 89, June 1976, pp. 22-25+.

2882. Confessions buy articles, too! B.Y. O'Dell. *Writer's Digest,* vol. 48, May 1968, pp. 64-65+.

2883. Cooking up the food/recipe article. Rona Zable. *Writer's Digest,* vol. 63, April 1983, pp. 30-33.

2884. Corresponding for the trades. Ed Morris. *Writer's Digest,* vol. 56, July 1976, pp. 26-27+.

2885. Craft of writing craft articles. N. Jackson. *Writer's Digest,* vol. 57, January 1977, pp. 35-37.

2886. Creating pictures for yourself and your readers, new approach to article writing. C.P. May. *Writer,* vol. 86, January 1973, pp. 13-15.

2887. Creative article. Marjorie M. Holmes. *Writer,* vol. 80, December 1967, pp. 16-19.

2888. Do you have the right angle to sell to TV guide? R. Malone. *Writer's Digest,* vol. 52, October 1972, pp. 22-24+.

2889. Don't be a wordy bird. Selma Glasser. *Writer,* vol. 96, March 1983, pp. 18-20.

2890. Don't give your opinions—sell them. Writing personal opinion pieces. S. Prange. *Writer,* vol. 96, January 1983, pp. 19-21+.

2891. Don't try to sell ice to Eskimos; freelancing. V.L. Oertle. *Writer's Digest,* vol. 48, November 1968, pp. 48-53.

2892. Fair play for freelances. *Author,* vol. 87, Summer 1976, pp. 63-64.

2893. Fifteen steps to winning the sports correspondence game. Steve Ellis. *Writer's Digest,* vol. 61, April 1981, pp. 35-38.

2894. Fillers and short items that sell; with list of markets. Selma Glasser. *Writer,* vol. 88, December 1975, pp. 19-22.

2895. First words are important. E. Marshall. *Writer's Digest,* vol. 49, April 1969, pp. 63-65.

2896. Five sales in one year to *Reader's Digest.* J. Mills. *Writer's Digest,* vol. 49, July 1969, pp. 38-43+.

2897. Five things I tell my class in article writing. J. Stocker. *Writer,* vol. 82, October 1969, pp. 25-26.

2898. Foreign markets for Yankee manuscripts. *Writer's Digest,* vol. 59, March 1979, pp. 38-42.

2899. Freelance article writer. M.M. Hunt. *Writer,* vol. 75, January 1962, pp. 18-19+.

2900. Freelance frustrations. *Author,* vol. 87, Summer 1976, pp. 65-66.

2901. Freelance job aid: promotion packet. C.G. Welton. *Writer's Digest,* vol. 51, August 1971, p. 27.

2902. Freelance job idea: convention freelancing. E. Engle. *Writer's Digest,* vol. 49, April 1969, pp. 42-43+.

2903. Freelance job idea: family histories. K. Carvell. *Writer's Digest,* vol. 51, July 1971, pp. 30-31+.

2904. Freelance job idea; pharmacy newsletters. C.J. Levin. *Writer's Digest,* vol. 49, May 1969, pp. 48-50.

2905. Freelance market report: Harcourt, Brace and Jovanovich trade journals. M.W. Fedo. *Writer's Digest,* vol. 51, November 1971, pp. 28-30.

2906. Freelance opportunities with associations. M.A. DeVries. *Writer's Digest,* vol. 50, September 1970, pp. 28-30+.

2907. Freelance specialty; recipe contests. V. Wines. *Writer's Digest,* vol. 52, April 1972, pp. 31-32.

2908. Freelance writers cite long list of woes but like independence. A. Kent MacDougall. *Wall Street Journal,* August 7, 1970, p. 1.

2909. Freelancing for newspapers. N. Kraft. *Writer's Digest,* vol. 56, March 1976, pp. 24-27.

2910. Fresh look at old ideas. L.L. Oldham. *Writer,* vol. 96, September 1983, pp. 31-32.

2911. From clippings to articles. William Miles. *Writer,* vol. 96, November 1983, pp. 18-20.

2912. From our rostrum; travelling with pen and camera. J.J. Chalmers. *Writer,* vol. 81, July 1968, pp. 26-30.

2913. From personal experience to article sales. P.Y. Guth. *Writer,* vol. 88, November 1975, pp. 28-29.

2914. Full-time freelance writer. J. Hale. *Writer's Digest,* vol. 49, March 1969, pp. 38-41.

2915. Full-time freelance writer: who is he? M. Renz. *Writer's Digest,* vol. 50, December 1970, pp. 24-26+.

2916. Full-time freelancer. O. Stewart. *Writer's Digest,* vol. 50, April 1970, pp. 23+.

2917. Full-time freelancing in rural route U.S.A. C. Stowers. *Writer's Digest*, vol. 51, April 1971, pp. 35-36+.

2918. Getting it write for *The Mother Earth News.* Report from an editor. David Petersen. *Writer*, vol. 97, August 1984, pp. 22-24.

2919. Getting started in freelancing. C.A. Smith. *Writer's Digest*, vol. 53, February 1973, pp. 17-18+.

2920. Getting the right article idea; excerpt from *Writing and Selling Nonfiction.* Hayes B. Jacobs. *Writer's Digest*, vol. 48, October 1968, pp. 34-37+.

2921. Give your how-to articles the voice of authority. Leonard McGill. *Writer's Digest*, vol. 64, August 1984, pp. 26-28.

2922. Good things come from small magazines. Ed Morris. *Writer's Digest*, vol. 60, December 1980, pp. 38-39.

2923. Happy hack. Derek Parker. *Author*, vol. 47, Autumn 1976, pp. 90-92.

2924. Harvesting a cash crop from farm magazines. Jeffrey Tennant. *Writer's Digest*, vol. 60, November 1980, pp. 25-30.

2925. Harvesting fruit from the writers' grapevine (networks). Kay Marie Porterfield. *Writer's Digest*, vol. 64, June 1984, pp. 36-38.

2926. Having wonderful time, wish you were there; travel writing. A.R. Pastore, Jr. *Writer*, vol. 84, October 1971, pp. 17-19+.

2927. Here at *The National Enquirer.* Frederick Woodress. *Writer's Digest*, vol. 57, July 1977, pp. 24-26.

2928. Hop aboard the music education bandwagon. Arthur J. Michaels. *Writer's Digest*, vol. 61, April 1981, pp. 39-43.

2929. How beginning writers can see their work in print and get paid for it; local newspapers. Doris E. Davis. *Writer*, vol. 87, December 1974, pp. 28-29.

2930. How fares the freelance writer? A. Geracimos. *Publishers Weekly*, vol. 201, March 6, 1972, pp. 30-33.

2931. How free is the freelance writer? N. Sayre. *Mademoiselle*, vol. 66, March 1968, pp. 177+.

2932. How I freelanced my way through Southeast Asia. F. Wells. *Writer's Digest*, vol. 52, August 1972, pp. 35-37+.

2933. How I sold my book again and again (book excerpts for magazine publication). Ralph Bugg. *Writer's Digest*, vol. 64, July 1984, pp. 26-29.

2934. How much your freelance time is worth. T. Crone. *Writer's Digest*, vol. 51, March 1971, pp. 28-29+.

2935. How to fictionize your article. H.D. Steward. *Writer's Digest,* vol. 48, August 1968, pp. 43-47.

2936. How to find and develop article ideas. B. Friedan. *Writer,* vol, 75, March 1962, pp. 12-15.

2937. How to find article ideas. Max Gunther. *Writer,* vol. 80, April 1967, pp. 24-27.

2938. How to generate hundreds of salable article ideas. Bob Kall. *Writer's Digest,* vol. 63, May 1983, pp. 22-28.

2939. How to get an article idea. P. Vandervoort. *Writer,* vol. 89, May 1976, pp. 15-17.

2940. How to go pro. Increase your article sales. Gary Turbak. *Writer,* vol. 97, July 1984, pp. 20-21+.

2941. How to learn what editors want and then write the article query. V. Guarino. *Writer's Digest,* vol. 48, April 1968, pp. 37-41.

2942. How to make money as a part-time writer. R. Hays. *Writer's Digest,* vol. 48, January 1968, pp. 25-26+.

2943. How to query an editor; advice to the writer of a magazine article. R.E. Greer. *Writer's Digest,* vol. 53, October 1973, pp. 9-11.

2944. How to research periodical articles by mail; facts to build magazine articles. Max Gunther. *Writer,* vol. 79, April 1979, pp. 13-16.

2945. How to sell articles to British magazines. F. Pasqualini. *Writer's Digest,* vol. 51, October 1971, pp. 25-27.

2946. How to sell the how-to article. K. Vining. *Writer's Digest,* vol. 48, July 1968, pp. 57-59.

2947. How to sell to the top religious magazines. E.H. Pitts. *Writer,* vol. 80, June 1967, pp. 31-33.

2948. How to write an article lead. Don McKinney (Editor, *McCall's). Writer,* vol. 95, December 1982, pp. 7-10.

2949. How to write and sell the round-up article. G. Evans. *Writer's Digest,* vol. 52, October 1972, pp. 27-29+.

2950. How to write articles for *Cosmopolitan.* Helen Gurley Brown. *Writer,* vol. 93, July 1980, pp. 12-13.

2951. How to write for specialized magazines. M.H. Endres. *Writer,* vol. 84, September 1971, pp. 24-25.

2952. How to write the science story. Ritchie Ward. *Writer's Digest,* vol. 58, February 1978, pp. 19-22.

2953. How to write your way through college. Lois Duncan. *Writer,* vol. 89, February 1976, pp. 29-30.

2954. Hows and whats of nonfiction ideas. F.A. Rockwell. *Writer,* vol. 88, September 1975, pp. 15-17.

2955. I am a lineman for the county?...?weeklies. Ed Woodward. *Writer's Digest,* vol. 62, October 1982, pp. 34-36.

2956. Idea a day. Frank A. Dickson. *Writer's Digest,* vol. 51, February 1971, pp. 12-13; March 1971, pp. 12+; June 1971, pp. 18-20; August 1971, pp. 16-17+.

2957. Idea Machine. D.R. Patterson. *Writer's Digest,* vol. 56, July 1976, pp. 22-23.

2958. If you want to sell to the *Reader's Digest:* the golden treasury of thou-shalt not's. E.T. Thompson (Editor-in-Chief, *Reader's Digest). Writer,* vol. 96, February 1983, pp. 12-14+.

2959. In journalistic search of the hillside strangler. Ted Schwarz. *Writer's Digest,* vol. 61, March 1981, pp. 20-25.

2960. Increase your article sales; marketing nonfiction. Omer Henry. *Writer,* vol. 88, April 1975, pp. 19-21+.

2961. Incredibly rich tabloid market. Larry Holden. *Writer's Digest,* vol. 57, July 1977, pp. 19-22.

2962. Interviewing for trade journal articles. M. Tyson. *Writer's Digest,* vol. 51, July 1971, pp. 25-27.

2963. Johnny deadline to the rescue: Bob Greene. Michael Schumacher. *Writer's Digest,* vol. 63, January 1983, pp. 30-33.

2964. Journalism's guerrillas; free lancers. A. Balk. *Saturday Review,* vol. 49, March 12, 1966, pp. 143-144.

2965. Keeping an eye on your figures (expense and overhead). Carl Kaft and Neil Kaft. *Writer's Digest,* vol. 64. October 1984, pp. 38-41.

2966. Leading with your best; writing introductory paragraphs. B. Vachon. *Writer's Digest,* vol. 56, August 1976, pp. 24-25+.

2967. Let's slay Procrustes. D. Toliver. *Writer,* vol. 89, November 1976, pp. 26-27.

2968. Little magazines; with list of markets. A.D. Winans. *Writer's Digest,* vol. 54, September 1974, pp. 24-27.

2969. Local history: a beginner's gold mine. A. Lynch *Writer,* vol. 84, February 1971, p. 26.

2970. Local human interest articles. Omer Henry. *Writer,* vol. 94, January 1981, pp. 22-24+.

2971. Long voyage; writing about far-off places. H. Innes. *Writer,* vol. 83, March 1970, p. 25.

2972. Look homeward angle: a guide to writing the city guidebook. Martin Fischhoff. *Writer's Digest,* vol. 58, December 1978, pp. 21-27.

2973. Magazine articles as art. A. Balk. *Saturday Review,* vol. 49, July 9, 1966, p. 57. Reply G. Walker, vol. 49, August 13, 1966, p. 60.

2974. Magic sentence. B. Lang. *Writer,* vol. 79, October 1966, pp. 20-21+.

2975. Make it personal; articles that communicate. G. Taber. *Writer,* vol. 82, April 1969, pp. 15-17.

2976. Making editors pay as you go (travel writing). L. Zobel. *Writer's Digest,* vol. 58, April 1978, pp. 18-25.

2977. Markets for the 90+ freelancer. M. Brodsky. *Writer,* vol. 96, November 1983, pp. 25-26.

2978. Memo from a late bloomer. V.J. Ross. *Writer,* vol. 95, June 1982, pp. 27-28.

2979. Moonlighting becomes you. Arturo F. Gonzalez, Jr. *Writer's Digest,* vol. 58, February 1978, pp. 23-25.

2980. Muscling in on the muscle magazines. Barry Sparks. *Writer's Digest,* vol. 60, June 1980, pp. 31-34.

2981. New sales in an "old" market: the antiques magazines. Ronald W. Pilling. *Writer's Digest,* vol. 60, September 1980, pp. 33-35.

2982. Nine to five, freelance style (time management). Paul Bernstein. *Writer's Digest,* vol. 62, August 1982, pp. 16-22.

2983. Nineteen hot markets to watch in 1984 (magazines representing new trends: *Vanity Fair, Sepia,* etc.). Robert D. Lutz. *Writer's Digest,* vol. 63, December 1983, pp. 24-29+.

2984. No Mounties, no maple leaves: writing for Canadian magazines. Cheryl MacDonald. *Writer's Digest,* vol. 60, August 1980, pp. 32-35.

2985. No where to go but down. Writing for the diving magazines. Ellsworth Boyd. *Writer's Digest,* vol. 61, January 1981, pp. 39-42+.

2986. Nonfiction, three to one. Samm S. Baker. *Writer,* vol. 82, January 1969, pp. 19-20+.

2987. Nothing ever sold in a desk drawer. Marjorie M. Holmes. *Writer,* vol. 89, September 1976, pp. 11-13.

2988. Occupational hazards of the professional article writer. D. Sherwood. *Writer's Digest,* vol. 52, November 1972, pp. 27-28+.

2989. On changing jobs: from fulltime to freelance. H. Bruback. *Mademoiselle,* vol. 83, December 1977, pp. 72-74.

2990. On one who wrote not wisely but to sell; magazine freelancing. M. Malone. *Nation,* vol. 224, May 14, 1977, pp. 597-598.

2991. On the road to becoming an off-road writer. Joe Zambone. *Writer's Digest,* vol. 60, July 1980, pp. 34-38.

2992. One idea: multiple sales. M.W. Fedo. *Writer's Digest,* vol. 51, June 1971, p. 31.

2993. Op-ed page market. S.E. Bleecker and D. Sandhage. *Writer's Digest,* vol. 56, June 1976, pp. 42-44.

2994. Out of the rough and into the green (golf freelance writing). *Writer's Digest,* vol. 60, October 1980, pp. 22-27.

2995. Part-time professional writer Steve Allen; an exclusive interview. *Writer's Digest,* vol. 52, December 1972, pp. 32-33+.

2996. Patterns for writing that first feature. M. Manor. *Writer's Digest,* vol. 56, November 1976, pp. 26-27.

2997. Personal essay; articles from experience. R. Hochstein. *Writer,* vol. 81, April 1968, pp. 9-12.

2998. Personal experiences, instant articles. M. Rozell. *Writer,* vol. 86, June 1973, pp. 26+.

2999. Phone interviewing. Kay Marie Porterfield. *Writer,* vol. 97, April 1984, pp. 18-20.

3000. Photos help sell your articles. Margaret Johnston. *Writer,* vol. 96, March 1983, pp. 25-26.

3001. Pit writer. J.J. Fookes. *New Statesman,* vol. 92, December 24-31, 1976, pp. 898-899.

3002. Plugging into the computer market: opportunities for freelance writers. *Writer,* vol. 97, April 1984, pp. 21-23.

3003. Pot boiler taken literally; recipes. P.E. Paden. *Writer's Digest,* vol. 48, September 1968, pp. 25-26.

3004. Pro looks at travel writing. A.R. Pastore, Jr. *Writer's Digest,* vol. 48, March 1968, pp. 42-45+.

3005. Reaching for the *Reader's Digest.* J.M. Allen. *Writer,* vol. 90, April 1977, pp. 26-28+.

3006. Red Smith in the final innings: interview with sportswriter. John Kern. *Writer's Digest,* vol. 62, June 1982, pp. 20-26.

3007. Report on the quarterlies. P.P. Witonski. *National Review,* vol. 20, November 5, 1968, pp. 1124-1126.

3008. Say when (seasonal articles). Rona Zable. *Writer's Digest,* vol. 64, June 1984, pp. 29-30.

3009. Scanning the CB market; writing for CB trade publications. *Writer's Digest,* vol. 56, July 1976, p. 40.

3010. Search the past for future sales. Allen J. McGill. *Writer,* vol. 97, May 1984, pp. 13-15.

3011. Secret of full-time freelancing: get a retainer. T. Rakstis. *Writer's Digest,* vol. 51, December 1971, pp. 28-30+.

3012. Selling the seasonal article is no piece of cake. Rebecca Muller. *Writer's Digest,* vol. 62, January 1982, pp. 40-43.

3013. Selling to men's magazines. Jack B. Olesker. *Writer,* vol. 97, May 1984, p. 10-12+.

3014. Selling what you write; freelancing. Crescent Dragonwagon. *Seventeen,* vol. 33, August 1974, p. 144.

3015. Selling your first article. D.C. Gleasner. *Writer's Digest,* vol. 49, May 1969, pp. 51-53.

3016. Service articles with a smile. George Campbell. *Writer's Digest,* vol. 60, October 1980, pp. 39-41.

3017. Service, shelter, store, and sex; writing for women's magazines. Don McKinney. *Writer's Digest,* vol. 55, February 1975, pp. 16-19.

3018. Shift into high gear. Writing for the auto hobby press. Chris Halla. *Writer's Digest,* vol. 61, February 1981, pp. 29-32+.

3019. Shoot your fish, in a barrel; selling selected articles to specialist magazines. T. McCarthy. *Writer,* vol. 81, November 1968, pp. 27-28.

3020. Short and, therefore, sweet. Shorties. Brief articles that focus on a single mood, idea, bit of information, or piece of humor. John Bryan. *Writer's Digest,* vol. 64, August 1984, pp. 29-31.

3021. Should the magazine article writer specialize? Freelancing. W.B. Furlong. *Writer's Digest,* vol. 48, May 1968, pp. 42-47+.

3022. Should your child be a freelance writer? Sara Pitzer. *Writer's Digest,* vol. 48, January 1968, pp. 44-46+.

3023. Small matter of truth (manuscript accuracy). Roger Caras. *Writer,* vol. 97, May 1984, pp. 7-9.

3024. Some new uses for the good old days; commemorative writing tips. M.S. Peterson. *Writer's Digest,* vol. 53, November 1973, pp. 14-17.

3025. Sources for feature articles. P. Robinson. *Writer,* vol. 75, June 1962, pp. 22-23.

3026. Special assignments: how to develop and capitalize on a writing specialty. Sandra Dark. *Writer's Digest,* vol. 63, March 1983, pp. 39-41.

3027. Special tabloid issue; writing for the tabloid press; symposium. *Writer's Digest,* vol. 57, July 1977, pp. 19-28.

3028. Starting your article right; six steps. Omer Henry. *Writer,* vol. 96, October 1983, pp. 18-20+.

3029. Successful article writing. C. Anderson. *Writer,* vol. 72, March 1959, pp. 5-7+.

3030. Surviving as a writer (freelance writing). S. Morton. *Writer,* vol. 93, September 1980, pp. 7-8.

3031. Syndicates: how they work, and how they can work for you. Candy Schulman. *Writer's Digest,* vol. 64, February 1984, pp. 31-34.

3032. Take five: the most common mistakes among beginning freelancers. M.L. Stein. *Writer's Digest,* vol. 56, February 1976, pp. 42-43.

3033. Tears before the mast; submitting work to periodical editors. Art Spikol. *Writer's Digest,* vol. 57, February 1977, pp. 14+.

3034. Ten article ideas that pay off. L. McLaughlin. *Writer,* vol. 79, June 1966, pp. 18-20.

3035. Ten ways to build article sales. K. Cruzic. *Writer,* vol. 90, December 1977, pp. 30-31.

3036. Thinking ahead: 34 article ideas for fall and winter. Frank A. Dickson. *Writer's Digest,* vol. 60, April 1980, pp. 33-35.

3037. Thought for food; with list of markets for the food writer. J. Pendergast and M. Pendergast. *Writer's Digest,* vol. 56, April 1976, pp. 23-26+.

3038. Three common errors in article writing. Samm S. Baker. *Writer,* vol. 79, December 1966, pp. 14-16.

3039. Three R's for revitalizing article sales. Larry Holden. *Writer's Digest,* vol. 60, January 1980, pp. 41-43.

3040. Tis pity he's a whore: writing for *Oui.* Ron Berler. *Chicago Magazine,* vol. 25, June 1976, p. 234.

3041. Tis the season for seasonal articles. C.E. Parker. *Writer's Digest,* vol. 55, December 1975, pp. 30+.

3042. Trials and joys of free-lance writing. Binnie S. Braunstein. *Serials Librarian,* vol. 7, Spring 1983, pp. 57-62.

3043. Try small newspapers. P. Nussman. *Writer's Digest,* vol. 57, March 1977, p. 35.

3044. Turn the "merchants page" to freelance opportunities. Nicholas Ahlfs. *Writer's Digest,* vol. 61, June 1981, pp. 30-31.

3045. Twelve money-making ideas for writers. Ted Schwarz. *Writer's Digest,* vol. 64, May 1984, pp. 37-38.

3046. Twelve ways to end your article gracefully. Robert L. Baker. *Writer's Digest,* vol. 62, October 1982, pp. 30-33.

3047. Twenty-five tips for writer-photographers. R. Rae. *Writer's Digest,* vol. 63, February 1983, pp. 32-35+.

3048. Twenty-five top-paying magazine markets. *Writer,* vol. 90, June 1977, pp. 29-31.

3049. Twenty-three tips for writer-photographers. Melissa Milar and William Brohaugh. *Writer's Digest,* vol. 58, June 1978, pp. 28-29.

3050. Two keys to instant magazine article sales. G. Jones. *Writer,* vol. 81, August 1968, pp. 25-26.

3051. Typewriter as time machine: the secrets of selling seasonal material. Jacqueline Shannon. *Writer's Digest,* vol. 64, November 1984, pp. 33-34.

3052. Uncle Sam wants you... on a freelance basis, of course. W.G. Williams. *Writer's Digest,* vol. 61, July 1981, pp. 29-31.

3053. Using anecdotes in article writing. Max Gunther. *Writer,* vol. 81, June 1968, pp. 11-15.

3054. Vast market for trade journal articles. *Writer,* vol. 96, February 1983, pp. 21-24. (List of journals, pp. 28-42.)

3055. Viewing with alarm. T. Curry. *Writer,* vol. 80, July 1967, pp. 29-30.

3056. What it's like to freelance. Rex Lardner. *Saturday Review,* vol. 54, January 9, 1971, pp. 47-49.

3057. What the city desk uses. N. Melnick. *Writer's Digest,* vol. 52, January 1972, pp. 22-23+.

3058. What writers should know about little magazines. Bruce McAllister. *Writer,* vol. 97, March 1984, pp. 10-12+.

3059. When you need a nonfiction idea. Max Gunther. *Writer,* vol. 89, January 1976, pp. 14-15+.

3060. Where to sell op-ed articles. *Writer,* vol. 90, May 1977, pp. 23-24.

3061. Where to sell op-ed articles. *Writer,* vol. 94, September 1981, pp. 24-25.

3062. Why freelance writers get nervous. J.N. Bell. *Saturday Review,* vol. 50, November 11, 1967, pp. 91-92. Dicussion, vol. 51, January 13, 1968, pp. 108-109.

3063. Write a query, get an assignment! magazine writers and editors. S.W. Olds. *Writer,* vol. 90, August 1977, pp. 15-19.

3064. *Writer's Digest 100:* magazines where you can expect fair, courteous, and prompt treatment. *Writer's Digest,* vol. 62, January 1982, pp. 21-30.

3065. Writing a magazine article. R. Dunlop. *Writer,* vol. 88, March 1975, pp. 14-16.

3066. Writing and selling the homespun how-to article. Gary Turbak. *Writer's Digest,* vol. 61, June 1981, pp. 26-29.

3067. Writing and selling the nearly perfect article. Charles V. Main. *Writer's Digest,* vol. 63, May 1983, pp. 29-31.

3068. Writing and selling to foreign markets. B. Quarteroni. *Writer's Digest,* vol. 59, February 1979, pp. 35-40.

3069. Writing article queries that sell. J. Fisher. *Writer,* vol. 84, June 1971, pp. 18-20+.

3070. Writing for regional magazines; with a list of markets. B. Vachon. *Writer,* vol. 89, September 1976, pp. 19-23.

3071. Writing for rock (music) magazines. Russell Shaw. *Writer's Digest,* vol. 58, March 1978, pp. 26-28.

3072. Writing for syndicates: how to get started as a syndicate writer. Valerie Bohigan. *Writer,* vol. 97, March 1984, pp. 16-18+.

3073. Writing for the men's magazines. Michael Schumacher. *Writer's Digest,* vol. 63, July 1983, pp. 24-32.

3074. Writing for the regional market. S.W. Martin. *Writer,* vol. 85, February 1972, pp. 24-25.

3075. Writing for the women's magazines. Elaine F. Shimberg. *Writer's Digest,* vol. 63, June 1983, pp. 20-23.

3076. Writing for the science and mechanics magazines. R.M. Benrey. *Writer,* vol. 84, November 1971, pp. 26-27.

3077. Writing life: Tom Wolfe. *Writer's Digest,* vol. 60, April 1980, pp. 18-19.

3078. Writing non-fiction. C.M. Curtis. *Writer,* vol. 80, January 1967, pp. 22-29.

3079. Writing queries that sell (magazines). Stephen Whitty. *Writer,* vol. 96, November 1983, pp. 12-14+.

3080. Writing sports for all sorts of magazines. Jay Stuller. *Writer's Digest,* vol. 62, April 1982, pp. 36-39.

3081. Writing the person-centered magazine article. Crescent Dragonwagon. *Writer,* vol. 96, August 1983, pp. 7-10+.

3082. Writing the roundup article. Gary Provost. *Writer's Digest,* vol. 60, June 1980, pp. 36-40.

3083. Writing with a legal twist. Lori B. Andrews. *Writer's Digest,* vol. 59, July 1979, pp. 28-31.

3084. Xerox-Salisbury-Esquire axis. A. Gingrich. *Esquire,* vol. 85, June 1976, pp. 8+.

3085. You are what you write; newspaper food articles. S. Middaugh. *Writer's Digest,* vol. 56, November 1976, pp. 38-39.

3086. You can write for horse magazines—if you avoid ten nagging mistakes. Byron Travis. *Writer's Digest,* vol. 60, March 1980, pp. 38-40.

3087. You don't have to be a mechanical genius to sell to mechanical magazines. Dick Barnett. *Writer's Digest,* vol. 59, October 1979, pp. 20-24.

3088. You meet such interesting people: diary of a freelancer. C. Schwalberg. *U.S. Camera,* vol. 32, January 1969, pp. 64-65+.

3089. Your smalltown newspaper needs you. M.A. Belyea. *Writer's Digest,* vol. 56, March 1976, pp. 28-30.

Technical Writing

"From a little distance one can perceive an order in what at the time seemed confusion."

—F. Scott Fitzgerald

Books

3090. Anderson, Paul V., and others. *New Essays in Technical and Scientific Communication; Research, Theory, and Practice.* Farmingdale, New York: Baywood, 1983. 254 pp.

The twelve previously unpublished essays in this collection represent important recent theoretical and practical communication concerns. They cover, among other topics, revision, topical focus, readable style, the role of models, and technical writing as a social act.

3091. Andrews, Clarence A. *Technical and Business Writing.* Boston: Houghton Mifflin, 1975. 243 pp.

This superior beginning text shows how to write and illustrate letters, technical reports, feasibility studies, various formal and informal reports, process papers, and materials destined for publication. It combines clearness with ample detail and offers the reader expert instruction regarding patterns in the technical sentence and technical paragraph, standards and specifications, and something called "technical software."

3092. Blicq, Ronald S. *Technically—Write! Communications in the Technical Era.* 2nd edition. Englewood Cliffs, New Jersey: Prentice-Hall, 1981. 381 pp.

Viewed as one of the better general introductions to the subject of technical writing, this work offers a broad range of techniques, most of which are based on actual situations. From planning and first draft through focus, brevity, clarity, and tone, there persists a heavy emphasis on basic communication skills. Writing types covered in-depth are letters, memoranda, inspections, investigations, proposals, feasibility studies, evaluations, briefs, and field trips. Appended is an extended glossary of technical usage.

3093. Brusaw, Charles T., and others. *Handbook of Technical Writing.* 2nd edition. New York: St. Martin's Press, 1982. 695 pp.

261

Called comprehensive and practical by its authors, this desktop reference is definitely both. It suggests five major steps to successful writing plus a "checklist of the writing process," but the bulk of the work concerns itself with usage, punctuation, and a variety of topics such as schematic diagrams, test reports, interviewing, documentation, and library research, all in easy-to-use dictionary form. Should be considered as a first purchase by new technical writers.

3094. Chandler, Harry E. *The "How to Write What" Book; For the Thousands of Writers in Science, Industry, Government, and Education Who Seek a Better Way to Present Information.* Metals Park, Ohio: American Society for Metals, 1978. 92 pp.

A short and reasoned statement on how to develop better content and organization in one's writing.

3095. Cypert, Samuel A. *Writing Effective Business Letters, Memos, Proposals, and Reports.* Chicago: Contemporary Books, 1983. 320 pp.

Filled with advice and examples on letters, memos, proposals, and reports, this valuable source relies on an audience-directed approach. Reviewers have noted its usefulness in the areas of research and writing rules.

3096. Damerst, William A. *Clear Technical Reports.* 2nd edition. New York: Harcourt, Brace, Jovanovich, 1982. 325 pp.

Arranged by major sections, such as clear communication, mastering the skills, presenting the finished product, and special finished products. A final section called "a technical writer's handbook" deals with usage, errors in diction, numbers, and abbreviations. Exercises follow each chapter.

3097. Day, Robert A. *How to Write and Publish a Scientific Paper.* 2nd edition. Philadelphia: ISI Press, 1983. 181 pp.

"Everything needed for the writing and production of a good paper is here. No scientist is too seasoned and no student too green not to have a good use for this." *Science Books and Films.* Day acts as managing editor of the American Society of Microbiology.

3098. Dodds, Robert H. *Writing for Technical and Business Magazines.* Malabar, Florida: Krieger, 1982. 194 pp. (Reprint of original 1969 Wiley imprint.)

Beginning with an explanation of the need for proficient technical writing, Dodds covers such matters as writing for an audience, text preparation, illustrations, and what to do after publication, including the use of reprints. Useful appendices covering style, copy reading symbols, and a list of publications that use contributed articles are included.

3099. Dumaine, Deborah. *Write to the Top; Writing for Corporate Success.* New York: Random House, 1983. 141 pp.

This pragmatic approach to business writing is divided into two parts. The first discusses the unabashedly manipulative uses of writing in a variety of business situations. The second part consists of a usage handbook.

3100. *Effective Communication for Engineers.* New York: McGraw-Hill, 1975. 216 pp.

An anthology of articles that originally appeared in the journal *Chemical Engineer.*

3101. Ewing, David W. *Writing for Results in Business, Government, the Sciences and the Professions.* 2nd edition. New York: John Wiley and Sons, 1979. 448 pp.

Called by the *Journal of Business Communications,* "The Rolls Royce of books on business writing," Ewing's book contains over one hundred cases and problems. Accompanied by a "Glossary of expungible words with substitutions" such as finalize—complete, I am in receipt of—I have, and It has been brought to my attention I have learned. Contains a succinct chapter on writing for business and scientific publications.

3102. Fear, David E. *Technical Communication.* 2nd edition. Glenview, Illinois: Scott, Foresman, 1981. 385 pp.

David Fear has become a name associated with superior technical writing texts. This volume is no exception. Under broad chapter headings, Fear offers expert advice about planning, writing, revising, and illustrating technical materials. Later, he deals with specific applications such as correspondence, reports, proposals, job descriptions, specifications, professional articles, and forms. His final contribution is a supplement on style, grammar and punctuation, spelling, and mechanics.

3103. ———. *Technical Writing.* Glenview, Illinois: Scott, Foresman, 1981. 385 pp.

Intended primarily for technical and industrial students, this is a beginning survey of writing techniques as they apply to technical letters, formal and informal reports, illustrations, and oral reports. Valuable additional features include worksheet planning, realistic case studies, and a job package on resumes, applications, and interviews.

3104. Fishbein, Morris. *Medical Writing; The Technic and the Art.* Springfield, Illinois: Charles Thomas, 1978. 203 pp.

Reflecting Fishbein's long association with such publications as *The Journal of the American Medical Association, Medical World News,* and *Excerpta Medica,* this work contains a wealth of sound advice on style, manuscript construction, numbers and abbreviations, bibliographies, illustrations, and indexing.

3105. Gould, Jay R. *Directions in Technical Writing and Communication.* Farmingdale, New York: Baywood, 1977. 152 pp.

Each of these outstanding articles, selected for their long-term value from the *Journal of Technical Writing and Communication,* covers a different approach to the subjects. The topics range from generally effective writing and readability to editorial viewpoint and technical sales literature. The result is an ar*hology of commendable quality.

3106. Grimm, Susan J. *How to Write Computer Manuals for Users.* Belmont, California: Lifetime Learning, 1982. 211 pp.

Directed to an audience that includes systems analysts and programmmers, as well as technical writers, this competently executed book tells how to "... research, plan, write, review, and maintain successful manuals." It offers concise coverage of an area about which very little else has been written. Included is a glossary of computer terms.

3107. Harty, Kevin J., editor. *Strategies for Business and Technical Writing.* New York: Harcourt, Brace, Jovanovich, 1980. 285 pp.

The twenty-five essays in this anthology, some of them classics, address such diverse topics as listening, the seven sins of technical writing, defensive writing, jargon and how to avoid it, as well as specific solutions to letter and report writing problems. Contains Morris Freedman's "The seven sins of technical writing" and "Gobbledygook" by Stuart Chase.

3108. Hill, Mary, and Wendell Cochran. *Into Print; A Practical Guide to Writing, Illustrating, and Publishing.* Los Altos, California: William Kaufmann, 1977. 175 pp.

The authors address the needs of those writing in technical fields and the professions in a tightly organized book that tells a little (sometimes too little) about every major consideration within its stated scope. Hints on finding ideas, writing, rewriting, using graphs and engineering drawings, indexing, and dealing with publishers are all included. References at the end of most chapters offer keys to additional information. Hill and Cochran are co-editors of *Geowriting: A Guide to Writing, Editing, and Printing in the Earth Sciences.*

3109. Holtz, Herman. *Persuasive Writing; Communicating Effectively in Business.* New York: McGraw-Hill, 1983. 256 pp.

Holtz addresses a wide range of situations that require the art of persuasion. Among these are speeches, new releases, resumes, and sales promotions. Frequent examples of how to and how not to round out this solid text.

3110. Holtz, Herman, and Terry Schmidt. *The Winning Proposal; How to Write It.* New York: McGraw-Hill, 1981. 381 pp.

Thought by some reviewers to be the single most useful source on proposal writing. The standard methods described include capturing interest, technical persuasion, program implementation, and competitive advantage. Case histories and examples of winning proposals round out this superior achievement.

3111. Houp, Kenneth, and Thomas E. Pearsall. *Reporting Technical Information.* 5th edition. New York: Macmillan, 1984. 549 pp.

This top-rated text for students and professionals in engineering and technology covers graphics, proposals, library research, measurement systems, and instructional manuals, in addition to full coverage of technical report writing and revision. A list of scientific reference materials and a series of exercises complete this comprehensive approach.

3112. Huff, Darrell. *How to Lie with Statistics.* New York: Norton, 1954. 142 pp.

While telling how readers are misled by statistics, Darrell also tells how not to delude oneself and one's readers. A classic.

3113. Huth, Edward J. *How to Write and Publish Papers in the Medical Sciences.* Philadelphia: ISI Press, 1982. 203 pp.

Intended for journal article writers in "medicine and closely related fields," this practical guide covers many topics not addressed by other works. Literature searching, case reports, case-series analysis, the editorial, book reviews, and many other chapters make for a comprehensive and understandable approach to a complex subject. Of particular value is the appendix called "twenty steps in planning, writing, and publishing a paper." Huth is editor of the highly respected *Annals of Internal Medicine.*

3114. Jacobi, Ernst. *Writing at Work; Do's, Don'ts, and How-to's.* Rochelle Park, New Jersey: Hayden, 1976. 198 pp.

Jacobi places a heavy emphasis on content and interest techniques, including theme, point of view, and problem stating, while at the same time warning against the dangers of over-outlining, which he feels can kill one's style. This work contains much good advice on avoiding common writing pitfalls and is an excellent companion to Strunk and White's *Elements of Style* (see entry 3698).

3115. Kapp, Reginald. *Presentation of Technical Information.* London: Constable, 1973. 184 pp.

Kapp's work appears frequently on recommended lists as a source that combines the deeper philosophical considerations with pragmatic do's and don'ts of technical writing.

3116. Lamphear, Lynn. *Shortcuts to Effective On-the-Job Writing.* Englewood Cliffs, New Jersey: Prentice-Hall, 1982. 179 pp.

Proven techniques and exercises for developing clarity of style and avoiding jargon. Concentrates on letters, memos, and reports with precise and concise writing as the ultimate goals.

3117. Lanham, Richard A. *Revising Business Prose.* New York: Scribner, 1981. 98 pp.

This admirable, short work tells how to achieve precision, accuracy, and directness, and how to remove the imprecise and impersonal from business English. It has been favorably compared with Strunk and White's *Elements of Style* (see entry 3698).

3118. Lannon, John M. *Technical Writing.* Boston: Little, Brown, 1982. 623 pp.

Widely praised for its comprehensiveness and use of concrete examples, this work concentrates on deliberate communication techniques, as well as on strategies for rhetoric and research, and applies such concepts to a wide assortment of technical writing situations, among which are letters, resumes, memos, form reports, proposals, and oral reports.

3119. McGehee, Brad M. *The Complete Guide to Writing Software Use Manuals.* Cincinnati: Writer's Digest, 1984. 300 pp.

Offers practical advice on creating manuals and finding markets once you have done so.

McGuire, Jerry. *How to Write, Direct, and Produce Effective Business Films and Documentaries.* See entry 517.

3120. Mambert, W.A. *Presenting Technical Ideas; A Guide to Audience Communication.* New York: Wiley, 1968. 216 pp.

Long considered a standard approach to the subject, this work covers, among other topics, audience, outlining, rehearsing, analysis, and delivery.

3121. Manko, Howard H. *Effective Technical Speeches and Sessions; A Guide for Speakers and Program Chairmen.* New York: McGraw-Hill, 1969. 174 pp.

Both respect and demand have kept this concise handbook in print. Covers creating interest, using the right vocabulary, visual aids, organizing a technical meeting, and parliamentary procedure.

3122. Michaelson, Herbert B. *How to Write and Publish Engineering Papers and Reports.* Philadelphia: ISI Press, 1982. 158 pp.

Questions such as reader interest, multiple authorship, planning and organizing, writing abstracts, avoiding information traps, using illustrations, constructing tables, compiling a bibliography, editing and marketing the manuscript, and dealing with potential critics are handled with competence and ease. Anyone contemplating engineering publication should have access to this first-rate work.

3123. Michaelson, Herbert B., Judson Monroe, and others. *Science of Scientific Writing.* Dubuque, Iowa: Kendall Hunt, 1977. 111 pp.

With emphasis on data management and organization, as opposed to style and grammar, this work covers visual aids, formats, proofreading, structure and meaning, and writing as conditioned behavior. The authors demonstrate how a scientist's basic skills of analysis and organization can be used to produce orderly and objective writing.

3124. Mitchell, John H. *Writing for Professional and Technical Journals.* New York: Wiley, 1968. 405 pp.

From the preface: "This book does two things. First it defines and illustrates the recognizable characteristics of professional and technical articles. Second, it anthologizes conflicting sections of the style guides issued for representative disciplines and illustrates those style guides by reprinting and reviewing representative articles." Though the original edition remains in print and serves to illustrate this aspect of writing for publication, a new edition is badly needed. Robert Day's *How to Write and Publish a Scientific Paper* (see entry 3097) should also be consulted, as should Harley Sachs's *How to Write the Technical Article and Get It Published* (see entry 3130).

3125. Morris, George E. *Technical Illustrating.* Englewood Cliffs, New Jersey: Prentice-Hall, 1975. 244 pp.

Covers the tools, techniques, and fundamentals of technical illustration. Has appendices for reproduction processes, typography, prefixes, and abbreviations.

3126. Mracek, Jan. *Technical Illustration and Graphics.* Englewood Cliffs, New Jersey: Prentice-Hall, 1983. 296 pp.

Designed for an era of "rapid change" and "accelerated technology," this comprehensive work covers drafting and drawing equipment, geometric construction, multiview drawing, isometric drawing, oblique drawing, perspective drawing, inking, printing and reproduction processes, and related topics. It provides an expert overview of a complex subject.

3127. Pearsall, Thomas E. *Audience Analysis for Technical Writing.* Beverly Hills, California: Glencoe Press, 1969. 113 pp.

The needs of each audience, be it layperson, executive, technician, or operator, will determine content and style, according to this wise and unique approach.

3128. Pearsall, Thomas E., and Donald H. Cunningham. *How to Write for the World of Work.* New York: Holt, Rinehart and Winston, 1982. 397 pp.

A business report and technical writing text designed for beginners.

3129. Pickett, Nell, and Ann Lester. *Technical English; Writing, Reading, and Speaking.* 4th edition. New York: Harper & Row, 1984. 722 pp.

This competent and popular text is divided into three major parts. The first part deals with principles and forms of communication in the industrial setting. The second consists of readings selected for their value to the technical student as well as for their relationship to part two. Part three is a handbook on usage.

3130. Sachs, Harley. *How to Write the Technical Article and Get It Published.* Washington, D.C.: Society for Technical Communication, 1976. 64 pp.

Intended for competent writers who are in need of guidance, this short but essential book covers ideas, research, interviewing, picking a title, leads and endings, rewriting, illustration, and marketing.

3131. Sheen, Anitra P. *Breathing Life Into Medical Writing; A Handbook.* St. Louis: Mosby, 1982. 108 pp.

Designed specifically for physicians, this short work covers such concepts as the central idea, clarity, jargon, accuracy, emphasis, metaphor and simile, and humor.

3132. Sherman, Theodore A., and Simon Johnson. *Modern Technical Writing.* 4th edition. Englewood Cliffs, New Jersey: Prentice-Hall, 1983. 512 pp.

This highly regarded text for engineers and scientists contains major sections on the general aspects of technical writing, reports and proposals, business correspondence, as well as a handbook of fundamentals. This comprehensive work is completed by a glossary, a list of technical abbreviations, and suggested additional readings.

3133. Smith, Terry C. *How to Write Better and Faster.* New York: Crowell, 1965. 220 pp.

A broad spectrum book aimed at helping almost anyone write clearly and correctly. Covers business reports and proposal writing, letters and memos, editing, and public relations as well as printing, copying, and illustration.

3134. Souther, James W., and Myron L. White. *Technical Report Writing.* New York: Wiley, 1977. 93 pp.

Placing emphasis on the writing process while at the same time providing both practical suggestions and an overall view of writing at the technical level, the authors of this excellent source first distinguish between technical and scientific writing. They then move on to analysis and design alternatives.

3135. Sparrow, W. Keats, and Donald Cunningham, editors. *Practical Craft; Readings for Business and Technical Writers.* Boston: Houghton Mifflin, 1978. 306 pp.

This collection of twenty-eight articles addresses the following major topics: What is business and technical writing and why study such writing? What style is appropriate for business and technical writing? What are some important writing strategies? What are some important types of letters and reports? What are the important formal elements of reports? Among the contributors are Rudolf Flesch, Morris Freedman, Paul Zall, S.I. Hayakawa, and Jacques Barzun.

3136. Thomas, T.A. *Technical Illustration.* 3rd edition. New York: McGraw-Hill, 1978. 280 pp.

Hundreds of illustrations, which range from isometric drawings, layouts, templates, and shading techniques to inking methods and oblique drawings, support the clear and even text. Without question, a superior work in all respects.

3137. Thorne, Charles. *Better Medical Writing.* London: Pitman, 1970. 96 pp.

Mainly concerned with articles and conference papers, this compact effort discusses style, correspondence with editors, rejection, and acceptance. Also covered are words to avoid and medical ethics.

3138. Tichy, Henrietta J. *Effective Writing for Engineers, Managers, and Scientists.* New York: John Wiley and Sons, 1966. 337 pp.

A respected approach to what is viewed as an abused area of writing. The chapter entitled "Two Dozen Ways to Begin" is a useful antidote for technical writer's block. Remains in print but would benefit from revision.

3139. Tracy, Raymond C., and Harold L. Jennings. *Writing for Industry.* Chicago: American Technical Society, 1973. 280 pp.

Intended for the vocational specialists, this clearly written text covers a variety of on-the-job reports and includes accident, inspection, project, and specification report writing as well as bids, proposals, letters, and job applications.

3140. Turner, Maxine T. *Technical Writing; A Practical Approach.* Reston, Virginia: Reston Publishing, 1983. 507 pp.

This comprehensive guide to style and mechanics, as well as to formats, addresses a number of issues that are not well covered elsewhere. The work abounds with useful examples. It is particularly valuable in its treatment of technical presentations and professional ethics.

3141. Ulman, Joseph N., Jr., and Jay R. Gould. *Technical Reporting.* 3rd edition. New York: Holt, Rinehart and Winston, 1972. 419 pp.

Covers grammar, punctuation, style, mechanics, tables, and illustrations, with heavy emphasis on layout and writing of reports. Considered a standard source by technical writers and editors.

3142. Van Til, William. *Writing for Professional Publication.* Boston: Allyn and Bacon, 1981. 332 pp.

In addition to receiving a wealth of advice on techniques for writing scholarly and professional books and articles, the reader is taken behind the scenes and shown style and production considerations facing editors. Text and popular book markets are explored, as are contract negotiations, index preparation, book reviewing, and the writing of yearbooks and anthologies. This work has more immediately useful information on the subjects it covers than any other book in print. It has received wide praise.

3143. Weisman, Herman M. *Basic Technical Writing.* 4th edition. Columbus, Ohio: Merrill, 1980. 414 pp.

This widely accepted text surveys the fundamentals of technical writing, including basic techniques, the role of the scientific method, investigative analysis, organizing data, graphic elements, and shorter technical writing forms such as technical correspondence and proposals. Appended material includes a variety of sample letters, reports, proposals, questionnaires, and articles.

3144. ————. *Technical Correspondence; A Handbook and Reference Source for the Technical Professional.* New York: Wiley, 1968. 218 pp.

Intended for the memo, letter, and report writing scientist and engineer. Contains a chapter on applied psychology in such writing. Weisman is a respected name among technical writers, as is this book.

3145. ————. *Technical Report Writing.* 2nd edition. Columbus, Ohio: Merrill, 1978. 181 pp.

Yet another superior contribution to the literature. Covers the elements and history of technical writing, semantics, organizing report data, and report writing techniques and style.

3146. Weiss, Edmond H. *Writing System for Engineers and Scientists.* Englewood Cliffs, New Jersey: Prentice-Hall, 1982. 274 pp.

Taking the premise that writing is a fundamental part of any engineer's or scientist's work day, Weiss provides what he calls a systems approach to planning and organizing one's writing, as well as to drafts, editing, layout, grammar, and mechanics. This is a rewarding short text which concentrates on process, procedure, and strategy.

3147. Wirkus, Tom E., and Harold Erickson. *Communication and the Technical Man.* Englewood Cliffs, New Jersey: Prentice-Hall, 1972. 237 pp.

In addition to covering visual, vocal, and listening skills in communication, this work treats technical communication in both formal and informal reports. Especially valuable is the chapter on the essentials of technical writing.

See also the chapter on Style Manuals (page 317) for book annotations containing references to technical writing.

Articles

3148. ABC's of good technical writing. H.M. Miller. *Supervisory Management,* vol. 10, August 1965, pp. 14-17.

3149. Adventures of a consultant writer; freelance business consultant. C.S. Blinderman. *Writer's Digest,* vol. 57, May 1977, pp. 25-26.

3150. Anatomy of a business report. William E. Spaulding. *Data Management,* vol. 11, July 1973, pp. 16-20.

3151. Annual report high-interest areas outlined in CSI study. *Journal of Accountancy,* vol. 145, February 1978, p. 8.

3152. Annual reports give ad plans more play; special report. P. Orth. *Printers' Ink,* vol. 294, May 12, 1967, pp. 11-14.

3153. Annual reports that fail. *Business Week,* October 18, 1976, p. 73.

3154. Are you an impressionist or an expressionist? C. Reimold. *Tappi,* vol. 64, September 1981, p. 193.

3155. Art of brief writing. F. Trowbridge Vom Baur. *Practical Lawyer,* vol. 22, January 15, 1976, pp. 81-93.

3156. Audio visuals: how to make a complex report understandable. *Association Management,* vol. 24, January 1972, pp. 39-42.

3157. Automated annual statement: preparation. Charles H. Holmes. *Interpreter,* vol. 38, August 1979, pp. 7-9.

3158. Automated internal financial statements. James R. Lesher. *Interpreter,* vol. 37, February 1978, pp. 14-15.

3159. Bad language in financial reports. Niall Lothian. *Accountancy,* vol. 89, November 1978, pp. 42-46.

3160. Better business writing; the audience comes first. Allen Weiss. *Supervisory Management,* vol. 22, April 1977, pp. 2-11.

3161. Better business writing; what's your communications IQ? R.R. Max. *Supervisory Management,* vol. 22, April 1977, pp. 12-15.

3162. Better business writing for banks. R.S. Mason. *Bankers Magazine,* vol. 162, January 1979, pp. 56-60.

3163. Better prospectuses? *Chemical Week,* vol. 102, June 1, 1968, p. 22.

3164. Blank page: don't let it keep you from sharing your good ideas. William Repp. *Supervisory Management,* vol. 23, October 1978, pp. 28-33.

3165. Brevity: soul of wit? R. Schoenfeld. *Chemical Technology,* vol. 12, January 1982, pp. 39-40.

3166. Bridging the corporate communications gap. Mary C. Bromage. *Advanced Management Journal,* vol. 41, Winter 1976, pp. 44-51.

3167. Business and trade journal market. Omer Henry. *Writer,* vol. 83, June 1970, pp. 24-26.

3168. Business writing styles. H.K. Mintz. *Business Horizons,* vol. 15, August 1972, pp. 83-87.

3169. Can bankers save reading time? M.J. Zoeller. *Journal of Commercial Bank Lending,* vol. 59, May 1977, pp. 45-50.

3170. Case for writing case histories. James A. Welser. *Writer's Digest,* vol. 61, October 1981, pp. 40-43.

3171. Choosing the best medium for the message. Allen Weiss. *Supervisory Management,* vol. 22, May 1977, pp. 16-24.

3172. Clear writing means clear thinking means ..... Marvin H. Swift. *Harvard Business Review,* vol. 51, January-February 1973, pp. 59-62.

3173. Clear writing needs clear thinking. A. Kuhl. *Supervisory Management,* vol. 12, October 1967, pp. 10-14.

3174. Clear writing: Rx for foggy audit reports. A. Maniak. *Internal Auditor,* vol. 38, August 1981, pp. 44-50.

3175. Collecting and organizing research materials. Allen Weiss. *Supervisory Management,* vol. 22, June 1977, pp. 18-27.

3176. Commercial effectiveness measures. K.J. Clancy and L.E. Ostlund. *Journal of Advertising Research,* vol. 16, February 1976, pp. 29-34.

3177. Communicating effectively through GAO reports. David M. Rosen. *GAO Review,* vol. 13, Winter 1978, pp. 18-21.

3178. Communications for the software consultant. G.T. Stacy. *Journal of Technical Writing and Communication,* vol. 6, Summer 1976, pp. 215-224.

3179. Computer and technical communication. William L. Benzon. *Journal of Technical Writing and Communication,* vol. 11, no. 2, 1981, pp. 103-114.

3180. Computer searching and the technical writer. Donna R. Dolan. *Journal of Technical Writing and Communication,* vol. 10, no. 3, 1980, pp. 183-188.

3181. Corporate report: a critique. R.B. Harrison. *CA Magazine,* vol. 107, December 1975—January 1976, pp. 26-33.

3182. Corporate report: where to from here? Derek Arnold Boothman. *Accountant,* vol. 174, March 25, 1976, pp. 354-356.

3183. Creative obfuscation. J.S. Armstrong. *Chemical Technology,* vol. 11, May 1981, pp. 262-264.

3184. Critical look at report writing. *Management Review,* vol. 64, December 1975, pp. 46-48.

3185. Developing your topic with sentence and paragraph. Allen Weiss. *Supervisory Management,* vol. 22, September 1977, pp. 25-32.

3186. Does your company practice affirmative action in its communications? Arnold R. Deutsch. *Harvard Business Review,* vol. 54, November/December 1976, pp. 16+.

3187. Drafting a meaningful annual report. *Financial Executive,* vol. 47, June 1979, pp. 26-30.

3188. Editing a company magazine. C. Hilliard. *Writer's Digest,* vol. 56, November 1976, pp. 40-43.

3189. Editor's view: ten common errors in technical writing. Clarence H. Annett. *Journal of Technical Writing and Communication,* vol. 12, no. 3, 1982, pp. 185-190.

3190. Effective financial reporting—to investors and management. Eugenio R. Reyes. *Accountants' Journal,* vol. 27, no. 1, 1977, pp. 7-15.

3191. Effective report crisis. John Caldwell. *Journal of Systems Management,* vol. 26, June 1975, pp. 7-12.

3192. Effective report writing. Gordon Wainwright. *Accountant,* vol. 157, October 1967, pp. 522-523.

3193. Effective report writing: a marketing research practitioner's view. Torrence R. Allsbrook. *University of Akron Business Review,* vol. 1, Spring 1970, pp. 5-9.

3194. Effective reporting structures. J.W. Wilkinson. *Journal of Systems Management,* vol. 27, November 1976, pp. 38-42.

3195. Effective systems reports. B. Menkus. *Journal of Systems Management,* vol. 27, September 1976, pp. 18-20.

3196. English is a high-level language (help EDP get its points across). G. James. *Infosystems,* vol. 24, January 1977, pp. 74+.

3197. Evaluate your technical writing. D.L. Flung. *Hydrocarbon Processing,* vol. 60, June 1981, pp. 155-156+.

3198. Evaluate your technical writing. D.L. Flung. *World Oil,* vol. 193, October 1981, pp. 245-246+.

3199. Evolution of published financial reporting. W.J. Jarvis. *Accountants Record,* no. 24, September/October 1978, pp. 10-12.

3200. Examination of the medical/scientific manuscript. Lottie Applewhite. *Journal of Technical Writing and Communication,* vol. 9, no. 1, 1979, pp. 17-25.

3201. Executive's guide to getting into print. C.W. Welch. *Management Review,* vol. 65, September 1976, pp. 25-30.

3202. Factors affecting the time lapse in report processing. Gilbert B. Bowers. *Federal Accountant,* vol. 23, March 1974, pp. 66-70.

3203. Fear of the blank page, and how to overcome it. Allen Weiss. *Advanced Management Journal,* vol. 43, Autumn 1978, pp. 22-29.

3204. Financial reports can be made more understandable. A.H. Adelberg and R. Lewis. *Journal of Accountancy,* vol. 149, June 1980, pp. 44-46+.

3205. Five basic elements of report writing. T. Darlington. *Supervisory Management,* vol. 9, October 1964, pp. 46-48.

3206. Flexibility as the ideal. Douglas Garbutt. *Accountancy,* vol. 84, October 1973, pp. 38+.

3207. Follow the rules—most of the time. Allen Weiss. *Supervisory Management,* vol. 22, November 1977, pp. 22-29.

3208. Four keys to effective writing. M.A. Dean. *Supervisory Management,* vol. 12, January 1967, pp. 41-43.

3209. Fowl language: 13 frequently observed writing lapses. R.M. Soldofsky and S. Kuiper. *Management World,* vol. 9, April 1980, pp. 13-15.

3210. Full-time freelancing in technical writing. P. Franklin. *Writer's Digest,* vol. 50, August 1970, pp. 20-22+.

3211. Gamesmanship in written communication. Mary C. Bromage. *Management Review,* vol. 61, April 1972, pp. 10-15.

3212. George Washington Carver and the art of technical communication. Stephen Gresham. *Journal of Technical Writing and Communication,* vol. 9, no. 3, 1979, pp. 217-225.

3213. Government news release: tedium need not be the message. W. Pedersen. *Public Relations Quarterly,* vol. 21, Winter 1976, pp. 17-20.

3214. Guidelines for abstracting. Clinton J. McGirr. *Technical Communications,* vol. 25, Second Quarter 1978, pp. 2-5.

3215. Help fight CPD: plan your report with your project—and optimize the quality of each. J.W. Hill. *Supervisory Management,* vol. 24, December 1979, pp. 8-14.

3216. Here's a formula for reports that really communicate. Sister Mary Martha. *Hospital Financial Management,* vol. 26, April 1972, pp. 24-25.

3217. How a business plan is read. Joseph R. Mancuso. *Business Horizons,* vol. 17, August 1974, pp. 33-42.

3218. How I buy at TAB; technical book publisher. K. Sessions. *Writer's Digest,* vol. 55, October 1975, pp. 17+.

3219. How to be your own editor. M. Whiting. *International Management,* vol. 30, June 1975, pp. 27-78.

3220. How to communicate with management. Jerry L. Ford. *Management Accounting,* vol. 60, March 1979, pp. 12-17+.

3221. How to communicate with your ADP analyst. George M. Cate. *Federal Accountant,* vol. 21, December 1972, pp. 56-66.

3222. How to define quality in engineering manuscripts. Herbert B. Michaelson. *Journal of Technical Writing and Communication,* vol. 11, no. 3, 1981, p. 245-250.

3223. How to defog your technical writing. D.L. Flung. *Electrical World,* vol. 196, January 1982, pp. 49-50.

3224. How to get your message across to doctors. H.R. Lewis. *Public Relations Quarterly,* vol. 22, Winter 1977, pp. 20-22.

3225. How to handle crash assigments. *Electrical World,* vol. 193, April 15, 1980, p. 60.

3226. How to overcome the annual report drag factor. W. Braznell. *Public Relations Journal,* vol. 34, August 1978, pp. 22-29.

3227. How to "right" a report. L.S. Bernstein. *Business Management* (London), vol. 98, September 1968, pp. 46-48.

3228. How to translate your thoughts into good technical writing. R.L. Miller. *Chemical Engineering,* vol. 87, August 11, 1980, pp. 163-164.

3229. How to write a better report. A.R. Pell. *Purchasing,* vol. 51, December 18, 1961, pp. 78-79+.

3230. How to write a poor report. Charles B. Smith. *Appraisal Journal,* vol. 41, April 1973, pp. 254-259.

3231. How to write a practical Q.A. Manual. E.V. Bravenec. *Mechanical Engineering,* vol. 100, November 1978, pp. 33-37.

3232. How to write a report. *Banking,* vol. 68, June 1976, pp. 43-44+.

3233. How to write a report. S. Dowst. *Purchasing,* vol. 64, March 21, 1968, pp. 89-90.

3234. How to write a report that will be read and acted upon. J.H. Lapperre. *Controller,* vol. 30, May 1962, pp. 250-251.

3235. How to write reports that won't be ignored. D. Fuller. *Machine Design,* vol. 51, January 11, 1979, pp. 76-79.

3236. How to write well in business. P. Hanft and M. Roe. *CA Magazine,* vol. 111, July 1978, pp. 46-47.

3237. Importance of report writing. John A. Edds and Dale Knowles. *Internal Auditor,* vol. 32, November/December 1975, pp. 73-75.

3238. Impress top management with your written reports. F. Benjamin. *Chemical Engineering,* vol. 86, March 26, 1979, pp. 179-180.

3239. Improve your method of preparing a technical study. S.L. Pitner. *Chemical Engineering,* vol. 85, April 24, 1978, pp. 105-106.

3240. Improve your report writing. M. Smith. *Supervisory Management,* vol. 13, December 1968, pp. 2-5; vol. 14, January 1969, pp. 7-9; vol. 14, February 1969, pp. 15-18.

3241. Improve your technical writing. Richard C. John. *Management Accounting,* vol. 58, September 1976, pp. 49-52.

3242. Improving communications between artists and writers. Susan Briles. *Technical Communication,* vol. 26, Fourth Quarter 1979, pp. 12-14.

3243. Improving technical and bureaucratic writing. Mohan R. Limaye. *Journal of Technical Writing and Communication,* vol. 11, no. 1, 1981, pp. 23-33.

3244. In praise of prepositions. R. Schoenfeld. *Chemical Technology,* vol. 11, June 1981, pp. 333-335.

3245. Increasing article acceptance. Leigh C. White. *Journal of Technical Writing and Communication,* vol. 9, no. 2, 1979, pp. 153-161.

3246. Instant stylistics. R. Schoenfeld. *Chemical Technology,* vol. 11, November 1981, pp. 676-677.

3247. Issue: annual report madness. *Public Relations Quarterly,* vol. 25, Spring 1980, pp. 21-23.

3248. Keep it simple, keep it clear. R. Crowe. *Writer's Digest,* vol. 55, October 1975, pp. 14-16.

3249. Kodak's financial information and reporting system. Arthur F. Brueningsen. *Management Accounting,* vol. 57, September 1975, pp. 21-24.

3250. Linguistic over kill. D.W. Mitchell. *Journal of Commercial Bank Lending,* vol. 55, June 1973, pp. 32-34.

3251. Look what's happened to annual reports. Robert F. Randall. *Management Accounting,* vol. 53, April 1972, pp. 61-63.

3252. Main job of the annual report: wooing investors. James H. Dowling. *Dun's Review,* vol. 112, September 1978, pp. 127-128+.

3253. Management report. Douglas Roy Carmichael. *Financial Executive,* vol. 46, November 1978, pp. 46-50.

3254. Marketing strategy for marketing knowledge—or how to publish and prosper. D.W. Twedt. *Journal of Marketing,* vol. 41, April 1977, pp. 69-72.

3255. Medical writing: problems and solutions. *Canadian Journal of Surgery,* vol. 19, November 1976, pp. 478-480.

3256. More about paragraphs: the orchestration of elements. Allen Weiss. *Supervisory Management,* vol. 22, October 1977, pp. 22-28.

3257. More effective sales force reporting. T.R. Wotruba and R. Mangone. *Industrial Marketing Management,* vol. 8, June 1979, pp. 236-245.

3258. Mystery of the business graduate who can't write. *Nation's Business,* vol. 65, February 1977, pp. 60-62.

3259. Need for clarity in business writing. J.D. Kimes. *Financial Executive,* vol. 47, January 1979, pp. 16-23.

3260. New technology and the technical author. Paul Berman. *Technical Communication,* vol. 25, Third Quarter 1978, pp. 2-7.

3261. Notes for a memorandum. C. Reimold. *Tappi,* vol. 64, October 1981, p. 131.

3262. Optimum readability formula. R.S. Silverman. *Chemical Technology,* vol. 12, February 1982, pp. 74-76.

3263. Organizing for forward motion. Frank Judd. *Management Accounting,* vol. 55, April 1974, pp. 23-24.

3264. Organizing to write. A.E. Witte. *Journal of Accountancy,* vol. 134, September 1972, pp. 105-106.

3265. Outlining: an indispensable tool for the business writer. A Weiss. *Supervisory Management,* vol. 22, July 1977, pp. 18-25.

3266. Personal observations on report writing. Nicholas Tereshenko. *GAO Review,* Winter 1973, pp. 59-64.

3267. Photographs in annual reports. John K. Courtis. *Accountants' Journal,* vol. 57, November 1978, pp. 390-392.

3268. Plain talk on business jargon. Barry Maude. *Accountant,* vol. 169, December 20/27, 1974, pp. 815-816.

3269. Planning an annual report; check-points for decision. W.E. Myers. *Public Relations Journal,* vol. 22, April 1966, pp. 34-36.

3270. Planning and coordination techniques of the annual statement process. Philip J. Guymont. *Interpreter,* vol. 37, June 1978, pp. 10-12.

3271. Planning and creating superior proposals. S. Morris. *Management Review,* vol. 53, November 1964, pp. 37-44.

3272. Planning the publication of a set of annual accounts. Alec Rabarts. *Accountancy,* vol. 89, June 1978, pp. 102-103.

3273. Plea for greater clarity. Richard Allen. *Accountancy,* vol. 86, March 1975, pp. 44, 46, 48, 50.

3274. Popular financial reporting in the public sector? Hal Peyer and Gerald Lonergan. *Governmental Finance,* vol. 5, May 1976, 32-39.

3275. Preparing a proposal step-by-step. H.M. Plotkin. *Journal of Systems Management,* vol. 23, February 1972, pp. 36-38.

3276. Primer on tables and figures. Alan G. Gross. *Journal of Technical Writing and Communication,* vol. 13, no. 1, 1983, pp. 33-55.

3277. Printer's point of view. Geoffrey Holmes. *Accountancy,* vol. 86, March 1975, pp. 52+.

3278. Problems in implementing an internal reporting system. A.G.H. Gilligan. *Accountants' Journal,* vol. 52, February 1974, pp. 253-254.

3279. Professional writing; why and how. D.R. Dilley. *Journal of Accountancy,* vol. 116, August 1963, pp. 59-65.

3280. Proposal resumes: a study of style. Tim Whalen. *Technical Communication,* vol. 27, Third Quarter 1980, pp. 26-29.

3281. Prose-polishing betters research's product. *Chemical Week,* vol. 86, April 2, 1980, pp. 35+.

3282. Punctuation; packaging in personality. C. Reimold. *Tappi,* vol. 65, May 1982, p. 189.

3283. Punctuation; the voice behind the writing. C. Reimold. *Tappi,* vol. 65, March 1982, p. 155; April 1982, p. 139.

3284. Put clarity in your writing. D. Mueller. *World Oil,* vol. 191, November 1980, pp. 154+.

3285. Put those reports to work. David K. Lindo. *Burroughs Clearing House,* vol. 59, February 1975, pp. 24-25+.

3286. Quality control methods for IBM computer manuals. Carl B. Wagner. *Journal of Technical Writing and Communication,* vol. 10, no. 2, 1980, pp. 93-102.

3287. Rate your own writing skills. R.M. Power. *Hydrocarbon Processing,* vol. 58, September 1979, pp. 313-314+.

3288. Readability and creativity in technical writing. Bert Edens. *Journal of Technical Writing and Communication,* vol. 10, no. 4, 1980, pp. 329-336.

3289. Reading annual reports can be fun. George Wasem. *Bankers' Monthly,* vol. 93, February 15, 1976, pp. 26-28, 30.

3290. Relativity of communication: Albert Einstein as technical writer. Michael J. Baresich. *Journal of Technical Writing and Communication,* vol. 10, no. 2, 1980, pp. 125-132.

3291. Removing the gobbledygook from government prose. Harold R. Fine. *GAO Review,* vol. 11, Winter 1976, pp. 25-34.

3292. Report writing—inverted pyramid structure. Guy Burnett. *Texas CPA,* vol. 47, July 1974, pp. 58-62.

3293. Reporting business performance. John Arnold and Anthony Hope. *Accounting and Business Research,* vol. 5, Spring 1975, pp. 96-105.

3294. Research report ethics. L.J. Zitnik. *Financial Analysts Journal,* vol. 22, January 1966, pp. 73-75.

3295. Rhetoric and technical writing. *Technical Communication,* vol. 25, Fourth Quarter 1978, entire issue.

3296. Role of a private research foundation in a technical writing program. Robert w. Kelton. *Journal of Technical Writing and Communication,* vol. 10, no. 1, 1980, pp. 59-64.

3297. Role of auditors in financial reporting: a behavioural approach. Nissim Aranya. *International Accountant,* vol. 44, July/September 1974, pp. 72-75.

3298. Scientific logic: a reader-oriented approach to technical writing. Marilyn S. Samuels. *Journal of Technical Writing and Communication,* vol. 12, no. 4, 1982, pp. 307-328.

3299. Search for venture capital—preparatory steps. Stephen D. Sholes. *Financial Executive,* vol. 42, August 1974, pp. 46+.

3300. Sentences that make sense. Mary C. Bromage. *Journal of Accountancy,* vol. 123, May 1967, pp. 56-60.

3301. Series of ideas to improve your presentations. Laurence E. Olewine. *Armed Forces Comptroller,* vol. 18, Fall 1973, pp. 24-25+.

3302. Seven steps to effective reports. *Office,* vol. 58, September 1963, pp. 20+.

3303. Seven ways to better client reports, presentations. Ann-Marie Lamb. *Infosystems,* vol. 27, May 1980, pp. 84+.

3304. Signed articles can boost corporate identity. J.M. Lufkin. *Public Relations Journal,* vol. 24, February 1968, pp. 29-32.

3305. Six steps to better written communications. D. Olson. *Office,* vol. 63, April 1966, pp. 69-76.

3306. Some psychological effects of syntax. Charles H. Sides. *Technical Communication,* vol. 30, First Quarter 1983, pp. 14-17.

3307. Some tips on improving your report writing. C.R. Ballard. *Practical Accountant,* vol. 13, November 1980, pp. 43-47.

3308. S.R.O.F. system of report writing. Edmund Carlson. *Internal Auditor,* vol. 32, November/December 1975, pp. 19-26.

3309. Style in analytical writing. P.S. Ley. *Journal of Commercial Bank Lending,* vol. 56, April 1974, pp. 61-66.

3310. Suggested practices for effective reports design. Norman D. Peterson. *Journal of Data Management,* vol. 6, November 1968, pp. 20-24.

3311. Targeting your vocabulary. Allen Weiss. *Supervisory Management,* vol. 22, December 1977, pp. 22-30.

3312. Technical editors look at technical editing. Lola Zook. *Technical Communication,* vol. 30, Third Quarter 1983, pp. 20-26.

3313. Technical publications can be entertaining. J. Gleason. *Chemical Engineering,* vol. 88, November 30, 1981, pp. 87-88+.

3314. Technical publicity means special handling. D.T. Van Deusen. *Public Relations Journal,* vol. 20, June 1964, pp. 26-28.

3315. Technical writer as naturalist: some lessons from the classics. Wayne A. Losano. *Journal of Technical Writing and Communication,* vol. 9, no. 3, 1979, pp. 227-237.

3316. Technical writers; loosen up. C. Reimold. *Tappi,* vol. 65, July 1982, pp. 113-114.

3317. Technical writers: what have they done for you lately? A.V. Swerz. *Management Review,* vol. 60, September 1971, pp. 20-26.

3318. Technical writing and translation. Ben Teague and Fran Teague. *Journal of Technical Writing and Communication,* vol. 12, no. 2, 1982, pp. 93-102.

3319. Technical writing; in defense of obscurity. W.J. Gallagher. *Management Review,* vol. 55, May 1966, pp. 34-36.

3320. Technical writing; the engineer's masterpiece. A.M. Andrews. *Electronics and Power,* vol. 26, June 1980, pp. 471-474.

3321. Technical writing: what it is and what it isn't. Charles R. Stratton. *Journal of Technical Writing and Communication,* vol. 9, no. 1, 1979, pp. 9-16.

3322. Ten report pitfalls: how to avoid them. Vincent Vinci. *Chemical Engineering,* vol. 82, December 22, 1975, pp. 45-48+.

3323. Ten steps toward better writing. Tom Stapleton. *Banking,* vol. 70, March 1978, pp. 63, 65.

3324. Ten ways to make your reports and publications unreadable. I. Parker. *Engineering,* vol. 218, February 1978, p. 145.

3325. Testing: how to increase the usability of computer manuals. Barbara Winbush and Glenda McDowell. *Technical Communication,* vol. 27, First Quarter 1980, pp. 20-22.

3326. Tips on working as a technical writer. P. Franklin. *Writer's Digest,* vol. 50, August 1970, p. 23.

3327. Transitions: the gates and bridges of a writer's journey. Allen Weiss. *Supervisory Management,* vol. 22, August 1977, pp. 20-27.

3328. User-driven approach to better user manuals. J. Maynard. *Computer,* vol. 12, January 1979, pp. 72-75.

3329. Wanted: "industrious" writers (industrial promotions and publicity). Robert Bly. *Writer's Digest,* vol. 64, February 1984, pp. 38-41.

3330. Well-written credit reports: a successful program. J.O. Morris. *Journal of Commercial Bank Lending,* vol. 56, July 1973, pp. 51-63.

3331. What to look for in technical communicators. F.W. Holder. *Personnel Journal,* vol. 51, October 1972, pp. 737-741.

3332. What's new in annual reports? F.E. Hewens. *Public Relations Journal,* vol. 24, April 1968, pp. 37-39.

3333. Who needs a technical editor? R.M. Power. *World Oil,* vol. 193, December 1982, p. 175.

3334. Why Johnny don't write good. L.H. Matthies. *Office,* vol. 72, September 1970, pp. 70+.

3335. Why your annual report won't be read. A.R. Roalman. *Industry Week,* vol. 204, March 3, 1980, pp. 4445+.

3336. Wording the management audit report. Mary C. Bromage. *Journal of Accountancy,* vol. 133, February 1972, pp. 50-57.

3337. Words, words, words (flowchart). L.A. Riney. *Production Engineering,* vol. 24, October 1977, pp. 24-26.

3338. World of technical books. Henry Miller. *Author,* vol. 84, Spring 1973, pp. 13-15.

3339. Writing a market research report. *International Trade Forum,* vol. 16, October/December 1980, pp. 22-27.

3340. Writing commercial reports for business. A. Mohre. *Writer's Digest,* vol. 52, June 1972, pp. 22-24.

3341. Writing company histories. W.J. Reader. *Author,* vol. 86, Winter 1975, pp. 143+.

3342. Writing for a public accounting practitioners' magazine. M. Block. *Accounting Review,* vol. 47, October 1972, pp. 814-818.

3343. Writing persuasive proposals. S.A. Edwards. *Medical Communications,* vol. 10, Summer 1982, pp. 34-39.

3344. Writing reports doesn't need to be difficult. W.H. Weiss. *Supervision,* vol. 40, December 1978, pp. 4-5.

3345. Writing reports that communicate. R. Houlehen. *Industry Week,* vol. 186, September 22, 1975, p. 46.

3346. Writing reports that lead to effective decisions. N.B. Sigband. *Supervisory Management,* vol. 15, June 1970, pp. 2-6.

3347. Writing to promote health and safety behaviors in occupational settings. D.T. Manning. *Journal of Technical Writing and Communication,* vol. 12, no. 4, 1982, pp. 301-306.

Translation

"A translator, like a witness on the stand, should hold up his right hand and swear to tell the truth, the whole truth, and nothing but the truth."

—Longfellow

Books

3348. Adams, Robert M. *Proteus, His Lies, His Truth; Discussion of Literary Translation.* New York: Norton, 1973. 192 pp.

Discusses various translation situations including Homer, William Faulkner, Ezra Pound, and Robert Lowell. Both nuance and poverty in translation are dealt with in this tightly organized and widely admired book.

3349. Arnold, Matthew. *On Translating Homer.* New York: AMS Press, 1971. 200 pp.

This work is considered one of the classic statements on the translator's art. Though of less immediate and practical utility to the modern translator than many of the works cited below, the principles and problems raised by Arnold are of lasting concern to all.

3350. Arrowsmith, William, and Roger Shattuck. *The Craft and Context of Translation; A Symposium.* Austin: University of Texas Press for Humanities Research Center, 1961. 206 pp.

This lively anthology contains such gems as "The poet as translator" by Kenneth Rexroth, "Translating for actors" by Robert Corrigan, and "The editor's problem" by Denver Lindley.

3351. Bassnett-McGuire, Susan. *Translation Studies.* London; New York: Methuen, 1980. 159 pp.

Not for the beginning writer/translator, this scholarly work discusses such issues as untranslatability, decoding, and the history of translation. The last part delves into some specific problems associated with translating, such as poetry and dramatic texts. A bibliography suggests books of an introductory nature for the novice, as well as further readings on translation theory.

3352. Belloc, Hillaire. *On Translation.* Oxford: Oxford University Press, 1931. 44 pp.

A near classic series of rules and prescriptions on what Belloc calls a subsidiary and derivative art.

3353. Brower, Reuben A. *On Translation.* Cambridge: Harvard University Press, 1959. 297 pp.

The concept of re-creation is central to these seventeen informed essays, many of which deal with the translation of fiction and poetry. Theory is tempered and examples abound. Included among the essayists are Edwin Muir, Vladimir Nabokov, and Justin O'Brien.

3354. Congrat-Butlar, Stefan. *Translation and Translators; An International Directory and Guide.* New York: R.R. Bowker, 1979. 241 pp.

This working tool includes a register of translators and interpreters with classifications under industrial, humanistic/literary, and conference translators. Also included are chapters on recent history and breakthroughs, associations, awards and grants, guidelines for contracts, copyright, and legislation, as well as an extensive bibliography of translation literature.

3355. Holmes, James S. *The Nature of Translation; Essays on the Theory and Practice of Literary Translation.* The Hague: Mouton, 1970. 232 pp.

The result of the International Conference on Translation as an Art held in Bratislava in May 1968, these essays address verse translation, images, style, and esthetics.

3356. Newmark, Peter. *Approaches to Translation; Aspects of Translation.* New York: Pergamon Press, 1981. 200 pp.

The basis for this text is the balance between semantic and communicative translation. This duality is covered in depth in Part 1, called "Aspects of Translation Theory." Part 2, "Some Propositions on Translation," elaborates "Linguistics of translation," "Theory of translation technique," "Aspects of meaning," "Punctuation," "Text analysis," "Wider questions," and "Technical translation." This work will be most useful for a variety of specific translation problems and should be on the desk of any working translator.

3357. Nida, Eugene Albert. *Language Structure and Translation; Essays.* Stanford, California: Stanford University Press, 1975. 284 pp.

This collection of essays by a noted Bible translator and translation theorist covers a wide variety of subjects, including the making of dictionaries, the role of languages in multilingual societies, and semantic structure. A liberal use of examples makes this a worthy tool for scholars involved in translating, especially for those concerned with the Bible or other religious texts.

3358. ———. *Toward a Science of Translating.* Leiden: E.J. Brill, 1964. 331 pp.

This frequently cited work addresses traditions of translation, linguistic meaning, emotive meaning, dynamic dimension in communication, principles of correspondence, and the role of the translator, to name a few of the technical and philosophical topics covered.

3359. Proetz, Victor. *Astonishment of Words; An Experiment in the Comparison of Languages.* Austin: University of Texas Press, 1971. 199 pp.

Selected poems of T.S. Eliot, e.e. cummings, Lewis Carroll, and others are translated into French and German to show what happens to English "quirky idioms" when inflicted upon another language, as well as other joys and difficulties associated with such translations.

3360. Raffel, Burton. *The Forked Tongue; Study of the Translation Process.* The Hague: Mouton, 1971. 181 pp.

By "process," Raffel refers to how one subjectively starts with a poem in one language and ends with it in another language. To adequately reflect this he relies upon his correspondence with several translators who, along with Raffel, discuss translating Beowulf, Indonesian poetry, and Old English poetry, and explore how to read a translation with a critical eye.

3361. Savory, Theodore Horace. *The Art of Translation.* Philadelphia: DuFour Editions, 1960. 159 pp.

Savory considers a variety of translation situations such as poetry, science, educational, Biblical, and classical translation. He also provides an historical perspective and a series of principles for translators.

3362. Steiner, George. *After Babel; Aspects of Language and Translation.* New York: Oxford University Press, 1975. 512 pp.

A lengthy but sometimes plodding discussion of a broad range of topics, including inner drama and aesthetics in translation.

3363. Tytler, Alexander F. *Essay on the Principles of Translation.* New York: E.P. Dutton, 1978. 239 pp.

An eighteenth-century British view of the subject, now considered a classic statement.

3364. Wilss, Wolfram. *The Science of Translation; Theoretical and Applicative Aspects.* Tubingen: Linguistik Beitragezur, 1982. 292 pp.

Filled with specific examples of problems in German/ English translation, this is a state-of-fine-art text which addresses text linguistics, error analysis, translation equivalence, and machine translation. More general chapters survey translation theory—past and present, problems of methodology, and translation as a modern means of communication. Wilss takes the position that modern translation theory has only begun.

3365. *World of Translation; Papers Delivered at The Conference on Literary Translation, New York City, May 1970.* New York: P.E.N. American Center, 1971. 384 pp.

Seen by many translators as one of the best collections of papers on the subject yet assembled, these forty-odd papers include Robert Payne's "On the impossibility of translation," Muriel Rukeyser's "The music of translation," Clara Malraux's "Translation and complicity," and I.B. Singer's "On translating my books."

Articles

3366. Art of translation. I.M. Hefzallah. *Babel,* vol. 16, no. 4, 1970, pp. 180-187.

3367. Art of translation. Vladimir Nabokov. *New Republic,* vol. 105, August 4, 1941, pp. 160-162.

3368. Can metaphor be translated? M.B. Dagut. *Babel,* vol. 22, no. 1, 1976, pp. 21-32.

3369. Craft of translation. R. Winston. *American Scholar,* vol. 19, 1950, pp. 179-186.

3370. Difficulties in translating Japanese into English and vice versa. K.I. Ishikawa. *Pacific Spectator,* vol. 9, 1955, pp. 95-99.

3371. Fit only for barbarians: the sound of translated poetry. K. Bosley. *World Literature Today,* vol. 55, Winter 1981, pp. 52-55.

3372. Further unanswered questions about translating. H. Carruth. *Poetry,* vol. 100, June 1962, pp. 198-200.

3373. How good is a translation? Fernando Alegria. *Americas,* vol. 6, May 1954, pp. 36-38.

3374. Into English, or into American English. Margaret Paroutand. *Babel,* vol. 18, no. 2, 1972, pp. 16-17.

3375. John Trevisa: scholar and translator. David G. Fowler. *Bristol and Gloucestershire Archaeological Society Transactions,* vol. 89, 1970, pp. 99-108.

3376. Lowells translations: questions of text and style. M. Bishop and H. Carruth. *Poetry,* vol. 100, April 1962, pp. 41-47.

3377. Merwin as translator. B. Gibbs. *Poetry,* vol. 101, February 1963, pp. 353-355.

3378. Modern translation. D.J.R. Bruckner. *New York Times Book Review,* vol. 88, September 18, 1983, p. 47.

3379. Modes of translation. J.W. MacFarlane. *Durham University Journal,* vol. 45, 1953, pp. 77-93.

3380. Mystery of translation. D. Wesling and A. LeFevre. *Babel,* vol. 16, no. 3, 1970, pp. 124-134.

3381. On quality in translation. David L. Gold. *Babel,* vol. 18, no. 1, 1972, pp. 10-11.

3382. On the necessity of translation. Norman Simms. *Landfall,* no. 131, September 1979, pp. 212-220.

3383. On the translation of form in poetry. Y. Bonnefoy. *World Literature Today,* vol. 53, Summer 1979, pp. 374-379.

3384. On translating Beowulf. Burton Raffel. *Yale Review,* vol. 54, June 1965, pp. 532-546.

3385. On translating Chinese philosophical terms. D. Bodde. *Far East Quarterly,* vol. 14, 1955, pp. 231-234.

3386. On translating poetry. H. Read. *Poetry,* vol. 98, April 1961, pp. 56-59.

3387. On translation. Hillaire Belloc. *Bookman,* vol. 74, 1931, pp. 32-39, 179-185.

3388. Onward and upward with the arts; a study of English and American poetry translated into German and French, with examples. Victor Proetz. *New Yorker,* vol. 47, May 22, 1971, pp. 82+.

3389. Phasing out the phrase book. Roger Green. *Observer,* October 21, 1979, p. 25.

3390. Poet as translator. C. Tomlinson. *Times Literary Supplement,* vol. 4043, September 26, 1980, pp. 1067-1068.

3391. Poetry and translation. H.W. Chalsma. *Babel,* vol. 11, no. 4, 1965, pp. 181-182.

3392. Poets and translators. D. Hine. *Poetry,* vol. 113, October 1968, pp. 35-59.

3393. Pony or Pegasus; problem of mistranslation in literature. Joel Agee. *Harpers,* vol. 263, September 1981, pp. 70-72+.

3394. Present and future technical aids to easier communication in foreign languages. Karl-Heinz Brinkman. *Babel,* vol. 26, no. 2, 1980, pp. 67-75.

3395. Problems of translation: international symposium looks to the future. *Bookseller,* June 2, 1973, pp. 2660-2661.

3396. Problems of translation: Onegin in English. Vladimir Nabokov. *Partisan Review,* vol. 22, 1955, pp. 496-512.

3397. Rhythm and meaning in liturgical translation. Michael Hodgetts. *Music and Liturgy,* vol. 2, Winter 1976, pp. 19-24.

3398. Rilke and the art of translation. S. Lautermilch. *Literary Review,* vol. 24, Summer 1981, pp. 519-529.

3399. Some thoughts on translation. B.R. Rees. *Greece and Rome,* vol. 21, October 1974, pp. 111-127.

3400. Taking the rough with the smooth; the translator as poet. K. Bosley. *World Literature Today,* vol. 54, Winter 1980, pp. 51-53.

3401. Translating Cesar Vallejo. C. Eshleman. *Nation,* vol. 204, April 24, 1967, p. 540.

3402. Translating in a multilingual society. A.E. Opubor. *Babel,* vol. 27, no. 1, 1981, pp. 6-8.

3403. Translating in transition. Peter Glassgold. *Publishers Weekly,* vol. 225, May 18, 1984, pp. 70-72.

3404. Translating isn't all beer and skittles. S. Putnam. *Books Abroad,* vol. 23, 1949, pp. 235+.

3405. Translating Shakespeare. Boris Pasternak. *Twentieth Century,* vol. 164, 1958, pp. 213-228.

3406. Translating Thomas Mann. H.T. Lowe-Porter. *Symposium,* vol. 9, 1955, pp. 260-272.

3407. Translation and bilingualism. K.A. Goddard. *Babel,* vol. 18, no. 2, 1972, pp. 18-23.

3408. Translation as a semiotic process. J.L. Ramos. *Comparative Literature Studies,* vol. 17, December 1980, pp. 376-390.

3409. Translation of literature: an approach. A. LeFevre. *Babel,* vol. 16, no. 2, 1970, pp. 75-79.

3410. Translation of plays. Max Beerbohm. *Saturday Review,* vol. 96, 1903, pp. 75-76.

3411. Translation, the art of failure. John Ciardi. *Saturday Review,* vol. 44, October 7, 1961, pp. 17-19.

3412. Translation: the speakable and the unspeakables. K.J. Dover. *Essays in Criticism,* vol. 30, January 1980, pp. 1-8.

3413. Translator at work. Rodney Milnes. *Opera,* vol. 26, March 1975, pp. 242-250.

3414. Translator's calling. Robert Bayers. *Times Literary Supplement,* December 7, 1979, pp. 97-98.

3415. Trial by translations: Plays of Corneille. Jacques Barzun. *New Republic,* vol. 127, December 8, 1952, pp. 20-21.

3416. Trials of the translator: *Les Miserables.* Norman Denny. *Bookseller,* July 17, 1976, p. 11.

3417. Trouble with translation. J.A. Kouwenhoven. *Harper's Magazine,* vol. 225, August 1962, pp. 38-44.

3418. Underdetermination of theory and indeterminacy of translation. R. Kirk. *Analysis,* vol. 33, June 1973, pp. 195-201.

3419. Verse translation as an interpretive art. T. Paul. *Hispania,* vol. 34, 1951, pp. 68-73.

3420. What is translation for? B.Q. Morgan. *Symposium,* vol. 10, 1956, pp. 322-328.

Book Reviewing

"Americans like fat books and thin women."
—Russell Baker

Books

3421. Drewry, John E. *Writing Book Reviews.* Boston: Writer, 1966. 230 pp.

A seasoned book reviewer and Dean of the University of Georgia School of Journalism delineates the types, styles, and techniques of reviewing and then concentrates on reviewing biography, history, contemporary thought, travel and adventure, poetry, and children's books. A final chapter titled "How the Experts Do It" provides a selection of exemplary reviews written by well-known reviewers.

3422. Jones, Llewellyn. *How to Criticize Books.* New York; Philadelphia: R. West, 1973. 190 pp.

Originally published in 1928, this short work retains its value as an examination of critical principles, philosophy, and mechanics.

3423. Kamerman, Sylvia, editor. *Book Reviewing; A Guide to Writing Book Reviews for Newspapers, Magazines, Radio, and Television; By Leading Book Editors, Critics, and Reviewers.* Boston: Writer, 1978. 215 pp.

Robert Kirsch of the *Los Angeles Times,* George A. Woods of the *New York Times,* Pulitzer-Prize-winner William McPherson, and seventeen others contribute short essays about the different forms reviews may take, how to choose books for reviewing, reviewing at the local level, reviewing children's books, and a variety of other topics of interest to potential and practicing reviewers.

3424. McCanse, Ralph Alan. *The Art of the Book Review; A Comprehensive Working Outline.* Madison: University of Wisconsin Press, 1963. 23 pp.

The most useful aspect of this short study is the extended outline which provides the prospective reviewer with a checklist of critical considerations.

3425. Oppenheimer, Evelyn. *Book Reviewing for an Audience; A Practical Guide in Technique for Lecture and Broadcast.* Philadelphia: Chilton, 1962. 132 pp.

Oppenheimer distinguishes between the review prepared for radio and other oral presentation and that intended for print. She then discusses one's intended public, marketing, and tools of the trade. Over half of this uneven work is devoted to the author's not very convincing sample reviews.

Articles

3426. A critic's power. *New York Times Book Review,* vol. 87, February 28, 1982, p. 39.

3427. Getting started in book reviewing. Lynne Schwartz. *Writer,* vol. 93, December 1980, pp. 23-26+.

3428. In praise of displeasure. James Atlas. *Atlantic,* vol. 248, August 1981, pp. 79-83.

3429. *LA Times,* Robert Kirsch (interview). *Publishers Weekly,* vol. 212, December 12, 1977, pp. 10-11.

3430. PW interviews: William McPherson, book editor of *The Washington Post. Publishers Weekly,* vol. 212, August 8, 1977, pp. 10-11.

3431. Reviewers on reviewing. T. Brown. *Journalism Quarterly,* vol. 55, Spring 1978, pp. 32-38.

3432. Shrivel of critics. Anthony Burgess. *Harpers,* vol. 254, February 1977, pp. 87+.

3433. Some thoughts on book reviewing. Paul Woodring. *Phi Delta Kappan,* vol. 63, February 1982, p. 422.

3434. Vanity in review. Paul Fussell. *Harpers,* vol. 264, February 1982, pp. 68-73.

3435. Which books should get a review? How ten magazines choose. Trisha Gorman. *Publishers Weekly,* vol. 220, November 6, 1981, pp. 23-26+.

Editor-Author and Publisher-Author Relationships: General

"Your talent seems to me to be a truely great one, and the sort...to be disciplined and curbed."
— Max Perkins to Thomas Wolfe

Books

3436. Balkin, Richard. *Writer's Guide to Book Publishing*. New York: Hawthorn, 1977. 236 pp.

This informative and highly regarded guide to dealing with publishers includes preparation of manuscripts, cover letters, and promotional efforts.

3437. Benjamin, Curtis G. *A Candid Critique of Book Publishing*. New York: Bowker, 1977. 187 pp.

Curtis Benjamin has logged over fifty years in publishing, many of them in leadership roles which led to his presidency of McGraw-Hill. His views on underpricing and overprinting, promotion and marketing, and what motivates people to enter and stay in the publishing world are controversial but informed. The chapter "Authors and publishers: an uneasy symbiosis" will be of most value to writers.

3438. Berg, Andrew Scott. *Max Perkins, Editor of Genius*. New York: Dutton, 1978. 498 pp.

The life story of the legendary editor of Fitzgerald, Hemingway, and Wolfe. (See also entries 3456, 3462, and 3463.)

3439. Burlingame, Roger. *Of Making Many Books; A Hundred Years of Reading, Writing, and Publishing*. New York: Scribners, 1946. 347 pp.

Charles Scribner's Sons' first hundred years in publishing are reviewed in intimate detail. Burlingame uses letters from the Scribners' files to show how authors and editors interact. For the practicing author and the student of literary history alike, this is a fascinating book.

3440. *Business of Publishing: A PW Anthology.* New York: Bowker, 1976. 303 pp.

A collection of forty-five articles taken from *Publishers Weekly* which covers topics of interest to agents, publishers, and authors.

3441. Cerf, Bennett. *At Random; The Reminiscences of Bennett Cerf.* New York: Random House, 1977. 306 pp.

Cerf recalls events from both his personal life and his participation in the rise of Random House from mere idea to multimillion dollar publishing house. He gives anecdotal accounts of authors and publishers such as William Faulkner, James Joyce, Eugene O'Neill, Horace Liveright, and Alfred Knopf. There is much here that enjoyably sheds light on the inner workings of a major publishing house as well as on publishing in the United States in the twentieth century.

3442. Commins, Dorothy. *What Is An Editor? Saxe Commins at Work.* Chicago: University of Chicago Press, 1978. 243 pp.

The papers of the late distinguished senior editor at Random House are used to show his interaction with authors such as Theodore Dreiser, Gertrude Stein, W.H. Auden, Stephen Spender, Sinclair Lewis, Eugene O'Neill, and S.N. Behrman.

3443. Compaine, Benjamin M. *Book Industry in Transition; An Economic Study of Book Distribution and Marketing.* White Plains, New York: Knowledge Industry Publications, 1978. 222 pp.

The five-billion dollar a year publishing industry is surveyed from distribution and marketing to author-publisher relationships. The author cites major problem areas, without suggesting radical change. He feels that, above all, "...a willingness to think and to work; courage to face facts and to experiment" are needed. A valuable and instructive study of a misunderstood industry.

3444. Coser, Lewis A., Charles Kadushin, and Walter Powell. *Books; The Culture and Commerce of Publishing.* New York: Basic Books, 1982. 411 pp.

This is a key book for anyone wishing to understand the history, traditions, hierarchies, and decision-making processes of the book publishing industry. Written by a team of distinguished sociologists, this book does for publishing what Oscar Lewis did for the study of urban and rural families in Latin America. It is a systematic text which investigates the organizational structure of publishing houses, the character of those who climb the editorial ladder, the role of literary agents, the interactions of book reviewers with publishers, and the role of authors in all of this.

3445. Dessauer, J.P. *Book Publishing; What It Is, What It Does.* New York: Bowker, 1981. 248 pp.

Dessauer has produced a work that is widely admired and used for its scope and grasp of the subject. If one must read only two books about the publishing world, this work would be one of those two. The other work to be so distinguished is the above cited Coser, Kadushin, and Powell.

3446. Faulkner, William, and Malcolm Cowley. *The Faulkner-Cowley File; Letters and Memories, 1944-1962.* New York: Viking, 1966. 184 pp.

This is the record of the remarkable editor-author relationship that led to the publication of the Viking *Portable Faulkner.*

3447. Gibson, Martin L. *Editing in the Electronic Era.* Ames: Iowa State University Press, 1979. 279 pp.

A more traditional discussion of the issues confronting editors and publishers than the word "electronic" in the title would suggest.

3448. Grannis, Chandler. *What Happens in Book Publishing.* New York: Columbia University Press, 1967. 467 pp.

Viewed by many as one of the better overviews of the book publishing industry, this anthology of expert opinion covers copyediting, advertising, publicity, production, and many other considerations. However, because of the rapid changes in the publishing world over the past decade, it should be supplemented by Dessauer and others.

3449. Greenfield, Howard. *Books; From Writer to Reader.* New York: Crown, 1976. 211 pp.

A seasoned author and editor skillfully relates the stages of activity that lead to a book's publication. Agents and their various roles, the publisher's decision to accept a given work, book design, proofing, indexing, and distribution are covered in depth. Completed by a glossary.

3450. Gross, Gerald, editor. *Publishers on Publishing.* New York: Grosset and Dunlap, 1961. 265 pp.

Essays by distinguished book publishers on a variety of subjects relating to the trade.

3451. Haydn, Hiram. *Words and Faces.* New York: Harcourt, Brace, Jovanovich, 1974. 346 pp.

A former editor of the *American Scholar* and editor for a number of large book publishing houses recalls his associations with Nat Wertels of Crown, David Chambers of Bobbs-Merrill, and Bennet Cerf of Random House. His encounters with authors included contacts with Jacques Barzun, Van Wick Brooks, William Faulkner, William Styron, Aldous Huxley, Ayn Rand, and Anais Nin. The distinguished Eric Moon said, "This is absolutely one of the most fascinating books about the world of publishing."

3452. Henderson, Bill. *Art of Literary Publishing; Editors and Their Craft.* Yonkers, New York: Pushcart, 1980. 268 pp.

A balanced sampling of magazine and book-editing opinion from Knopf, Harper and Row, the *Partisan Review,* and other trade publishers, little magazines, and small presses.

3453. Hollstein, Milton, and Larry Kurtz. *Editing with Understanding.* New York: Macmillan, 1981. 342 pp.

Stressing "... editing as judgement rather than mechanics," this combination textbook and workbook provides a somewhat less than even treatment of the subject. It is strongest in providing exercises but fails to reach the goal of teaching judgement and editorial understanding.

3454. Jovanovich, William. *Now Barabbas.* New York: Harper and Row, 1964. 228 pp.

The perceptions and wit of a major twentieth-century American editor and publisher are repeatedly revealed in these eleven essays on the rights, duties, and dangers of being in such a position.

3455. Kaufmann, William. *One Book Five Ways; The Publishing Procedures of Five University Presses.* Foreword by Joyce Kachergis; Introduction by Chandler Grannis. Los Altos, California: Kaufmann, 1978. 337 pp.

A documented account of how five different university presses would have produced the same book. Budget, production, layout, correspondence, sales strategy, and the like are given for each press in this informative and altogether unique look at the inner workings of university presses.

3456. Kuehl, John, and Jackson Bryer, editors. *Dear Scott, Dear Max; The Fitzgerald-Perkins Correspondence.* New York: Charles Scribner's Sons, 1971. 282 pp.

Letters between editor Maxwell Perkins and F. Scott Fitzgerald on writing, revising, and editing.

3457. Kujoth, Jean. *Book Publishing; Inside Views.* Metuchen, New Jersey: Scarecrow Press, 1971. 519 pp.

An anthology of essays by various publishers, editors, and authors on economics, ethics, editorial roles, and the interactions of authors, editors, and publishers.

3458. Lee, Marshall. *Bookmaking; The Illustrated Guide to Design and Production.* New York: Bowker, 1965. 399 pp.

Considered to be one of the best over-all introductions to the physical making of books, but the user is cautioned that computer composition and other innovations are rapidly changing this field.

3459. Legat, Michael. *Dear Author; Letters From a Working Publisher to Authors, Prospective and Practised.* London: Pelham Books, 1972. 160 pp.

These letters offer no-nonsense advice about the publishing world. Legat is a publisher of long reputation and gives the reader many insights into that realm which, for so many writers, is an enigma only slightly less mysterious than the afterworld. Though this book has a British point of view, it also has much to reveal to Americans and other English-speaking nationalities.

3460. Madison, Charles A. *Irving to Irving; Author—Publisher Relations, 1800-1974.* New York: Bowker, 1976. 453 pp.

This work profiles some thirty author-publisher relationships, including those of Washington Irving, Nathaniel Hawthorne, Louisa May Alcott, Mark Twain, Robert Frost, and Clifford Irving. The bias seems to be in favor of publishers.

3461. Meyer, Carol. *The Writer's Survival Manual; The Complete Guide to Getting Your Book Published Right.* New York: Crown, 1982. 310 pp.

The managing editor of Harcourt Brace Jovanovich's trade book department knows whereof she speaks on the subjects of finding a publisher, employing and using a literary agent, preparing the manuscript, negotiating subsidiary rights including paperback rights, and a variety of business considerations such as royalties, taxes, and self-publication. Her views on publicity, advertising, promotion, and other marketing approaches are especially valuable. William Jovanovich has called this information-filled work "...the best book of its kind I've read." It is written by a professional for those with genuine professional interests.

3462. Mitchell, Burroughs. *The Education of an Editor.* Garden City, New York: Doubleday, 1980. 163 pp.

This short work tells how Mitchell served an editorial apprenticeship under Maxwell Perkins and acted as an

editor for James Jones and others. It is rich with insight
and anecdote.

3463. Perkins, Maxwell Evarts. *Editor to Author; The Letters of Maxwell
E. Perkins.* Selected and edited, with commentary and an
introduction by John Hall Wheelock and a new introduction by
Marcia Davenport. New York: Charles Scribners, 1979. 315 pp.

3464. Shatzkin, Leonard. *In Cold Type; Overcoming the Book Crisis.*
Boston: Houghton Mifflin, 1982. 397 pp.

A perceptive critique of what Shatzkin feels is wrong with
the industry along with solutions the author sees as
essential. Like *The Blockbuster Complex* (see entry 3469),
this is required reading for any who would know book
publishing.

3465. Tebbel, John. *A History of Book Publishing in the United States.* 4
vols. New York: Bowker, 1972—.

This monumental effort is the most complete statement on
the subject yet published. Exhaustive if not definitive.

3466. Unwin, Stanley, and Philip Unwin. *The Truth about Publishing.* 8th
edition. London: Allen and Unwin, 1976. 256 pp.

One of the few truly classic statements on publishing.
Begun in the 1920s, it retains its wit and venom.

3467. Weeks, Edward. *Breaking Into Print; An Editor's Advice on Writing.*
Boston: Writer, 1962. 145 pp.

Less a technical handbook than an accumulation of one
editor's wisdom over the span of a long career. This work
combines style and wit.

3468. ———. *Writers and Friends.* Boston: Atlantic/Little Brown, 1982.
323 pp.

A distinguished, former editor of *The Atlantic Monthly*
during what many feel were its best years recalls a lifetime
of associations with writers.

3469. Whiteside, Thomas. *The Blockbuster Complex; Conglomerates, Show
Business, and Book Publishing.* Middletown, Connecticut: Wesleyan
University Press, 1981. 207 pp.

This is an assessment of the big-money and big-hype
mentality that has become increasingly evident among
many larger publishing companies. Though Whiteside has
convincingly portrayed a trend in a part of the industry
which has to do with power politics and show-biz antics, it
is hard to extend his dark projections to the industry as a
whole. As others have pointed out, if the public need is not
being served by existing publishing houses, new ones will
spring up to meet that need. Whiteside's book is

nonetheless a landmark work which has been widely quoted.

See also the chapters on Legal Aspects (page 335), Manuscript Preparation (page 311), Marketing (page 323), and Royalties and Payments (page 341) for book annotations containing references to editor-author and publisher-author relationships.

Articles

3470. Another example of successful mail research; questioning authors about editorial changes. A. Kotula. *Writer's Digest,* vol. 55, June 1975, pp. 17-19.

3471. Art of publishing; James Laughlin (interview). *Paris Review,* no. 89, 1983, pp. 154-193.

3472. At the business end: the author and his publisher. Siegfried Unseld. D.J. Enright. *Times Literary Supplement,* October 3, 1980, pp. 1079, 1082.

3473. Author's alterations: are they really necessary? comments at American Book Publishers Council conference. B.L. Stratton. *Publishers Weekly,* vol. 187, April 5, 1965, pp. 21-22.

3474. Author's and editor's responsibility; excerpts from *A Practical Style Guide for Authors and Editors.* M. Nicolson. *Publishers Weekly,* vol. 191, April 17, 1967, pp. 28-30.

3475. Authors give their views on British publishers. *Bookseller,* September 13, 1980, p. 1122.

3476. Author's signing sessions: conflicting views at Publishers Publicity Circle. *Bookseller,* March 29, 1975, pp. 1918+.

3477. British publishers: what authors say. A survey. *Author,* vol. 91, Autumn 1980, pp. 1, 15-20.

3478. British publishers: what the authors say. *Bookseller,* September 13, 1980, pp. 1136+.

3479. Copyright war between editors and writers. Norman Schreiber. *Writer's Digest,* vol. 59, January 1979, pp. 18-21.

3480. Critical interface between authors and publishers (Bookbinders Guild of New York's Seminar on Typesetting/Electronic Update). Jerome P. Frank. *Publishers Weekly,* vol. 220, September 4, 1981, pp. 37-38.

3481. Do editors steal? Gary Provost. *Writer's Digest,* vol. 63, April 1983, pp. 21-24.

3482. Editing in America. W.J. Weatherby. *Author,* vol. 91, Summer 1980, pp. 83-86.

3483. Editor and author in a university press. D. Davin. *Times Literary Supplement,* no. 3432, December 7, 1967, p. 1191.

3484. Editor and writer. T.J. Fleming. *Writer,* vol. 72, December 1959, pp. 10-12.

3485. Editor has a headache. Margaret Hill. *Writer,* vol. 72, September 1959, pp. 19-20.

3486. Editor: midwife or meddler? Catherine Drinker Bowen. *Writer,* vol. 72, June 1959, pp. 18-22.

3487. Editor over my shoulder. L. McLaughlin. *Writer,* vol. 79, May 1966, pp. 29-30+.

3488. Editor to author. E.M. Hutter. *Writer,* vol. 89, February 1976, pp. 26-28.

3489. Editors and their authors; excerpts from interviews. M. Saxton. *Writer,* vol. 88, February 1975, pp. 22-23.

3490. Editors are helpful ogres. R.C. Payes. *Writer,* vol. 78, March 1965, pp. 27-28.

3491. Editors are nuts about nuts and bolts. Gary Provost. *Writer's Digest,* vol. 63, January 1983, pp. 34-38.

3492. Eternal triangle: writer-editor-reader relationship. L. Conger. *Writer,* vol. 85, April 1972, pp. 11-12.

3493. Getting tough (with editors). Robert Bahr. *Writer's Digest,* vol. 59, April 1979, pp. 22-28.

3494. George Plimpton (interview). *Writer's Digest,* vol. 54, June 1974, pp. 16-18.

3495. Give your book a promotion (promotion tips). James Ennes. *Writer's Digest,* vol. 62, September 1982, pp. 30-32+.

3496. Heirs to Maxwell Perkins: seven American writers tell what they think about their editors. R. Rosen. *Horizon,* vol. 24, April 1981, pp. 50-53.

3497. How to behave like an author; advice from an editor. E. Heidt. *Writer,* vol. 81, October 1968, pp. 20-21+.

3498. How to promote your book on radio and TV interviews. Raymond Hull. *Writer's Digest,* vol. 51, August 1971, pp. 28-30+.

3499. How to read an editor's mind and manuscripts. M. Nord. *Writer's Digest,* vol. 59, September 1979, pp. 26-27.

3500. How to turn an editor into a friend. B. Ullman. *U.S. Camera and Travel,* vol. 29, October 1966, pp. 16+.

3501. I am tired of lazy writers. E. Jacobson. *Writer,* vol. 86, August 1973, pp. 18-19+.

3502. I want to know, can you trust editors? M.B. Parrott. *Writer,* vol. 74, November 1961, pp. 22-23.

3503. In defense of editing. N. Podhoretz. *Harper's Magazine,* vol. 231, October 1965, pp. 143-147.

3504. Is there a conflict between authors and publishers over book prices? S.K. Layson. *Southern Economic Journal,* vol. 48, April 1982, pp. 1057-1060.

3505. Is your editor really necessary? Sarah Neilan. *Bookseller,* November 15, 1975, pp. 2394-2395.

3506. Learning from editors. D.B. Kidney. *Writer,* vol. 95, January 1982, pp. 27-28.

3507. Letter from an unknown editor. *Writer,* vol. 85, September 1972, pp. 18-20.

3508. Letters to the editor (cover, query, confirmation, rights, etc.). Gary Turbak. *Writer's Digest,* vol. 62, March 1982, pp. 34-38.

3509. Looking at literary authors. R. Hayman. *Author,* vol. 88, Winter 1977, pp. 144-147.

3510. Martin Levin (editor): the good humor man. L. Taylor. *Writer's Digest,* vol. 57, October 1977, p. 29.

3511. Meet the manuscript editor. G.D. Griffin. *Writer's Digest,* vol. 48, July 1968, pp. 42-47+.

3512. Now I sit me down; pleasing the editor. W. Chamberlain. *Writer,* vol. 79, February 1966, pp. 22-24.

3513. Obligations of publishers and authors. Henry Cecil. *Bookseller,* October 6, 1973, pp. 2206-2209.

3514. One jump ahead of the editors. H. Schell. *Writer,* vol. 85, October 1972, pp. 28-29.

3515. Orphans' tales; what to do when your editor leaves your publishing house. Daryln Brewer. *Coda,* vol. 11, September/October 1983, pp. 10+.

3516. Panning for gold in the slush. (Reflections of a senior editor.) David Groff. *Writer,* vol. 97, September 1984, pp. 9-12+.

3517. Publisher and the pep talk. E. O'Connor. *Writer,* vol. 80, April 1967, pp. 31-32.

3518. Publisher as the Mad Hatter, or the writer as Alice. M. Holroyd. *Publishers Weekly,* vol. 197, March 16, 1970, pp. 24-26.

3519. Publishers' decision making: what criteria do they use in deciding which books to publish? *Social Research,* vol. 45, Summer 1978, pp. 227-252.

3520. Publishing parties: their do's and don'ts. *Publishers Weekly*, vol. 188, December 6, 1965, pp. 33-34.

3521. PW interviews; Doubleday's California editor. L. Nichols. *Publishers Weekly*, vol. 206, December 9, 1974, pp. 6-7.

3522. PW interviews; Doubleday's European editor. B. Gordey. *Publishers Weekly*, vol. 204, December 10, 1973, pp. 6-7.

3523. PW interviews; editor of the *Times Literary Supplement.* J. Gross. *Publishers Weekly*, vol. 210, August 9, 1976, pp. 12-13.

3524. PW interviews; West Coast editor for *Atlantic Monthly Press.* W. Abrahams. *Publishers Weekly*, vol. 210, November 22, 1976, pp. 6-7.

3525. Question of power. C. Gavin. *Writer*, vol. 93, December 1980, pp. 15-17.

3526. Real and ideal editor; excerpts from address. C. Canfield. *Publishers Weekly*, vol. 195, March 31, 1969, pp. 24-27.

3527. Role of a publisher's editor. David Farrer. *Bookseller*, July 19, 1975, pp. 182-183.

3528. Should an editor edit? H. Brucker. *Saturday Review*, vol. 50, January 14, 1967, pp. 116-117+.

3529. Strange relationships between author and editor. C.M. Smith. *Publishers Weekly*, vol. 207, January 20, 1975, pp. 50-51.

3530. Total word management comes to a publishing house (word processing/typesetting continuum at William H. Sadler, Inc.). R. Merritt. *Publishers Weekly*, vol. 218, November 7, 1980, pp. 47-48+.

3531. Toward a more perfect union: handling problem editors. Arthur S. Green. *Writer's Digest*, vol. 54, April 1974, p. 30.

3532. What HBJ is looking for (Harcourt Brace Jovanovich). W. Gladstone. *Writer*, vol. 94, September 1981, pp. 22-23.

3533. What have you done to my words? (editorial changes). Brian Vachon. *Writer's Digest*, vol. 62, July 1982, pp. 22-26.

3534. What is a book editor? J. Kahn. *Writer*, vol. 87, December 1974, pp. 22-24.

3535. What's ahead for writers? Comments by leading authors and editors. *Writer*, vol. 90, April 1977, pp. 20-22.

3536. Writers and editors: the publishing lifeline. B.A. Bannon. *Publishers Weekly*, vol. 201, pt. 2, April 10, 1972, pp. 100-106.

3537. Writers and publishers. Charles A. Madison. *American Scholar*, vol. 35, Summer 1966, pp. 531-541.

3538. Writers and their editors: notes on an uneasy marriage. J. Fischer. *Harper's Magazine,* vol. 219, October 1959, pp. 12+.

3539. Writers vs. editors. Art Spikol. *Writer's Digest,* vol. 57, September 1977, pp. 14-15.

Literary Agents

"It is very much the same as entering a marriage: you do not have to be in love but you better be damn good friends. Good agents, like good marriage partners, are hard to find."
—Donald MacCampbell

Books

3540. Cleaver, Diane. *The Literary Agent and the Writer; A Professional Guide.* Boston: Writer, 1984. 131 pp.

Describes both agents' and the publishers' points of view in such matters as the query, the submission, subsidiary rights, and marketing. Written by a best-selling author, experienced editor, and successful literary agent.

3541. Curtis, Richard. *How to Be Your Own Literary Agent.* Boston: Houghton Mifflin, 1983. 219 pp.

An experienced agent shares his knowledge about marketing manuscripts, contract negotiations, and the like.

Goldin, Stephen, and Kathleen Sky. *The Business of Being a Writer.* See entry 3713.

3542. *Literary Agents; A Complete Guide.* New York: Poets and Writers, 1978. 40 pp.

Answers basic questions and includes a list of agents who consider unsolicited work.

3543. *Literary Agents of North America; Marketplace, 1983-84. The Complete Guide to Over 450 U.S. and Canadian Literary Agencies: Profiles/Policies, Interests/Specialities, Collaboration/Ghostwriting and Services, Attitudes toward the New Writer, and Unsolicited Manuscripts. Includes Geographical and Subject Indexes. Essential for Writers Looking for an Agent, Planning to Change Agents, Looking for the Right Agent.* New York: Author Research Associates International, 1983. 128 pp.

3544. MacCampbell, Donald. *Don't Step on It—It Might Be a Writer; Reminiscences of a Literary Agent.* Los Angeles: Aherbourne, 1972. 190 pp.

MacCampbell provides what is mainly a memoir dealing with his own career as an agent in the mass market paperback field. His book is filled with anecdotes and reflexive (as opposed to reflective) opinions. This is an entertaining view of the man and of the world of agents and publishers during the mid-twentieth century.

MacCampbell, Donald. *The Writing Business.* See entry 3722.

Meredith, Scott. *Writing to Sell.* See entry 3725.

3545. Reynolds, Paul Revere. *The Middle Man; The Adventures of a Literary Agent.* New York: Morrow, 1972. 223 pp.

The anecdotal recollections of a life-long literary agent, discussing his pioneering agency and how authors, publishers, editors, motion picture executives, and agents interact.

3546. Strauss, Helen M. *A Talent for Luck; An Autobiography.* New York: Random, 1979. 315 pp.

Strauss recalls her twenty-three years as agent and founder of the literary department of the William Morris Agency, during which she represented an impressive array of authors and negotiated lucrative contracts for them.

3547. *Writer's Guide to Agents, Associations, and Services.* New York: Bowker, 1984. Approx. 100 pp.

This affordable spin off from the more expensive *Literary Market Place* (see entry 3721) provides names and addresses and other information for literary agents, writers' associations, awards, conferences, workshops, editorial services, and typing and word processing services.

Articles

3548. Agent as catalyst. A. Wood. *Esquire,* vol. 58, December 1962, pp. 216-218.

3549. Agent as provocateur. *Bookseller,* October 28, 1972, pp. 2222-2223.

3550. Agents and publishing: matters of taste and tax shelters. T. Weyr. *Publishers Weekly,* vol. 205, January 14, 1974, pp. 72-76.

3551. Agents and publishing: midwives, middlemen and auctioneers. T. Weyr. *Publishers Weekly,* vol. 205, January 7, 1974, pp. 34-38.

3552. Agent's changing role. Michael Sissons. *Author,* vol. 90, Summer 1979, pp. 53-56.

3553. Agents: writing with a dollar sign. *Time,* vol. 91, March 8, 1968, pp. 96+.

3554. All about agents. Diane Cleaver. *Writer's Digest,* vol. 60, June 1980, pp. 20-30.

3555. Authors and agents. *Author,* vol. 86, Summer 1975, pp. 60-62.

3556. Best way to get an agent. Comments by editors and publishers. *Writer,* vol. 90, October 1977, pp. 22-25.

3557. Birth of an agency; Peterborough Literary Agency. P. Nathan. *Publishers Weekly,* vol. 204, July 30, 1973, p. 58.

3558. Care and feeding of the artist. M.A. Guitar. *Mademoiselle,* vol. 70, November 1969, pp. 166-167.

3559. Counteragent. *Publishers Weekly,* vol. 196, August 18, 1969, pp. 35-37.

3560. Double trouble agents. Janice Young Brooks. *Writer's Digest,* vol. 58, June 1978, pp. 26-27.

3561. Editor-agent, with a difference. John L. Hochmann and T. Lask. *New York Times Book Review,* vol. 83, July 30, 1978, p. 35.

3562. Engel's millions: book producer. A. Myers. *Writer's Digest,* vol. 57, October 1977, pp. 35-36.

3563. Erich Linder: the role of an international agent. H.R. Lottman. *Publishers Weekly,* vol. 202, November 13, 1972, p. 26.

3564. Gail Hochman: literary agent. P. Jacobi. *Mademoiselle,* vol. 84, August 1978, p. 101.

3565. Garage sale; the story of Bert Briskin. Jacqueline Briskin. *Writer's Digest,* vol. 57, December 1977, pp. 48+.

3566. Getting an agent. Paul Revere Reynolds. *Writer,* vol. 85, October 1972, pp. 16-17+.

3567. Harold Ober, literary agent; a personal reminiscence. Catherine Drinker Bowen. *Atlantic,* vol. 206, July 1960, pp. 35-40.

3568. Helpful companion. W.D. Bayless. *Writer,* vol. 75, December 1962, pp. 16-18+.

3569. How to be a Hollywood literary agent. N. Brown. *Publishers Weekly,* vol. 206, December 9, 1974, pp. 40-42.

3570. How to get a literary agent. *Writer,* vol. 97, June 1984, pp. 21-24.

3571. How to get an agent. J.O. Brown. *Writer,* vol. 87, October 1974, pp. 17-19.

3572. Literary agent. N.R. Kentfield. *New York Times Book Review,* December 7, 1980, pp. 9+.

3573. Literary agent and book publishing. J. Cushman. *Publishers Weekly,* vol. 201, April 10, 1972, pp. 112-114.

3574. Literary agent and the freelance writer; questions and answers. E. Jacobson. *Writer,* vol. 85, July 1972, pp. 13-14.

3575. Literary agent; excerpt from *Writer and His Markets*. Paul Revere Reynolds. *Writer,* vol. 73, February 1960, pp. 8-13.

3576. Literary agent; his function, life, and power. Paul Revere Reynolds. *Saturday Review,* vol. 49, October 8, 1966, pp. 113-114.

3577. Literary agents. J.O. Brown. *Writer,* vol. 80, July 1967, pp. 15-17.

3578. Literary agents come of age. H. Rubinstein. *Times Literary Supplement,* vol. 3848, December 12, 1975, p. 1490.

3579. Literary agent's notebook. Paul Revere Reynolds. *Writer,* vol. 84, December 1971, pp. 15-17+.

3580. Literary hustler; Scott Meredith. P.D. Zimmerman. *Newsweek,* vol. 87, March 1, 1976, pp. 76-77+.

3581. Man in the middle; excerpts from *The Middle Man*. Paul Revere Reynolds. *Publishers Weekly,* vol. 200, October 18, 1971, pp. 21-23.

3582. Mary Kling; walking the tightrope as an agent in Paris. H.R. Lottman. *Publishers Weekly,* vol. 207, April 14, 1975, p. 30.

3583. Matchmakers. *Forbes,* vol. 119, March 15, 1977, p. 29.

3584. Michelle Lapautre. H.R. Lottman. *Publishers Weekly,* vol. 211, May 30, 1977, pp. 25-26.

3585. Mort Janklow: friends make the man. L. Wolfe. *New York,* vol. 11, February 13, 1978, pp. 41-44.

3586. Paperback talk; Charles B. Bloch and Associates. R. Walters. *New York Times Book Review,* vol. 83, July 23, 1978, pp. 31-32.

3587. Rights and permissions; agents relatively scarce in most countries. P. Nathan. *Publishers Weekly,* vol. 188, November 22, 1965, p. 56.

3588. Rights and permissions; tools for the profession. P. Nathan. *Publishers Weekly,* vol. 194, August 19, 1968, p. 62.

3589. Role of the literary agent today; excerpts from address. A. Elmo. *Writer,* vol. 89, April 1976, pp. 17-19+.

3590. Should every writer have an agent? excerpts from *Writing and Selling of Fiction*. Paul Revere Reynolds; reply. G. Hackel. *Saturday Review,* vol. 48, January 9, 1965, pp. 69-70+; reply February 13, 1965, p. 67.

3591. Should you really have an agent? *Writer,* vol. 84, July 1971, pp. 13-15; discussion, vol. 84, September, October, November 1971, pp. 3-5.

3592. Ten percent fantasy figure. L. Conger. *Writer,* vol 83, June 1970, pp. 7-8+.

3593. Ten percent solution. A. Diamant. *Writer,* vol. 92, January 1979, pp. 19-21.

3594. Ten percent solution: David Obst, super agent. D.K. Mano. *Esquire,* 86, November 1976, pp. 44+.

3595. Those ancient ritual insults: an agent replies. Michael Sissons. *Bookseller,* June 21, 1975, pp. 2922+.

3596. Trade winds (interview). Edited by C. Amory. Paul Revere Reynolds. *Saturday Review,* vol. 55, March 18, 1972, pp. 10-11.

3597. What beginning writers want to know (agents). J. Reach. *Writer,* vol. 76, October 1963, pp. 10-12.

3598. What can an agent do for you? D. Tritsch. *Writer's Digest,* vol 57, May 1977, p. 28.

3599. What every writer needs to know about literary agents. E. Levine. *Writer,* vol. 96, January 1983, pp. 13-15+.

3600. What my agent does for me. W.J. Slattery. *Writer's Digest,* vol. 57, May 1977, p. 29.

3601. Why you can't get a literary agent. E. Christman. *Writer's Digest,* vol 55, November 1975, pp. 13-15.

3602. Working with an agent (excerpt from *The Business of Being a Writer).* Stephen Goldin and Kathleen Sky. *Writer's Digest,* vol. 62, April 1982, pp. 22-26+.

3603. Writers, agents and manuscript sales. Paul Revere Reynolds. *Writer,* vol. 75, January 1962, pp. 20-21+.

3604. Writing as business (agents). N. Joseph. *Writer,* vol. 75, June 1962, pp. 13-15.

Manuscript Preparation, Including Revision, Rewriting, and Word Processing

Books

3605. Fluegelman, Andrew, and Jeremy Hewes. *Writing in the Computer Age; Word Processing Skills and Style for Every Writer.* New York: Doubleday, 1983. 256 pp.

This thorough introduction to word processing asserts that computers not only speed the writing process, but also creatively enhance one's thinking.

3606. Gadney, Alan. *Busy Person's Guide to Selecting the Right Word Processor; A Shortcut to Understanding and Buying, Complete with Checklists and Product Guide.* Glendale, California: Festival, 1983. 304 pp.

Billed as a "crash course in word processing," this comprehensive work provides selection criteria and detailed information about keyboards, memory, printers, software, and training.

3607. Knight, Gilfred N. *The Art of Indexing; A Guide to the Indexing of Books and Periodicals.* London: Allen Unwin, 1979. 208 pp.

A detailed guide to the basic principles of indexing.

Larsen, Michael. *How to Write a Book Proposal.* See entry 4255.

3608. McCunn, Donald H. *Write, Edit, and Print; Word Processing with Personal Computers.* San Francisco: Design Enterprises, 1982. 527 pp.

Covers "... four essential word processing programs from the Word Worker system, including BASIC word processing program, the extended writing program, and the editing program, written in microsoft compatible BASIC with specific conversions for Apple II, IBM-PC, PET/CBM, and computers using BASIC-80."

3609. McWilliams, Peter. *The Word Processing Book; A Short Course in Computer Literacy.* Los Angeles: Prelude Press, 1982. 240 pp.

Designed for those without prior computer background, this slightly irreverent but always readable introduction by a "word processing poet," covers equipment and software in both a buyer's and a user's contexts. This admirable work has received high marks from the reviewing community.

3610. Mullins, Carolyn. *The Complete Manuscript Preparation Guide.* Englewood Cliffs, New Jersey: Prentice-Hall, 1982. 276 pp.

Includes "typing and format rules for all major styles, word processing applications, business tips, and copyright rules, guidelines for books, articles, theses, dissertations, plays, poems, greeting cards, and training manuals."

3611. Olsen, Udia G. *Preparing the Manuscript.* Boston: Writer, 1976. 154 pp.

This is a functional, step-by-step introduction to the mechanics of preparing a manuscript for submission to popular markets. It treats page layout, grammar, punctuation, indexing, author's rights, and permissions.

3612. Poynter, Dan. *Word Processors and Information Processing; A Basic Manual on What They Are and How to Buy.* Santa Barbara, California: Para Publishing, 1982. 172 pp.

This work is intended mainly for commercial office applications, but many of the concepts will apply to free-lance writers. The information on specific kinds of equipment will need continual updating.

3613. Zinsser, William. *Writing with a Word Processor.* New York: Harper, 1983. 128 pp.

The author of the classic *On Writing Well* and executive editor of the Book-of-the-Month Club takes the fear and myth out of electronic writing by discussing his own experiences with a word processor. He has created a humorous informal manual for those about to take the plunge.

See also the chapter on Style Manuals (page 317) for book annotations containing references to manuscript preparation.

Articles

3614. Authors advocate do-it-yourself typesetting for more books. P. Doebler. *Publishers Weekly,* vol. 206, October 7, 1974, pp. 24+.

3615. Basic guide to packaging and mailing your words. Bruce Joel Hillman. *Writer's Digest,* vol. 62, November 1982, pp. 30-31+.

3616. Chocolate mouse pie (typos). N. Kraft. *Writer's Digest,* vol. 62, December 1982, pp. 37-39.

3617. Computer as super-typewriter. *Consumer Reports,* vol. 48, October 1983, pp. 540-543+.

3618. Critical interface between authors and publishers. Seminar on typesetting/electronic update. Jerome P. Frank. *Publishers Weekly,* vol. 220, September 4, 1981, pp. 37-38+.

3619. Electronic freelancer: a peek at the freelance life, circa 1991. G.L. Beiswinger. *Writer's Digest,* vol. 61, April 1981, pp. 26-30.

3620. From computer to silver screen; word processing software for scriptwriters. Barbara Elman. *Writer's Digest,* vol. 63, October 1983, pp. 35-38.

3621. Get your book's index on the right track with fast-track indexing. Frank R. Wallace and Mark Hamilton. *Writer's Digest,* vol. 62, October 1982, pp. 42-44.

3622. Goodbye, typewriter; hello word processor. W.J. Hawkins. *Popular Science,* vol. 220, February 1982, pp. 79-81+.

3623. How to get along with your typist. B. Foy. *Writer's Digest,* vol. 54, August 1974, p. 42.

3624. How to prepare a professional manuscript. D. Balkin. *Writer's Digest,* vol. 54, January 1974, pp. 44-46.

3625. How to save money on your MSS. Nixon Smith. *Author,* vol. 86, Winter 1975, pp. 135+.

3626. How to submit a book manuscript. *Writer,* vol. 89, July 1976, p. 41.

3627. How to submit a book manuscript. *Writer,* vol. 90, July 1977, p. 31.

3628. Keyboard configuration: an example of how you might approach customizing your computer keyboard. William Brohaugh. *Writer's Digest,* vol. 64, March 1984, p. 62.

3629. Living with a computer. J.M. Fellows. *Atlantic,* vol. 250, July 1982, pp. 84-91.

3630. Low cost word processing for TRS-80 users. C.L. Wolf. *On Computing,* vol. 3, Summer 1981, pp. 43+.

3631. Maker's eye: revising your own manuscripts. D.M. Murray. *Writer,* vol. 86, October 1973, pp. 14-16.

3632. Me and my typewriter. Gay Talese and others. *Writer's Digest,* vol. 61, January 1981, pp. 28-32.

3633. Mixing the media (authors needed for home computer programming; views of R. Kasser). J.F. Baker. *Publishers Weekly,* vol. 218, October 31, 1980, p. 61.

3634. Neatness counts. Art Spikol. *Writer's Digest,* vol. 57, April 1977, pp. 12+.

3635. Over the transom. What happens when a book manuscript is submitted to a publisher. Jim Menick. *Writer,* vol. 93, November 1980, pp. 18-19+.

3636. Pain-by-the-numbers. Getting the numbers right. Steve Carper. *Writer's Digest,* vol. 63, January 1983, pp. 40-42.

3637. Plugged-in prose (authorship use). J.D. Reed and J. North. *Time,* vol. 118, August 10, 1981, pp. 68+.

3638. Portable feast: the writer's guide to portable typewriters. Ronald J. Donovan. *Writer's Digest,* vol. 63, June 1983, pp. 26-29.

3639. Publication process: an editor's perspective (manuscript preparation). F.M. Berardo. *Journal of Marriage and the Family,* vol. 43, November 1981, pp. 771-779.

3640. Revision as a creative process. B. Weigl. *English Journal,* vol. 65, September 1976, pp. 67-68.

3641. Revision: nine ways to achieve a disinterested perspective. G.J. Thompson. *College Composition and Communication,* vol. 29, May 1978, pp. 200-202.

3642. Revisions and rewrites: a checklist. Phyllis A. Whitney. *Writer,* vol. 96, April 1983, pp. 12-14.

3643. Revisions can work magic. G.C. Little. *Writer,* vol. 85, November 1972, p. 28.

3644. Right title for your book. Patricia Tompkins. *Writer,* vol. 97, June 1984, pp. 13-15.

3645. Self-evaluation strategies of extensive revisers and nonrevisers. R. Beach. *College Composition and Communication,* vol. 27, May 1976, pp. 160-164.

3646. Should you use a Ms typing service? E. Depperman. *Writer's Digest,* vol. 49, January 1969, pp. 60-63.

3647. Style of manuals: in the age of the word processor. Typing on a manual is the choice of a tool over a machine. Jennifer Crichton. *Publishers Weekly,* vol. 222, October 22, 1982, pp. 26-28.

3648. Super Text II: one writer's appraisal. V.A. Glover. *On Computing,* vol. 3, Summer 1981, p. 40.

3649. Ten typewriter problems you can correct yourself. Wayne Gash. *Writer's Digest,* vol. 64, October 1984, pp. 33+.

3650. That all-important rewrite. Lois Duncan. *Writer,* vol. 86, December 1973, pp. 20-22.

3651. Three hints for successful revision. Jesse Hill Ford. *Writer,* vol. 73, September 1960, pp. 11-12.

3652. Unkindest cut of all. John Grossman. *Writer's Digest,* vol. 64, January 1984, pp. 28-30+.

3653. Using local typists. E.M. Rogers. *Writer's Digest,* vol. 49, January 1969, p. 63.

3654. When you submit a book manuscript. *Writer,* vol. 81, February 1968, pp. 23-25+.

3655. Why a word processor? C.J. Mullins. *Writer,* vol. 95, August 1982, pp. 19-22.

3656. Word machines for word people (authorship use). G. Courter. *Publishers Weekly,* vol. 219, February 13, 1981, pp. 40-43.

3657. Word processing. H. Friedman. *Radio-Electronics,* vol. 53, April 1982, pp. 83-85+.

3658. Word processing. Peter McWilliams. *Popular Computing,* vol. 1, March 1982, pp. 52+.

3659. Word processing. L. Werner. *Popular Electronics,* vol. 19, August 1981, pp. 29-32.

3660. Word processing. *Money,* vol. 11, November 1982, pp. 88-89.

3661. Word processing: keys to the future (keyboards). *Writer's Digest,* vol. 64, January 1984, pp. 46-48.

3662. Word-processing programs. *Consumer Reports,* vol. 48, October 1983, pp. 544-545+.

3663. Word processing: the A to Z of software. Robin Perry. *Personal Computing,* vol. 6, March 1982, pp. 72+.

3664. Word processor and I: a question of speed. Isaac Asimov. *Popular Computing,* June 1982, pp. 24+.

3665. Word processor and I: a true story from the master of science fiction. Isaac Asimov. *Popular Computing,* February 1982, pp. 32+.

3666. Writer's guide to buying a word processor. Mrinal Bali. *Writer,* vol. 97, April 1984, pp. 5-8.

3667. Writer's guide to "smart" typewriters. Ronald J. Donovan. *Writer's Digest,* vol. 62, April 1982, pp. 27-35+.

3668. Writer' guide to typewriters. Ronald J. Donovan. *Writer's Digest,* vol. 61, January 1981, pp. 20-27.

3669. Writer's guide to word processing printers. Ronald J. Donovan. *Writer's Digest,* vol. 64, March 1984, pp. 31-34.

3670. Writer's guide to word processors. Robin Perry. *Writer's Digest,* vol. 61, April 1981, pp. 21-30.

3671. Writing made easier with personal computers. Ronald J. Donovan. *Writer's Digest,* vol. 62, September 1982, pp. 33-42.

3672. Writing poetry on a word processor. Peter McWilliams. *Popular Computing,* February 1982, pp. 38+.

Style Manuals

"Fine writing is generally the effect of spontaneous thought and a labored style."

—William Shenstone

Books

Note: The following list of style manuals is by no means a complete inventory of all such publications, but it includes many that are currently in common use. Periodical and book publishers commonly employ their own internally produced style manuals or style sheets. It is usually best to ask a prospective publisher about such requirements when doubt exists.

3673. American Chemical Society. *Handbook for Authors.* Washington, D.C.: American Chemical Society Publications, 1978. 122 pp.

Covers manuscript preparation, terms, illustrations, and a variety of other information of use in submitting one's work to ACS journals.

3674. American Mathematical Society. *Manual for Authors of Mathematical Papers.* Providence, Rhode Island: AMS, 1980. 20 pp.

A concise style sheet which originally appeared in the *AMS Bulletin.*

3675. American Medical Association. *Style Book and Editorial Manual.* 6th edition. Acon, Massachusetts: Pub. Sciences Group, 1976. 161 pp.

Mainly intended for AMA publications but good for other medical writing as well.

3676. American Psychological Association. *Publication Manual.* 3rd edition. Washington, D.C.: American Psychological Association, 1983. 160 pp.

Intended as a standard for APA publications, this respected guide now reaches a wider range of writers. It covers manuscript preparation and format, editorial style, punctuation and use of numbers, proofreading, and a generous inventory of specific examples.

Bates, Jefferson D. *Writing with Precision.* See entry 3933.

3677. Bishop, Elna E., Edwin B. Eckel, and others. *Suggestions to Authors of the United States Geological Survey*. 6th edition. Washington, D.C. U.S. Government Printing Office, 1978. 273 pp.

The most widely accepted style manual in the earth sciences, this orderly approach covers illustration, manuscript preparation, stratigraphic nomenclature and expression, computer-related aspects, and basic elements of style as seen by the Geological Survey.

3678. Campbell, William G., Stephen V. Ballou, and Carol Slade. *Form and Style; Theses, Reports, Term Papers*. 5th edition. Boston: Houghton Mifflin, 1982. 212 pp.

With a goal of providing assistance to students who are writing scholarly papers, this widely consulted manual treats quotations, footnotes, bibliographies, tables, charts, computer materials, and manuscript format.

3679. Cappon, Rene J. *Associated Press Guide to Good Writing*. Reading, Massachusetts: Addison-Wesley, 1982. 140 pp.

"Shoptalk" on language, usage, feature writing, and other topics of interest to journalists.

3680. *Chicago Manual of Style*. 13th edition. Chicago: University of Chicago Press, 1982. 752 pp.

One of the most widely cited and respected general and scholarly style manuals, this clearly written work gives detailed coverage of footnotes, bibliographies, tables, punctuation, book production and printing, illustrations, rights and permissions, and a vast number of other topics.

3681. Council of Biology Editors. *CBE Style Manual*. 3rd edition. Washington, D.C.: American Institute of Biological Sciences, 1972. 297 pp.

Covers usage, punctuation, scientific style, formulas, tables, illustrations, indexing, bibliographic citations, and other specialized data.

3682. Dirckx, John H., M.D. *Dx + Rx; A Physician's Guide to Medical Writing*. Boston: G.K. Hall, 1977. 238 pp.

Discusses the writing of medical papers and monographs. Emphasis is on style, editing, and readability. The three culminating chapters deal with the "pathology" of writing.

3683. Fleischer, Eugene B. *Style Manual for Citing Microform and Nonprint Media*. Chicago: American Library Association, 1978. 66 pp.

A concise guide to the footnoting and bibliographic citation of bibliographically difficult materials.

3684. Grinsell, Leslie, and others. *The Preparation of Archaeological Reports.* New York: St. Martin's, 1974. 105 pp.

Provides succinct advice about publication grants, abstracts, illustrating one's report with drawings and maps. Also treats the differences between excavational and nonexcavational reports, and discusses final editor-author revisions.

3685. Graves, Robert, and Alan Hodge. *The Reader over Your Shoulder; A Handbook for Writers of English Prose.* New York: Collier, 1966. 446 pp.

Billed by its publisher as "...an unreverent and patient instructional guide to the confusions, peculiarities, abuses, and good uses of English prose from King Alfred to James Joyce, with twenty-five principles of clear statement and hundreds of famous and infamous illustrations of every kind...," this widely respected and entertaining usage manual searches the writings of the great and near great for the ambiguous phrase and the confused metaphor to show us that no matter how good one gets, there is always room for one more proofreading.

3686. Helm, Eugene, and Albert T. Luper. *Words and Music; Form and Procedure in Theses, Dissertations, Research Papers, Book Reports, Programs, and Theses in Composition.* Totowa, New Jersey: European American Music, 1982. 91 pp.

Along with Irvine (see entry 3688), one of the two essential sources for writing about music.

3687. Howell, John B. *Style Manuals of the English Speaking World; A Guide.* Phoenix, Arizona: Oryx Press, 1983. 152 pp.

Divided into two sections, this unique aid first describes government, commercial, and university press manuals "designed for general use." Part 2 describes manuals intended for individual disciplines such as education, biology, and physics. Included also is a brief historical sketch of the development of style manuals. A must for scholarly and technical writers.

3688. Irvine, Demar. *Writing about Music.* 2nd edition. Seattle: University of Washington Press, 1968. 211 pp.

Covers style considerations and procedure and provides an abundance of examples.

3689. Longyear, Marie. *McGraw-Hill Style Manual; A Concise Guide for Writers and Editors.* New York: McGraw-Hill, 1983. 333 pp.

Longyear has been director of publishing services at McGraw-Hill. She provides not only specific insight about that publisher's style requirements, but also a refreshing approach to punctuation, copy editing, and standards for writing in science and technology. Her manual has been hailed by reviewers as first aid for "editorial emergencies."

3690. McCartney, Eugene S. *Recurrent Maladies in Scholarly Writing.* Ann Arbor: University of Michigan Press, 1953. 141 pp.

After a lifetime of experience at the University of Michigan Press, McCartney comments upon a wide range of grammatical errors and failures of logic and style which are common to many of the manuscripts that he has considered for publication. This is an excellent short review of the pitfalls to be avoided in scholarly writing.

Miller, Casey and Kate Swift. *The Handbook of Nonsexist Writing for Writers, Editors, and Speakers.* See entry 4257.

3691. Modern Humanities Research Association. *M.H.R.A. Style Book; Notes for Authors, Editors, and Writers of Dissertations.* 2nd edition. London: Modern Humanities Research Association, 1978. 72 pp.

Reflects current British academic practice with regard to punctuation, spelling, abbreviations, italics, quotations, footnotes, and final manuscript preparation in the humanities. Also includes a table of British proof correction marks.

3692. Modern Language Association of America. *MLA Handbook for Writers of Research Papers, Theses, and Dissertations.* New York: Modern Language Association, 1977. 163 pp.

The standard publication to be used by American writers in language and literature.

3693. Montgomery, Michael, and John Stratton. *The Writer's Hotline Handbook.* New York: New American Library, 1981. 384 pp.

This work had its origins in a successful word-usage phone service for authors. Though it is full of practical answers to common questions, it is organized in a way that will frustrate quick access to that information.

3694. National Education Association of the United States. *Style Manual; NEA Style Manual for Writers and Editors.* Washington, D.C.: National Education Association, 1974. 92 pp.

Covers abbreviations, capitalization, dates and time, italics, plurals, punctuations, appellations, footnotes, bibliographies, and copy preparation in the field of education.

3695. New York Times. *Style Book for Writers and Editors.* New York: McGraw-Hill, 1962. 124 pp.

A concise guide to punctuation, word division, and abbreviations as prescribed by *New York Times* editorial policy.

3696. Repp, William. *Complete Handbook of Business English.* Englewood Cliffs, New Jersey: Prentice-Hall, 1982. 448 pp.

Designed for executives, secretaries, and other business professionals, this is a comprehensive approach to spelling, word usage, and grammar.

3697. Skillin, Marjorie, Robert M. Gay, and others. *Words into Type.* 3rd edition. Englewood Cliffs, New Jersey: Prentice-Hall, 1974. 585 pp.

This highly respected work provides advice about grammar, usage, style, and production methods in the publishing world. Divided into lengthy sections that address the manuscript, copy and proof, copy editing style, typographical style, grammar, use of words, typography, and illustration. Carefully indexed. Has a glossary of printing and allied terms. The 3rd edition deals with recent technical innovations in the publishing world such as lithography cathode ray tube equipment, cold type composition, and computer applications. The 3rd edition also responds to the "greater flexibility of style" currently allowed in the publication world and is thus less rigid and prescriptive.

3698. Strunk, William, Jr., and E.B. White. *The Elements of Style.* 3rd edition. New York: MacMillan, 1973. 85 pp.

No guide as short as this has ever been so widely praised for its apt use of examples and general perceptiveness. This nonpareil work covers usage, composition, form, and style in ways that will delight. To be, at once, wisely corrected and entertained is no small trick.

3699. Swanson, Ellen. *Mathematics into Type; Copy Editing and Proofreading of Mathematics for Editorial Assistants and Authors.* Providence, Rhode Island: American Mathematical Society, 1982. 90 pp.

Always clear and concise, Swanson covers copy editing, typography, mathematical expressions, usage, manuscript and proof techniques, publication style considerations, and composition trends. A glossary and bibliography complete this admirable short work.

3700. Timmons, Christine, and Frank Gibney, editors. *Britannica Book of English Usage.* Garden City, New York: Doubleday/Britannica, 1980. 655 pp.

A radical yet welcome departure in usage manuals, this admirable work begins with the evolution of the English language, then deals with grammar, pronunciation, spelling, and abbreviations. A final section addresses writing and speaking effectively. Each chapter is written by an expert in the field under consideration.

3701. Turabian, Kate L. *Manual for Writers of Term Papers, Theses, and Dissertations.* 4th edition. Chicago: University of Chicago Press, 1973. 216 pp.

Incorporating material from the *Chicago Manual of Style* (see entry 3680), this, along with Campbell's *Form and Style* (see entry 3678), is one of the most widely consulted guides for student writing. It addresses formats, abbreviations and punctuation, quotations, footnotes, bibliographies, and illustrations. A special section of this clearly written work deals with the scientific paper.

3702. U.S. Government Printing Office. *Style Manual.* Washington, D.C.: Government Printing Office, 1973. 548 pp.

A widely used source which covers rules of the G.P.O. on punctuation, abbreviations, foreign languages, and the like.

3703. Van Leunan, Mary-Claire. *A Handbook for Scholars.* New York: A.A. Knopf, 1978. 354 pp.

Van Leunen's effort might better have been titled "A Handbook for Scholars in the Social Sciences and Humanities" for it has little to do with scholarly activity in the behavioral and pure sciences. While much attention is given to what the author considers proper bibliography and footnote forms, little or no information is provided about the confoundingly different requirements from one scholarly discipline to the next. Beyond its misleading title, this is an informative and competent survey of the general aspects of form and style. It should, however, be used in conjunction with a style manual particular to one's own discipline.

Zinsser, William. *On Writing Well.* See entry 4017.

See also the chapter on Manuscript Preparation (page 311) for book annotations containing references to style manuals.

Marketing: Queries, Proposals, Submissions, and Rejections

"Your manuscript is both good and original; but the part that is good is not original, and the part that is original is not good."

—Samuel Johnson

Books

3704. Adelman, Robert H. *What's Really Involved in Writing and Selling Your Book.* Los Angeles: Nash, 1972. 171 pp.

This is a work that offers a method for getting almost any kind of book written, though it contains little about literary technique. Adleman assumes that his reader is already trying to write a book or at least has an idea for one. He stresses self-discipline and goal-setting. Using a question and answer style, he covers outlining, precis writing, research, manuscript marketing, and promotion. He also offers advice on dealing with agents, editors, and publishers, as well as practical suggestions on writing as a business. This book contains valuable professional advice from a self-supporting author.

3705. Appelbaum, Judith, and Nancy Evans. *How to Get Happily Published.* New York: Harper & Row, 1978. 272 pp.

By means of entertaining anecdotes and practical advice, two editors offer systematic advice on writing mechanics, manuscript preparation, sales, and promotion. An appendix of resources adds to a source that is among the best recently published works of its kind.

3706. Astbury, Raymond, editor. *Writer in the Market Place; Papers Delivered at a Symposium Held at Liverpool School of Librarianship, April 1968.* London: Archon Books, 1969. 176 pp.

Dealing with such specialized topics as public lending rights, the historical novelist, and the relationship among booksellers, authors, and librarians, these are views of the British writing and publishing world. Several of the essays, such as Joe Martindale's "The New Author," and Michael Sissons' "The Author and the Literary Agent," have more universal appeal.

3707. Clark, Bernadine. *Writer's Market, 1984.* Cincinnati: Writer's Digest, 1984. 1008 pp.

For anyone who has not yet discovered this amazing annual publication, let it be said that there is nothing else quite like, it both for surveying broader market segments and for determining a book or magazine publisher that may be just right for one's projected or recently completed manuscript. Thousands of magazine publishers and hundreds of book publishers are listed, along with addresses, who to contact, what they buy, manuscript requirements, and royalty rates.

3708. *Directory of Publishing Opportunities in Journals and Periodicals.* 5th edition. Chicago: Marquis Academic Media, 1981. 844 pp.

Detailed entries for nearly four thousand journals appear in this indispensable resource intended for academic, professional, and related specialized uses. Divided into categories such as literature, education, urban studies, botany, and environmental sciences, the entries are up to 2,400 words in length and include such diverse information as desired manuscript length, payments (if any), response time, and positions of editors on simultaneous submission.

Fredette, Jean M. *Fiction Writer's Market.* See entry 1109.

3709. Fulton, Len, and Ellen Ferber. *International Directory of Little Magazines and Small Presses.* 19th edition, 1983-84. Paradise, California: Dustbooks, 1983. 586 pp.

Small presses and little magazines represent a vital publishing medium. This essential source continues to be the most comprehensive guide to such publications. Entries are arranged alphabetically and vary from quite brief to over 2,500 words. They provide editors' names, addresses, phone numbers, material needed, manuscript requirements, and payment scales. Subject and regional indexes plus a guide to agents, jobbers, and distributors complete the work. *Wall Street Journal* has called this directory "the bible of the business."

3710. Gearing, Philip J., and E.V. Brunson. *Breaking into Print; How to Get Your Work Published.* Englewood Cliffs, New Jersey: Prentice-Hall, 1977. 131 pp.

Tells how to find a publisher, how to negotiate a contract, and other marketing considerations. Also included are evaluative criteria with regard to quality and readability.

3711. Gedin, Per I. *Literature in the Marketplace.* London: Faber & Faber, 1977. 211 pp.

A European view of book markets and the events that are rapidly changing them.

3712. Giles, Carl H. *Writing Right—To Sell.* Cranbury, New Jersey: A.S. Barnes and Company, 1970. 216 pp.

Giles, a professor of journalism, reveals his own system for writing commercially. The main emphasis of this once-over-lightly account is on magazine article writing. With chapters on writing for such markets as industrial, trade, religious, adventure, travel, and outdoor, this book is accompanied by short sample articles in each category.

3713. Goldin, Stephen, and Kathleen Sky. *The Business of Being a Writer.* New York: Harper & Row, 1982. 321 pp.

Among the best of those books that set out to describe the business aspects of professional writing, this work covers marketing, record keeping, contracts, royalties, copyright, fair use, taxes including advice about the dreaded self-employment tax, publicity techniques, advice about editors and agents, and up-to-date appendices of writers' organizations and addresses of interest to professional writers. Goldin and Sky, whose combined talents have produced over twenty novels, developed this book from experience gained through teaching a course in writers' business aspects at one of the California state universities. The resulting trial and revision is reflected in this readable and highly informative work.

3714. Gordon, Barbara, and Elliot Gordon. *How to Survive in the Freelance Jungle—A Realistic Plan for Success in Commercial Art And Photography.* New York: Executive Communications, 1980. 118 pp.

William A. Fisher, writing for *Journalism Quarterly,* considered this short work essential for the freelance writer's or photographer's library. It discusses markets, promotion, and how much to charge, and it includes a valuable section on developing a salable portfolio.

3715. Halpern, Frances. *Writer's Guide to West Coast Publishing.* Los Alamitos, California: Hwong Publishing, 1980. 252 pp.

3716. Hill, Mary, and Wendell Cochran. *Into Print; A Practical Guide to Writing, Illustrating, and Publishing.* Los Altos, California: William Kaufmann, 1977. 175 pp.

Describes the widest possible range of writing and publishing situations, including advertising and promotion, self-publishing, and rewriting for a new editor.

3717. *International Literary Market Place, 1983-84.* New York: Bowker, 1983. 545 pp.

Intended as an extension of *Literary Market Place* (see entry 3721), this standard source is arranged by country and includes information about book trade organizations, book publishers, literary agents, literary prizes, translation agencies, and the like. Also included are international copyright conventions and international literary prizes.

3718. Joan, Polly. *Guide to Women's Publishing.* Paradise, California: Dustbooks, 1978. 296 pp.

Covers nonsexist book and periodical markets as well as resources, archives, library collections, bookstores, and distributors.

3719. Kuswa, Webster. *Sell Copy.* Cincinnati, Ohio: Writer's Digest, 1979. 205 pp.

Spanning public relations, speech writing, direct mail, advertising, and editorial freelancing, this competent work relfects Kuswa's thirty years of experience, which ranges from copywriter and public relations director to company president. It contains wise advice on client relations and self-organization.

3720. Levin, Joel. *Getting Published; The Educators' Resource Book.* New York: Arco, 1983. 352 pp.

Along with an extensive directory of book and journal publishers, this work discusses author-publisher relationships and contracts.

3721. *Literary Market Place; 1984. A Directory of American Book Publishing with Names and Numbers.* New York: Bowker, 1983. 908 pp.

Long recognized as the unequaled standard approach to the contemporary U.S. book publishing industry, this "Sears Catalog" size work lists U.S. and Canadian book publishers (and important individuals in each by division), book clubs, literary agents, awards and prizes, editorial services, review media, and a wide range of associated businesses and organizations. If you want to know, for example, who is the editor in charge of scientific and academic editions at Van Nostrand, this book will tell, and include an official title as well.

3722. MacCampbell, Donald. *The Writing Business.* New York: Crown, 1978. 120 pp.

A successful professional writer sets out to acquaint new writers with the needs of publishers for new material and talent, stressing at the same time the fact that as much as 90 percent of literary material is currently brought to market by agents.

3723. *Magazine Industry Market Place: 1984; The Directory of American Periodical Publishing with Names and Numbers.* New York: Bowker, 1983. 720 pp.

This hefty volume is to the U.S. magazine industry what *Literary Market Place* (see entry 3721) is to the book industry. Publications are arranged by type of magazine such as Farm, Art, Engineering, and the like. Also included are awards, contests and prizes, illustration agents, art services, translators, and a broad range of technical support services.

3724. Mathieu, Aron M. *Book Market; How to Write, Publish, and Market Your Book.* New York: Andover Press, 1981. 474 pp.

An experienced author concentrates mainly on the business aspects of writing, with inside accounts of transactions with editors and publishers. A good companion volume to Richard Balkin's *A Writer's Guide to Book Publishing* (see entry 3436) and Judith Appelbaum's *How to Get Happily Published* (see entry 3705).

3725. Meredith, Scott. *Writing to Sell.* 2nd revised edition. New York: Harper & Row, 1974. 232 pp.

Writing to Sell has been a standard of its kind since 1950. Meredith, a well-known literary agent and author, approaches writing as a business and stresses marketing, author-agent-publisher relationships, and contracts. A number of chapters are devoted to the technical aspects of writing fiction, as well as nonfiction.

3726. *MLA Directory of Periodicals; A Guide to Journals and Series in Languages and Literatures.* 1984-85 edition. New York: Modern Language Association, 1984. 745 pp.

This companion volume to the *MLA International Bibliography* contains information about 3102 journals. The listings for each journal include average length of article published, length of book reviews published, average time lapse before publication decision, number of reviewers, and disposition of rejected manuscripts.

3727. Oleksy, Walter G. *1000 Tested Money-Making Markets for Writers.* New York: Harper & Row, 1974. 225 pp.

This book is mainly a group of lists of magazine and book publishers, with addresses, payments, and types of material published by each. Categorized into fifteen writing areas, such as travel and outdoor, juvenile and teenage, and science and technical, each list is preceded by a short essay which offers an overview of the market. *Writer's Market* (see entry 3707) is more comprehensive and is regularly updated.

3728. *Political and Social Science Journals; A Handbook for Writers and Reviewers.* Santa Barbara, California: ABC-Clio, 1983. 236 pp.

Covers nearly 450 English-language publications and includes such diverse information as submission requirements, style manual used, and editorial policies.

3729. Raffelock, David. *Writing for the Markets.* New York: Funk & Wagnalls, 1969. 150 pp.

Addressing writing as an increasingly fragmented and specialized business, Raffelock provides a short chapter on each of fourteen markets. From motion picture and stage script markets to juvenile and religious magazine markets, he attempts to give an overview of each area. What should be said about a book with a chapter that disposes of the book publishing market in only thirteen pages? That it is largely insufficient to the needs of any serious inquiry? Yes. But this book has the advantage of giving the beginner a concise view of market options in an honest and systematic manner. Accompanied by good index. The book as a whole is becoming dated.

3730. Reynolds, Paul Revere. *Professional Guide to Marketing Manuscripts.* Boston: Writer, 1968. 170 pp.

Reynolds gives a 111-page introduction to a variety of writing markets and considerations. This is supplemented by a series of useful sample contracts and releases, as well as information relating to literary agents and writers' organizations. Of limited usefulness because it badly needs updating and lacks an index.

3731. *Standard Periodical Directory, 1983-84.* 8th edition. New York: Oxbridge, 1982. 1613 pp.

The entries in this exhaustive compilation are brief, being mainly restricted to names, editors, addresses, telephone numbers, contents, and subscription and advertising information. But with over 60,000 entries the user will find publications listed here that can be found nowhere else. Arrangement is by major subject such as Banking and Finance, Baseball, Biophysics, and Boating.

3732. Thomas, David St. John, and Herbert Bermont. *Getting Published.* New York: Harper & Row, 1974. 188 pp.

With an emphasis on specialty and trade nonfiction, this book gives advice from a British editor to the individual who wishes to write a book on a subject related to his or her profession, vocation, or hobby, but who will never be a full-time professional writer. In a phrase, for people who have something to say and want to know how to organize and forcefully state it in a way that is "editorially viable." In tone and style this is a straightforward book which gets directly to the business at hand. It should be of particular use to writers interested in the British market.

3733. White, John. *Rejection.* Reading, Massachusetts: Addison-Wesley, 1982. 192 pp.

Tells how over two hundred notable artists, authors, musicians, and inventors coped with multiple rejections. For example, James Joyce's *Dubliners* was turned down by twenty-two publishers before being accepted by one. You are not alone!

3734. *Writers' and Artists' Yearbook. A Directory for Writers, Artists, Playwrights, Writers for Film, Radio, and Television, Photographers, and Composers.* London: Adam and Charles Black, 1983. (U.S.distributor: Writer's Digest Books.)

Addressed primarily to those interested in British and Commonwealth markets, this standard source lists hundreds of newspaper, magazine, and journal publishers as well as a wide range of book publishers. Addresses, editorial requirements, and payments are also included. Theatre, television, and radio markets appear, as do lists of literary agents, prizes, and writers' organizations. A series of short essays covers topics ranging from libel and taxation to Britain's interesting experiment with public lending rights.

3735. Writer's Digest Magazine. *The Basics of Selling Your Writing.* Cincinnati: Writer's Digest, 1983. 112 pp.

This quick guide for beginners covers contemporary writing opportunities in fiction, poetry, screenwriting, and nonfiction. It also discusses agents and publishers, manuscript preparation, taxes, and copyright.

See also the chapter on Freelancing (page 237) for book annotations containing references to marketing.

Articles

3736. ASJA insider report; submitting manuscripts to many publishers. S.S. Fader. *Writer's Digest,* vol. 56, January 1976, pp. 10+.

3737. Basic guide to selling your words. Gary Provost. *Writer's Digest,* vol. 62, November 1982, pp. 24-29.

3738. Brevity is the soul of sales. M. Weisinger. *Writer's Digest,* vol. 56, December 1976, pp. 17-19.

3739. Change your rejection slips into checks. E. Shepherd. *Writer's Digest,* vol. 52, August 1972, pp. 25-26.

3740. Confessions of a first reader. N. Henderson. *Writer's Digest,* vol. 54, May 1974, pp. 20-24.

3741. Do your queries pass the IQ test? Clay Schoenfeld. *Writer's Digest,* vol. 62, February 1982, pp. 43+.

3742. Don't lick the stamp yet. B. Robinson. *Writer,* vol. 76, September 1963, pp. 11-13+.

3743. Don't query editors; propose to them. Herman Holtz. *Writer's Digest,* vol. 64, September 1984, pp. 33-35.

3744. Editors regret: phrasing of rejection slips. John Ciardi. *Saturday Review,* vol. 48, January 2, 1965, p. 24.

3745. Final approach. M. Lodeesen. *Writer,* vol. 78, July 1965, pp. 12-13.

3746. Four point system for writing a selling query letter (interview). C. Handley. *Writer's Digest,* vol. 49, August 1969, pp. 48-51.

3747. Great paper-clip robbery and other related crimes. S. Gish. *Writer's Digest,* vol. 55, October 1975, pp. 21-23+.

3748. Growing market for paperback originals. *Writer,* vol. 89, July 1976, pp. 25-26.

3749. Hanging in there; adapting to the market, with excerpts from letter. F. Bonham. *Writer,* vol. 87, September 1974, pp. 13-15+.

3750. Hey! You! See! Sold! (sales technique). Margaret L. Aubuchon. *Writer's Digest,* vol. 62, November 1982, p. 40.

3751. How book publishing decisions are made: with questions and answers. *Writer,* vol. 86, April 1973, pp. 17-19+.

3752. How to be rejected. L. Conger. *Writer,* vol. 79, May 1966, pp. 7-8.

3753. How to break the barriers of getting a book published. R.E. Wolseley. *Journalism Educator,* vol. 32, January 1978, pp. 32-34.

3754. How to effectively query an editor. Iris S. Jones. *Writer's Digest,* vol. 55, June 1975, p. 28.

3755. How to market your articles. Lorene Hanley Duquin. *Writer,* vol. 97, January 1984, pp. 19-21.

3756. How to pre-sell an editor. W.B. Mueller. *Writer,* vol. 91, August 1978, pp. 19-21+.

3757. How to write a nonfiction book proposal that sells. R. Roesch. *Writer,* vol. 93, September 1980, pp. 16-20.

3758. How to write a query letter. W.F. Hallstead. *Writer,* vol. 89, August 1976, pp. 23-25+.

3759. If you were an editor, could you turn these down? Query letters. *Writer's Digest,* vol. 55, June 1975, p. 29.

3760. It's been done before. Samm S. Baker. *Writer,* vol. 88, February 1975, pp. 14-16.

3761. It's push, not pull. L. Conger. *Writer,* vol. 83, February 1970, pp. 9-10.

3762. I've turned down more best-sellers than you have. A. Orrmont. *Writer's Digest,* vol. 53, July 1973, pp. 9-14.

3763. Keep those manuscripts coming, folks! D. Copps. *Writer's Digest,* vol. 55, October 1975, pp. 22-23.

3764. Knowing the market you write for. C.R. Stoertz. *Writer,* vol. 89, March 1976, pp. 28-29.

3765. Language of rejection. M.E. Marty. *Christian Century,* vol. 92, December 10, 1975, p. 1143.

3766. Let's up the ante! (asking editors for a raise). Jay Stuller. *Writer's Digest,* vol. 62, December 1982, pp. 22-25.

3767. Letters to the editor (cover, query, confirmation, rights, etc.). Gary Turbak. *Writer's Digest,* vol. 62, March 1982, pp. 34-38.

3768. Make your query letter work for you. R. Langley. *Writer,* vol. 87, August 1974, pp. 20-22.

3769. Memo from the market editor; pros and cons of sending photocopies of manuscripts to publishers. L. Ellinwood. *Writer's Digest,* vol. 52, April 1972, p. 25.

3770. Ms. that was rejected 123 times. Meg Hill. *Writer's Digest,* vol. 54, June 1974, pp. 10-11.

3771. Multiple queries, simultaneous submissions; writers and editors speak out. *Writer,* vol. 86, June 1973, pp. 19-25.

3772. Nicholas Meyer's do-it-yourself solution (author of *The Seven-Per-Cent Solution).* Christine Rose. *Writer's Digest,* vol. 58, July 1978, pp. 30-31.

3773. Nonfiction; query letters. Art Spikol. *Writer's Digest,* vol. 56, March 1976, pp. 10+.

3774. Nor rhyme nor reason. Judson Jerome. *Writer's Digest,* vol. 55, December 1975, pp. 19-21.

3775. On reading a rejection letter. Jane H. Yolen. *Writer,* vol. 94, March 1981, pp. 5-6.

3776. Opportunity is like a train. Phyllis A. Whitney. *Writer,* vol. 87, November 1974, pp. 11-13+.

3777. Over the transom (submitting a book manuscript). Jim Menick. *Writer,* vol. 93, November 1980, pp. 18-19+.

3778. Over the transom and into print: how to give an unsolicited manuscript the best chance. *Coda,* vol. 6, June/July 1979, pp. 15-18.

3779. Paperback talk. *New York Times Book Review,* vol. 86, August 2, 1981, pp. 31-32.

3780. Partial road to complete writing success (partial manuscript submissions). Chet Cunningham. *Writer's Digest,* vol. 59, June 1979, pp. 18-21.

3781. Penny for my thoughts. Brigid Brophy. *Observer,* August 6, 1972, p. 4.

3782. Power for the writer. Michael Korda. *Writer's Digest,* vol. 58, July 1978, p. 31.

3783. Put yourself in the editor's chair; rejected articles. C. Darlington. *Writer,* vol. 77, October 1964, pp. 26-27.

3784. Reference notebook: how books get published. *Writer's Digest,* vol. 51, April 1971, p. 31.

3785. Rejection is a rejection is an acceptance; correspondence between Gertrude Stein and E. Sedgwick. *Writer's Digest,* vol. 55, August 1975, pp. 19-23.

3786. Rejection slip. Don Gold. *New York Times Magazine,* August 22, 1976, p. 87.

3787. Rejection slips? So what? H.E. Neal. *Writer's Digest,* vol. 56, May 1976, pp. 22-23.

3788. Rejections: reaping between the lines. R.M. Fuerst. *Writer's Digest,* vol. 56, October 1976, pp. 50-51.

3789. Rewards of persistence. Elizabeth Yates. *Writer,* vol. 76, January 1963, pp. 19-20+.

3790. Sell what you write. L. Zobel. *Writer,* vol. 82, November 1969, pp. 26-27.

3791. Sell your nonfiction. Omer Henry. *Writer,* vol. 95, July 1982, pp. 14-17.

3792. Successful query letters. W. Casewit. *Writer,* vol. 76, December 1963, pp. 15-17.

3793. Theory of the silver bullet. L.S. Bernstein. *Writer,* vol. 90, August 1977, pp. 28-29.

3794. There's gold in them thar files (unsold manuscripts). Mansfield Latimer. *Writer's Digest,* vol. 62, November 1982, pp. 32-33.

3795. Thomas Wolfe on publishers: reaction to rejection. P. Reeves. *South Atlantic Quarterly,* vol. 64, Summer 1965, pp. 385-389.

3796. Timing the submission. A.S. Harris, Jr. *Writer,* vol. 90, March 1977, pp. 19-21+.

3797. Too many books? An author's experience. A. Netboy. *Publishers Weekly,* vol. 207, February 10, 1975, pp. 32-33.

3798. Truth about nonfiction book proposals. B. Toohey and J. Biermann. *Writer's Digest,* vol. 55, March 1975, pp. 9-10.

3799. Trying to sell your book. Frank Fernyhough. *Author,* vol. 87, Spring 1976, pp. 10-12.

3800. Twenty-four little sins. Art Spikol. *Writer's Digest,* vol. 56, November 1976, pp. 14+.

3801. Ultimate rule (finding an editor who will buy your manuscript). John Ashmeade, and others. *Writer's Digest,* vol. 63, November 1983, pp. 39-40.

3802. Unsolicited, unloved MSS (fiction manuscripts). D. Menaker. *New York Times Book Review,* vol. 86, March 1, 1981, pp. 3+.

3803. Vanishing manuscript. R. Dobbs. *Writer,* vol. 85, March 1972, pp. 27-28.

3804. What do editors mean when they say ... sorry, but the motivation is missing. Dean R. Koontz. *Writer's Digest,* vol. 49, March 1969, pp. 42-47.

3805. What I look for in a manuscript. L.P. Ashmead. *Writer,* vol. 87, July 1974, pp. 15-17.

3806. When you finish your book. Richard Stern. *Writer,* vol. 95, February 1982, pp. 9-11.

3807. When you query, write it right! L. Olfson. *Writer,* vol. 80, March 1967, pp. 14-15+.

3808. When you submit a book manuscript. *Writer,* vol. 81, February 1968, pp. 23-25+.

3809. Why do editors use form rejection slips? *Writer,* vol. 89, January 1976, pp. 16-19.

3810. Why editors get gray hair. Joe Zambone. *Writer's Digest,* vol. 58, October 1978, p. 39.

3811. Write to sell; a three-part checklist that works. Samm S. Baker. *Writer,* vol. 97, November 1984, pp. 9-20.

3812. Writing article queries that sell. J. Fisher. *Writer,* vol. 84, June 1971, pp. 18-20+.

3813. Writing proposals for nonfiction books. James Heacock and Rosalie Heacock. *Writer,* vol. 97, February 1984, pp. 21-23.

3814. Writing the query letter. Max Gunther. *Writer,* vol. 85, September 1972, pp. 13-15+.

3815. Writing the query letter. B. Pesta. *Writer,* vol. 88, July 1975, pp. 15-18.

3816. Your book rejected by an inch? D. Richards. *Writer's Digest,* vol. 48, March 1968, pp. 52-54+.

Legal Aspects, Including Copyright and Contracts

"People say law but they mean wealth."
—Ralph Waldo Emerson

Books

3817. Ashley, Paul P., and Camden M. Hall. *Say It Safely; Legal Limits in Publishing, Radio, and Television.* 5th edition. Seattle: University of Wasington Press, 1976. 238 pp.

This widely quoted work discusses libel, contempt of court, obscenity, invasion of privacy, and other issues in a way that is understandable to those without a legal background.

3818. Beil, Norman, editor. *The Writer's Legal and Business Guide; A Presentation of the Beverly Hills Bar Association Barristers Committee for the Arts.* New York: Arco, 1984. 210 pp.

Though the emphasis is on film and television writing, this admirable and much needed collection will appeal to all writers with commercial interests. Written by industry lawyers and other experts, it is a series of essays on such subjects as copyright law, protection of ideas, liability for defamation and invasion of privacy, tax considerations, and basic contract law as it applies to writers. Sample contracts and forms, such as writer-agency forms and collaboration agreements, are conveniently included.

3819. Bonham-Carter, Victor. *Authors by Profession.* Los Altos, California: Kaufmann, 1978. 252 pp.

A lively history of authors' organizations and copyright and the continuing struggle of writers for a reasonable return from their efforts.

3820. Cavallo, Robert M., and Stuart Kahan. *Photography; What's the Law?* 2nd edition. New York: Crown, 1979. 155 pp.

Court cases, copyright laws, and careful analysis for photographers and photographer-writers.

3821. Chernoff, George, and Hershel Sarbin. *Photography and the Law.* New York: AM-Photo, 1971. 158 pp.

Covers rights of privacy, loss or damage to film, obscenity, copyright, libel by photograph, and photographs as evidence. Also provided is a table of significant legal citations for each principle of law discussed.

3822. Chickering, Robert B., and Susan Hartman. *How to Register a Copyright and Protect Your Creative Work; A Basic Guide to the New Copyright Law and How It Affects Anyone Who Wants to Protect Creative Work.* New York: Charles Scribner's Sons, 1981. 216 pp.

A "no-nonsense" guide to registration, protection, and limits of protection under the latest U.S. copyright law. Takes one through the steps of registering copyright and answers frequently asked questions about literary protection.

3823. *Complete Guide to the New Copyright Law by the "New York Law School Review."* Dayton, Ohio: Lorenz Press, 1977. 448 pp.

Based on essays originally appearing in the *New York Law Review.*

3824. Crawford, Tad. *The Writer's Legal Guide.* New York: Hawthorn Books, 1977. 271 pp.

Written by a lawyer, this work will be most useful for its treatment of contracts, copyright, censorship, taxes, libel, and privacy. It will be of particular interest to freelance writers.

3825. Davidson, Marion, and Martha Blue. *Making It Legal; A Law Primer for the Craft Maker, Visual Artist, and Writer.* New York: McGraw-Hill, 1979. 242 pp.

Written in clear language, this work contains legal forms, cites cases, and tells when to consult a lawyer.

3826. Glassman, Don. *Writers' and Artists' Rights.* Washington, D.C.: Writers Press, 1978. 104 pp.

Covering copyright, contracts, and a variety of other authors' rights issues, this is a short but instructive overview.

3827. Haight, Anne Lyon. *Banned Books 387 B.C. to 1978 A.D.* 4th edition. Updated and enlarged by Chandler Grannis. New York: Bowker, 1978. 196 pp.

Three hundred significant books are discussed in the context of their having been censored. Appendices provide commission reports, court decisions, censorship trends, and selected U.S. laws and regulations.

3828. Herron, Caroline, editor. *Writer's Guide to Copyright.* New York: Poets and Writers, 1979. 49 pp.

Provides a quick overview of a complex subject.

3829. Johnston, Donald F. *Copyright Handbook.* New York: Bowker, 1978. 309 pp.

Johnston has done the near-impossible. He has made the convoluted concepts of the new copyright law understandable to the legally uninitiated reader. A reader's first choice on the subject.

3830. MacCampbell, Donald. *The Writing Business.* New York: Crown, 1978. 120 pp.

Contracts, agents, and rights are among the business topics discussed.

3831. Morris, Clarence. *Modern Defamation Law.* Philadelphia: American Law Institute/American Bar Association, 1978. 76 pp.

3832. Patton, Warren L. *An Author's Guide to the Copyright Law.* Lexington, Massachusetts: Lexington Books, 1980. 192 pp.

The Copyright Act of 1976 and subsequent interpretations are addressed with regard to permissions, dedication, infringement, ownership and transfer, fair use, and foreign countries. From the writer's point of view this is one of the most useful sources available on the subject.

3833. Polking, Kirk, and Leonard S. Meranus, editors. *Law and the Writer.* Cincinnati: Writer's Digest, 1981. 258 pp.

An anthology of articles covering contracts, taxation, obscenity, freedom of speech, rights and permissions, and the 1978 copyright law. Provides sources of additional information.

3834. Sarna, Lazar. *Authors and Publishers; Agreements and Legal Aspects of Publishing.* West Yarmouth, Massachusetts: Butterworth, 1980. 167 pp.

Written from a Canadian perspective.

3835. Strong, William S. *The Copyright Book; A Practical Guide.* Cambridge, Massachusetts: MIT Press, 1981. 210 pp.

Overall of less value than Chickering, but tax treatment and international law are treated in ways not covered elsewhere.

3836. Wittenberg, Philip. *Protection of Literary Property.* Boston: Writer, 1978. 308 pp.

One of the standard reference works on the subject of copyright, libel, privacy, censorship, and related issues. Wittenberg is an attorney with a lifetime of experience in cases involving literary property.

Articles

3837. Authors' contracts: the need for a new deal (British). Richard Findlater. *Author,* vol. 91, Autumn 1980, pp. 12-14.

3838. Authors guild urges reform of "satisfactory ms." clause. M. Reuter. *Publishers Weekly,* vol. 218, November 14, 1980, pp. 12+.

3839. Basic Books sues author for breach of contract; case of D. Kearns. D. Maryles. *Publishers Weekly,* vol. 207, June 2, 1975, pp. 13-14.

3840. Book business; contracts. Alan Green. *Saturday Review,* vol. 54, October 30, 1971, p. 48+.

3841. Book contracts: trial and terror. D. Waitley. *Writer's Digest,* vol. 57, September 1977, pp. 49-50.

3842. Book that Du Pont hated (G.C. Zilg's suit against Prentice-Hall for breach of contract). R. Sherrill. *Nation,* vol. 232, February 14, 1981, pp. 172-176.

3843. Copyright: a guide to "Author's law." Ellen M. Kozak. *Writer's Digest,* vol. 64, March 1984, pp. 26-30.

3844. Court upholds "best efforts" clause in author's contract; with editorial comment. *Publishers Weekly,* vol. 201, March 6, 1972, pp. 38, 44.

3845. Fair deal for authors; contract prepared by the Authors Guild. G. Borchardt. *Publishers Weekly,* vol. 204, August 6, 1973, pp. 26-27.

3846. Finding your way around the new copyright law. *Publishers Weekly,* vol. 210, December 13, 1976, pp. 38-41.

3847. From royalties to options: five thorns in the book contract. *Coda,* vol. 5, June/July 1983, pp. 14-17.

3848. How to "bulletproof" your manuscripts. Bruce Henderson. *Writer's Digest,* vol. 64, April 1984, pp. 28-32.

3849. Last word in book contracts. J.T. Casale. *Writer's Digest,* vol. 55, November 1975, pp. 16-17.

3850. Law and the writer. W. Francois. *Writer's Digest,* vol. 54, July 1974, p. 48.

3851. Legal rights for writers. J. Pollett. *Writer,* vol. 84, April 1971, pp. 22-24.

3852. Lessons from Sweden: Swedish writer and his rights, by the Swedish Institute. *Author,* vol. 91, Winter 1980, pp. 50-52.

3853. Morrow vs. Safire: the author keeps his money, but loses the issue; contract dispute. D. Maryles. *Publishers Weekly,* vol. 207, January 20, 1975, p. 21.

3854. New protection for the author: libel insurance. J. Wilderman. *Macleans,* vol. 95, August 16, 1982, p. 46.

3855. Nice girls do—get sued (M. Margolis' claim that he co-authored I. Kassorla's bestseller). *Time,* vol. 119, April 19, 1982.

3856. On contracting with publishers: or what every author should know. W.J. Bawmol and P. Heim. *AAUP Bulletin,* vol. 53, March 1967, pp. 30-46.

3857. Once again, into the bank; selling reprint rights to Sunday newspaper-magazine editors. F.J. O'Rourke. *Writer's Digest,* vol. 57, September 1977, p. 54.

3858. Over the transom to a book contract. Carol Meyer (editor, Trade Division, Harcourt Brace Jovanovich). *Writer,* vol. 95, December 1982, pp. 14-16.

3859. Predictions: sub rights splits. *Publishers Weekly,* vol. 214, July 24, 1978, p. 54.

3860. Prentice-Hall to pay lost royalties on Du Pont book, court says (resolution of G. C. Zilg Case). J. Mutter. *Publishers Weekly,* vol. 221, May 7, 1982, pp. 12+.

3861. Publish and be damned: a comparative survey of book contracts issued by 60 British publishers. David Caute. *New Statesman,* June 13, 1980, pp. 892-899.

3862. Publishers and authors in court. H.F. Pilpel and Alan U. Schwartz. *Publishers Weekly,* vol. 204, September 3, 1973, pp. 20-21.

3863. Publishing contracts. Termination of contracts. Mark LeFanu. *Author,* vol. 93, Winter 1982, p. 120.

3864. Simple business contract for writers. Mike Major. *Writer's Digest,* vol. 61, September 1981, pp. 39-41+.

3865. Success may be top drawer, but Workman's preppies find it's tension city when disputes arise (contributors to *The Official Preppy Handbook* unhappy over lack of credit). Wendy Smith. *Publishers Weekly,* vol. 219, February 13, 1981, pp. 61+.

3866. To be continued (magazine and newspaper serials). R. Dahlin. *Publishers Weekly,* vol. 218, October 31, 1980, pp. 54-56+.

3867. Trends and changes in international contracts; a survey of the position in countries that buy U.S. rights. *Publishers Weekly,* vol. 206, September 23, 1974, pp. 70-80.

3868. Volunteer lawyers for the arts: legal assistance for financially strapped writers. Jerome Richard. *Writer's Digest,* vol. 63, April 1983, pp. 25-26.

3869. What right has an author? Address June 13, 1966. D. Home. *Publishers Weekly,* vol. 190, July 4, 1966, pp. 26-31.

3870. What to do if your publisher starts getting arbitrary. M. Maese. *Writer's Digest,* vol 55, May 1975, p. 11.

3871. Wills. Important for everyone, essential for writers. *Coda,* vol. 6, no. 4, April/May 1979, pp. 3-8.

Royalties and Payments

"Ready money is Aladdin's lamp."

—Byron

See the chapters on Editor-Author and Publisher-Author Relationships (page 293), Legal Aspects (page 335), and Marketing (page 323) for book annotations containing numerous references to royalties and payments.

Articles

3872. Anthology rates (British). *Author,* vol. 91, Summer 1980, p. 86.

3873. Australia boosts writer's income. *American Libraries,* vol. 6, March 1975, pp. 143-144.

3874. Authors guild report urges reform in royalty procedure. *Publishers Weekly,* vol. 205, May 6, 1974, p. 24.

3875. Authors guild reports on royalty statements. M. Reuter. *Publishers Weekly,* vol. 209, June 21, 1976, p. 30.

3876. Authors unsympathetic to bookseller plea on royalties (proposal by J. Ripley). J.F. Baker. *Publishers Weekly,* vol. 219, January 2, 1981, p. 16.

3877. Bill 'em. David F. Curran. *Writer's Digest,* vol. 62, May 1982, p. 46.

3878. Book ruckus marks opening of Halberstam case; royalties from book on murderer B.C. Welch. H. Fields. *Publishers Weekly,* vol. 219, April 24, 1981, pp. 32+.

3879. Computers join royalty statement fray. *Publishers Weekly,* vol. 223, March 18, 1983, pp. 16+.

3880. Delicate question of payment. J.R. Ackerley and J.M. Keynes. *Encounter,* vol. 43, November 1974, pp. 24-28.

3881. Eighty-four dollar egg; writing for money. L. Conger. *Writer,* vol. 85, June 1972, pp. 6-8.

3882. How I do it (payments). *Writer's Digest,* vol. 56, December 1976, pp. 24-31.

3883. How much to charge. *Writer's Digest,* vol. 54, September 1974, p. 10.

3884. How to establish a retainer. B. Palmer. *Writer's Digest,* vol. 51, December 1971, p. 30.

3885. How to read a royalty statement. G. Borchardt. *Publishers Weekly,* vol. 205, February 18, 1974, pp. 60-62.

3886. Invisible writers (payments). Brigid Brophy. *Observer,* November 27, 1977, pp. 13+.

3887. Jack Abbott's other victims fight back, suing for royalties that came with his fame. G. Diliberto. *People Weekly,* vol. 17, February 8, 1982, pp. 76+.

3888. Japanese royalties: two points of view. T. Mori and L.E. Kern, Jr. *Publishers Weekly,* vol. 199, May 3, 1971, pp. 17-18.

3889. Kind of wealth; earnings of authors. L. Conger. *Writer,* vol. 88, September 1975, pp. 7-8.

3890. Letter from London: Question of royalties in Great Britain. Frank Kermode. *New Republic,* vol. 173, August 2, 1975, pp. 23-25.

3891. Patronage and writing: the Piccadilly paymasters. *Author,* vol. 88, Autumn 1977, pp. 89-93.

3892. Publishers' profits and authors' pay. M. Oram. *Author,* vol. 85, Winter 1973, pp. 153+.

3893. Quiet revolution: Norton reforms the royalty statement. J.A. Hennessee. *Publishers Weekly,* vol. 213, April 10, 1978, pp. 24+.

3894. Royalties and rights: a report on publishers' payments (British). Richard Findlater. *Author,* vol. 93, Winter 1982, pp. 102-105.

3895. So you want to be an author. J.D. Atwater. *Money,* vol. 11, July 1982, pp. 73-74.

3896. Three-act guide to selling non-fiction to T.V. and movies. Ted Schwarz. *Writer's Digest,* vol. 62, May 1982, pp. 21-25.

3897. What should writers do? (payments). B.S. Johnson. *Author,* vol. 84, Summer 1973, pp. 57-59.

3898. What should writers do? (payments). C. Osborne. *Author,* vol. 84, Summer 1973, pp. 61-63.

3899. What should writers do? (payments). Gordon Gordon. *Author,* vol. 84, Summer 1973, pp. 53+.

3900. What should writers do? (payments). H. Rubinstein. *Author,* vol. 84, Summer 1973, pp. 49-53.

3901. What should writers do? (payments). M.T. Smith. *Author,* vol. 84, Summer 1973, pp. 59-66.

3902. What should writers do? (payments). Richard Findlater. *Author,* vol. 84, Summer 1973, pp. 63+.

3903. Writers and money. L. Conger. *Writer,* vol. 84, May 1971, pp. 7-8.

3904. Writers and money. P. Meyer. *Writer's Digest,* vol. 56, April 1976, pp. 13-17+.

3905. Writing under inflation (payment). A. Harrison. *Author,* vol. 87, Spring 1976, pp. 13-15.

3906. Yes, I write for money. Nicholas Monsarrat. *Writer's Digest,* vol. 49, August 1969, pp. 56-59.

Tax Considerations

"There is one difference between a tax collector and a taxidermist—the taxidermist leaves the hide."

—Mortimer Caplan

Books

3907. *Tax Guide for College Teachers and Other College Personnel.* Washington, D.C.: Academic Information Services, 1983. Annual. 368 pp.

Although this comprehensive work is geared for the academic community, book royalties and writing "write-offs" are covered in a way that will benefit almost any author with a cash flow. Of particular interest is the section on Keogh plans, which afford an excellent opportunity to shelter writing business income.

Articles

3908. Authors League irked by IRS ruling on R&D costs. S. Wagner. *Publishers Weekly,* vol. 209, January 19, 1976, p. 28.

3909. Authors League protests tax reform act inequities. S. Wagner. *Publishers Weekly,* vol. 212, December 5, 1977, p. 19.

3910. Authors League speaks out on writers' tax problems. S. Wagner. *Publishers Weekly,* vol. 208, August 18, 1975, p. 20.

3911. Begorra! No income taxes for writers! (Ireland). Arturo F. Gonzalez, Jr. *Writer's Digest,* vol. 56, November 1976, p. 25.

3912. Deep in the heart of taxes; tax records and returns for freelance writers. A. Ruder. *Writer's Digest,* vol. 54, January 1974, pp. 9-21.

3913. Investment guide for writers. Andrew Tobias. *Writer's Digest,* vol. 59, November 1979, pp. 20-25.

3914. Keeping the writer out of tax trouble. J. Block. *Writer's Digest,* vol. 55, January 1975, pp. 9-14.

3915. Little bit of haven; tax free Ireland. *Time,* vol. 110, October 10, 1977, pp. 115-116.

3916. Modest proposal on foreign authors' taxes: proposal of Authors League of America. R.H. Smith. *Publishers Weekly,* vol. 201, May 15, 1972, p. 38.

3917. More of your taxing questions answered. J. Block. *Writer's Digest,* vol. 55, February 1975, pp. 23-24.

3918. Office-in-home deduction for writers. Steve Tucker. *Writer's Digest,* vol. 64, November 1984, p. 26.

3919. On taxes—the Keogh plan. S. Jarvis. *Writer's Digest,* vol. 54, September 1974, pp. 13-14.

3920. Rates of spring. Patricia Fox. *Writer's Digest,* vol. 57, March 1977, pp. 20-21.

3921. Reality, fantasy, and the IRS. L. Conger. *Writer,* vol. 89, April 1976, pp. 7-8.

3922. Tax-reform bill has good news for writers. S. Wagner. *Publishers Weekly,* vol. 210, August 23, 1976, pp. 22+.

3923. Tax tips from freelancers. M. Lasky. *Writer's Digest,* vol. 54, January 1974, p. 12.

3924. Taxes and the writer. B. Francois. *Writer's Digest,* vol. 52, April 1972, pp. 6+.

3925. Those shameless tax loopholes for writers. Tad Crawford. *Writer's Digest,* vol. 55, February 1975, pp. 20-22.

3926. Writer's primer on taxes. Rosalie Minkow. *Writer's Digest,* vol. 62, March 1982, pp. 43-45+.

General Advice and Inspiration about Writing, Including Writer's Block

"Writing every book is like a purge; at the end of it one is empty... like a dry shell on the beach, waiting for the tide to come in again."

—Daphne Du Maurier

Books

3927. Allen, Walter. *Writers on Writing.* Boston: Writer, 1948. 258 pp.

Under such topics as inspiration and calculation, poetry and symbolism, novelists at work, and the shape and structure of the novel, such authors as William Blake, Charlotte Bronte, George Eliot, Gustave Flaubert, Henry James, Leo Tolstoy, Anthony Trollope, and W.B. Yeats are quoted at length.

3928. Anderson, Sherwood. *The Modern Writer.* San Francisco: Lantern Press, 1925. 44 pp.

Anderson addresses the question of an American national literature and how young writers can become a part of it.

3929. Anderson, Sherwood, and others. *The Intent of the Artist.* Edited and introduced by Augusto Centeno. New York: Russell and Russell, 1970. 162 pp.

Anderson writes on "Man and his imagination," Thornton Wilder offers "Some thoughts on playwrighting," Roger Sessions writes on the "message" of musical composition, and William Lescaze discusses buildings, architecture, and "documents" in this wide-ranging approach to imagination, creativity, and continuing artistic effort.

3930. Asimov, Isaac. *In Joy Still Felt; The Autobiography of Isaac Asimov, 1954-1978.* New York: Doubleday, 1980. 828 pp.

Chronicles Asimov's career as a full-time author and, to quote *Library Journal,* "...offers a fascinating insight into the personal life and working habits of this most prolific author."

3931. Bader, Arno Lehman. *To the Young Writer. Hopwood Lectures, Second Series.* Ann Arbor: University of Michigan Press, 1965. 196 pp.

Lectures to young writers given at the University of Michigan on the occasion of the presentation of the Hopwood Awards for essay, drama, poetry, and fiction. These range from a technical analysis of what makes a poem tick to a blueprint for college courses in creative writing. Included are suggestions for sources of artistic material, as well as observations on how to cope with success.

3932. Barzun, Jacques. *On Writing, Editing, and Publishing; Essays Explicative and Hortatory.* Chicago: University of Chicago Press, 1971. 130 pp.

These articles, which appeared individually over a twenty-five-year period in the *Atlantic Monthly, Partisan Review,* and the *American Scholar,* are concerned with the difficulty of being a writer, the problems of accurate translation, the agonies of getting permission to quote, as well as with Lincoln's style and Poe's proofreading. Collectively and individually they exhibit the precision, depth, and critical savvy that we have come to expect from so brilliant a mind as Barzun's. "A Writer's Discipline" and "Advice to a Young Writer" are particularly noteworthy. Throughout, Barzun is true to his principle of "protecting the work and not the self."

3933. Bates, Jefferson D. *Writing with Precision; How to Write So That You Cannot Possibly Be Misunderstood. Zero Based Gobbledgook.* Washington, D.C.: Acropolis, 1978. 213 pp.

Contains excellent examples and advice about mastering the art of clear writing, including grammar, style, and vocabulary.

3934. Beasley, Maurice, and Richard Harlow. *Voices of Change; Southern Pulitzer Winners.* Latham, Maryland: University Press of America, 1979. 145 pp.

Artful interviews which reveal that careful analysis, acquired knowledge, and rewriting are the keys to such prize-winning efforts.

3935. Bradbury, Ray. *Zen and the Art of Writing and the Joy of Writing; Two Essays.* Santa Barbara, California: Capra Press, 1973. 34 pp.

A few gem-like thoughts from a master craftsman.

3936. Brittain, Vera M. *On Being an Author.* New York: Macmillan, 1948. 218 pp.

Called "lively," "sensible," and "sound" by reviewers, this work depends largely upon the author's recollections of her rise in the literary world. As one might expect of the woman who wrote *Testament of Youth,* it is filled with integrity.

3937. Bruccoli, Matthew J. *Conversations with Writers.* 2 vols. Detroit: Gale Research Co., 1977.

Interviews with James T. Farrell, Irvin Faust, Anita Loos, James Michener, and Ishmael Reed, among others.

3938. Burack, Sylvia K., editor. *The Writer's Handbook.* Boston: Writer, 1983. 838 pp.

Divided into four parts. The first three consist of articles on professional writing taken from *Writer* magazine and range from "background for writers," through techniques in fiction, nonfiction, poetry, juvenile and teenage writing, and special fields, to "the editorial and business side". Part four deals with markets. Publications and publishers are categorized according to type of market involved and accompanied by a short descriptive annotation. *Writer's Market* (see entry 3707) generally does a more comprehensive job of isolating and describing specific markets than does section four of *The Writer's Handbook.* However, with some markets, such as that for television plays, *The Writer's Handbook* can be more reliable. Among the authors who have contributed to this volume are John D. MacDonald, Shirley Ann Grau, Paul Gallico, E.B. White, Frank G. Slaughter, Joyce Carol Oates, Norah Lofts, Irving Stone, Phyllis Whitney, Barbara Tuchman, May Sarton, Elizabeth Honness, Charlotte Zolotow, and Neil Simon. *The Writer's Handbook* has been issued annually since 1936.

3939. Charlton, James, editor. *The Writer's Quotation Book; A Literary Companion.* New York: Penguin, 1981. 71 pp.

As with other quotation books, there is something here for nearly every writer, but given the wealth of quotations available, one wonders at Charlton's brevity.

3940. Clark, Bernadine. *Writer's Resource Guide.* Cincinnati: Writer's Digest, 1983. 480 pp.

This valuable compendium contains over 1,600 listings from libraries, museums, companies, and other organizations which are considered prime information sources. They are divided into subject areas such as arts, hobby, public affairs, and the like. Each entry tells whom to contact and what services are offered.

Corwin, Stanley J. *How to Become a Bestselling Author.* See entry 4249.

3941. Cousins, Norman, editor. *Writing for Love and Money; Thirty-Five Essays Reprinted from "The Saturday Review of Literature."* New York: Longsman, Green, 1949. 278 pp.

Authors in a broad range of literary fields speak on writing novels, short stories, history, biography, science, and criticism, as well as more general aspects of writing.

3942. Cox, Sidney. *Indirections for Those Who Want to Write.* New York: Alfred A. Knopf, 1947. 139 pp.

This has been called "... a book for anyone who has written or thought about writing," and indeed it is. Quotable and highly concentrated, it provides a kind of mental acupuncture for writers of serious fiction, poetry, or criticism. In its lyrical style, this slim volume tells not so much how to write as why. It acts as a codified value-system to be consulted whenever a writer feels adrift. To quote Cox, "... you may have always known that the most stable thing in a flood is a man or woman who can ride it."

3943. Daigh, Ralph. *Maybe You Should Write a Book.* Englewood Cliffs, New Jersey: Prentice-Hall, 1977. 181 pp.

This is a shallow book which panders to the most self-defeating instincts of the "Gee, I'd like to write" crowd. Those readers seeking a feast of "inside" information will find here only crumbs from the table.

3944. Davidson, Marshall B. *American Heritage History of the Writers' America.* New York: American Heritage Publishing Company, 1973. 416 pp.

A lavishly illustrated overview of the development of American letters. Written in a popular style, this volume combines quotations, photography, art work, and commentary which bring its vast subject to life.

3945. Davidson, Peter, and others, editors. *Literary Taste, Culture, and Mass Communication.* Vol. 10. Teaneck, New Jersey: Somerset House, 1978. 385 pp.

Includes timeless essays, such as George Orwell's "Why I Write," Jacques Barzun's "Artist Against Society," Stephen Spender's "Modern Writers in the World of Necessity," William Barrett's "Writers and Madness," and James T. Farrell's "Fate of the Writer in America."

3946. Egri, Lajos. *Your Key to Successful Writing; A Handbook for the Layman Who Wants to Write, and for the Writer Who Wants to Understand the Layman.* New York: Cornell Books, 1952. 208 pp.

A string of theoretical catchwords such as "unity of opposites," "orchestration," and "motivation" serve as springboards for discussion of Egri's views.

3947. Elbow, Peter. *Writing with Power; Techniques for Mastering the Writing Process.* New York: Oxford, 1981. 384 pp.

This is a valuable pragmatic handbook intended for a wide range of writing situations. It offers proven techniques for writing, revising, setting a tone for a given audience, and gaining feedback, and it stresses both critical objectivity and creativity in a way that allows these seemingly exclusive approaches to complement one another. From a simple business memo or a student essay to the massive marketing report or complex novel, this wise and original work has the potential for improving almost any kind of writing.

3948. Fairfax, John, and John Moat. *The Way to Write.* New York: St. Martin's Press, 1982. 96 pp.

In this short but valuable work, the authors present a "power system" for writing which involves the use of images and well-chosen words.

3949. Flesch, Rudolf. *The Art of Readable Writing.* 25th Anniversary edition. New York: Harper, 1974. 288 pp.

Flesch is considered by many to have had a major impact on the verbal expression of his time. Chapters in this work such as "How to Operate a Blue Pencil," "Our Shrinking Sentences," and "How to be Human Though Factual" retain their original freshness and wit. His prescriptions and tests for readability have been widely employed.

3950. Gorky, Maxim, and others. *On the Art and Craft of Writing.* Moscow: Progress Publishers, 1972. 298 pp.

In twenty-four separate essays, Maxim Gorky tells "How I learned to write," Alexei Tolstoy discusses his working methods and the nature of the short story, Vladimir Mayakovsky writes on the construction of verse, and Konstantin Fedin gives his views on craftsmanship, notebooks, and the nature of language.

3951. Hall, Donald. *Modern Stylists; Writers on the Art of Writing.* New York: Free Press, 1968. 186 pp.

Prose style and its proper fashioning is the subject of this anthology of short selections from the likes of James Thurber, E.B. White, George Orwell, H.L. Mencken, Robert Frost, Gertrude Stein, William Carlos Williams, Georges Simenon, Virginia Woolf, Mary McCarthy, Truman Capote, and H.B. Fowler. Though many of these essays, such as Orwell's "Politics and the English Language," are widely known, they contain sufficient wit and wisdom to justify reprinting. A subject index is appended and gives the book added appeal as a quick reference source.

3952. Hall, Donald, editor. *The Oxford Book of American Literary Anecdotes.* New York: Oxford, 1981. 360 pp.

This companion volume to Sutherland's *Oxford Book of Literary Anecdotes* (see entry 4000) covers over 100 American authors.

3953. Harding, Rosamond Evelyn Mary. *An Anatomy of Inspiration.* With an appendix on *The Birth of a Poem* by Robert B.M. Nichols. 2nd edition with corrections. New York: Barnes and Noble, 1967. 145 pp.

This valuable examination of the habits and methods that contribute to invention in literature and science includes references to a wide range of writers.

3954. Hellyer, Clement D. *Making Money with Words.* Englewood Cliffs, New Jersey: Prentice Hall, 1981. 262 pp.

The seemingly limitless range of writing opportunities is contrasted with the finite and sobering prospects of earning a reasonable return for one's efforts. Written by a veteran professional writer and writing teacher, this honest assessment of the world of authorship is less a "how-to" account than it is a grand tour of writing options.

3955. Hemingway, Ernest. *Ernest Hemingway on Writing.* Edited by Larry W. Phillips. New York: Scribner, 1984. 140 pp.

Assembles quotations, maxims, and extended advice from the entire corpus of Hemingway's work.

3956. Hendrickson, Robert. *The Literary Life and Other Curiosities.* New York: Viking, 1981. 352 pp.

Filled with anecdotes and improbable facts about writing and writers, this unindexed compendium is a sort of *Book of Lists* for the literary world.

3957. Hooker, Zebulon Vance. *An Index of Ideas for Writers and Speakers.* Chicago: Scott, Foresman, 1965. 304 pp.

Arranged in thirty-four sections, these "thought starters" cover some 14,000 topics and are variously intended to initiate, provoke, and inspire.

3958. Horgan, Paul. *Approaches to Writing; Reflections and Notes on the Art of Writing from a Career of Half a Century.* With a provisional bibliography of the author's work by James Kraft. New York: Farrar, Straus and Giroux, 1974. 233 pp.

Horgan offers plot ideas, character outlines, and a plenitude of detail about his techniques, experience, and development as a writer. Horgan, who has been a prolific writer of novels, poetry, biography, stories, reviews, and articles, believes that writing must be "caught," not taught.

Horowitz, Lois. *Knowing Where to Look: The Ultimate Guide to Research.*
See entry 4252.

3959. Howarth, William L. *The Book of Concord; Thoreau's Life as a Writer.* New York: Viking, 1982. 288 pp.

Howarth concentrates on Thoreau's Journals to show "... the processes by which the writer, developing from early confusion to mature and original vision, transmitted the literal into metaphor, facts into truth, and turned landscape—a beanfield, a mountain, a pond—into internal vision."

3960. Hughes, Riley. *Finding Yourself in Print; A Guide to Writing Professionally.* New York: Watts, 1979. 292 pp.

Spanning fiction and nonfiction, this work competently stresses markets, research, and basic writing techniques. "The book is readable, and the author is knowledgeable." *Journalism Quarterly.*

Hugo, Richard. *The Triggering Town: Lectures and Essays on Poetry and Writing.* See entry 4253.

3961. Hull, Helen R., editor. *Writer's Book; Presented by the Authors Guild.* New York: Harper, 1956. 353 pp.

Forty authors write on forty different aspects of their craft. Topics range from writing biography and mysteries to more general subjects such as imagination and social criticism. Authors include Helen R. Hull, Pearl S. Buck, Ira Wolfert, Thomas Mann, John Hersey, Ann Petry, Francis Steegmuller, Richard Lockridge, Rex Stout, Arthur Koestler, Faith Baldwin, Jacques Barzun, W.H. Auden, Thomas R. Coward, James A. Michener, Richard Summers, Paul Gallico, Ware Torrey Budlong, Margaret Culkin Banning, Myron David Orr, Lajos Egri, Christopher Lafarge, Lionel Trilling, Mabel Louise Robinson, Joel Sayer, Katharine Anthony, Frederick Lewis Allen, William L. Laurence, Henry F. Pringle, Babette Deutsch, Lenora Speyer, Phyllis McGinley, Niven Busch, Erik Barnouw, Max Ehrlich, Winston Churchill, Rudolf Flesch, Harold Freedman, and Dr. Beatrice Hinkle.

3962. Hull, Helen R., and Michael Drury. *Writers' Roundtable; Presented by the Author's Guild.* New York: Harper, 1959. 201 pp.

Intended as a follow-up volume to the *Writer's Book* (see entry 3961), these twenty-one essays address the short story, the historical novel, the paperback, translation, literary agents and book reviewing, to name a few of the topics covered.

3963. Hutchinson, Eliot D. *How to Think Creatively.* New York: Abington-Cokesbury Press, 1949. 237 pp.

Quotations from questionnaires sent to musicians, artists, scientists, and authors regarding the wellsprings of their creativity are combined with Hutchinson's observations on the nature of creative mental ability. Under broad chapter headings such as "The Stage of Preparation," "The Stage of Frustration," "The Stage of Achievement," "Emotions in Creation," Hutchinson investigates the patterns of insight, intuition, and sustained effort that lead to masterpieces and significant discoveries.

3964. International Congress of the P.E.N. Clubs. *The Writer as Independent Spirit; Proceedings.* New York: International Congress of the P.E.N. Clubs, 1968. 320 pp.

Among the topics given extended treatment are the writer in the electronic age, literature and science, the writer as collaborator, and the writer as public figure.

3965. Ireland, Norma Olin. *Index to Inspiration; A Thesaurus of Subjects for Speakers and Writers.* Westwood, Massachusetts: F.W. Faxon, 1976. 506 pp.

Provides intensive subject indexing for over 220 books in English, from Norman Vincent Peale's *Treasury of Courage and Confidence* to James Schermerhorn's *1500 Anecdotes and Stories.* Writers should not underestimate the potential value of this fine work.

3966. Janeway, Elizabeth. *Writer's World; Presented by the Author's Guild, Incorporated.* New York: McGraw-Hill, 1969. 415 pp.

A collection of literary discussions by Joseph Heller, Wallace Markfield, Jane Jacobs, Kenneth Clark, and others.

3967. Josipovici, Gabriel. *Writing and the Body.* Princeton, New Jersey: Princeton, 1982. 142 pp.

Illustrates the ways artists, including writers, have used or avoided metaphors for the human body. Josipovici is a recognized writer of fiction, poetry, drama, and essays.

3968. Knott, Leonard. *Writing for the Joy of It.* Cincinnati: Writer's Digest, 1983. 204 pp.

Concentrating on the non-commercial, Knott discusses the joys of verse, recipe, journal, and local drama writing. He brings humor and a deft touch to writers who may be in need of both.

3969. Lambuth, David, and others. *The Golden Book on Writing.* Foreword by Budd Schulberg. New York: Penguin Press, 1976. 80 pp.

Stressing clear thinking, natural order, and economy, this is a short collection of practical suggestions rather than a rigid codification of rules.

3970. Leacock, Stephen B. *How to Write.* New York: Dodd, Mead and Co., 1943. 264 pp.

A noted humorist offers witty and wise advice to young writers about the art of narration, the use of language, and the writing of historical novels, poetry, and humor.

3971. Lewis, Wyndham. *The Writer and the Absolute.* London: Methuen, 1952. 202 pp.

The questions of liberty in society and the writer's freedom of expression are explored in depth in these critical essays. Lewis comments at length on Orwell, Sartre, Malraux, and Camus.

3972. Lovett, Robert Morse, and others. *Writer and His Craft; (Twenty Hopwood Lectures to the Young Writer, by Robert Morse Lovett and Others).* Foreword by Roy W. Cowden. Ann Arbor: University of Michigan Press, 1956. 297 pp.

Part of the distinguished Hopwood Series. (See also entries 3931, 3975, and 4008.)

3973. Mack, Karin, and Eric Skjei. *Overcoming Writing Blocks.* Los Angeles: Tarcher, 1979. 240 pp.

Intended for "the millions of people who must write" memos, business letters, school papers, and the like, as well as for the professional writer, this work defines the problem of block, discusses why it happens, and then provides an in-depth analysis of unblocking techniques in four broad areas: preparing to write, organizing your material, the rough draft, and revision. In a final section, called "Unblocking Techniques at Work," we see this system applied to business writing, student writing, technical, academic and professional writing, and personal writing. This inspirational work is seasoned by quotes from major writers about how they have met and overcome block.

3974. Madden, David, and Richard Powers. *Writer's Revisions; An Annotated Bibliography of Articles and Books about Writers' Revisions and Their Comments on the Creative Process.* Metuchen, New Jersey: Scarecrow, 1981. 241 pp.

In addition to the section on revision, this work also contains references to "how-to" manuals and articles as well as interviews with well-known writers, all of which combine into a total of over 350 articles and books. Of particular value is the five-part analytical index.

3975. Martin, Robert, editor. *Writer's Craft; Hopwood Lectures, 1965-81.* Ann Arbor: University of Michigan Press, 1982. 286 pp.

Contains, among other essays, Walker Percy's "The state of the novel," Joan Didion's "Making up stories," and Denise Levertov's "Origins of a poem."

3976. Maurois, Andre. *The Art of Writing.* New York: Dutton, 1960. 320 pp.

Twelve essays dealing with such figures as Tolstoy, Proust, and Voltaire reveal Maurois' broad range as a biographer and critic. Though the title of this book is misleading, it is an excellent source for peripheral reading.

3977. Melton, William, editor. *"I Get My Best Ideas in Bed," and Other Words of Wisdom from 190 of America's Best-Selling Authors.* Foreword by Richard Armour. Los Angeles: Nas, 1969. 307 pp.

Melton, a columnist for the *Santa Anna Register* and reviewer for the *Los Angeles Times,* draws on 190 of his author interviews to assemble relevant quotations under chapter headings such as "Writing Habits," "Critics," and "What They Think of Other Writers." The results are, as with most interview material, chatty, catty, and revealing. What makes this collection different is the presentation of a series of different answers to each question. The comments on writing techniques and habits are probably the most valuable parts of this book.

3978. Montague, Charles Edward. *A Writer's Notes on His Trade.* Port Washington, New York: Kennikat Press, 1969. (Originally published in 1930). 254 pp.

These are the interesting but random thoughts of a noted British journalist and man of letters about style and cadence.

3979. Munson, Gorham B. *The Written Word; How to Write for Readers.* New York: Crowell, Collier, and Macmillan, 1962. 256 pp.

Elementary advice to beginning writers. Topics range from self-discipline as a writer to vocabulary building and identification with the needs of the reader. An uncommonly diverse book which draws on Munson's wide reading and in-depth reflections.

3980. ———. *The Writer's Workshop Companion.* New York: Greenwood Press, 1968. 310 pp.

Addressed to the advanced writer, this is a compendium of writing shoptalk for both fiction and nonfiction authors. This useful book is filled with the advice and experience of noted writers of the past.

Nelson, Victoria. *Writer's Block and How to Use It.* See entry 4258.

3981. Newquist, Roy. *Conversations.* New York: Rand McNally, 1967. 505 pp.

These interviews with writers, editors, critics, and publishers include such figures as Helen Gurley Brown, Hortense Calisher, Rachel Carson, Will and Ariel Durant, Evan Hunter, Christopher Isherwood, Rona Jaffe, Ogden Nash, Edith Sitwell, and Arnold Toynbee.

3982. Olsen, Tillie. *Silences.* New York: Delacorte, 1978. 306 pp.

In tone, *Silences* is a lament. In subject it is a recitation of those barriers (family responsibilities, inadequate finances, and the vagaries of the literary marketplace) which thwart those who would write. In demonstrating her point, Olsen captures the frustration of writers, such as Herman Melville, Thomas Hardy, Gerard Manley Hopkins, Virginia Woolf, and Emily Dickinson, by quoting from diaries and letters. *Silences* addresses, most particularly, the plight of women writers, whom Olsen sees as a struggling minority in the world of creative letters. Along with a sense of desolation, the solutions are left to the reader. Comprehensive index.

3983. Olson, Gene. *Sweet Agony; A Writing Manual of Sorts.* Grants Pass, Oregon: Windridge Press, 1972. 122 pp.

A sketchy but entertaining set of personal views from a professional writer on the subjects of establishing a writing discipline and avoiding common writing ailments.

3984. Polking, Kirk, editor. *Writer's Encyclopedia.* Cincinnati: Writer's Digest, 1983. 480 pp.

Provides definitions and cross references for some 1200 terms and concepts such as royalties, rights, and agents. Standard practices are carefully explained, and a series of idea stimulators are also included.

3985. Polking, Kirk, and Jean Chimsky, editors. *Beginning Writer's Answer Book.* 2nd revised edition. Cincinnati: Writer's Digest, 1977. 168 pp. (A revision of the *Beginning Writer's Handbook,* entry 3986.)

Provides hundreds of answers about manuscript preparation, queries, submissions, interviewing, collaboration, agents, editors, plagiarism, legal rights and responsibilities, and a miscellany of other fundamental questions. Though the coverage is shallow, this will give novice writers a valuable overview.

3986. Polking, Kirk, and Jean Chimsky. *Beginning Writer's Handbook.* Cincinnati: Writer's Digest, 1968. 168 pp.

Grouped in thirty-eight subject categories, these short statements provide answers to questions most frequently asked of the editors of *Writer's Digest* and cover such issues as rights, agents, pen names, and query letters, to name only a few.

3987. Price, Jonathan. *Thirty Days to More Powerful Writing; A Step-by-Step Method for Developing a More Dynamic Writing Style.* New York: Fawcett, 1981. 192 pp.

The developing of a powerful writing style, the use of concrete images, the uses of description, how to arouse emotions, how to sharpen contrast, and how to expertly revise are but a few of the concepts covered by this practical text designed for almost any kind of writing.

3988. Priestley, John Boynton. *The Writer in a Changing Society.* Aldington, Kent: Hand and Flower Publishers, 1956. 29 pp.

A plea for taking chances, rather than the safe course. Tells little about writing, but a great deal about the serious writer's purpose.

3989. Provost, Gary. *Make Every Word Count; A Guide to Writing that Works: For Fiction and Nonfiction.* Cincinatti: Writer's Digest, 1980. 256 pp.

This "guide to more effective writing" offers sentence and paragraph control based on proven techniques.

3990. *Publishers Weekly* editors and contributors. *The Author Speaks; Selected P.W. Interviews, 1967-1976.* New York: Bowker, 1977. 540 pp.

These two-to-three page "quick takes" originally appeared in the trade journal, *Publishers Weekly.* They provide biographical tidbits, opinions both outrageous and conventional, and some sense of the events and ideas that influenced the authors who have been included in the anthology.

3991. Rosenbaum, Jean, and Veryl Rosenbaum. *The Writer's Survival Guide; How to Cope with Rejection, Success, and 99 Other Hang-ups of the Writing Life.* Cincinnati: Writer's Digest, 1982. 252 pp.

Two mental health professionals use interviews, case histories, and self-tests to prescribe antidotes to the stresses of rejection, success anxiety, and other barriers to creative productivity.

3992. Quiller-Couch, Sir Arthur Thomas. *On the Art of Writing.* New York: G.P. Putnam, 1916. 302 pp.

This enduring classic by a distinguished British author and critic retains its energy as a counter to jargon and an inducement to accuracy and persuasive style. Quiller-Couch includes chapters on verse, prose, and the "lineage of English literature." Based on the author's lectures at

Cambridge, this is less a handbook than a highly personal set of observations.

3993. Rico, Gabriele L. *Writing the Natural Way; Using Right Brain Techniques to Release Your Expressive Powers.* Los Angeles: Tarcher, 1983. 272 pp.

Designed to stimulate blocked writers, this work draws upon psychological and neurological studies for evidence and techniques on the uses of the right and left hemispheres of the brain.

3994. Rivers, William L. *Writing; Craft and Art.* Englewood Cliffs, New Jersey: Prentice-Hall, 1975. 214 pp.

Expository, descriptive, narrative, and persuasive writing techniques are covered in this short text. The final chapter gives essential principles of punctuation, grammar, spelling, and usage.

3995. Rose, Mike. *Writer's Block; The Cognitive Dimension.* Carbondale, Illinois: Southern Illinois University Press, 1984. 132 pp.

Rose sees genuine writer's block as "an inability to begin or continue writing for reasons other than a lack of skill or commitment," and goes on to analyze the problem according to cognitive psychology models. In doing so, Rose isolates such causes as inflexible composing rules and planning strategies and develops remedies which he suggests may lead to more effective writing. While the main emphasis of this work is on college classroom situations, anyone with a serious interest in the subject of writer's block will come away with a wide range of new information.

3996. Salis, Richard. *Motives; 46 Contemporary Authors Discuss Their Life and Work.* Translated from the German and introduced by Egon Larsen. London: Oswald Wolff, 1975. 228 pp.

Billed as a "valuable reference collection," this is merely another assembling of brief and entertaining comments by authors who include Heinrich Boll and Gunter Grass.

Shedd, Charlie. *If I Can Write, You Can Write.* See entry 4259.

3997. Shimberg, Elaine F. *How to Be a Successful Housewife/Writer; Bylines and Babies Do Mix.* Cincinnati: Writer's Digest, 1979. 254 pp.

This book is a partial answer to the "not enough time" laments expressed by Tillie Olsen in *Silences* (see entry 3982), being a crash course in organizing one's life so that there is time for writing. In addition it contains many marketing suggestions and writing tips for the beginner.

Society of Magazine Writers. *A Treasury of Tips for Writers.* See entry 2857.

3998. Stein, Gertrude. *How to Write.* With a new preface and introduction by Patricia Meyerowitz. New York: Dover, 1975. 416 pp.

In an attempt to demonstrate her beliefs about the nature of language and its potentials, Stein provides numerous cryptic but quotable observations, such as, "There are two things. A dictionary and a country," and, "There is grammar in verification." The product of her effort is a work that provokes one into looking for pattern, movement, and alternative meanings in written communication.

3999. Sternburg, Janet. *Writer on Her Work.* New York: Norton, 1980. 265 pp.

The reflections of sixteen American authors on their own efforts. Included are Mary Gordon, Margaret Walker, Alice Walker, Jane Burroway, Susan Griffin, Ann Tyler, Joan Didion, Erica Jong, Gail Godwin, and Maxine Hong Kingston. This collection covers such subjects as "Why I Write" and "Blood and Guts: The Tricky Problem of Being a Woman Writer in the Late Twentieth Century."

4000. Sutherland, James, editor. *The Oxford Book of Literary Anecdotes.* Oxford: Clarendon Press, 1975. 382 pp.

Over 400 British and Irish authors are represented in this entertaining collection.

4001. Teeters, Peggy. *How to Get Started in Writing.* Cincinnati: Writer's Digest, 1980. 220 pp.

4002. Turner, Robert. *Some of My Best Friends Are Writers But I Wouldn't Want My Daughter to Marry One.* Los Angeles: Sherbourne Press, 1970. 253 pp.

Taking the position that odds are against anyone who wishes to "make it" as a professional writer, Turner recounts his own career as a freelancer and offers an "old pro's" ideas on what works and what does not. This is more of a meandering memoir than an organized text on writing.

4003. Ueland, Brenda. *If You Want to Write.* New York: Putnam, 1938. 179 pp.

More a work that seeks to motivate and inspire than a set of techniques, this book encourages writers to ask the best of themselves. To quote Ueland, "The work, the effort, the search is the important and exciting thing."

4004. Val Baker, Denys. *How to Be an Author.* London: Hartvill Press, 1952. 191 pp.

Penetrating British wit applied to the subject of writing and writers. His dedication is an example: "To the reading public with heartfelt sympathy."

4005. White, E.B. *Letters of E.B. White.* New York: Harper & Row, 1976. 686 pp.

This memorable work reflects the frustrations and joys of writing as seen by one of the *New Yorker's* most widely admired authors. The letters themselves clearly reveal how White's writing style matured.

4006. White, Edward M., editor. *The Writer's Control of Tone; Readings, with Analysis, for Thinking about Personal Experience.* New York: Norton, 1970. 221 pp.

This excellent anthology-text with commentary examines tone from three perspectives: child and adult, school and institutions, and meaning in large and small experiences. Among the contributors are James Baldwin, George Orwell, James Joyce, and John Updike.

4007. White, Stephen. *The Written Word and Associated Digressions Concerned with the Writer as Craftsman.* New York: Harper, 1984. 256 pp.

In addressing the specific demands of expository writing, White stresses that lucidity must be of prime importance at all times. To be used with such classics as Zinsser's *On Writing Well* (see entry 4017).

4008. *Writer and His Craft, Being the Hopwood Lectures, 1932-1952.* Ann Arbor: University of Michigan Press, 1954. 297 pp.

Balanced statements on craftsmanship, form, and content comprise the bulk of these lectures. They were delivered by Norman Cousins, Robert Penn Warren, Christopher Morley, and others of equal reputation and ability.

4009. Writers at Work. *The Paris Review Interviews.* First Series. New York: Viking, 1958. 309 pp.

Interviewees include E.M. Forster, Francois Mauriac, Joyce Cary, Dorothy Parker, James Thurber, Thornton Wilder, William Faulkner, Georges Simenon, Frank O'Connor, Robert Penn Warren, Alberto Moravia, Nelson Algren, Angus Wilson, William Styron, Truman Capote, and Francoise Sagan.

4010. Writers at Work. *The Paris Review Interviews.* Second Series. New York: Viking, 1963. 368 pp.

Interviewees include Robert Frost, Ezra Pound, Marianne Moore, T.S. Eliot, Boris Pasternak, Katherine Anne Porter, Henry Miller, Aldous Huxley, Ernest Hemingway, S.J.

Perelman, Lawrence Durrell, Mary McCarthy, Ralph Ellison, and Robert Lowell.

4011. Writers at Work. *The Paris Review Interviews.* Third Series. New York: Viking, 1967. 368 pp.

Interviewees include William Carlos Williams, Blaise Cendrars, Jean Cocteau, Louis-Ferdinand Celine, Evelyn Waugh, Lillian Hellman, William Burroughs, Saul Bellow, Arthur Miller, James Jones, Norman Mailer, Allen Ginsberg, Edward Albee, and Harold Pinter.

4012. Writers at Work. *The Paris Review Interviews.* Fourth Series. New York: Viking, 1974. 459 pp.

Interviewees include Isak Dinesen, Conrad Aiken, Robert Graves, John Dos Passos, Vladimir Nabokov, Jorge Luis Borges, George Seferis, John Steinbeck, Christopher Isherwood, W.H. Auden, Eudora Welty, John Berryman, Anthony Burgess, Jack Kerouac, Anne Sexton, and John Updike.

4013. Writers at Work. *The Paris Review Interviews.* Fifth Series. New York: Viking, 1981. 384 pp.

Interviewees include P.G. Wodehouse, Archibald MacLeish, Pablo Neruda, Isaac Bashevis Singer, Henry Green, John Cheever, Irwin Shaw, Kingsley Amis, James Dickey, Joseph Heller, William Gass, Gore Vidal, Jerry Kosinski, Joan Didion, and Joyce Carol Oates.

4014. *Writer's Manual.* Palm Springs, California: ETC Publications, 1979. 987 pp.

Covers the how to and where to of fiction, nonfiction, term papers, academic publishing, and foreign markets.

4015. Yates, Edward D. *The Writing Craft.* Raleigh, North Carolina: Contemporary Publishing, 1981. 235 pp.

Though a little short on specific examples, this is a broad introduction to writing for both print and non-print media. The emphasis is on effective communication through proven techniques. This is a competent and insightful work.

4016. Ziegler, Isabelle Gibson. *The Creative Writer's Handbook; What to Write, How to Write It, Where to Sell It.* 2nd edition. New York: Barnes & Noble, 1975. 138 pp.

Ziegler provides a guide to techniques, terms, and markets. She avoids detailed theories of writing in favor of a pragmatic approach. The chapters on tone, style, and structure seem all too brief, but the author presents a useful introductory overview for the beginning writer. Though not indicated by title, this book contains several chapters on nonfiction.

4017. Zinsser, William. *On Writing Well; An Informal Guide to Writing Nonfiction.* New York: Harper, 1979. 176 pp.

Zinsser discusses a series of writing principles, rather than how-to prescriptions, for producing good, popular journalism. The book grew out of a course he teaches at Yale and has been called best short guide to writing since Strunk and White's *Elements of Style* (see entry 3698). The sample quotations are well chosen, and the chapters on science and sports writing, travel writing, and humor are outstanding. Never preachy, Zinsser counsels simplicity, brevity, and order.

Articles

4018. Advice to a young writer. W. Van Atta. *Writer's Digest,* vol. 56, August 1976, pp. 15-19

4019. Advice to myself ten years ago. W. Cross. *Writer,* vol. 75, April 1962, pp. 25-27+.

4020. And where do you get your ideas?. R.W. Wells. *Writer,* vol. 77, January 1964, pp. 24-25+.

4021. Anyone can not. L. Conger. *Writer,* vol. 83, September 1970, pp. 7-8.

4022. Apology for literature. P. Goodman. *Commentary,* vol. 52, July 1971, pp. 39-46.

4023. Are writers made, not born? R. Diers. *Saturday Review,* vol. 48, August 14, 1965, pp. 52-53.

4024. Are you making the most of your talent? Marjorie M. Holmes. *Writer,* vol. 88, January 1975, pp. 9-11+.

4025. Beat the block. S. Shaphren. *Writer,* vol. 91, April 1978, p. 26.

4026. Beating writer's block. *Time,* vol. 110, October 31, 1977, p. 10.

4027. Becoming a writer. Nancy Willard. *Michigan Quarterly Review,* vol. 21, Winter 1982, pp. 77-84.

4028. Beginning at the beginning, sort of. W.J. Slattery. *Writer's Digest,* vol. 56, August 1976, p. 25.

4029. Beginnings. S. Rothchild. *Writer,* vol. 88, April 1975, pp. 16-18+.

4030. Best advice I've ever received. M.H. Comfort. *Writer,* vol. 89, April 1976, pp. 25-27.

4031. Block, failure, and depression. Patricia Highsmith. *Writer,* vol. 80, October 1967, pp. 23-26.

4032. Book is born (satire). M. Bennett. *Publishers Weekly,* vol. 204, October 1, 1973, pp. 36-37.

4033. Booze and the writer. Kate Millett and others. *Writer's Digest,* vol. 58, October 1978, pp. 25-33.

4034. Brainstorming; generating ideas. S.F. Asher. *Writer,* vol. 86, December 1973, pp. 24-25.

4035. Breaking the writers' block; a five-point plan. Lois Duncan. *Writer,* vol. 82, March 1969, pp. 17-19.

4036. Camus at Stockholm: acceptance of the Nobel prize. Albert Camus. *Atlantic,* vol. 201, May 1958, pp. 33-34.

4037. Camus' last answers. Albert Camus' answers to questions by R.D. Spector. *Mademoiselle,* vol. 51, May 1960, pp. 102-103.

4038. Can a complete s.o.b. be a good writer?. Malcolm Cowley. *Esquire,* vol. 88, November 1977, pp. 120-211+.

4039. Can writing be taught? C. Bartholomew. *Writer,* vol. 80, September 1967, pp. 18-20+.

4040. Caveat scriptor. E. Strainchamps. *Harper's Magazine,* vol. 221, August 1960, pp. 24-27.

4041. Check your game plan. Tom McCormick. *Writer,* vol. 86, February 1973, pp. 27-28.

4042. Conscience of a writer. Benjamin Tammuz. *Pointer,* vol. 9, Spring 1974, pp. 6-10.

4043. Could you write more? John Creasey. *Writer,* vol. 73, January 1960, pp. 18-20.

4044. Creative cycle. S. Grafton. *Writer,* vol. 90, December 1977, pp. 11-15.

4045. Day in whose life? John Hall. *New Society,* September 29, 1977, pp. 663-664.

4046. Defense of the bedside pad. W. Brown. *Writer,* vol. 78, September 1965, pp. 15-17.

4047. Developing a sense of audience. B.M. Kroll. *Language Arts,* vol. 55, October 1978, pp. 828-831.

4048. Dig for buried treasure. A.W. Lyons. *Writer,* vol. 84, June 1971, pp. 15-17.

4049. Diligence and inspiration. R. Potts. *Times Educational Supplement,* vol. 3186, June 25, 1976, p. 45.

4050. Does genius have a gender? Janet Burroway and C. Ozick. *Ms.,* vol. 6, December 1977, pp. 56-57+.

4051. Does practice make perfect?. M.J. Crowder. *Writer,* vol. 94, January 1981, p. 28.

4052. Does the woman writer exist? Report of symposium sponsored by Doubleday. M. Reuter. *Publishers Weekly,* vol. 209, April 5, 1976, pp. 24+.

4053. Don't let your mother look over your shoulder. Nancy Thayer. *Writer,* vol. 97, June 1984, pp. 10-12+.

4054. Edmund Wilson on writers and writing. (Wilson's correspondence with various American authors.) *New York Review of Books,* vol. 24, March 17, 1977, pp. 10+.

4055. Eighteen tricks that make writing more fun. Don C. Reed. *Writer's Digest,* vol. 63, July 1983, pp. 41-42.

4056. End of it all; a modern fable (satire). B.J. Chute. *Writer,* vol. 82, January 1969, pp. 15-18.

4057. Essence of good writing. T. Caldwell. *Writer,* vol. 74, January 1961, pp. 5-8.

4058. Essence of writing. Shirley Ann Grau. *Writer,* vol. 87, May 1974, pp. 14-15.

4059. Exploitation and manipulation on tour (interview). Kate Millett. *Writer's Digest,* vol. 53, October 1973, pp. 21-22.

4060. Faith of a writer; remarks. E.B. White. *Publishers Weekly,* vol. 200, December 6, 1971, p. 29.

4061. Family skeleton with solid gold teeth. V. Henry. *Writer,* vol. 78, April 1965, pp. 14-15+.

4062. Few words to a beginning writer. J. Krantz. *Writer,* vol. 93, December 1980, pp. 18-19.

4063. Finding time to write. Richard Armour. *Writer,* vol. 81, April 1968, pp. 23-24+.

4064. First words are important. E. Marshall. *Writer's Digest,* vol. 49, April 1969, pp. 63-65.

4065. For beginners only. E.R. Paxton. *Writer's Digest,* vol. 48, June 1968, pp. 66-67.

4066. From the land of me...to the land of you. W.F. Nolan. *Writer,* vol. 83, June 1970, pp. 18-20.

4067. Giant killer: drink and the American writer. Alfred Kazin. *Commentary,* vol. 61, March 1976, pp. 44-50.

4068. Give me time. B.M. Devaney. *Writer,* vol. 74, May 1961, pp. 21-22.

4069. Good word for greed. L. Conger. *Writer,* vol. 79, July 1966, pp. 8-10.

4070. Grain of pleasure. A. Iverson. *Writer,* vol. 81, December 1968, pp. 11-13.

4071. Great American things; a prologue. Thomas Wolfe. *Esquire,* vol. 84, December 1975, pp. 83-84+.

4072. Helping hand for a literary upstart. J. Fischer. *Harper's Magazine,* vol. 227, September 1963, pp. 20+. Discussion, vol. 227, November 1963, pp. 10+.

4073. How a book grows. Marchette Chute. *Library Journal,* vol. 84, September 1 1959, pp. 2431-2432.

4074. How an anthology is made. T.M.H. Blair. *Writer,* vol. 80, March 1967, pp. 16-20+.

4075. How do you cure writer's block?. Jerome E. Kelley. *Writer's Digest,* vol. 56, October 1976, pp. 27-28+.

4076. How to be madder than Captain Ahab; excerpt from *Literary Cavalcade.* Ray Bradbury. *Writer,* vol. 87, February 1974, pp. 21-22.

4077. How to cope with the stress of writing. Tom Mach. *Writer's Digest,* vol. 61, July 1981, pp. 22-28.

4078. How to feed your brain and develop your creativity. Chuck Loch. *Writer's Digest,* vol. 61, February 1981, pp. 20-25.

4079. How to keep from writing. Nancy Hale. *Saturday Review,* vol. 45, April 7, 1962, pp. 11-13+.

4080. How to put perspective in your nonfiction. Bob Baker. *Writer's Digest,* vol. 61, December 1981, pp. 29-31.

4081. How to put your best foot forward. C. Schwalberg. *Writer,* vol. 82, August 1969, pp. 25-26+.

4082. How to put your rhythms to work on your blues. B. Bigham. *Writer's Digest,* vol. 55, August 1975, pp. 14-15.

4083. How to write in spite of yourself. T. Jewell Collins. *Writer,* vol. 96, October 1983, pp. 29+.

4084. I could write a better book than that! Marilyn Durham. *Writer,* vol. 85, December 1972, pp. 11-14.

4085. I have an idea.... George H. Scithers. *Writer's Digest,* vol. 64, November 1984, pp. 31-32.

4086. I never think of posterity. J. Sayles. *New York Times Book Review,* vol. 86, September 6, 1981, pp. 3+.

4087. If an artist wants to be serious and respected and rich, famous and popular, he is suffering from cultural schizophrenia. Robert Brustein. *New York Times Magazine,* September 26, 1971, pp. 12-13+; discussion, October 24, 1974, p. 16.

4088. In defense of a writing career. Norman Cousins. *Michigan Alumnus,* Autumn 1950, pp. 22-28.

4089. In defense of professionalism. R. Hayman. *Author,* vol. 91, Autumn 1980, pp. 4+.

4090. Inspiration. V. Nabokov. *Saturday Review of the Arts,* vol. 1, January 1973, pp. 30-32.

4091. Inspiration for every writer. R. Weinstein. *Writer's Digest,* vol. 54, December 1974, pp. 16-17.

4092. Interest curve. John Ball. *Writer,* vol. 83, July 1970, pp. 9-12.

4093. Interviews with psychiatrists who treat writers block; symposium. Edited by J. Charnay. *Writer's Digest,* vol. 54, July 1974, pp. 15-16.

4094. Is art all there is? Annie Dillard. *Harper's,* vol. 261, August 1980, pp. 61-66.

4095. Is greatness everything? J.F. Fixx. *Saturday Review,* vol. 45, Noverber 17, 1962, p. 24.

4096. Is there really such a thing as talent? (excerpt from address). Annie Dillard. *Seventeen,* vol. 38, June 1979, p. 86.

4097. Isaiah Berlin (interview). *Partisan Review,* vol. 50, no. 1, 1983, pp. 7-28.

4098. It's been done before. Samm S. Baker. *Writer,* vol. 88, February 1975, pp. 14-16.

4099. It's never too late to get started. M.L. Barr. *Writer's Digest,* vol. 51, January 1971, p. 31.

4100. Joys of inexperience. P. Moyes. *Writer,* vol. 86, August 1973, pp. 11-13+.

4101. Left hand, right hand. Joan Aiken. *Writer,* vol. 88, December 1975, pp. 9-12+.

4102. Leg-up for ditched centipedes; an author's confusion over ideas. L. Conger. *Writer,* vol. 79, September 1966, pp. 6-8.

4103. Let the would-be writers beware. D. Dempsey. *Saturday Review,* vol. 46, July 13, 1963, pp. 22-23.

4104. Letter to a son who has declared his ambition to become a writer. B. Deal. *Writer,* vol. 87, November 1974, pp. 20-23.

4105. Life expectancy of a writer. Margaret Culkin Banning. *Writer,* vol. 73, March 1960, pp. 7-11.

4106. Life is the raw material. R. Standish. *Writer,* vol. 77, July 1964, pp. 20-21+.

4107. Literary mind. Alfred Kazin. *Nation,* vol. 201, September 20, 1965, pp. 203-206.

4108. Literary roundtables: the writer as victim; summary of discussions. *Publishers Weekly,* vol. 190, July 18, 1966, pp. 36-40.

4109. Living with a writer. L. Conger. *Writer,* vol. 84, September 1971, pp. 9-10.

4110. Look! Look! Mommy can write! A.T. Serb. *Writer's Digest,* vol. 56, October 1976, pp. 17-21.

4111. Making it: with Mailer, Miller and Capote. James Fallows. *Washington Monthly,* vol. 6, June 1974, pp. 57+.

4112. Matter of respect. L. Conger. *Writer,* vol. 82, September 1969, pp. 7-8.

4113. Mechanics of magic. R. Blythe. *Times Educational Supplement,* vol. 3171, March 12, 1976, pp. 18-19.

4114. Middle of the book blues. Ten ways to get your novel back on track. Phyllis A. Whitney. *Writer,* vol. 97, July 1984, pp. 9-12.

4115. Middle of the journey. R. Marius. *Sewanee Review,* vol. 85, Summer 1977, pp. 460-467.

4116. Million words of practice writing. M.L. Falkowski. *Writer,* vol. 84, March 1971, pp. 23-25.

4117. Most important questions unpublished writers ask. M. Pollack. *Writer,* vol. 80, February 1967, pp. 14-16+.

4118. Must we always write for money? Patricia Highsmith. *Writer,* vol. 88, June 1975, pp. 9-10+.

4119. My battle with booze. Kent Hackett. *Writer's Digest,* vol. 58, October 1978, pp. 22-24.

4120. My love affair with English. M. Apple. *New York Times Book Review,* vol. 86, March 22, 1981, p. 9+.

4121. Mystique of the writer. S.F. Asher. *Writer's Digest,* vol. 56, December 1976, pp. 41-42.

4122. Myths, delusions, detours, and delays. L. Conger. *Writer,* vol. 89, June 1976, pp. 7-8.

4123. Norman Mailer; correspondence. Richard Lee-Fulgham. *Writer's Digest,* vol. 61, Jan. 1981, pp. 72+.

4124. "Not enough time" to write a book? Ha! (author who found time to write novels while working regular jobs). P. Bernstein. *Los Angeles,* May 22, 1977, p. 23+.

4125. Obsession of writers with the act of writing. Stephen Spender. *Michigan Quarterly Review,* vol. 21, Fall 1982, pp. 553-560.

4126. On becoming a dictator. H. Gardner. *Psychology Today,* vol. 14, December 1980, pp. 14+.

4127. On becoming a writer; excerpt from *Shadow and Act.* Ralph Ellison. *Commentary,* vol. 38, October 1964, pp. 57-60.

4128. On persisting as a writer. M. Apple. *Michigan Quarterly Review,* vol. 21, Winter 1982, pp. 21-25.

4129. On reading and writers. Oliver Warner. *Author,* vol. 86, Autumn 1975, pp. 101-104.

4130. On reading/writing/freedom (address). Kurt Vonnegut. *Mademoiselle,* vol. 83, August 1977, pp. 96+.

4131. On women writers: discussion at the Modern Language Association meeting. C.A. Denne and K.M. Rogers. *Nation,* vol. 221, August 30, 1975, pp. 151-153.

4132. On writing and bad writing. John Ciardi. *Saturday Review,* vol. 45, December 15, 1962, pp. 10-12.

4133. On writing well. R.S. Wolper. *Nation,* vol. 224, March 19, 1977, pp. 345-346.

4134. One way out. E. Savage. *Writer,* vol. 85, September 1972, pp. 9-10.

4135. Organizations for writers. *Writer,* vol. 88, October 1975, pp. 25-28.

4136. Originality paradox. T. McFarland. *New Literary History,* vol. 5, Spring 1974, pp. 447-476.

4137. Outside the ivory tower. B.J. Chute. *Writer,* vol. 96, January 1983, pp. 9-12.

4138. Overcoming the ultimate writer's block. Lawrence Block. *Writer's Digest,* vol. 64, April 1984, pp. 20-24.

4139. Pack every word with power. Gary Provost. *Writer's Digest,* vol. 63, February 1983, pp. 21-23.

4140. Paperback writer. F. Howe. *Atlantic,* vol. 236, November 1975, pp. 112+.

4141. Party of one; how to live happily with a split personality. C.D. Lewis. *Holiday,* vol. 33, March 1963, pp. 32+.

4142. Patience is a game of solitaire. L. Conger. *Writer,* vol. 86, March 1973, pp. 7-8.

4143. Pattern of common mistakes. Joan L. Nixon. *Writer,* vol. 85, September 1972, pp. 25-26.

4144. Pen is a heavy oar (writer's block). R. Rosen. *New York Times Book Review,* vol. 86, April 12, 1981, pp. 3+.

4145. Per ardua ad astra. J. Porter. *Writer,* vol. 81, August 1968, pp. 16-18.

4146. Perils of the female writer. Olivia Manning. *Spectator,* vol. 233, December 7, 1974, pp. 734-735.

4147. Plugging away and throwing away. G.N. Fletcher. *Writer,* vol. 74, September 1961, pp. 13-15.

4148. Privacy and production. Peggy Simson Curry. *Writer,* vol. 83, March 1970, pp. 9-11+.

4149. Professional attitude. K. Nelson. *Writer,* vol. 76, December 1963, pp. 9-11+.

4150. Psychotherapy and me. Dudley Lynch. *Writer's Digest,* vol. 58, March 1978, pp. 18-23.

4151. PW interview. William Zinsser: the four cardinal virtues of good writing are simplicity, clarity, economy, and warmth. *Publishers Weekly,* vol. 225, June 29, 1984, pp. 106-107.

4152. Rx for stuck playwrights. Louis E. Catron. *Writer,* vol. 97, September 1984, pp. 20-23+.

4153. Self confrontation and the writer. C. Brooke Rose. *New Literary History,* vol. 9, Autumn 1977, pp. 129-136.

4154. Seven beacons of excellent writing. Gary Provost. *Writer's Digest,* vol. 64, March 1984, pp. 35-38.

4155. Seventh thing: writer's need for a thick skin. L. Conger. *Writer,* vol. 85, January 1972, pp. 6-8.

4156. Should a public man write. R.L. Neuberger. *Saturday Review,* vol. 43, April 9, 1960, pp. 24-25.

4157. Should I be a writer? J. Gores. *Writer,* vol. 85, May 1972, pp. 17-19+.

4158. Should I try to be a writer? L.T. Henderson. *Writer,* vol. 77, April 1964, pp. 21-23.

4159. Silences when writers don't write (adaption of address). Tillie Olsen. *Harper's Magazine,* vol. 231, October 1965, pp. 153-161.

4160. Six burrs in the blanket. F. Flora. *Writer,* vol. 80, August 1967, pp. 24-26.

4161. Six most-asked questions on writing. Samm S. Baker. *Writer,* vol. 89, December 1976, pp. 15-18.

4162. Slight case of library fever; or How not to write a book. M.K. Sanders. *Harper's Magazine,* vol. 224, April 1962, pp. 68-71.

4163. So it's all been done before. H. Rezatto. *Writer,* vol. 77, Novermber 1964, pp. 27-28+.

4164. So you want to write a book (black authors). E.F. Ruffin. *Black Enterprise,* vol. 11, December 1980, pp. 61-62+.

4165. So you want to write a book; excerpt from *The Writing and Selling of Nonfiction.* Paul Revere Reynolds. *Saturday Review,* vol. 46, July 13, 1963, pp. 48-50; reply, vol. 46, August 10, 1963, p. 43.

4166. So mething to discover. Thomas Williams. *Writer,* vol. 82, June 1969, pp. 11-13.

4167. Stand it on its head! L. Alfson. *Writer,* vol. 87, March 1974, pp. 15-16+.

4168. Standing in the wings. J. Cunningham. *Writer,* vol. 89. November 1976, pp. 18-20+.

4169. Successful scribes (writing behavior of succesful writers). L. J. Peter. *Human Behavior,* vol. 6, September 1977, pp. 10+.

4170. Susan Sontag (interview). *Publishers Weekly,* vol. 222, October 22, 1982, pp. 6-8.

4171. Taking self-inventory. L.D. Peabody. *Writer,* vol. 78, August 1965, pp. 26-28.

4172. Ten pitfalls and how to avoid them. J.Z. Owen. *Writer,* vol. 79, July 1966, pp. 15-17+.

4173. Ten steps to greater writing productivity. Michael A. Banks. *Writer's Digest,* vol. 64, July 1984, p. 33.

4174. Testament to perseverance. Carol Amen. *Writer,* vol. 97, October 1984, pp. 13-15.

4175. Theodore H. White (interview). *Writer's Digest,* vol. 55, July 1975, pp. 21-24.

4176. Think piece; excerpt from *Prose by Professionals,* ed. by T. Morris. R.L. Heilbroner. *Writer,* vol. 75, October 1962, pp. 16-19.

4177. This constant struggle, this manual and psychic labor that we perform. T. Solotaroff. *Michigan Quarterly Review,* vol. 21, Winter 1982, pp. 66-76.

4178. Thomas Thompson, celebrity? Interview with author of *Blood and Money* and *Serpentine. Writer's Digest,* vol. 62, October 1982, pp. 22-29.

4179. Thou shalt not bore. C. Hanley. *Times Educational Supplement,* vol. 3094 supp., September 13, 1974, p. 11.

4180. Time of the assassins (inspiration can come from many sources). William Burroughs. *Crawdaddy,* February 1977, p. 16.

4181. Time of the assassins (thoughts on writing and enlightenment). William Burroughs. *Crawdaddy,* October 1976, pp. 12+.

4182. To a young writer. Wallace Stegner. *Atlantic,* vol. 204, November 1959, pp. 88-91.

4183. To be a writer. W.B. Ready. *Catholic World,* vol. 193, May 1961, pp. 113-116.

4184. To him who would a writer be. Granville Hicks. *Saturday Review,* vol. 49, January 1, 1966, pp. 23-24.

4185. To writers, with love. R. Fontaine. *Writer,* vol. 73, April 1960, pp. 5-7.

4186. Truth, beauty, and the wolf at the door (famous writers' early efforts). *Playboy,* vol. 20, December 1973, pp. 228+.

4187. Two writers' reasons for writing books; address June 22, 1959. H.A. Overstreet and B.W. Overstreet. *Wilson Library Bulletin,* vol. 34, October 1959, pp. 131-133.

4188. Unbeatable combination: ignorance and confidence. L. Conger. *Writer,* vol. 81, November 1968, pp. 7-8+.

4189. Use your creative memory. Jane H. Yolen. *Writer,* vol. 82, September 1969, pp. 16-17+.

4190. Versatility. W.F. Nolan. *Writer,* vol. 81, March 1968, pp. 9-11+.

4191. Way of seeing. J.H. Kay. *Writer,* vol. 84, May 1971, pp. 24-26.

4192. Way to writing. Paul Horgan. *Intellectual Digest,* vol. 3, July 1973, pp. 56+.

4193. What beginning writers want to know. J. Reach. *Writer,* vol. 76, October 1963, pp. 10-12.

4194. What Dick Powell taught me about writing. W.J. Slattery. *Writer's Digest,* vol. 57, March 1977, pp. 4-5.

4195. What is an author? M. Foucault. *Partisan Review,* vol. 4, 1975, pp. 603-614.

4196. What is the writer's social responsibility? N. Cousins. *Writer's Digest,* vol. 50, January 1970, pp. 30-31+.

4197. What is writing? S. Cloete. *Writer,* vol. 75, May 1962, pp. 5-7+.

4198. What makes a pro a pro? L. Conger. *Writer,* vol. 81, May 1968, pp. 7-8.

4199. What makes a writer write? C. Leslie. *Writer,* vol. 82, July 1969, pp. 17-20.

4200. What makes an opus? F. De Armond. *Writer,* vol. 72, October 1959, pp. 18-19.

4201. What's wrong when you can't write. M. Hewson. *McCalls,* vol. 108, November 1980, p. 27.

4202. What's wrong with full-time authorship?. David St. John Thomas. *Author,* vol. 91, Summer 1980, pp. 81-82.

4203. What to do till the Muse returns; how 21 famous authors fight writer's block. *Writer's Digest,* vol. 53, July 1973, pp. 18-19.

4204. When the writer comes of age (reprint). B.J. Chute. *Writer,* vol. 79, November 1966, pp. 20-24.

4205. When to follow the rules. S. Bauer. *Writer,* vol. 84, June 1971, p. 23.

4206. When to ignore advice. T. Burnam. *Writer,* vol. 81, March 1968, pp. 18-19.

4207. When writers talk about writing: papers presented at the international conference in Lahti, Finland, with notes by N. Cousins. E. Kos, N. Cousins, and J. Myrdal. *Saturday Review,* vol. 49, August 13, 1966, pp. 11-17+.

4208. Where do you get your ideas? Lawrence Block. *Writer's Digest,* vol. 56, September 1976, pp. 15-17+.

4209. Where to find ideas. C. Stephens. *Writer's Digest,* vol. 51, March 1971, pp. 33-35.

4210. Why does a writer write? William Saroyan. *Saturday Review,* vol. 44, February 25, 1961, pp. 24+.

4211. Why writers matter (excerpt from *Human Options).* N. Cousins. *Saturday Review,* vol. 8, June 1981, pp. 7-8.

4212. Why writers need islands. C.N. Parkinson. *Saturday Review,* vol. 5, January 7, 1978, pp. 33-34.

4213. Wings on your mind; address, April 6, 1972. C.D. Owsley. *Vital Speeches,* vol. 38, May 15, 1972, pp. 477-479.

4214. Without prospect or retrospect. L. Conger. *Writer,* vol. 82, May 1969, pp. 7-8.

4215. Works in progress (symposium). *New York Times Book Review,* vol. 87, June 6, 1982, pp. 11+.

4216. World of forms. S. Babb. *Writer,* vol. 86, July 1973, pp. 11-13.

4217. Write before writing. D.M. Murray. *College Composition and Communication,* vol. 29, December 1978, pp. 375-381.

4218. Write within your means. Margaret Culkin Banning. *Writer,* vol. 75, December 1962, pp. 11-13.

4219. Writer and the sea; symposium. *Yachting,* vol. 140, July 1976, pp. 48-53.

4220. Writer as a master craftsman. Jane H. Yolen. *Writer,* vol. 86, September 1973, pp. 18-20.

4221. Writer as editor: compiling an anthology. L. Zimpel. *Writer's Digest,* vol. 56, March 1976, pp. 13-17.

4222. Writer as revolutionary. A flight from openness? Ferdinand Mount. *Encounter,* vol. 45, November 1975, pp. 52-53+.

4223. Writer as sexual guru. Erica Jong. *New York Magazine,* vol. 7, May 20, 1974, pp. 80-82.

4224. Writer can write anywhere, can he? Richard Armour. *Writer,* vol. 72, November 1959, pp. 12-13.

4225. Writer in America. J.P. Sisk. *Commonweal,* vol. 75, December 8, 1961, pp. 271-274.

4226. Writer in his heavenly house. W.H. Scheib. *Writer,* vol. 90, January 1977, pp. 27-29.

4227. Writer: lens or catalyst. N. Clad. *Writer,* vol. 72, November 1959, pp. 5-9.

4228. Writers and reading. R.E. Wolseley. *Writer,* vol. 86, October 1973, pp. 28-29.

4229. Writers are people; address, May 10, 1961. R.T. Oliver. *Vital Speeches,* vol. 27, July 1, 1961, pp. 571-576.

4230. Writer's block. L. Conger. *Writer,* vol. 86, May 1973, pp. 9-10.

4231. Writer's block. N. Henderson, K. Salzinger, and C. Farley. *Writer's Digest,* vol. 55, August 1975, pp. 16-18.

4232. Writer's block: why words fail them. Owen Edwards. *New York Magazine,* vol. 6, April 1973, pp. 61+.

4233. Writers' colonies: sixteen creative havens for freelancers. Rose Adkins. *Writer's Digest,* vol. 63, August 1983, pp. 36-39.

4234. Writer's demotion to solid-citizen status. J.W. Aldridge. *Saturday Review,* vol. 54, September 18, 1971, pp. 35-36+.

4235. Writers in glass houses. D. Betts. *Writer,* vol. 88, February 1975, pp. 9-11.

4236. Writer's life; symposium. *Harper's Magazine,* vol. 231, October 1965, pp. 141-156+; November 1965, pp. 141-171.

4237. Writer's place can even be in the home. Carolyn Lane. *Writer's Digest,* vol. 55, February 1975, pp. 11-12.

4238. Writer's requisites. A. Seton. *Writer,* vol. 80, August 1967, pp. 19+.

4239. Writers, take heart. Faith Baldwin. *Writer,* vol. 73, October 1960, pp. 10+.

4240. Writer's world. M. Forster. *Writer,* vol. 81, October 1968, pp. 11-13.

4241. Writers, writing, and the written; symposium. *Bulletin of the Atomic Scientists,* vol. 19, November 1963, pp. 13-28; December 1963, pp. 19-33.

4242. Writing as temperature. T. Merton. *Sewanee Review,* vol. 77, Summer 1969, pp. 535-542.

4243. Writing effectively—and economically; address, July 12, 1976. W. Pedersen. *Vital Speeches,* vol. 42, August 15, 1976, pp. 661-663.

4244. Writing for the pure joy of it. Leonard Knott. *Writer's Digest,* vol. 64, January 1984, pp. 22-26.

4245. Writing from the inside out. C. Edwards. *Writer,* vol. 72, September 1959, pp. 11-13.

4246. Writing in retirement. G.D. Kratz. *Writer,* vol. 79, April 1966, pp. 26-28.

Addendum

Books

4247. Barnhart, Helene. *How to Write and Sell the Eight Easiest Article Types.* Cincinnati: Writer's Digest, 1985. 256 pp.

Covers how-to-do-it, nostalgia, people profiles, personal experiences, inspirational, travel, pet peeve/think pieces, and humor.

4248. Brenner, Alfred. *The T.V. Scriptwriter's Handbook.* Cincinnati: Writer's Digest, 1985. 322 pp.

Describes the mechanics of writing professional scripts in such areas as drama, comedy, mini-series, serials, specials, and animated programs. The author is an Emmy-winning scriptwriter.

4249. Corwin, Stanley J. *How to Become a Bestselling Author.* Cincinnati: Writer's Digest, 1984. 256 pp.

Includes advice on promotion and publicity, proper title, proposals, contracts, and relations with publishers. Corwin has extensive experience as a book marketer.

4250. Davis, Sheila. *The Craft of Lyric Writing.* Cincinnati: Writer's Digest, 1984. 252 pp.

This introduction to songwriting by a composer and lyricist covers rhyme, meter, lyrics, beat, and the basics of rewriting songs for more polished results.

4251. Delton, Judy. *The Twenty-nine Most Common Writing Mistakes and How to Avoid Them.* Cincinnati: Writer's Digest, 1985. 108 pp.

A light and humorous approach aimed at increasing sales.

4252. Horowitz, Lois. *Knowing Where to Look; The Ultimate Guide to Research.* Cincinnati: Writer's Digest, 1984. 444 pp.

Covers statistics, quotes, facts, and photographs, among others.

4253. Hugo, Richard. *The Triggering Town; Lectures and Essays on Poetry and Writing.* New York: Norton, 1979. 109 pp.

In what has been viewed as one of the more inspiring recent statements on the writer's art, Hugo discusses the original inspiration or "triggering" for poems, teaching creative writing, faith in writing, and other fundamentals. To quote the *New York Times Book Review,* "Every page reads like a man talking, a man who celebrates, blames, remembers, argues, praises, and reveals."

4254. Kauffman, Stanley. *Albums of Early Life.* New Haven: Tickner and Fields, 1980. 229 pp.

An exercise in wit and self perception, this autobiography of a major motion picture critic allows us to understand the forces which shaped Kauffman's inimitable style.

4255. Larsen, Michael. *How to Write a Book Proposal.* Cincinnati: Writer's Digest, 1985. 124 pp.

An agent and writer touches on compelling description, placing the concept in market perspective, and attractive physical format.

4256. Marston, Doris K. *A Guide to Writing History.* Cincinnati: Writer's Digest, 1950. 258 pp.

Covers interviewing, biographical writing, short articles, historical poetry, historical fiction, the nonfiction history book, local and regional history, and marketing.

4257. Miller, Casey and Kate Swift. *The Handbook of Nonsexist Writing for Writers, Editors, and Speakers.* New York: Lippincott and Crowell, 1980. 134 pp.

Combines humor and passion in an effort to substitute genderless language for what is seen as that which is "distractions, ambiguous, and injurious." One example: "What is a working wife? One whose arms and legs move?"

4258. Nelson, Victoria. *Writer's Block and How to Use It.* Cincinnati: Writer's Digest, 1985. 204 pp.

Addresses "...the inner conflicts that are causing block." The author conducts seminars on writer's block at conferences and with writing programs.

4259. Shedd, Charlie. *If I Can Write, You Can Write.* Cincinnati: Writer's Digest, 1984. 152 pp.

A bestselling inspirational writer offers rules for good writing and other advice to the beginner.

Select List of Literary Agents

Dominick Abel Literary Agency, Inc.
498 West End Avenue
New York, New York 10024

Author Aid Associates
350 East 52nd Street
New York, New York 10022

Bleecker Street Associates, Inc.
88 Bleecker Street
New York, New York 10012

Brandt and Brandt Literary Agents, Inc.
1501 Broadway
New York, New York 10036

Georges Borchardt, Inc.
136 East 57th Street
New York, New York 10022

Jane Jordan Browne Multimedia Product Development, Inc.
410 South Michigan Avenue
Room 828
Chicago, Illinois 60605

Howard Buck Agency
86 Eighth Avenue
Suite 1107
New York, New York 10011

Ruth Cantor
156 Fifth Avenue
New York, New York 10010

Hy Cohen Literary Agency, Ltd.
111 West 57th Street
New York, New York 10019

Molly Malone Cook Literary Agency, Inc.
Box 338
Provincetown, Maine 02657

Robert Cornfield Literary Agency
5 West 73rd Street
New York, New York 10021

Liz Darhansoff
1220 Park Avenue
New York, New York 10028

Anita Diamant
51 East 42nd Street
New York, New York 10017

Ann Elmo Agency, Inc.
60 East 42nd Street
New York, New York 10165

John Farquharson, Ltd.
250 West 57th Street
New York, New York 10107

Sanford J. Greenburger Associates, Inc.
825 Third Avenue
New York, New York 10022

Edite Kroll
31 East 31st Street
Apartment 2E
New York, New York 10016

Bill Kruger Literary Services
1308 Canterbury Road North
St. Petersburg, Florida 33710

Peter Lampack Agency, Inc.
551 Fifth Avenue
Suite 2015
New York, New York 10017

Barbara Lowenstein Associates, Inc.
250 West 57th Street
New York, New York 10107

Thomas Lowry Associates, Inc.
156 West 86th Street
New York, New York 10024

Donald MacCampbell, Inc.
12 East 41st Street
New York, New York 10017

Renate B. McCarter
823 Park Avenue
New York, New York 10021

McIntosh & Otis, Inc.
475 Fifth Avenue
New York, New York 10017

Denise Marcil Literary Agency, Inc.
316 West 82nd Street
New York, New York 10024

Scott Meredith Literary Agency,
Inc.
845 Third Avenue
New York, New York 10022

William Morris Agency
1350 Avenue of the Americas
New York, New York 10019

Otte Co.
9 Goden Street
Belmont, Massachusetts 02178

Ray Peekner Literary Agency
3210 South Seventh Street
Milwaukee, Wisconsin 53215

Paul R. Reynolds, Inc.
12 East 41st Street
New York, New York 10017

Marie Rodell-Frances Collin Literary
Agency
110 West 40th Street
New York, New York 10018

Jack Scagnetti Talent Agency
5258 Cartwright Avenue
North Hollywood, California
91601

Susan Schulman Literary Agency
165 West End Avenue
New York, New York 10023

Philip G. Spitzer Literary Agency
1465 Third Avenue
New York, New York 10028

Gloria Stern Agency
1230 Park Avenue
New York, New York 10028

Warren-Hilton, Literary Agents
13131 Welby Way
North Hollywood, California
91606

Ruth Wreschner, Authors'
Representative
10 West 74th Street
New York, New York 10023

Mary Yost Associates, Inc.
75 East 55th Street
New York, New York 10022

George Ziegler
160 East 97th Street
New York, New York 10029

For a more complete listing of literary agents, please consult sources cited in this book under Literary Agents (page 305) and Marketing (page 323).

Select List of Organizations for Writers

Academy of American Poets
177 East 87th Street
New York, New York 10028

American Medical Writers
Association
5272 River Road
Suite 410
Bethesda, Maryland 20816

American Society of Journalists &
Authors, Inc.
1501 Broadway
Suite 1907
New York, New York 10036

American Translators Association
109 Croton Avenue
Ossining, New York 10562

Authors League of America, Inc.
234 West 44th Street
New York, New York 10036

Aviation/Space Writers Association
1725 K Street NW
Washington, D.C. 20006

Council of Writers Organizations
1501 Broadway
Suite 1907
New York, New York 10036

Education Writers Association
Box 281
Woodstown, New York 08098

International Women's Writing
Guild
244 East 86th Street
New York, New York 10028

Mystery Writers of America, Inc.
150 Fifth Avenue
New York, New York 10011

National Association of Science
Writers, Inc.
Box 294
Greenlawn, New York 11740

National Writers Club, Inc.
1450 South Havana
Suite 620
Aurora, Colorado 80012

Outdoor Writers Association of
America
3101 West Peoria Avenue
Suite A207
Phoenix, Arizona 85029

PEN American Center
47 Fifth Avenue
New York, New York 10003

Poetry Society of America
15 Gramercy Park South
New York, New York 10003

Poets & Writers, Inc.
201 West 54th Street
New York, New York 10019

Science Fiction Writers of America
P.O. Box H
Wharton, New Jersey 07885

Society for Technical
Communication
815 15th Street N.W.
Suite 506
Washington, D.C. 20005

Society of American Business and
Economic Writers
San Jose Mercury News
750 Ridder Park Drive
San Jose, California 95190

Society of American Travel Writers
1120 Connecticut Avenue NW
Suite 940
Washington, D.C. 20036

Society of Children's Book Writers
Box 296
Mar Vista Station
Los Angeles, California 90066

Western Writers of America, Inc.
1052 Meridan Road
Victor, Montana 59875

Writers Guild of America-East
555 West 57th Street
New York, New York 10019

Writers Guild of America-West
8955 Beverly Blvd.
Los Angeles, California 90048

For more complete listings of writers' organizations, please consult *Literary Market Place, Writer's Handbook,* or *Writer's Guide to Agents, Associations and Services.*

Author Index

Gross, Alan G.   3276
Gross, B.   189
Gross, Gerald   3450
Gross, J.   3523
Grossman, John   3652
Gruber, F.   656
Guarino, V.   2941
Guerard, A.J.   1836
Guest, J.   213
Guitar, M.A.   3558
Gundell, Glenn   2826
Gunn, P.   1519
Gunther, Max   2827, 2878, 2937, 2944, 3053, 3059, 3814
Gustafson, R.   829
Guth, P.Y.   2913
Guthrie, A.B., Jr.   67
Guyer, D.D.   800, 844
Guymont, Philip J.   3270
Gwynn, Frederick L.   1100

Hackel, G.   3590
Hackett, Francis   1084
Hackett, Kent   4119
Hackwer, S.   2192
Hager, Jean   2315
Haight, Anne Lyon   3827
Hailey, Elizabeth Forsythe   1500
Haines, John   674
Halberstadt, J.   278
Hale, J.   2914
Hale, Nancy   1121, 1274, 4079
Haley, Alex   236, 2808
Hall, Camden M.   3817
Hall, Donald   675, 843, 3951, 3952
Hall, Douglas K.   2407, 2445
Hall, John   4045
Hall, Karen   652
Hall, Mark W.   511
Halla, Chris   3018
Hallett, C.A.   451
Halliburton, D.   742
Hallstead, W.F.   3758
Halperin, John   27
Halpern, Frances   3715
Halpern, J.W.   2673
Halpern, M.   476
Hamilton, D.   1490
Hamilton, Donald   112, 1568
Hamilton, Mark   3621
Hammett, Dashiell   2172, 2299
Hammond, Karla   765
Hampe, B.   589
Hanania, Joseph   631, 645

Handley, C.   3746
Hanft, P.   3236
Hanley, C.   4179
Hannibal, E.   958, 1216
Hansen, Joseph   1048, 2267, 2281
Hanson, Nancy E.   2828
Harding, J.   457
Harding, Rosamond Evelyn Mary   3953
Hardt, Lorraine   2455, 2500
Hardwick, E.   290
Hardy, Barbara Nathan   860
Hardy, Thomas   1086, 1122, 1718, 3982
Harlow, Richard   3934
Harmon, Barbara   1885
Harnett, C.   1931
Harris, A.S., Jr.   3796
Harris, C.   1951, 1975
Harris, David M.   2567
Harris, Joel Chandler   1070
Harris, L.M.   952
Harris, Mark   37
Harris, Wilson   1083
Harrison, A.   3905
Harrison, B.G.   2207
Harrison, R.B.   3181
Harrison, William   1118, 1541
Harsh, J.D.   2149
Hart, Moss   322, 385
Hartley, L.P.   210
Hartman, G.   1830
Hartman, Susan   3822
Hartmann, Sadakichi   676
Harty, Kevin J.   3107
Haugland, J.   1609
Hawes, E.   1589
Hawkes, John   156, 157, 197, 1083, 1092, 1135, 1152, 1219, 1287
Hawkins, P.S.   2531
Hawkins, W.J.   3622
Hawthorne, Nathaniel   54, 1076, 1123, 3460
Hay, M.   381
Hayakawa, S.I.   3135
Haydn, Hiram   3451
Hayes, R.E.   1029
Hayman, R.   405, 3509, 4089
Haynes, L.   2875
Hays, R.   2942
Heacock, James   3813
Heacock, Rosalie   3813
Heaney, Seamus   672
Hearn, Betsy   1950

Weatherby, W.J.   3482
Weaver, Elvira   2138
Webb, J.   2206
Weeks, Edward   3467, 3468
Weigl, B.   3640
Weinkauf, Mary S.   2625
Weinstein, R.   4091
Weisbord, Marvin   2857
Weisinger, M.   3738
Weisman, Herman M.   3143, 3144, 3145
Weiss, Allen   3160, 3171, 3175, 3185, 3203, 3207, 3256, 3265, 3311, 3327
Weiss, Edmond H.   3146
Weiss, Peter   347
Weiss, W.H.   3344
Welch, C.W.   3201
Welles, O.   596
Wells, A.M.   2177, 2655
Wells, F.   2932
Wells, H.G.   96, 848, 2558
Wells, Henry W.   335
Wells, R.W.   4020
Welser, James A.   3170
Welsh, A.   1838
Welton, C.G.   2901
Welty, Eudora   905, 964, 971, 1135, 1183, 1200, 1256, 1312, 1328, 1432, 1440, 1446, 1764, 1790, 1798, 4012
Wendelburg, T.   1683
Werner, L.   3659
Wersba, Barbara   1886
Wertheim, Arthur Frank   544
Wescott, Glenway   1112
Wesker, Arnold   347, 408, 456
Wesling, D.   3380
West, B.   555
West, E.J.   342
West, Jessamyn   1200
West, John Foster   1245, 1803
West, Morris   137, 1258
West, Nathanael   190
West, P.   1422
West, Ray Benedict   1184
West, Rebecca   850, 1200, 2767
Westervelt, Virginia   2535
Westheimer, D.   138, 182, 1610
Weston, J.   1340
Wetering, Janwillem van de   2157
Wetzsteon, R.   233
Weyr, T.   3550, 3551
Whalen, Tim   3280
Whaley, C.T.   885

Wharton, Edith N.   1185
Wharton, G.C.   2514
Wheatcroft, J.   784
Wheatley, D.   2331
Wheelock, John Hall   718, 3463
Whitcomb, D.   874, 1002, 1697, 1756
White, E.B.   1911, 1912, 1929, 3698, 3938, 3951, 4005, 4060
White, Edward M.   4006
White, John   3733
White, Leigh C.   3245
White, Mimi   585
White, Myron L.   3134
White, R.   295
White, Stephen   4007
White, Theodore H.   4175
Whiteside, Thomas   3469
Whiting, M.   3219
Whitman, Alden   2763
Whitman, Walt   676, 703
Whitney, Phyllis A.   181, 1186, 1337, 1342, 1386, 1411, 1433, 1476, 1578, 1778, 1786, 1813, 1868, 2232, 2347, 2381, 3642, 3776, 3938, 4114
Whittington, H.   966
Whittlesey, Marietta   2861
Whitty, Stephen   3079
Wibberley, L.   1502, 1630
Wiesenfarth, Joseph   118, 1097
Wilber, Richard   1118
Wilbur, L. Perry   2862, 2872
Wilbur, Richard   718, 791, 1099, 1119
Wilcox, C.   2344
Wilde, Oscar   323
Wilder, Gene   522
Wilder, Thornton   310, 323, 432, 3929, 4009
Wilderman, J.   3854
Wildsmith, Brian   1855
Wilkinson, J.W.   3194
Wilkinson, S.   1461
Willard, Barbara   1849
Willard, Nancy   1966, 4027
Willeford, C.   632
Willett, J.   1646
Williams, J.   1816
Williams, M.   293, 1293, 1400
Williams, Nan Schram   2119, 2774
Williams, Tennessee   317, 336, 347, 348, 461
Williams, Thomas   1639, 4166
Williams, W.G.   3052

Book Title Index

(Numbers refer to entry numbers.)

Subject Index